KNOWLEDGE AND INFORMATION

PERSPECTIVES AND PROSPECTS

G. J. NARAYANA

Ess Ess Publications
New Delhi

Knowledge and Information
Perspectives and Prospects

ISBN: 978-81-7000-607-7

Rs.1675/-

First Published 2010

Published by:
Ess Ess Publications
4837/24, Ansari Road,
Darya Ganj,
New Delhi-110 002.
INDIA
Phones: 23260807, 41563444
Fax: 41563334
E-mail: info@essessreference.com
www.essessreference.com

Cover Design by *Patch Creative Unit*

Printed and bound in India at Salasar Imaging Systems.

Dedicated to

my grand children

PRANAV RAO, KASTURI RAO,

HIMANI BHAT, MANDIRA BHAT,

and ***ATUL HERLE***

CONTENTS

PREFACE

The idea of writing this book originated from my doctoral thesis, titled *Information as a Commodity: An Inquiry into the Characteristics of Knowledge*, approved by the University of Poona, India in 1991. The thesis was limited mainly to the study of the commodity aspects of information, and some of the principal characteristics of knowledge. The two aspects of knowledge covered in the thesis have been retained after thoroughly revising and reshaping them. These are only two facets of knowledge, whereas the world of knowledge consists of numerous facets and innumerable concepts.

Reasons compelling the study of knowledge could be many. Such studies centre on human society, its actors, and actions vis-à-vis knowledge and information. Knowledge has many uses, such as: satisfy one's curiosity, uplift one's spirit, help in solving problems, aid economic advancement, and create new knowledge. Knowledge also has an institutional dimension. Even though knowledge phenomena take place at the individual's level it is influenced by society, and also exploited institutionally. Since knowledge is associated with and results from human thinking and actions from the times of recorded human history, it has as many facets as the human beings could think of. The attempt here is to provide the perspectives and prospects of the fields of knowledge and information. The chapters are arranged in the natural order of: Fundamentals, Dimensions, Domains, Access and servicing of knowledge and information, and Fulfillment.

in one chapter or context often appear in another chapter or context following a different angle or same angle of approach. This may give the reader a feeling of repetition, whereas it shows the mutually non-exclusive nature of knowledge. What is important is that we realize as mentioned above that knowledge, information, and data are only the means to achieve a desired purpose, and not an end in itself. The definitions and usage of these terms are only to help us retain the focus.

In writing this book, I have been strengthened by the scrutiny of each chapter by experts in respective fields. Many others also have helped me in different ways. I wish to express my thanks to all of them through "Acknowledgement".

G. J. Narayana

ACKNOWLEDGEMENT

I wish to pay my homage to the following scholars, who are deceased : Prof. B. Anderson of the University of Bombay, my Ph.D. guide; Shri. N.M. Ketkar, former Director, Social Science Documentation Centre, New Delhi with whom I had spent a number of days discussing about knowledge and information; Prof. Venkatagiri Gowda, Professor of Economics, Bangalore University; and Prof. D.M. Nanjundappa, the former Chairman of the Planning Commission of Karnataka for their insightful comments on the economic portion of the Ph.D. thesis from which the text has benefitted.

I am indebted to following scholars, experts, and professional colleagues who have helped me by offering their valuable suggestions while writing this book:

Prof. S. Mahadevan. Head, Department of Molecular Reproduction, Development and Genetics, Indian Institute of Science, Bangalore for reviewing the chapter "Biological Basis of Information".

Dr. Manjunatha Bhat. Head, Life Sciences Department, Winston Salem State University, North Carolina, (and my son-in-law) for reviewing the chapter "Biological Basis of Information" and helping me in graphics.

Prof. N. Mukunda. Vice President, Indian Academy of Science, Bangalore for reviewing the chapter "Science and Scientific Knowledge. Technology".

Prof. M. G. Narasihman. Fellow, National Institute for Advanced Studies, Banglore for reviewing the chapter "Knowledge in Philosophy".

Prof. A. Neelameghan. Former Professor and Head, Documentation Research and Training Centre, Indian Statistical Institute, Bangalore for reviewing the chapters "Knowledge, Information and Wisdom", "Organization, Communication and Transfer", "Characteristics of Knowledge", "Cognitive and Intellectual Processes", "Utilization and Growth of Knowledge", "Users and Information Processes", "Libraries, Internet and Web sites", and "Knowledge Society". Besides reviewing these chapters, he has been extremely generous to review the entire text, and has offered valuable suggestions for which I am doubly thankful.

Prof. V. S. Parthasarathy. Former Associate Professor of Sociology, Institute for Social and Economic Change, Bangalore for reviewing the chapters " Social Knowledge", and "Sociology of Knowledge".

Prof. M. R. Riswadkar. Former Professor in the Department of Library and Information Science, University of Poona, Pune for his valuable suggestions made at the draft stage.

Prof. K.S. Raghavan. Professor, Documentation Research and Training Centre, Indian Statistical Institute, Bangalore for reviewing the chapter "Time, Space and Knowledge".

Prof. V. V. Raman. Emeritus Professor of Physics and Humanities, Rochester Institute of Technology, New York for reviewing the chapter "Information as Physical Reality".

Prof. B. Sheshadri. Former Professor of Economics, Hampi University, Hampi for reviewing the chapters "Knowledge and Information as Goods", " Information as a Factor of Production", and " Information as Economic Signals".

I am thankful to Sarada Ranganathan Endowment for Library Science, Bangalore for permitting me to update and include Chapter 7 Change: A Precursor of Knowledge, which appeared in *Library and Information Systems* (2009).

I am indebted to Dr. K.N. Prasad, Executive Director, Sarada Ranganathan Endowment Trust for Library Science, Bangalore for his help in preparing the text for publishing and in many other ways, and to Mr. M. Nadiger, my former colleague for his bibliographic aid and providing the index. I am extremely thankful to the authorities of the Indian Institute of Science, the Indian Institute of Management (IIM), the Institute for Social and Economic Change (ISEC), and the Indian Statistical Institute, all from Bangalore for permitting me to use their library and information facilities, and to the U.S. Educational Foundation in India for awarding me a Senior Fulbright Fellowship which helped me to build the initial knowledge base by tapping the U.S. information resources.

Special thanks are due to Mr. Chikkamallaiah, the former Librarian of IIM; K. Venkatesh of ISEC; my brothers-in-law Prof. K.R. Hande and Dr. K.S. Hande; my friend Shri. H. Achhutha; and my wife Smt. G.N. Vedavathi for their enthusiastic support. Also, I thank my grand children Shri. P.N. Pranav Rao and Km. P. N. Kasturi Rao for their assistance in computer work.

Fundamentals

1
KNOWLEDGE, INFORMATION AND WISDOM

Knowledge is a phenomenon that is unique to human beings. Other species in nature are also endowed with some awareness or sensing capacity, which is limited to carryout survival functions, such as locating food, sensing danger, and adjusting to the variations in the surrounding environment. What is unique to human beings is that they can think, understand, and communicate with others. It is these characteristics that give human awareness the status of knowledge or consciousness. The study of knowledge may be said to begin with the dawn of civilization, although knowledge existed and used to a limited extent by pre-civilization people. It is the invention of language, particularly the development of speech, that made knowledge a wide spread social and cultural phenomenon, and gave knowledge its transfer characteristic. The invention of writing further enhanced the preservation and dissemination characteristics of knowledge. In all civilizations, philosophical and religious aspects of life were a dominant theme. This emphasis accorded religious and philosophical knowledge a superior status over other facets of knowledge, including practical knowledge. As societies progressed and their social functions increased, knowledge too became a multi-faceted phenomenon. Information, on the other hand, did not receive the attention it is given now because of its deemed lower order in the social value system compared to knowledge. Information, as a subject of study, came into prominence when communication engineers began to study the mechanism of information process. Another reason for the increased attention paid to information studies is the enormous growth of information and records, particularly in the domains of science and technology, and the need for efficient organization and management of information and records. With the computer and communication technologies revolutionizing the whole pattern of knowledge and information generation, processing and utilization, we are now in an entirely new world-the cyber world. What follows in this chapter and the chapters ahead is an account of the various facets of knowledge and information.

The terms "knowledge", "information" and "wisdom" connote familiar concepts, and yet determining in concrete terms what they are or arriving at their generally acceptable definitions has eluded thinkers for long. It is more so in defining the relationship between knowledge and information. The intractability of the problem can be seen from the fact that Machlup who justified the use of the term "knowledge" to that of "information" in his classical work on knowledge switched over to the use of the term information in a later work (Machlup, 1984). The problem is compounded by the fact that there are too many interpretations making the task of defining formidable. There is also an extreme belief that attempting to define knowledge and information is unproductive, and the study of knowledge is irrelevant. Knowledge is the subject of study of epistemology, a branch of philosophy. Epistemological treatment of knowledge is confined to ascertaining how man as an individual comprehends knowledge, and the study of its nature (see chapter 8). The problem with epistemology is that it studies knowledge at an abstract philosophical level, away from the demands of the practical world. In addition, classical epistemology faces the charge of ignoring the role of social factors in shaping one's knowledge and the impact of social forces on the creation, production, distribution and utilization of knowledge. Therefore, it is all the more necessary to study knowledge phenomenon as seen in practice, relevant to its day-to-day handling and utilization, i.e., in the context of the reality of everyday life.

KNOWLEDGE FORMATION - A MENTAL PROCESS

Knowledge formation is the resultant of cognitive processes acting on stimuli and a priori knowledge in the brain. It is an integral part of mind. Brain is the centre that receives stimuli from the outside world, converts it into awareness, stores it in memory, and recalls it when needed. There are two aspects to the working of the brain - physiological and mental. Much progress has been achieved in our understanding the physiological process of receiving sense stimulus, the electrical and biochemical mechanisms involved, and the role of neurons in internal transmission and interpretation of messages (see chapter 9). How electro-chemical impulses become awareness is still a mystery of nature. The portion of activity of the brain that encompasses sense perception, feeling and emotion, traits of character and personality, the volitional aspects of human life, and in a narrow sense, the intellectual phenomena represents mind (Encyclopaedia Britannica, 2007. Vol.24). Mind is taken to be the sum total of the conscious state of an individual. A cognitive science view of meaning following Oxford English Dictionary, is that the action of knowing is cognitive— the ways in which we become acquainted with things, i.e., becoming aware. Awareness, consciousness, and reality — all meaning knowledge is the result of complex interaction between the brain and the external and internal stimuli reaching brain. Awareness is caused by stimuli (including information) undergoing cognitive processes in the brain (empirical). Thus, the study of knowledge is concerned with consciousness — being conscious of something or some phenomenon and other cognitive aspects of mind. The cognitive aspect encompasses both percept and thought. Perception is an automatic process (reflexive) that produces the stream of consciousness in us about the real world. Thought is reflective awareness, a controlled process (Lieberman et al., 2002). For example, when I see a fast moving object at a far distance in the sky, I may perceive it initially as a bird. However, on pondering (reflecting) over it, I may come to the conclusion that it is an aeroplane, and not a bird. Thus, knowledge formation involves both perception and thinking.

We express knowledge, i.e., our awareness of things in terms of concepts, imagery, attention and comprehension. Other concepts related to knowledge include intelligence (informational sagacity, quickness of understanding), intuition or immediate insight (creativity, problem solving), personal acquaintance or social knowledge and categorizing (personal cognition, concepts, memory and schemata), skill (reasoning, practical knowledge, expertise), and understanding (including judgement, decision-making, language and comprehension) (Benjafield, 1996).

The nature of knowledge phenomena may be explained by taking a practical example of knowledge transfer through teaching. The process of acquiring and transmitting knowledge by a teacher includes the following steps:

1. The teacher reads (one of the methods) the text books and other source materials on the topic to be taught.
2. As a result of reading, the content of the texts (conveyed through language) is carried to the brain through the sense organs.
3. Knowledge content carried as stimulus to the brain is recognized with the active participation of memory.
4. Recognition process may identify (compare/ differentiate) the incoming sense-data with an already existing percept,

(i.e., awareness) as same, or related to it, or entirely new.

5. If the new sense-data and existing percept are same, then there may not be any change in the teacher's existing state of knowledge.
6. If it is new or related to an existing percept in some way, the existing knowledge state gets modified.
7. Teacher, then selects the mental knowledge text, original or modified, to be conveyed to the class.
8. The knowledge to be transmitted to the class is transformed or coded by the brain into language and other modes like gestures and signals.
9. The teacher conveys the knowledge through the mode of speech, writing, demonstration, and other means to the students.
10. The delivery of information by the teacher is also influenced by teacher- taught interaction. The process of interaction between the teacher and the taught adds or modifies the existing state of awareness in the taught that "something or other is the case".

The above analysis shows in bare outlines how speech, reading, writing, and gestures constituting stimuli caused by sense-data (in this case it is information) by undergoing cognitive processes in the brain become knowledge in the minds of students. The actual mental processes of learning are complicated as many other cognitive and psychological factors come to play. Creation of new knowledge as in research involves other cognitive steps.

Knowledge in its most general and fundamental sense is "recognition, the recognition that something new appearing before the consciousness is identical to, similar to, or in some way related to something that the mind already knows. The strictly novel elements of our knowledge are products of our sensibility: new colors, sounds, etc. At the beginning, the mind has available to it only certain concepts that arise from its ability to act and are thus involved in every act of thought, and, similarly, certain characteristics of its sensibility that in a corresponding way color or form all we derive through the senses. Knowledge arises through acts of understanding, which may be taken as the designation of the productive faculty of the mind" (Jones, 1964, p. 68).

The key elements of knowledge in the above interpretation are: cognition, sense perception, and awareness. A straight forward approach to understand knowledge is to go by the operative concept "to know" in the word "knowledge". However, " to possess the information which the dictionary provides about the accredited uses of the English word 'to know', or the corresponding words in other languages, is no doubt a necessary qualification for giving an analysis of knowledge; but it is not sufficient" (Ayer, 1956, p.9). The dictionary's "to know" to become knowledge must answer further questions on the attributes such as special state of mind, truth, certainty, belief, reality and many others to establish the nature of knowledge (Ayer, 1956). This sets the conditions under which consciousness becomes eligible to be treated as knowledge. In the context of practical knowledge, philosophers' insistence on test of validity based on certainty, truth etc. will be unproductive as unverified or even false knowledge has practical implications and utility.

Classifying knowledge at the cognitive level into "procedural" knowledge relating to skills, reasoning, problem solving, and the like; and "declarative" knowledge which pertains to facts and descriptions; "semantic" knowledge referring to knowledge about the world which is shared by many; and "episodic" knowledge which limits knowledge to one's own experience and linked to a particular space and time gives knowledge contextual clarity (see chapters 8 and 9). Categorizing knowledge at the pragmatic level into "tacit" or "implicit" knowledge referring to what is in the mind, and "explicit" knowledge meaning knowledge existing outside the mind in the form of information and records is helpful.

INFORMATION

To distinguish between knowledge and information in an objective manner is difficult. Their states may possibly be considered to be somewhat analogous to the state of particles in quantum physics. Knowledge through the process of communication gives rise to information. Information is "that which is transmitted by the act or process of communication, it may be a message, a signal, a stimulus"(Shera, 1972, p.164). The communicated information then becomes a form of stimulus capable of interacting with the mind giving rise to knowledge. The teacher to become aware (steps 1 to 6 and 10 in the example), and to transmit that awareness to students (steps 7 and 8) there has to be communication (step 9). Information is thus, a manifestation of knowledge (projected as an object of mind, description or stimuli) that exists independently and externally. Information is a product or form or consequence of knowledge and it cannot be created without knowledge.

In the above example, what the teacher learns from reading, and later conveys through speech to the class is knowledge drawn out of his mind. There is a difference between awareness as it exists in the mind, which is termed *implicit* knowledge by Noam Chomsky, the noted language scholar, and the knowledge in the mind communicated as an external manifestation termed *explicit* knowledge. This external manifestation is related to, but independent of the mind, and in this state knowledge is information. Unless the teacher acquires relevant knowledge on the selected topic, he cannot relay (the act of communication) it to the class. Information acquires its quality only when it has the characteristic to interact with the mind and participate in the cognitive processes. In other words, it must have significance or must be meaningful to some one.

Sound, sign, symbol, touch, and smell by themselves do not convey sense unless their meaning is pre-established by a common convention by the group using them. Further, they convey information only when a person exposed to them is able to derive meaning from it. Shera names it as the response-potential of information (Shera, 1972).

As observed earlier, information is not a part of the mind. It is a sensation or stimulus carried by sense organs. The cognitive processes in the brain transform information into knowledge. Boulding seems to mean this when he states that message encountering the image and affecting it is information (Boulding, 1956). Here, the image refers to knowledge and message to information.

Consciousness is a part of the mind. Information being the external manifestation of knowledge is not knowledge itself. Hence information is independent of the individual, whereas knowledge is not. Information can be related to knowledge and data through an information concept. Information concept has the consequence that: a) information and data are not identical; b) information is independent of the state of the individual; and c) effective information changes the state of knowledge of the receiver (Boulding, 1956; Brookes, 1975).

INFORMATION- KNOWLEDGE DUALITY

Knowledge may be defined as *image* of the world perceived by an individual, which has an implication of validity, of truth (Boulding, 1956). In this definition, knowledge is perceived as a cognitive structure or patterns in mind caused by information. The element of significance enables a knowledge structure to realize an image of the future which exists in the present (Boulding, 1970). Whether it is image or structure, it refers to awareness. In Machlup's view "information is the *activity* or *process* of informing and getting informed; knowledge is the *state* of knowing". By "getting *informed* about something, the recipient may reach *a state of* knowing the *contents* of the information" (Machlup, 1980, p. 56-57). Still, it does not make clear what information is, though the contents of information stand for knowledge. Further, it does not explain the implications, if any, of information being an activity, and knowledge a state of mind.

Knowledge is also created without the use of information, but from other external stimuli, and through the processes of thinking and reflection. In the example, the teacher uses reading which is only one of the means employed to gain knowledge. Brain also receives sense-data from other sense organs directly from objects and phenomena in nature or through internal stimuli. Because knowledge cannot be conveyed without employing some communication mode, knowledge outside its mental environment may be explained by using the concept of surrogate. Then, information becomes the surrogate of knowledge. Information becomes descriptive and takes the forms of speech, signs, symbols or touch. If information is different from knowledge, then the surrogate concept explains neatly the relationship between the two. In other words, information is to be considered as a representation or surrogate of (internal) knowledge (Farradane, 1976). Knowledge-information conundrum may be better understood by beginning with natural information. Natural information is the pattern of organization of matter and energy in the material world. Natural information gets represented through the process of encoding or embedding. The encoded information, which we encounter in our social and perceptual world, is based on patterns of organization derived from the use of symbols, language or signals. Embedded information is the corporeal expression or manifestation of information previously encoded. Information "given meaning and integrated with other contents of understanding" is knowledge (Bates, 2006, p.1044).

The brain, and thereby mind is constantly exposed to various sense-data or stimuli. As a result, the state and character of an existing knowledge structure keep changing by cognitive and emotional processes taking place in the brain. However, not all stimuli reaching the brain alter an existing knowledge state. Information, on the other hand, does not change for the reason that it does not get affected. The inference is that knowledge is dynamic, and information is static. Information thus becomes an external manifestation of knowledge. In the knowledge process information acts as stimuli serving as an input. The interrelationship between information and knowledge is shown in Fig. 1.

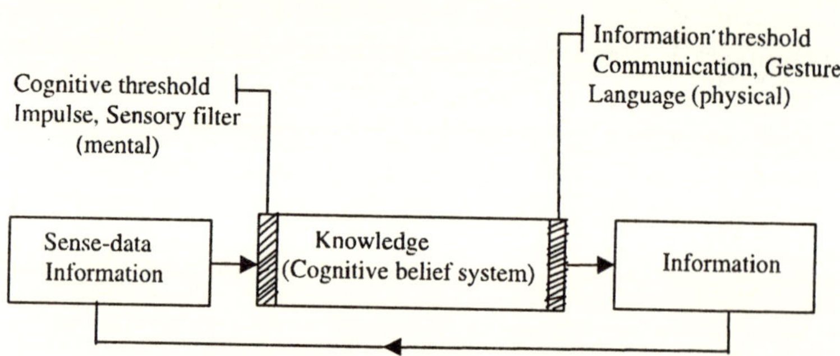

Fig.- 1. Information-knowledge duality

Knowledge and information constitute a duality. Fig.1 explains the nature of this duality. Knowledge and information are interdependent; one leads to the other. The interdependency is accounted by transformation process involving neural phenomena, memory, and cognitive and physical processes. The critical elements in the transformation process are: the cognitive threshold, and the information threshold. Sense-data and information, which are physical in nature and conveyed by sense organs, passing through the cognitive threshold gets transformed into knowledge, a cognitive product stored in memory. In a reverse way, knowledge held in memory gets transformed into information, a physical entity, after passing through information threshold. Communication is the main process and language is the chief agent acting at the information threshold. Information as a physical phenomenon follows the principles of science, such as Shannon's theory of information, compression of information, and even quantum principles. Brain theory and cognitive psychology try to explain the cognitive processes. The mysterious phase in the transformation of electrical impulses to consciousness/knowledge remains unsolved.

Knowledge and information phenomena can also be considered as an input to output conversion process. As seen in Fig. 1, sense-data and information constitute the input, knowledge the output; and information, an output of knowledge. It is a continuous process with brain (particularly cortex) acting as the processor unit. Output information and new sense-data conveyed by sense organs become the new input.

Integration and Consolidation of Knowledge. Contemplation and reflexive thinking take decisive part in the knowledge creation phenomenon. In the present context, the use of the term reflexive thinking has a wider meaning than in the context of sociology. Contemplation and reflexive thinking constantly going on in the mind about a given knowledge item occupying the mind develop it into a relatively enduring knowledge of substance. Whether it is Einstein's theory of relativity or knowledge about Mohenjo-Daro culture or any other account of knowledge advancement is not just the result of unitary acts of sensation being converted into knowledge of substance. It is the sustained acts of pondering, and reflecting, which include the application of intellectual processes like reasoning, correlating, combining, discarding, and testing the various entities and aspects of the knowledge item, lead to the creation of the final structure of the itemed knowledge at a given point of time. The cognitive efforts involve the play of various intellectual processes such as analysis, reasoning, comparison, logical thinking, intuition, making of hypothesis, verifying and testing the hypothesis, which finally shape the unitary units of knowledge in the mind into an integrated knowledge text of substance; it is not a case of simple conversion of stimulus/ data into knowledge, the instant the former is registered in brain. In contrast, instant discoveries, routine and ephemeral knowledge do not seem to undergo the process of contemplation and reflexive thinking.

Integrated knowledge is the resultant of continuous, intended cognitive activities taking place at the personal and institutional levels. Higher level cognitive processes play a predominant role in the act of consolidation. Consolidation has an important role in the development of theories, perspectives, and reviews. Without integration and consolidation our world of knowledge will be mere accumulated thoughts stored in memory. The integrated knowledge texts following the processes of identification, organization, ordering, and communication lead to the formation of disciplines and sub-disciplines, which together constitute the universe of knowledge. The universe of knowledge forms the base from which further growth of knowledge takes place. Consolidation is a primary step in the conversion of data to information, and information to knowledge (covered later in the chapter).

IGNORANCE

Ignorance is not being aware. All human beings have at least some knowledge that is essential for living. The range and amount of knowledge is growing in step with advances in civilization. It is impossible for any one individual to be aware of or knowledgeable about all things, of all times. Just as knowledgability refers to the state of awareness the lack of it, i.e., the state of unawareness, is commonly known as ignorance. Ignorance corresponds to a less crowded state of mind, knowledge-wise. Hence, there seems to be some truth in the proverb that "ignorance is bliss".

Types of Ignorance. Going by the effects of ignorance on individuals and society, ignorance can be classified into three types: a) ignorance of nil consequence; b) ignorance of deprival consequence; and c) ignorance of extended or third party consequence.

Ignorance of Nil Consequence. The universe of knowledge is so vast and varied that no one individual can be aware of all knowledge or even a substantial portion of it, yet individuals and cultures survive, if the requirement of minimum knowledge stock is met. Ignorance of all or any part of the total knowledge stock falling outside the minimum is of no serious consequence to the individual or the society to which he or she belongs. For example, not being aware of the pattern of crustacean life on the ocean bed or what is happening inside a distant galaxy is of no practical consequence to ordinary people, at least immediately. So is the case with a car driver living in Japan being ignorant of the Indian road traffic regulations.

Deprival Consequence. Knowledge is one of the main driving forces behind human life and progress. A person being ignorant of certain items of essential knowledge is likely to be deprived of the benefits flowing from that knowledge. A citizen may not even know, if he is deprived of the benefits of fundamental rights guaranteed by the constitution in a truly democratic setup, if he is ignorant of his rights, at least in general terms. An individual ignorant of the nutritive values of different food items is likely to deprive himself the safety of health due to wrong selection of diet. Ignorance does matter (or becomes important) only when it becomes distressing or harmful (Buckland, 1983).

Extended or Having Public Consequence. Acts of an individual done under ignorance may result in positive or negative consequences not only for the self, but also to others, such as neighbors and the larger society. A smoker of tobacco may be aware of the harmful effects of tobacco on his health, but may be ignorant of its hazardous impact on the health of the community and wellbeing of society to which he or she belongs— a case of ignorance with public or social consequence. A forest fire caused by the ignorant act of throwing a burning cigarette butt is another example of extended consequence of ignorance.

Acts of Ignorance and Accountability. All of us are ignorant of so many things happening in the world around us. In daily life we engage ourselves in many activities knowingly or unknowingly, which will have repercussions on the individual responsible for the act and on others in society. If the consequences are the outcome of acts committed under ignorance — invincible or vincible, i.e., real or contrived, and harm others, the question arises whether the committer of the act can disclaim all responsibility for the consequences of such acts pleading ignorance. On moral and compassionate grounds the plea of ignorance may be accepted by many, but not by courts of law. This principle is one of the tenets on which the English "law of torts" is founded. The individual is accountable for the consequences of his or her actions, and cannot take cover under the plea of ignorance. Ignorance is also employed by some as a tactical means to avoid facing embarrassing situations.

Reducing the Level of Ignorance. In individuals, ignorance of a particular knowledge field or items can be removed or reduced by acquiring knowledge of those domains through learning and experiencing. This calls for efforts on the part of the individual, and also from social institutions including the state. More often, benefit-cost consideration, i.e., balancing the perceived importance or the benefits likely to follow from a particular item of knowledge to the individual against the efforts or resources needed to acquire it decides the issue. In addition, one's mental makeup, external influences such as culture, tradition, social and political movements, economic necessity, geography, and the like account for one's state of ignorance.

Epistemic (or Knowledge) Syndrome. Ignorance also has a psychological dimension, which takes the form of a psychological tendency in many people. Such people want to show that they are knowledgeable, even though they are not, about a given knowledge position; they want to prove that they are not ignorant. This tendency is more often seen in interpersonal interactions; and it is different from knowledge-standpoints arising out of genuine perceptional or value differences. Such a tendency has the potential to create ignorance-centered conflicts. On the other hand, there are cases of persons for whom pursuit of knowledge is an intense activity bordering on affliction to the exclusion of all other pursuits and values in life.

Another psychological facet of knowledge is knowledge phobia. It takes the form of aversion towards knowledge and disliking of intellectuals.

Technical Approach to Ignorance. Ignorance dealt with so far is on the lines of a general interpretation. In the general approach ignorance is seen through the window of common sense and general perception. There is another approach to the study of ignorance, which may be called "technical" or "managerial". A technical approach developed by Michael Smithson studies ignorance, its characteristics and effects applying statistical laws, organizational management findings, and social behaviour research. In this view, the prime causes of ignorance are error and irrelevance. Error occurs due to incomplete comprehension of facts, meaning or distorted view of things. Irrelevance related ignorance is caused by intended ignorance. Irrelevances are of different types, e.g., ignorance caused by the usage of language. Keeping information secret also leads to ignorance (Smithson, 1988). In organizations, if the logic of right to privacy is intended to keep those outside the "need to know" ignorant, "right to information" acts are enacted to reduce ignorance by providing access to information falling under the public domain.

WISDOM

Generally, wisdom may be categorized into- spiritual

wisdom, and practical wisdom. The Hindu philosophy expresses the two types of wisdom beautifully by the terms "paramarthika" viveka and "vyavaharika" or "loukika" viveka. Spiritual wisdom deals with larger issues of life, like existence, self realization, and cosmic reality. It is metaphysical and spiritual in nature. In this sense, Perry comments, wisdom is true knowledge that "leads to the recovery of the Primordial Self, 'lost or obscured' through the process of individualism implied in existence, but which in essence 'we' have never ceased to be" (Perry, 1971, p. 19). It is that knowledge which leads to identification of the "pattern of the human personality in the cosmos that is unerringly consistent, clear, and struck through with a resonance infallible in its ever renewed reverberations of the same reality" (Perry, 1971, p.21).

Practical wisdom, on the other hand, refers to knowledge that promotes material, social and cultural well-being of individuals and society in relation to earthly existence. It is knowledge wisely used for the benefit of individuals, society and mankind as against misuse of knowledge that would add to human misery and violation of nature's sanctity. Wisdom connotes qualities of goodness and harmony; it is distinct from other qualities of knowledge such as intelligence and creativity. Often, one associates wisdom with one's maturity of mind, experiential and analytic insights, and capacity to reflect and judge what is good. Wisdom carries with it the essence of cumulative knowledge. It is subjective, and what is considered as wisdom at one point of time may not be valid for all times, to all societies or to all situations. A critical aspect of wisdom that guards us against obsessiveness is the use of power of selection — the ability to grasp the essential features that matters in a given problem or action situation, and ignore the irrelevant aspects (Midgley, 1989).

Scholarly usage shows that the relationship between knowledge and information is one of subjective values and ranking. Machlup refers to the fact that the characteristic of information content-wise being secondary and concrete, as against original, abstract, general or universal in knowledge has suggested to many hierarchical ranking, giving knowledge a superior status and information an inferior one (Machlup, 1980). For this same reason wisdom is ranked higher than knowledge.

Sectoral Wisdom. Wisdom is also seen as having practical perspectives, and moral and social perspectives as its major components. Based on the analysis of these perspectives it is suggested that wisdom:

1. Is embedded in, or exhibited by action.
2. Involves the sophisticated and sensitive use of knowledge.
3. Accommodates multiple realities, and wider social and ethical considerations, and is exercised in decision-making and in the implementation of decisions (Rowley, 2006).

In Knowledge Management. Some "Knowledge Management" specialists recognize organizational wisdom to be distinct from wisdom in general and make it (along with managerial leadership), the basis of "Wisdom Management" (Bierly et al., 2000). Distinguishing organizational wisdom from common wisdom makes sense, as in the former the characteristics unique to organizations and their problems are traced; and they are made use of in shaping wisdom relevant to organizational management. Similarly, one can recognize wisdom shaped by special characteristics of particular professions or broad fields of engagement, distinct from general wisdom, e.g., medical wisdom, and legal wisdom. Such a sectoral wisdom carries with it the best counsel available at the given point of time. However, the fact remains that wisdom is a qualitative, cognitive phenomenon of the mind, which is unique to each person. A "wisdom" manager can only advice or give his wise counsel. On the other hand, if Wisdom

Management means managing wisdom for others, then we may have to add one more line " Where is the wisdom we have lost in Wisdom Management" to T.S Eliot's famous lines "Where is the wisdom we have lost in knowledge; Where is the knowledge we have lost in information" (Eliot, 1939, p. 157).

Carriers of Wisdom. Not withstanding Marxist's ideological conclusion of a ruling class claiming monopoly of political and economic wisdom to rule, claim to wisdom is not limited to any particular section of society, such as intellectuals or specific specialist groups. Extreme specialization may sometimes blur one's wisdom. In fact, extreme specialization in any field has the possibility of a specialist loosing sight of elementary factors associated with a given situation, which are easily discerned by common sense or ordinary professionals in the particular field. Several examples supporting this fact are seen in the field of medical treatment of patients. The limitation caused by specialist bias is tried to overcome by access to group consultation and multiple refereeing. An example for nonrestrictive nature of wisdom is "folk wisdom". Many of the proverbs composed centuries ago carry well tested wisdom, which are found valid even in the current era of modernity. To give one example is the proverb "a stitch in time saves nine" is not only valid, but also is the basis of preventive maintenance in factory management.

Foolishness. Lack of application of wisdom in decision-making and in human transactions is a sign of foolishness. It is said to be the opposite of wisdom. Wisdom is different from intelligence and smartness. Intelligence is no protection against foolishness. One could be smart, yet foolish. Wisdom is situation and knowledge domain bound. The nature and the growth of wisdom is influenced by the cultural, social, psychological, and philosophical surroundings of the individual. Wisdom may take a collative form in larger social units like a community or a society (Sternberg, 2005). One may be acting wisely in a particular situation or in a particular field, but may be foolish in another situation or another domain. The term wisdom is used in two senses: a) meaning the content of wisdom or the kind of information that a particular person deems wise at a given time, and b) an individual's capacity to think or act wisely (Csikszentmihalyi and Nakamura, 2005).

DATA

Encyclopedia of Statistical Sciences defines "datum" (in statistics) as a fact from which a conclusion may be drawn. A datum contains information, whereas a number, adjective, or other form of description may not. When numbers and adjectives convey information (facts) about some entity such facts are denoted as data (Kotz, 1982). A common man's perception of data is facts and figures pertaining to items such as population, trade statistics, household income and expenditure, items in a calendar, timetables, and also facts and figures collected from scientific observations of phenomena and experiments as in research. Data form the basis for reasoning, discussion or calculation, and drawing conclusions. Raw data collected from observations and experiments may include redundant or irrelevant items as well as useful facts and figures, and must be refined to be meaningful. The description of the characteristics of data is called metadata (Gelbstein, 2003).

In the context of knowledge, data may be considered as a form of information. It is largely unitary in character, less complex and limited in scope. Data become information when subjected to cognitive processes, such as recognition, analysis evaluation, correlation and synthesis. Information can be considered as specifically structured data which act to transform a state of knowledge or knowledge structure. Data is a (taken as a) physical symbol of some sort which represents a message. Data undergo the process of cognition to form a specific data structure called information function of data. The information function then operates on the recipient's knowledge-structure, resulting in a new knowledge-structure (Belkin, 1975). A similar interpretation holds that data turns into "information", when we identify a particular use for it, and structure it so that it can be used. It takes knowledge to turn data into information (Blair, 2002). This makes data the primary building blocks in the knowledge- information structure.

FROM DATA TO ENLIGHTENMENT

Data, information, knowledge, wisdom and enlightenment (and genius) constitute a spiral of awareness, with data forming the base and enlightenment the vertex, which is shown in Fig. 2.

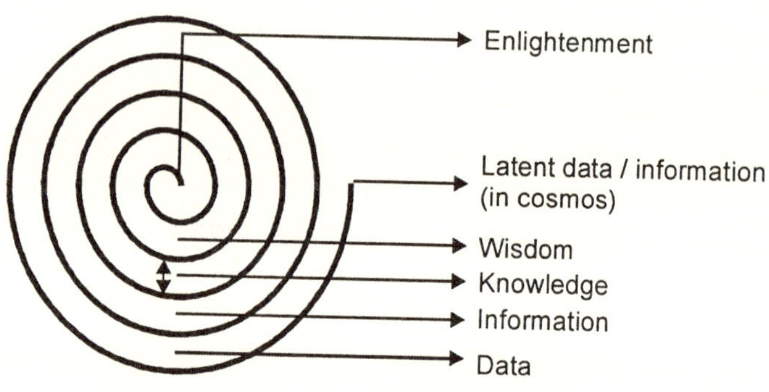

Fig. 2. Spiral of data, information, knowledge, wisdom and enlightenment

When we speak of totality of knowledge we seem to imply universe of knowledge, the knowledge that human beings are aware of. This universe of known knowledge is only a part of the cosmos, which includes awareness yet to be discovered by man. We have no idea about the quantum as well as the nature of awareness hidden in the undiscovered portion of the cosmos other than what the fundamental constituents of nature can explain. Nature neither reveals its secrets easily nor within a fixed time-frame; it depends on nature herself, and the human efforts to extract the hidden knowledge. What we are sure of is that the boundaries of known knowledge universe are constantly expanding through exploration of hidden awareness in the cosmos, and by playing with the units and entities in the known knowledge universe. The known knowledge universe shown in Fig. 2 categorizes data, information, knowledge, wisdom and enlightenment based on value relations between them, which are subjective. They are related structurally by quantity, quality, depth and value following the process of mental distillation. As we proceed from the base of the spiral, i.e., data to the vertex, i.e., enlightenment, the volume of each segment decreases and the quality, depth, and value increases. Enlightenment is the pristine final outcome of wisdom; and one does not know, when, where and how it appears. Probably, higher level intuition and the qualities of genius are parts of it.

RECORDS

Records do not belong to the same category as that of knowledge, information and data. Records are considered here as they are physically related to information. Though, the transmission of knowledge through speech preceded writing, it is the written record that made possible: a) access to information independent of time and space, b) give permanency to knowledge, and c) ease of use. A record is a physical medium on which information is embodied through the use of a communication mode such as language. Records help in reconstructing the past, access the present, and can also serve as an external memory aid. Records constitute an important means of carrying public knowledge. Popper links records with objective knowledge in his "World 3", the world of our conscious experiences and the world of the logical contents of books, libraries, computer memories and the like (Popper, 1972). Records being physical entities stand at a different level than that of knowledge, information and data. The following example illustrates the relationship between knowledge, information and record. A book is a record, a physical good. If a book, say a treatise on advanced level calculus is read by a voice reader to a blind mathematician, the hearing of the text is information, and his mental grasping of what he has heard is knowledge. The numbers and individual terms in the treatise read to him or expressed by him is data, and the notes or comments he may dictate on the treatise becomes a record of information or record of the commentator's knowledge.

CLOSURE

The formation of knowledge is the resultant of mental processes acting on stimuli and a priori knowledge held in memory. Knowledge in its most general and fundamental sense is recognition. A straight approach to understand knowledge is to go by the operative concept "to know" in the word knowledge. According to classical epistemology, knowledge is justified true belief. In the context of practical life insistence on the criteria of justification and truth will be unproductive as unverified or even false knowledge has practical implications and utility. Contemplation and reflexive thinking help integrate and consolidate knowledge in the mind.

Information is the external manifestation of knowledge, i.e., a surrogate for knowledge. Information also serves as stimulus and is independent of the individual, where as knowledge is not. Ignorance is not being aware of existing knowledge. Ignorance may be grouped under: ignorance of nil consequence, of deprival consequence, and of extended or third-party consequence. Perceived deficiency of knowledge and attempts to camouflage it leads to *epistemic syndrome*. Level of ignorance in individuals and society may be reduced by learning, education and experiencing. Study of ignorance by applying statistical laws, organization science, and social behaviour yields new insights having practical applications. Wisdom is knowledge refined and distilled through maturity of mind, improved by experiential or analytic insights; and is the capacity to reflect and judge what is good. Data are the basic units constituting a message or meaningful signals made out of stimuli. Data stand independently, are less complex, and limited in scope. Data becomes knowledge by cognitive structuring. Data, information, knowledge, wisdom and enlightenment constitute a spiral of awareness in the order of increasing value.

Defining knowledge, information and data emphatically having universal acceptance is almost impossible. This is mainly due to the abstract nature of these entities, and the limitless area in which they operate. The definitions vary from one context to another due to the different emphasis laid in the approaches— mental or pragmatic. Mental approach is characterized more by philosophic and psychological bias of the definer, where as pragmatic approach is influenced by the physical nature of these phenomena. Thus, the definition framed by a philosopher or a cognitive psychologist differs from that of a scientist, which differs from that of an economist or computer specialist or knowledge management practitioner. Each approach is valid in the given context or domain.

Categorizing knowledge at the pragmatic level into "tacit" or "implicit" knowledge referring to what is in the mind, and "explicit" knowledge meaning knowledge existing outside the mind in the form of information and records is helpful. Classifying knowledge at the cognitive level under "procedural" knowledge relating to skills, such as reasoning, problem solving and the like and "declarative" knowledge which pertains to facts and descriptions; "semantic" knowledge referring to knowledge about the world which is shared by many and "episodic" knowledge, which limits knowledge to one's own experience and linked to a particular space and time gives knowledge contextual clarity. Ultimately what counts most is how these entities are understood and put to use. The accounts of knowledge, information, ignorance, wisdom, data and record covered in this chapter serve as the platform for moving on to next chapters.

REFERENCES

Ayer, A. J. The Problem of Knowledge. Harmondsworth (Middlesex), Pengin Books, 1956.

Bates, Marcia J. Fundamental forms of information. *Journal of the American Society for Information Science* 57 (8): 1033-1045, June 2006.

Belkin, N.J. Towards a Definition of Information for Informatics. Pp. 53-54. *In* Horsenell, Verina. Ed. Informatics 2. London, Aslib, 1975.

Benjafield, John G. Cognition. Ed. 2. Upper Saddle River (N.J.), Prentice-Hall, 1996.

Bierly, P.E. III; Kessler, E.H. and Christensen, E.W. Learning, knowledge and wisdom. *Journal of Organizational Change Management* 13 (6): 595-618, 2000.

Blair, David C. Knowledge management: Hype, hope, or help? *Journal of the American Society for Information Science and Technology* 53(12): 1019-1028, 2002.

Boulding, K.E. Knowledge as a Commodity. In Beyond Economics: Essays on Society, Religion and Ethics. Ann Arbor, University of Michigan Press, 1970.

Boulding, K. E. The Image: Knowledge in Life and Society. Ann Arbor, University of Michigan Press, 1956.

Brookes, B.C. The Fundamental Problem of Information Sciences. Pp. 42-49. *In* Horsnell, Verina. Ed. Informatics 2. London, Aslib, 1975.

Buckland, M. K. Library Services in Theory and Context. New York, Pergamon Press, 1983.

Csikszentmihalyi, Mihaly and Nakamura, Jeanne, The Role of Emotions in the Development of Wisdom. Pp.220-242. In Sternberg, Robert J. and Jordan, Jennifer. Ed. A Handbook of Wisdom: Psychological Perspectives. Cambridge (NY), Cambridge University Press, 2005.

Eliot, T.S. Collected Poems, 1909-1935. London, Faber and Faber, 1939.

Encyclopaedia Britannica, The New. Ed.15. Chicago, Encyclopaedia Britinica, 2007. Vol.24. Pp.152-161:Mind.

Farradane, J. Towards a true information science. *Information Scientist* 10 : 91-101, 1976.

Gelbstein, Eduardo. Data, Information, and Knowledge. *In* Encyclopaedia of Information Systems. Vol.1. Pp. 469- 4 , 2003.

Jones, P.C. The Nature of Knowledge. New York, Scarecrow Press, 1964.

Kotz, Samuel. Ed . Encyclopedia of Statistical Sciences, Vol. 2. New York, Wiley, 1982.

Lieberman, Matthew D. et al. Reflexion and reflection: A social cognitive neuroscience approach to attributional inference, Pp. 199-249. *In* Zanna, Mark P. Ed. *Advances in Experimental Social Psychology*. Vol. 34, 2002.. San Diego (CA.), Academic Press.

Machlup, Fritz. Knowledge: Its Creation, Distribution, and Economic Significance. Vol. 1: Princeton University Press, 1980.

Machlup, Fritz. Knowledge: Its Creation, Distribution, and Economic Significance.Vol.3: The Economics of Information and Human Capital. Princeton, Princeton University Press, 1984.

Midgley, Mary. Wisdom, Information and Wonder: What is Knowledge For? London, Routledge, 1989.

Perry, W. N. A. Treasury of Traditional Wisdom. New York, Simon and Schuster, 1971.

Popper, K.R. Objective Knowledge; An Evolutionary Approach. London, Oxford University Press, 1972.

Rowley, Jennifer. Where is the wisdom that we have lost in knowledge? *Journal of Documentation* 62 (2): 252-270, 2006.

Shera, J.H. The Foundations of Education for Librarianship. New York, Wiley-Becker and Hayes, 1972.

Smithson, Michael. Ignorance and Uncertainty: Emerging Paradigms. New York, Springer-Verlag, 1988.

Sternberg, Robert J. Foolishness. Pp.331-352. *In* Sternberg, Robert J. and Jordan, Jennifer. Ed. A Handbook of Wisdom: Psychological Perspectives. Cambridge (NY), Cambridge University Press, 2005.

2

ORGANIZATION, COMMUNICATION AND TRANSFER

Human knowledge to become useful and to build upon it further, all items of knowledge or concepts that make up the human universe need to be organized so that they can be easily identified and retrieved. Knowledge is stored in memory that may be compared to a closed system. Entropy, enshrined in the Second Law of Thermodynamics, is the study of energy contents of closed systems in the physical universe. Entropy also relates energy with the level of disorder in a system. An increase in entropy increases disorder. To increase order in a system entropy is to be decreased, which means expenditure of energy. In the case of human memory, expenditure of energy amounts to putting increased efforts, i.e., cognitive labour. Increasing order means organizing thoughts, and items of knowledge held in memory so that they can be easily recalled when needed. Universe of knowledge consists of knowledge items stored in individual human memories, and information relating to past as well as present stored in various physical media. Thus, to bring order to the universe of knowledge cognitive efforts are to be put in, which is the function of organization. Before proceeding to organizational aspects of knowledge, it is necessary to define the scope of knowledge field so that one knows what knowledge is to be organized.

SCOPE OF KNOWLEDGE

A practical approach to the organization of knowledge must take knowledge in its broadest sense, and in the commonly understood usage, and must include anything that is known by somebody. Since most of religious knowledge is considered to be of "revealed" and "divine" creation, which falls outside the human origin, is excluded from consideration throughout this book. However, the influence of religious knowledge on the thinking and living of millions and millions of people has to be accepted. The following scope of knowledge is adapted from Levitan's view on the scope of information as it conveys more clearly what constitutes knowledge: knowledge refers not just the subject or the message, not just to its media or technologies, not just to the processes involved, but to all of these interrelated and interdependent factors taken together as one system. This is true whether the knowledge is in the mind of an individual and is available only to that person (personal knowledge) or whether it is possessed collectively by a society and made available to that society through its records (social knowledge) (Levitan, 1978). Thus, the scope of knowledge takes under its purview "knowing that" and "knowing how", and knowledge that is profound as well as mundane, scholarly as well as ordinary, permanent as well as transitory, basic as well as applied, abstract as well as concrete, intellectual as well as sensual, scientific as well as nonscientific and unscientific, private as well as public, acquired in everyday experience as well as through conscious efforts of learning, research and other means, such as intuition. In other words, the percept of knowledge must include awareness of all that concerns and interests human beings and society. This is because the types of knowledge that affect and shape human life are varied, and hence the study of knowledge cannot ignore any of them.

For understanding the various aspects of knowledge, their effects and implications, it is necessary to recognize the components of a knowledge situation. These are:

1. Knowing as well as what is known by a human being, i.e., what the human mind thinks, perceives, creates, senses, and feels.
2. Communication mode, i.e., the manner in which knowledge or what is known by one human being is conveyed to another human being by means, such as sound or speech, symbol, odor, touch, and expression.
3. Communication medium (the physical medium), i.e., any physical object like paper, a sound record, a computer CD, a hard disk, and others employed by the communicator to transmit knowledge.

Because of the amorphous nature of knowledge phenomena, and the lack of precise usage of terminology in discussing knowledge, communication mode and physical medium are often used as surrogates for knowledge. Neither communication mode nor physical medium can resurrect knowledge outside the human brain.

ORGANIZATION OF KNOWLEDGE

Society is based on organization. The more advanced a society is, the more complex will be its organization. Organization needs structure, and structure is based on division of labour and specialization of functions. Such a division gives rise to fuctionalization of activities and thoughts. Organization in social, political, and economic spheres is based on will and purposes, and it largely depends on the progressive functional organization of relevant thoughts arising from varied, syntactic knowledge. This takes the form of intellectual organization, professional organization, and the organization of rational purpose, which in turn depends on the organization of relevant knowledge (Bliss, 1929). Unlike social and physical organization, knowledge organization is an intellectual organization, and its purpose is to facilitate use of knowledge, and to support the growth of knowledge. The organization is in relation to abstract knowledge units.

In the case of individuals, items of knowledge stored in human memory to be recalled its organizational part is taken care of by the mental processing mechanism of the brain, e.g., the phenomena of long-term and short-term memory, and "associationism", i.e., learning brought about by association of ideas and events. On the other hand, when it comes to the universe of knowledge consisting of thousands of concepts further organization by external agencies becomes necessary. No single mind can be aware of even a minor segment of the entire universe of knowledge. The chief function of knowledge organization is to make available to a mind a panoramic structured view of the contents of the universe and its phenomena, including the human thoughts, as grasped by individuals as well as collective human mind over time and space. It is also to serve as a topography, guide map, and aid memoir. Another vital function of organization is to identify items of knowledge, and help recall any item of knowledge when wanted.

Intellectual Organization. Without the organization of knowledge, world is a vast jumble of entities — thoughts, ideas, concepts and subjects. The first stage in the process of knowledge organization is identification of thousands of entities constituting the knowledge world. The only pragmatic and natural way, we know, of identifying these entities is by name, that is by a word. One can also think of identifying by numbers. Identification by numbers alone will not serve any purpose as each number has to be correlated with the entity it represents to make it meaningful, which means the use of names. A word is "the symbol, the core, the matrix that unifies and preserves abstracted, integrated, and synthesized experience... It functions without recall of the pertinent experiences. It is the 'shorthand' that allows experiences to be fed into the infinitely complex 'electronic computer' of the human mind" (Lawther, 1984, p.519). The human learning process generally begins with the word "maa" or "mom" of English language (and its corresponding sound words in other languages). A word becomes a "concept" as a result of the associative skill of linking the abstract with the concrete, which develops in stages from early childhood. Knowledge identification thus becomes naming of concepts by means of words; in other words, it means construction of vocabulary. Most of the words we use in ordinary life are traced to our cultural and linguistic origin, and learning. The building of nomenclature, in general, is a part of our endeavors, such as scientific, artistic and professional pursuits. The first step in organization of knowledge is labeling of knowledge entities, which is done by the use of vocabulary. Fortunately, labeling words are coined mostly by the creators of knowledge, and to some extent by the users of knowledge. With the scope of knowledge defined, and vocabulary for identifying knowledge entities and concepts in place, we move on to the next step in organization, and that is establishing order amongst the concepts or entities of knowledge. Classification brings order, but may not be the right solution for all types of accessing knowledge world. Even a classified order of entities needs to be supplemented by an alphabetical index to the classified portion. Alphabetical arrangement, in spite of its many limitations in providing complete coverage within reasonable efforts and time, forms the most familiar and primary means of providing access. In the world of Internet and web sites, words linked with relational cognitive support has become the only way of reaching texts in the electronic form with ease and least effort.

CLASSIFICATION OF KNOWLEDGE

Classification is one of the basic methods employed by the human brain in organizing thoughts and concepts. The purpose of classification is to bring out the differences, recognize commonalities, discern relationships, indicate the variety and scope of entities in a given area of knowledge, and thereby establish order. Classification of knowledge "is a form of analysis and often it can be more enlightening than definition in establishing the nature and function of knowledge in society" (Shera, 1972, p.119). An intricate problem in classifying knowledge is defining knowledge and its scope. It is also necessary to pre-establish the purpose to be served by classification. The purpose of classifying the universe of knowledge is to help us in providing a holistic view of the entire knowledge field and also to know its types, characteristics, relations, growth, utilization and impact.

Besides arrangement, classification facilitates identification, display of items, correlation, comparison, synthesis and prediction. It gives a total view of a field of knowledge, and shows the pattern of development of its constituent parts. A less explored aspect of classification is its use in producing new knowledge and exploitation of the predictive power of classification. A study of the vacant classes in a classification table can help to produce new knowledge (Ranganathan, 1952). Combining logical and conceptual relationships between classes can lead to prediction of fruitful areas of research and research findings (Jolley, 1973). Classifying a given set of objects by every possible attribute relevant to the field could show the hidden properties of the object world, and relations so apparent that could exist between the members of the group, e. g., classifying books applying the characteristics of size, colour, weight, period of publication, cost, language of the text, citation, place of publication, number of pages, and the like show unexpected relationships existing between texts.

Recognition of different types of thoughts was a part of Greek philosophic tradition. The first systematic taxonomy, i.e., biological classification was given by Aristotle. Aristotle in his work *Nicomachean Ethics* refers to five different forms of thought, which may be presented as five divisions of knowledge:

1. *Episteme* : Factual or scientific knowledge.
2. *Techne* : Skills-based technical and action-oriented knowledge.
3. *Phronesis* : Experiential self-knowledge or practical wisdom based on experience.
4. *Nous* : Intuition.
5. *Sophia* : Theoretical knowledge of universal truths or first principles (Schwartz, 2006).

In modern times knowledge has been classified in different ways depending upon the purpose to be served, such as the needs of philosophy, science, biology, education, libraries, economics, and so on. Traditionally, Bliss notes, that knowledge is organized in several stages or kinds— mental synthesis, social organization of knowledge, the organization of a special branch of knowledge, the organization of a field of knowledge in a class of books or other records, and the organization of many fields of knowledge as in an encyclopaedia or library. This approach is represented by the tree of knowledge (Bliss, 1929). With the growth of knowledge, particularly in science and technology, the tree approach is neither sufficient nor capable of showing the multi-dimensionality of knowledge, and its complex relationships. Others have divided knowledge into "scientific and historical", "general systemic" (or "general abstract") and "particular - concrete", "permanent" and "transitory", "basic" and "applied", and "knowing how" corresponding to *wissen and konnen* in German language. Classifying knowledge into permanent and transitory, basic and applied are helpful in identifying knowledge in terms of relative utility and functional relationship, respectively. Still the categorization is subjective and relative.

A more appropriate classification is the one based on the end use of knowledge. Following this criterion, Max Scheler categorizes knowledge into:

1. Knowledge for the sake of action or control (*Herrschaftswissen*).
2. Knowledge for the sake of material culture (*bildungswissen*).
3. Knowledge for the sake of salvation (*Erlosungswissen*) (Scheler,1926).

Machlup provides a more detailed and practical scheme, in which knowledge is classified into:

1. Practical knowledge, i.e., knowledge useful in work, decision-making and actions. It is further divided into: professional knowledge, political knowledge, business knowledge, household knowledge, work-man's knowledge, and other practical knowledge.
2. Intellectual knowledge, i.e., knowledge satisfying intellectual curiosity as in liberal arts, education, and scientific research.
3. Small-talk and pastime knowledge, i.e., knowledge satisfying non-intellectual curiosity or providing light entertainment.
4. Spiritual knowledge.
5. Unwanted knowledge, i.e., knowledge outside one's interests, accidentally acquired, aimlessly retained (Machlup, 1980).

Sometimes it may be more useful to think knowledge in terms of systems of knowledge. A system of knowledge is made up of several subsystems which are distinct, and stand independently; but are bound by a central common theme, and may have several common features. An example for systems of knowledge is the systems of medicine representing-Allopathic, Ayurvedic, Unani, Homoeopathic and Tribal practices. Systems of knowledge approach makes comparing and contrasting of systems easy and focused. Often, these systems constitute diverse and unique knowledge. Hence, any attempts to homogenize them by applying the new technological methods of producing, preserving and accessing the research results will harm the integrity of that knowledge (Birdsall, 2005).

Both knowledge and information, irrespective of their natures, need to be communicated, if they are to be used. Further, transfer of knowledge is a social necessity and fulfils a psychological need. Thus, the study of knowledge must necessarily include the study of the relevant aspects of human communication. Engineering theory of physical transmission of information is dealt with in a later chapter.

COMMUNICATION AND KNOWLEDGE

In the context of knowledge, the phenomenon of communication may be deemed to connote a deep, dynamic and complex series of processes operating together—perception, memory, information analysis and processing, symbolic transformation, delivery and feedback (Neelameghan, 1979). Considered in a general way, communication takes place, "when one mind so acts upon its environment that another mind is influenced, and in that other mind an experience occurs which is like the experience in the first mind, and is caused in part by that experience" (Richards, 1955, p.177). This general definition explains the process of communication, and distinguishes between contents of the messages and their transmission. Other dimensions of communication are its psychological, behavioural, mathematical, and mechanical aspects. The study of knowledge is also concerned with communication of thoughts in humans. The impact of mass communication media has been so pervasive that it made McLuhan to state "the medium is the message" (McLuhan, 1964). Though medium has a tremendous influence on the diffusion of knowledge, it is the message that is vital. Moreover, mass communication is only one type of communication, while there are other aspects and forms that are of interest to knowledge, namely, persuasive communication, processes of interpersonal communication as mediator, dynamics of verbal and nonverbal communication between individuals, perception of different kinds of communication, uses of communication technology for social, educational and artistic purposes, and development of relevant criticism for artistic endeavors (Encyclopaedia Britannica, 2007. Vol. 16).

Language. Most of the knowledge comes to us from speaking to and hearing from others, reading and writing. New knowledge is built upon the knowledge that has already accumulated. Transfer of knowledge in society is largely based on oral, written, and visual communication. Thus, knowledge is intertwined with communication. Though communication takes place through signals, signs, symbols, sound, gestures and other means, it is language based on speech and symbols that dominates communication of knowledge in human society.

A language is "a system of arbitrary vocal symbols by means of which a social group cooperates" (Bloch and Trager, 1942, p. 5). It provides an associative link between an easily transmitted sign and the idea which it represents. Language and thinking are so closely interrelated that some logicians conclude that thinking is not possible without language. Apart from transmitting information, language also serves a few other purposes, such as: to establish relations among people, to express or clarify thoughts, for play, for creative mental activity. Interdependence of language and thought which is known as "linguistic relativity" is generally accepted, but their exact relationship is yet to be established (Chomsky, 2003). Language as a communication mode has advantages as well as disadvantages. Speech has the advantage of speed and its emotional connotation can convey hidden meaning better than the written word. On the other hand, a written word is easy to use and conveys a concept more accurately (Perry, 1956).

Symbolic Character of Learning. Speech and symbolic representation, particularly language, of natural phenomena and human activities constitute the most effective tools of learning. As one grows from childhood, objects, phenomena and acts acquire symbolic counterparts which can be in lieu of the original. Symbolization provides unlimited scope for learning. Shera points out that "symbols make possible: a) the effective communication of experience from person to person or group to group; b) the compression, or short circuiting, of experience through the efficiency of symbolic manipulation; and c) the utilization of past experience through storage and manipulation in the memory of symbolic representations" (Shera, 1972, p.19).

A major disadvantage of language is that it cannot completely represent our observations, reflections and perceptions. Hence, there is an inherent risk of misunderstanding and misinterpretation. Further, it cannot transmit emotions and senses. Use of uniform graphic codes, such as standardized symbols in mathematics and formulae in chemistry serve as universal language without giving rise to ambiguity as to their meaning. Pictorial representation of knowledge has the advantage of duplicating a multiplicity of individual observations and their relationship, but is unable to furnish all the details (Perry, 1956). The invention of computer, and programming languages based on Boolean algebra, the development of high density storage media, and high speed transmission, and over the earth communication have revolutionized the whole field of machine processing of language texts and their physical transmission.

From the standpoint of knowledge, the main problems in communicating through language are : how to convey meaning/knowledge, how to convey it fast and at the least cost without distortion. Communication and dissemination of knowledge largely depend on language. Hence the study of language and its usage becomes crucial in processing knowledge.

Psychology of Communication. Communication is complete, from the point of view of conveyor, only when the message communicated elicits the desired response from the recipient. Communication makes demands on the recipient and is interrelated with the emotions, values and expectations of the recipient (Drucker, 1975). This is true of communication in organizations, in learning, and to a lesser extent in scientific interactions. Symbols and terminology have emotional connotations which play a significant role, particularly, in the fields of law, economics and public affairs. Existence of socially forbidden words is a common feature in all languages. Knowledge processing through language cannot ignore the psychological aspects of communication. Effective communication has to overcome the psychological and motivational barriers.

LEARNING AND EDUCATION

The progress of the human society is sustained by its ability to transmit knowledge by means of learning. The human brain is endowed with unique mechanisms of cognition and memory which make learning a highly developed function not found in other species. This has tempered the role of instinct in human beings. From birth until death, a person is in constant interaction with the environment, and thus engaged in learning. Learning is defined by Garry as the process by which behaviour is originated or changed through practice (Garry and Kingsley, 1970). *The Dictionary of Psychology* (Colman, 2001) defines learning as: a) any lasting change in behavior resulting from experience, especially conditioning, and b) the act or process of acquiring knowledge or skill, gained by study.

LEARNING

Survival of species rests on homeostatic mechanisms like

maintenance of constant body temperature, reflexive actions like one's instinctive withdrawal from a danger zone, and learning acquired through one's interaction with the environment for meeting basic needs like food, water and other sources of satisfaction. The learning process provides an organism with the flexibility it needs to survive under a wide variety of environmental conditions. Most of the theories of learning follow *proximate explanations* of behaviour to the near exclusion of *ultimate explanations* of behaviour. Proximate explanation refers to events in an organism's immediate environment like deprivation conditions, environmental stimuli, reinforced contingencies, and the immediate learning history of the organism, whereas ultimate explanation means traits and behaviour of organisms acquired through natural selection (Hergenhahn and Olson, 2005). Learning theories are broadly classified into- a) connectionist or stimulus-response theories, b) field or cognitive theories, and c) functionalist theories. The addition of evolutionary theories, and neurophysiologic theories have enlarged the field.

Connectionist Theories. Central to connectionist theories are stimulus, response and conditioning, the core concepts associated with behaviour. Stimulus is any event, agent, or influence, internal or external, that excites or is capable of exciting a sensory receptor, and of causing a response in an organism. Response is any physical or psychological reaction of an organism to a stimulus caused by stimulation of a sensory receptor. Skinner's behaviorism also includes a purely mental reaction. Conditioning is the process of learning through which the behaviour of organisms becomes dependent on environmental stimuli (Colman, 2001).

Under appropriate conditions, when stimuli act on sense organs, the organism, i.e., the individual's brain, automatically responds and such a response is "unlearned response". But in learning the nervous system of the brain connects specific stimuli to responses that are favorable, an act of *connectionism*.

Learning theories developed by Thorndike, Pavlov, and Skinner are based on connectionist principle. Connectionist theories are based on the findings that stimulus S leads to (or connected with) response R. This relationship is symbolically represented by $S \longrightarrow R$.

Field Theories. For supporters of field theories learning is the resultant of constant interaction between two dynamic energy systems, the learner and the larger universe, in which the mind plays its cognitive role in co-relating and interpreting events (stimuli and response) in time. Since learning events are bound to a wider field consisting of natural elements, learning theories are called field theories. Field theories are also known as Gestalt psychology or cognitive theories. The prominent cognitive theories are:

Functional Theories. As the name indicates, functional theories deal with learning process in parts covering specific functional aspects of learning, like motivation, transfer of learning, aging, rather than an integrated whole. Hence there is disagreement among psychologists to call it as theory.

Environmental theories and neurophysiological theories. The names clearly convey the principles behind these theories.

Thorndike's Stimulus-Response Theory. Edward Thorndike discovered the connectionist principle, and developed his theories of learning around it. His three laws: the law of readiness, the law of exercise, and the law of effect explain when and how a connection is accomplished. The law of readiness, which deals with the types of annoyance/ satisfaction associated with the state of readiness of mind in conducting a connection, was later de-emphasized. The law of exercise states that the strength of the connection between stimulus and response depends on the frequency of occurrence of the connection, higher the frequency greater is the strength. The law of effect states that when a connection between a stimulus and response is followed by a satisfactory result, the connection is strengthened, i.e., it becomes the established pattern for subsequent repetitions of the connection.

Based on the results of his experiments on animals, Thorndike reported that the most basic form of learning is by trial-and-error; and learning is an incremental process. His discovery of the phenomenon of "transfer of training" has left deep impact on the later day developments in the field of learning theories. Transfer of training means that the responses learned in one situation may be recalled and become applicable in a new situation. If the transfer of training is positive, then the new learning will become easier; and if it is negative, the new learning becomes difficult as it involves relearning. The number of elements that are common to the earlier and the new situations shape the response in a new unfamiliar situation. Transfer of training theory rejects the theory of punishment (Anderson,1964; Hergenhahn and Olson, 2005).

Pavlov, Ivan Petrovich (1849-1936) of Russia introduced *conditioning* theme to the development of learning theories. He found that an organism's natural response to a natural stimulus can also be *conditioned* through artificial stimulus to produce the same natural response. By his experiments on dogs, he showed that an artificial stimulus like the sound of a bell could also elicit the same natural response of salivation caused by natural stimulus of food. By this, Pavlov showed that an organism can be made to learn by conditioning.

B. F. Skinner, the behavioural psychologist from America, concluded that learning occurs as a consequence of behavioural change, called *operant conditioning.* In operant conditioning the response is elicited not by stimuli, but by the organism itself. Further, he stressed that positive reinforcement is more effective in teaching than negative reinforcement like punishment. Based on the concept of positive reinforcement, he developed the technique of *programmed learning,* and a *teaching machine* presenting programmed teaching material.

Drive Theory by Clark L. Hull. Hull's learning theory is based on his work *Principles of Behavior* (Hull, 1943). Hull's theory is similar to that of Thorndike, but more elegant. Hull emphasizes the role of human drive factor in learning. Accordingly, learning occurs because of the drive to satisfy a need. A drive is a tension state resulting from a need, which causes the organism to become stimulated and produces its own response. What causes the response that reduces the drive is *reinforcement.* The reinforcement causes a change in the nervous system known as a habit (Anderson, 1964).

Connectivity theories have been criticized on the grounds that they relay on the results of experiments on simple behaviour, where as learning is a complex process involving multiple stimuli, and responses with different motivational factors playing dominant part (Hilgard and Bower, 1956).

Cognitive Theories. Gestalt Psychology. Gestalt psychology originated in Germany in 1912, and its origin is traced to Max Wertheimer (1880-1943). Gestalt school explains learning process in terms of the principles of *organization in perception*, and they are:

1. The human mind through sense perception gives organizational structure to the objects and phenomena in the environment, and that is how the organism becomes aware of the environment. The implication of the principle is that response is not just a connecting system, but involves transformation providing meaning to the stimuli.
2. The organism and the larger environment together constitute a "pattern" or "configuration" — the English equivalent of "Gestalt". In this configuration, organism is constantly adapting to the environment — a process of organization and reorganization. The recurring changes in the adaptation process is called learning.
3. Higher organisms have the ability to learn in ways other

than trial-and-error and conditioning routes. The German Gestalt psychologist Wolfgang Köhler through his experiments on chimpanzees, and later on chicken in early 1900s discovered *insightful* learning. Insightful learning is finding solutions to a problem by comprehending total situation, and often, the solution occurs suddenly. The salient features of insightful learning are: a) the transition from pre-solution state to solution is sudden and complete; b) performance based on a solution gained by insight is usually smooth and free of errors; c) solution to a problem gained by insight stays fairly long; and d) a principle gained by insight can be easily applied to other problems (Hergenhahn and Olson, 2005).

Tolman's Sign Learning. Edward Chase Tolman's (1886-1959) approach to learning is on the lines of Gestalt psychology. Moreover, he believed that the proper study of behaviour has to begin with higher level concepts or purpose and need, as opposed to elemental theories of stimulus-response connectionism. The purpose is response related and not that of mental disposition. The stimulus that produces the response being learned takes on a meaning in terms of the learner's perception of the stimuli. Thus, stimuli become a "sign", whose action results in a response satisfying a purpose. In other words, the learner through his mental action organizes the stimuli, attaches meaning to them and responds accordingly (Anderson, 1964).

Learning Stages of Jean Piaget. According to Jean Piaget (1896-1980), the Swiss psychologist, a baby's experiencing of the world around it at birth is limited because of the nascent state of the sensorimotor schemata of the brain. As child grows, the nerve structure modifies to accommodate new elements in the environment. The sensory schemata with the beginning of interiorization process enable a child to deal with symbolic manipulation of real things— the cognitive act of understanding the environment. Piaget describes that learning process in children is a gradual, but continuous process, and he sees four stages in it. Piaget's unique contribution is his concepts of assimilation and accommodation. Assimilation and accommodation "identify two different types of learning experience. Both are learning; both entail the acquisition and storage of information. Assimilation, however, is a static kind of learning limited by the current cognitive structure; accommodation is a progressive growth of the cognitive structure that changes the character of all subsequent learning" (Herganhahn and Olson, 2005, p.308). Cognitive theories of learning rely on the expectancy that a particular event will lead to a particular consequence. Expectancies imply awareness of the goal. Thinking and other cognitions intervene between stimuli and the behavioural response (Luthans, 1981).

Evolutionary Theory. Evolutionary theory of learning draws its strength from evolutionary psychology (some call it sociobiology), which is developed from Darwin's theory of *natural selection*. A prominent contribution to the field is by Robert C. Bolles from America. The essential features of natural selection are:

1. There is natural variability within a species. This variability may appear as greater visual acuity, greater physical strength or more rapid learning.
2. As a general rule variation caused by genetic mutations or environmental events, and learned variations in behaviour are not heritable. Evolutionary theory is concerned only with heritable variability.
3. The interaction between the attributes of an organism and the demands of the environment in which it lives allows natural selection to operate.

Evolutionary psychology has been widely applied to the understanding of human behaviour. It is assumed that learning is guided by innate predispositions, and is influenced by our evolutionary history. Like other animals, we are prone to innate response biases, particularly when guided by strong, biologically significant motivational states. Both culture and biology must be considered to fully understand human behaviour. (Hergenhahn and Olson, 2005).

Neurophysiological Theory. Neurophysiological theory founded by Donald Hebb of Canada explains learning and other psychological phenomena in terms of fundamental relationship between synaptic, and all higher-order brain functions. According to Hebb, our experiencing the thought of an event involves a complex pattern of neurons called *cell assembly,* and a neurologically, but temporarily integrated cell assemblies called *phase sequence*. Even a single cell assembly when gets excited stimulates the entire phase sequence, which leads to our experiencing a stream of thoughts, i.e., a series of ideas arranged in some logical order. Childhood learning follows *assoociationism,* and is caused by slow development of cell assemblies and phase sequence. Subsequent learning is more insightful, and probably involves rearrangement of phase sequences.

Arousal Theory. Hebb states that stimulus has an arousal function impacting on the *reticular activating system* located in the brain, just below thalamus and hypothalamus. The level of arousal affects the optimal performance of a task. Anything done to adjust the arousal level required to maintain optimal performance is reinforcing. Sensory deprivation disrupts our normal cognitive functioning, including learning, because it interferes with the neural circuit-environmental equilibrium. Hebb's work inspired many later-day research workers who have made outstanding contributions, which include: the discovery of reinforce centers in the brain, research on right-brain left-brain asymmetry and associated dichotomies; computer simulation of mental functions; development of (artificial) neural networks; and demystifying the cellular mechanisms of learning (Hergenhahn and Olson, 2005).

Brain Research and Learning. Recent findings of brain research has contributed to our in-depth understanding of learning mechanism as well as other cognitive phenomena of the brain. Some of the important findings (Sousa, 2006) are:

1. Neuroplasticity is a property of the human brain to reorganize messages and meaning from the input received on a continuous basis. The input drawn from the environment (home and school in the case of young children) shapes the neural circuit formation, and thereby shapes the process of learning.
2. Contrary to earlier assumption on the production of spoken language, the brain uses other neural networks in the left hemisphere besides Broca's area and Wernicke's area. The cognitive state of brain at the birth is not blank (*tabula rasa*). The brain is receptive to sound impulses from the birth. Language learning and speech develop very fast in the first three years and continue up to the age of ten to twelve years. The visual cortex processes stimuli including reading. At birth, the brain responds first to *prosody* (the rhythm), cadence, and pitch of the mothers' voice. Later, the brain begins to recognize *phonemes,* the minimal unit of sound which combines to form syllables and words. Earlier theory on learning of grammar relied on "universal grammar" hypothesis proposed by Noam Chomsky in the 1950's. According to Chomsky, all languages follow certain universally applicable grammar rules; and language acquisition is an innate characteristic of the human mind. The brain has genetically programmed circuits that follow these rules. The present thinking is that the brain responds more to the statistical regularities found in the flow of the native tongue than to the universal rules. More a child is exposed to spoken language in early years, more quickly it learns to distinguish between phonemes and recognize word boundaries. The exposure to

produce result has to come from natural human interaction or by mechanical devices like television, and the latter can impair the growth and functioning of brain in a child.

3. Since there is no specifically assigned area in the brain that attends to reading, the task of reading becomes a difficult cognitive act for a child. The process of reading involves integration of three neural systems- the visual processing system, wherein the visual cortex processes visual stimuli formed by the written/printed word; the auditory processing system which processes sounds; and the frontal lobe integrates the information to produce meaning. The angular gyrus helps decode the visual word recognition signal for further processing in the Broca's and the Wernicke's area.
4. Emotions affect learning, memory, and recall.
5. Movement and exercise improve mood, increase brain mass, and enhance cognitive processing.
6. Circadian rhythms, i.e., daily time cycles of high and low aptitudes to do mental work, has deep bearings on our learning moods. This has implications for finding effective time for deriving maximum effectiveness out of teaching/learning.
7. Sleep deprivation and stress impacts on learning and memory.
8. Intelligence and creativity are separate abilities, and both can be modified by the environment and schooling.

There is a close relationship between the principles of learning and educational practices. The introduction of programmed learning, teaching machines, and computer assisted instruction are just a few examples of how learning research has contributed to the further development of educational practices. For instance, computer assisted instruction systems "allow the student to progress at his own speed, at his own place and time, free of the sometimes oppressive scrutiny of teacher and peers" (Mowshowitz, 1976, p. 107). Learning constitutes a primary means of acquiring and transmitting knowledge and skills. Through learning one acquires knowledge, which is already known to others and exists in society (sharing) or generates new knowledge through direct observation, experiencing and thinking (discovering and creating). Man makes use of accumulated knowledge rather than replicate the whole process of knowing by direct experiencing or redoing. Thousands of years of experience of man cannot be acquired by each individual of every generation by direct experiencing and experimentation, but through the process of learning and education. Learning and education thus form an important link in the chain of creation, transmission, dispersion and utilization of knowledge by individuals and the whole society.

EDUCATION

The terms 'education' and 'training' are often used together. While education is broader in content, training is on the job learning. The purpose of education is to transmit the values and accumulated knowledge of a society to its every new entrant, i.e., *socialization*. As per Goode's *Dictionary of education,* education is the art of making available to each generation the organized knowledge of the past (Goode, 1973). Education is also to equip individuals and groups to progress further in whatever activities they are interested to pursue or enter new fields of activities. Education is a process invented by society to guide each new-born in the world to learn the culture to which it is born or adopted, mould its behaviour in the ways of adulthood, and to prepare it to play its eventual role in that society. The term education is also used in a narrow sense to mean the influence of the school consciously brought to bear through the agency of the teacher upon the pupil; and in the broadest sense, truest sense, refers to the sum total of the influences of life that educate a man (Sharma, 2005). In primitive societies the need for institutionalized form of education was not felt as living was simple, though harsh, and needed only rudimentary knowledge, which was learnt by experience or told by other members of the tribe. As civilization advanced, society became more complex and knowledge to be learnt got expanded. The method invented to inculcate knowledge is education — a formal institutionalized learning pattern. The development of education is directly linked with the invention of language, writing and printing, and now electronic networks like Internet. Formalized education is "predicated on the assumption that the efficiency of the learning process can be improved through controlled exposure to vicarious experience, though individuals differ in their responses" (Shera, 1972, p.16).

The modern educational system is built on the foundation of historical, social, philosophic, scientific and structural principles. Historical part of the foundation consists of evolution of educational institutions through times; social component relates it to culture, social change, political ideology, minority interests, role of religion, law and the courts; the philosophic part includes it's relationship to philosophy, knowledge and value, educational theories, logic and analysis, challenge of existentialism and aesthetics; scientific dimension consists of world of science, teaching and technology perspectives from sociology, political socialization, economics, research, contents and methods; and the structural part is identified with practice in terms of organization and management, knowledge and the curriculum, stages of education, vocational education, the learning society; and international perspectives focus on change and modernization (Kneller, 1971). Though the principles, contents and practice described above was in the context of America, half a century ago, they are still valid not only to America, but also to many other countries, including India.

As education is to meet the requirements of each society

in the context of their history and culture, political system, stage of their social, economic and technological development, future vision of progress, no educational system can be transplanted from one society to another. It is the environment, the culture, and the genius of the people in a given society will determine and device appropriate education system or modify the existing system in the light of their requirements. When we speak of an education system to suit the genius of the people, 'gurukula' pattern of education that existed in ancient India is a fine example. The constitution of the National Knowledge Commission by the government of India in 2005 (India. National Knowledge Commission, 2007), and the constitution of earlier Commissions on education testify how a nation responds to its educational needs. The recommendations of the National Knowledge Commission cover a wide area including education, science and technology, agriculture and industry, development, intellectual property rights, knowledge application, knowledge capabilities in governance, libraries, translation, and information networks.

The general pattern of education is based on the teacher, the taught and the curriculum. The institutions of education range from schools and colleges, to universities and polytechnics; the educational segments from general, technical, professional and vocational to child, adult, women, labour and physically handicapped, mentally retarded, minorities, and so on; the mode of education from direct contact to self-study, and remote access; the educational materials from books (including e-books), films and cassettes to models; the techniques of education from oral, visual and practical to simulated; and the sources of sustenance and innovation from psychology, philosophy, history, economics, sociology and management to science, technology and artificial intelligence.

Keeping with the demands of the changing environment, the focus of educational policies and frameworks is constantly getting revisited and reframed in all countries, but the foundational components of education referred to earlier remain more or less intact. The new developments are shaped by the Internet, the computer and communication technologies, the demands of globalization of economy, needs of human resource development, public-private partnership, emphatic awareness among the rural and working-class section of the population about the importance of educating their wards, and other socio-cultural and technological developments. Education is now considered a basic need and a fundamental right. With pervasive use of Internet and web sites, newer applications of computers, and the use of advanced communication systems a new phase in education has started. Education being the dominant and most effective mode of transferring knowledge to new minds, and refreshing the old minds, the seekers, producers, transmitters and disseminators of knowledge, governments and the society at large have become stakeholders faced with the task of creating new knowledge and optimizing the use of existing knowledge.

CLOSURE

To access and to work upon knowledge, it needs to be organized. Organizing knowledge is a cognitive phenomenon of the mind; its purpose is to facilitate use of knowledge and support growth of knowledge. The system of organization consists of cognitive processes, such as identification of each unit or concept of knowledge in the universe of knowledge; classification of these concepts; and devising a means of communicating knowledge. Before proceeding to organizational aspects of knowledge, it is necessary to define the scope of the field. The field must include all items of knowledge in the universe. It cannot exclude any item, even if it is ephemeral in nature or unscientific or false as they are part of the human universe. Identification is done by labeling of knowledge entities or concepts in memory. The labels are names identifying the concepts, which are coined in memory mostly by the creators of knowledge, and to some extent by the users of knowledge.

The main purpose of classification is to bring order to the collection of items/concepts constituting the world of knowledge. The ordered collection should be able to project the panoramic view of the universe of knowledge indicating the relationships between the different categories of concepts, and between the concepts within a category. From the panoramic view it should be possible to show the pattern of growth of knowledge. Sometimes, it is more beneficial to think of knowledge in terms of systems of knowledge. This makes comparing categories within a system easier and focused, e.g., systems of medicine.

To express the identified/labeled, classified and stored items of knowledge in the memory to oneself or to others needs a mechanism, which is done by the process of communication. Though communication takes place through signals, signs, symbols, sound, and other means, it is the speech and symbol based language that forms the primary vehicle of communication in human society.

Transmission of knowledge from one mind to another mind takes place through the processes of learning and education. The values and accumulated knowledge of a society are transmitted to its every new entrant through socialization. Learning is the process of bringing lasting change in behaviour caused by experience, especially conditioning. Learning theories are broadly categorized into: stimulus-response theories, cognitive or field theories, evolutionary theory, and functional theory. Learning process is explained in terms of neuroplasticity, a property of the human brain to reorganize messages and meaning from the input received on a continuous basis. The inputs drawn from the environment (home and school in the case of young children) shape the neural circuit formation, which represents a learning state. Speech and symbolic representation, particularly through language, of natural phenomena and human activities constitute the most effective tools of learning. As one grows from childhood, objects, phenomena and acts acquire symbolic counterparts in lieu of the original.

Recent findings of brain research show that: a) the cognitive state of brain at the birth is not blank (*tabula rasa*); b) brain is receptive to sound impulses from the birth; c) visual cortex region of the brain processes stimuli pertaining to vision, including reading; d) at birth the brain responds first to *prosody* (the rhythm*)*, cadence, and pitch of the mothers' voice, and later the brain begins to recognize *phonemes*, the minimal unit of sound which combines to form syllables and words. Noam Chomsky's 1950's hypotheses states that all languages follow certain universally applicable grammar rules; and language acquisition is an innate characteristic of the human mind. The present thinking is that the brain responds more to the statistical regularities found in the flow of the native tongue than to the universal rules.

The process of reading involves integration of three neural systems - the visual processing system, wherein the visual cortex processes visual stimuli formed by the written/printed word; the auditory processing system processes sounds; and the frontal lobe integrates the information to produce meaning. The angular gyrus helps decode the visual word recognition signal for further processing. A number of other factors like emotions, daily time cycles, sleep deprivation, and a few others influence learning. The principles of learning and educational practices are linked.

The modern educational system is built on the foundation of historical, social, philosophic, scientific and structural principles. Historical part consists of evolution of educational institutions through times; social component relates to culture, social change, political ideology, minority interests, role of religion, law and the courts; the philosophic part deals with the relationship with philosophy, knowledge and value, educational theories, logic and analysis, challenge of existentialism and aesthetics; scientific dimension consists of world of science, teaching and technology perspectives from sociology, political socialization, economics, research, contents and methods; the structural part is identified with practice in terms of organization and management, knowledge and the curriculum, stages of education, vocational education, the learning society and the international perspectives focus on change and modernization. Every society develops its education system to suit its requirements and the genius of its people. Information and computer technologies are having a revolutionary impact on the development of education. Thus, organization, communication and transfer form the fundamental processes on which the use and growth of knowledge and information are based.

REFERENCES

Anderson, G. Lester. Basic Learning Thoery for Teachers. Pp. 389-416. *In* Skinner, Charles E. Ed. Educational Psychology. Ed. 4. 1964. New Delhi, Prentice-Hall of India, 1984. Reprint.

Birdsall, William F. Principal Investigator, Research Team. Towards an Integrated Knowledge Ecosystem: A Canadian Research Strategy. A Report Submitted to the Canadian Association of Research Libraries/ L'Association des bibliothe'ques de recherche du Canada (CARL/ ABRC). January 2005. http://creativecommons.org/licenses/by-nc-nd/2.0/ca/

Bliss, H. E. The Organization of Knowledge and the System of the Science. New York, Henry Holt, 1929.

Bloch, Bernard and Trager, G. L. Outline of Linguistic Analysis. Baltimore (Md.), Linguistic Society of , America, 1942.

Chomsky, Noam. Language and Responsibility. English Translation and Revision, 2003. Pp. 1-212. *In* Chomsky, Noam. On Language. New Delhi, Penguin Books, 2003.

Colman, Andrew M. A Dictionary of Psychology. Oxford, Oxford University Press, 2001.

Drucker, P .F. Management: Tasks, Responsibilities, Practices. Bombay, Allied Publishers, 1975. (Indian edition).

Encyclopaedia Britannica, The New. Ed.15. Chicago, Encyclopaedia Britinica, 2007. Vol.16. Pp. 611-616: Communication.

Garry, Ralph and Kingsley, H. L. The Nature and Conditions of Learning. Ed.3. Englewood Cliffs (N J), Prentice-Hall, 1970.

Goode, C. V. Ed. The Dictionary of Education, Ed. 3. New York, McGraw-Hill, 1973.

Hergenhahn, B.R. and Olson, Matthew, H. An Introduction to Theories of Learning. Ed.7. Upper Saddle River (N.J.), 2005.

Hilgard, E.R. and Bower, G.H. Theories of Learning. Ed.3. New York, Appleton-Century-Crofts, 1956.

Cf. Hull, Clark L. Principles of Behavior. D. Appleton Century, 1943.

India, National Knowledge Commission. Compilation of Recommendations on Education. (Chairman: Sam Pitroda). New Delhi, 2007.

Jolley, J.L. The Fabric of Knowledge: A Study of the Relations between Ideas. London, Duckworth, 1973.

Kneller, G. F. Ed. Foundations of Education. New York, Wiley, 1971.

Lawther, John D. Learning Motor Skills and Knowledge. Pp. 499-525. *In* Skinner, Charles E. Ed. Educational Psychology. Ed. 4. 1964. New Delhi, Prentice-Hall of India, 1984. (Reprint).

Levitan, Karen. Clarifying the concept of private-public interaction. Pp. 198-201. In The information age in perspective. (Proceedings of the ASIS Annual Meeting 1978, Vol. 15). New York, Knowledge Industry, 1978.

Luthans, Fred. Organizational Behavior. Ed.3. Tokyo, McGraw-Hill, 1981.

Machlup, Fritz. Knowledge: Its Creation, Distribution, and Economic Significance. Vol. 1: Knowledge and Knowledge Production. Princeton, Princeton University Press, 1980.

McLuhan, Marshall. Understanding Media: The Extensions of Man. New York, McGraw-Hill, 1964.

Mowshowitz, Abbe. The Conquest of Will: Information Processing in Human Affairs. Reading (Mass.), Addison- Wesley, 1976.

Neelameghan, A. Expressions of Time in Information Sience and Their Implications. Pp. 103-118. *In* Greenway, Frank. Ed. Time and the Sciences. Paris, Unesco, 1979.

Perry, J.W. The Characteristics of Recorded Knowledge. Pp. 80-83. *In* Shera, J. H. et al. Documentation in Action. New York, Reinhold, 1956.

Ranganathan, S.R. Library classification: Its added uses. *Libri* 2:31-36, 1952.

Richards, I. A. Principles of Literary Criticism. Ed. 2. London, Routledge & Kegan Paul, 1955.

Scheler, Max. Die Wissensformen und die Gesellschaft. Leipzig, Neue-Geist Verlag, 1926. Pp. 250-251.

Schwartz, David G. Aristotelian View of Knowledge Management. Pp.10-16. *In* Schwartz, David G. Encyclopaedia of Knowledge Management. London, IDEA Group Reference, 2006 .

Sharma, Promila. Philosophy of Education. New Delhi, A.P.H. Publishing, 2005.

Shera, J. H. The Foundations of Education for Librarianship. New York, Wiley-Becker and Hayes, 1972.

Sousa, David A. How the Brain Learns. Ed.3. Thousand Oaks (Calif.), Corwin Press, 2006.

3

CHARACTERISTICS OF KNOWLEDGE

The study of the characteristics of knowledge is an aspect of the study of knowledge phenomenon. Some of the features that characterize knowledge, such as knowledge-information duality, organization and transfer of knowledge have been examined in the previous chapters. The characteristics of knowledge and information determine and enable the use of knowledge in particular ways. In this chapter we examine the phenomenon of knowledge to find its characteristics that are fundamental in nature and applicable to the entire universe of knowledge. The fundamental characteristics differ from particular form of cognition-related or context and domain bound characteristics.

AS A BASIC NEED

Knowledge is a basic need of man. The human brain, except in a state of coma, processes knowledge non-stop. The subconscious mind is continuously engaged in processing knowledge, as the brain cannot remain blank except perhaps in very rare cases. It is not always necessary to have external stimuli for cognitive activities of the brain. Knowledge generation and processing can take place by auto-stimuli and delayed action of the brain based on previously stored knowledge. The need to receive and process new information and to mull over already held knowledge in memory is an inherent characteristic of the human brain. It is a psychological necessity. As a biological and social entity, human species seeks and inputs energy and the information necessary to satisfy his biological, emotional, intellectual, spiritual, economic and cultural needs (Neelameghan, 1979). Knowledge is a basic need of man (Platt, 1959). Solitary confinement is a well established form of psychological punishment. It is not that all knowledge fulfils a basic need. It is possible to draw a hierarchy of the types of knowledge, and then determine the type or types that constitute a basic need. It has been established that the brain utilizes only a small portion of its capacity to process knowledge. Although, this capacity varies from individual to individual, it is roughly constant for each individual. Utilization of the knowledge processing capacity below a certain minimum level seems to impair the brain (Shera, 1972). The reverse, that is, forcing the brain to process knowledge beyond its capacity is bound to affect the working of the brain. School going children forced by parents to study beyond their brain capacity ending up as psychic cases is not unknown. Thus, a limitation of the brain to receive information/stimulus and convert it into knowledge is an important aspect of knowledge phenomenon.

Human brain has its own sieving mechanism that selects, retains and processes stimuli and converts them into knowledge. Our memories are quite selective. A vast number of messages that reach the brain through the senses are ignored or dropped out of our memories instantaneously. Brain research has shown that the left hemisphere of the brain deals with verbal skills associated with knowledge of the external world and reason, and the right hemisphere with that of nonverbal and symbolic skills identifiable with artistic and emotional traits, and knowledge of self (Poggio and Koch, 1987; Arbib, 1995). Further, it has been established that we make use of only a small portion of our mental capacity. It is believed that we humans use less than 10% of the capacity of our brain, which is made of an estimated 100 billion neurons (Read, 1998). All these features of human brain reflect a complexity that is not seen in other species. The complex structure of the brain with its astonishing ways of functioning has been designed to serve a specific purpose intended by nature. The purpose seems to insert knowledge phenomenon as a unique design in human species, and assign it the characteristic of a basic need like food and affection. Without the need function of knowledge, the human species will not be able to act the role assigned to it by nature. The need characteristic of knowledge seems to coalesce well with Darwin's theory of survival of the fittest. There is underutilization of knowledge processing capacity of the brain. The role of the need characteristic of knowledge in furthering the cause of knowledge creation and use calls for further study.

ENVIRONMENTAL EFFECTS

It is generally agreed now that human behaviour is conditioned by genetics (heredity) and the environment. The same principle governs knowledge phenomena. Since genetic characteristics are predetermined, an individual has no control over genetic foundation of knowledge phenomena. However, this may not be completely valid now with the arrival and use of recently developed DNA manipulation techniques. Genetic component determines the basic traits of mental quality, capacity, and special abilities of individual human beings. Environmental components act upon the genetically effected knowledge in mind and modify it. In many cases the environmental factors support further development of existing mental abilities. Environment we live in is made up of natural environment and human-created environment. Natural environment is characterized by time and space, geography, climate, flora and fauna, and other creations of nature. Natural environment supports knowledge phenomena by setting the background that prescribes mood, emotions and attitudes.

Engaging in intellectual activities like reading, learning and thinking are often influenced by natural environmental factors like weather and daily time cycles. Human created environment is evolved through social, cultural, economic, political and other societal phenomena. The Parsi society is an example that shows how environment affects the knowledge front. Parsis migrated from Persia (modern Iran) a thousand years ago and settled down in Western India. Knowledge stock of Parsis is a blend of the features of three sub-environments. They have retained their original faith system and the associated religious tradition, and certain food habits. The impact of the Indian environment is reflected in their dress, adoption of Gujarathi language, and even surnames based on their vocations in the new land. They have also been among the first to be influenced by some of the features of the Western human created environment. Even though the impact of human created environmental factors are comparatively less on scientific knowledge, still it affects in important ways as in the selection of scientific projects, data collection, and the like.

If knowledge phenomenon is affected by environment, then it should be possible to control and manage it. This is particularly true in the case of human created environment. For illustration, we may consider here motivation an aspect of human created environment. Motivation, especially the desire of individuals to fulfill their social, economic and psychological needs, plays an important positive role; and frustration a negative role in human actions. This affects one's knowledge acquiring disposition. Another example is the impact of environment on knowledge seeking behaviour. To acquire knowledge, at least to meet one's minimum need for survival, is one of the natural characteristics of human mind, which is greatly influenced by wonder and curiosity. Wonder and curiosity in turn sustain knowledge-seeking urge in individuals. The causes of wonder are difficult to explain. Familiarity inhibits wonder. If a thing is familiar enough, one unconsciously assumes that he knows all that need to be known about it. Familiarity acts as a barrier to our acceptance of new knowledge whenever this new knowledge requires an appreciable change in our normal conception of any familiar thing (Jones, 1964). Wonder and curiosity (other than those caused by nature) in our daily living come from our exposure to varied social behaviour, cultural acts and facts, and from the external man-created environment. Social institutions like museums, planetariums, botanical gardens, aquariums and zoos are all designed to arouse or fulfill curiosity and wonder. Necessity also drives human beings to seek and create knowledge. This is true of individuals, of organizations, and of societies. The new necessities are the outcome of modern life, and are designed to overcome the tensions of living in high technology society or to create and supply newer forms of pleasure or luxury or to economize. The new social environment in turn creates new knowledge and finding new applications of existing knowledge.

Ultimately, it is the society that controls creation, transmission, and utilization of knowledge. This is achieved by controlling the knowledge environment and the resource to be invested on knowledge producing activities. For example, collecting records of knowledge, and providing universal access to them through institutional mechanisms become a part of the intellectual environment needed for maximizing knowledge generation and its utilization in society. There is a close relationship between environmental and psychological factors, and both of them take part in shaping an individual's knowledge behaviour. A suitable knowledge environment can enhance and activate the cognitive processes in the brain. Some of the environmental factors affecting an individual's knowledge behaviour are physical environment; moral, religious and cultural forces; and the social, economic and technological factors that constitute the environment. Lack of educational and experiencing opportunities limit one's state of knowledge.

Cultural environment of an individual influences the value interpretation of knowledge. Often, the human mind refuses to recognize certain items of knowledge. If it recognizes them, it may refuse to accept them, if that knowledge is contrary to the one assiduously held as true by the individual (Bourne et al., 1970). This is a consequence of belief and conviction shaped partly by the social and cultural environment. The hold of astrology on individuals, and in certain cultures people's belief in the effects of eclipses on their lives are examples of how belief and faith influence knowledge induced actions. These behavioural changes are attributed to halo effect, projection, and stereotyping (Castello and Zalkind, 1963). One's judgment and perceptions of events are influenced considerably by circumstances embedded in the environment. Exercise of parental, religious and political authorities also shapes knowledge behaviour. Communication and language, the products of cognitive, social and cultural environment directly influence one's perception, conceptualization, and understanding of knowledge. Language, particularly denotation and connotation of words, affects one's ways of understanding. However, in many cases, it is possible to change one's belief and convictions by appropriate environmental influences.

By controlling intellectual freedom, material needs, cognitive environment, and other motivating forces, the knowledge acquiring capacity of individuals can be increased or restricted. Similarly, the rate of increase of knowledge and the direction of such increase can be activated, promoted, or curtailed by society by direct as well as indirect means. There is a close relationship between environmental and psychological factors, and both of them take part in shaping an individual's knowledge behaviour. The results of such actions by the society on an individual are not always predictable because of the uniqueness of the human mind to respond according to differing perception of the environmental factors involved. One way of controlling knowledge generation in society and its appropriate use is by allocation of manpower. Suitable incentives, appropriate allocation of resources, monetary and prestige value that goes with a knowledge field influence manpower deployment in different knowledge fields. Apart from general environment, scientific method, a feature of scientific environment is another favorable factor for the development of knowledge. It has been inferred from studies that knowledge flourishes in societies in which intellectual freedom, liberal attitude towards learning and research, and opportunity for cross-fertilization of cultures exist. Scientific method accelerates knowledge creation, as witnessed in ancient Greece and Renaissance period of Europe (Lewis, 1955). Knowledge brings in change in society in the form of social good, cultural resource, economic means, and political power (Diener, 1984). Being a human phenomenon, knowledge acquisition and processing are greatly influenced by the norms, policies, values and ethos of the society, which in turn influence society. This implies that creation, organization, management, and servicing of knowledge must center on the pattern of human thinking, human behaviour, human needs and human actions in the societal context; and must take into consideration both genetic and environmental dimensions of knowledge.

LIMITATIONS OF KNOWLEDGE

Knowledge has certain limitations. These limitations are imposed by the quality of the cognitive part of the brain, capacity of the human memory, and the response range of sense organs in processing knowledge. There are other limitations too. To study them, it is necessary to go into the dynamics of knowledge. Observation, analysis, correlation and interpretation of entities, phenomena in nature and the acts of man result in the creation of new knowledge, and modification of already existing knowledge structure. This is a continuous process. The capacity of human sense organs to observe and that of the brain to fully process the observed data are limited. Human sense organs are very limited in their sensitivity to: a) the forms of energy to which they respond (e.g., magnetic field), and b) the different types of energy (e.g., range of electromagnetic radiation). This puts severe limitations on our access to information carried by energy at large in the universe. Thus, wider the range of energy to which our senses give us access, the greater the raw materials of our knowledge (O'Conner and Carr, 1982). Observable facts/ phenomena in the universe are varied, infinite, and changing. As a result, the development of knowledge takes place continuously, over a wide range of time, place and situations, the change appearing in bits and pieces or in a large burst. Because of change, knowledge undergoes the processes of review, consolidation, elimination, reformulation, and addition of new chunks of knowledge on a continuous basis. Thus, knowledge is by its nature incomplete, fragmentary and provisional in character (Perry, 1956). This characteristic is known as "falliblism" in philosophy. Bertrand Russell affirms that all human knowledge is uncertain, inexact, and partial (Russell, 1948). However, this characteristic of knowledge does not imply that because knowledge is incomplete, partial and provisional, it is invalid or useless. What it means is that the knowledge world is not static, but dynamic in nature; and in applying knowledge, one must be aware of this limitation.

Another limitation of particular interest to information processors emanates from the characteristics of communication. Communication, "by its very nature, comes to be closely associated with the symbolic representation of attributes of observed phenomena, and such representation is, as a consequence, also linked with the analysis of phenomena and with their correlation. There is, in short, an important relationship between human communication and the correlation of observations to establish those general patterns of action..." (Perry, 1956, p. 71). The communication problem centers on the ability to represent completely and exactly the attributes of observed phenomena in nature and in society through signs and symbols. This primarily refers to the limitations of language in communicating knowledge.

Limitations of knowledge impose a qualitative pre-requirement of ascertaining accuracy, extent of completeness, and validity of a given chunk of knowledge before use. Consolidation of evaluated knowledge, in the form of compendiums, codes, reviews and summaries in record form, is one important method of overcoming some of the limitations inherent in the creation, processing and utilization of knowledge. Development of suitable communication modes and media capable of representing knowledge in a precise, comprehensive and effective way, and training in the use of language are other means of overcoming or minimizing the adverse effects. Incomplete, fragmentary and provisional nature of knowledge is precisely the reason that keeps knowledge growing.

MEASURABILITY

Knowledge is not measurable by quantitative means. There is no physical yardstick to measure knowledge. Often, we hear people saying that "so and so is a knowledgeable person." One understands what it means; but it does not answer the question "How knowledgeable is that person?" More precisely, "How much knowledge does the knowledgeable person has?" This leads to the issue of measuring or quantifying knowledge. There is no quantitative yardstick for measuring knowledge. Addressing this aspect of knowledge, Boulding concludes: "knowledge is not merely a pile of bits of information; and the 'wit' which seems to be the appropriate term for a unit of knowledge, is far more complex than a mere capitalized 'bit'. The idea of knowledge as an improbable structure is still a good place to start. Knowledge, however, has a dimension which goes beyond that of mere information improbability. This is a dimension of significance which is very hard to reduce to quantitative form" (Boulding, 1970, p.142).

What is measurable is the physical units of language employed for conveying the mental text (number of words, bits and bytes) or the material medium used for communication (number of pages) or the time engaged (the time a TV programme lasts) or numerical scale assigned to expressed knowledge content (as in evaluating answer papers in schools). Information theory provides a basis for measuring the physical aspects of communication and not the cognitive elements of knowledge. On the other hand, effects of knowledge and the results of application of knowledge are measurable. The number of students passing out of a school shows a quantitative measure. Similarly, when knowledge items have utility, such items may get a price in terms of money. This is more so in the case of technological knowledge, when one pays for transfer of technology which implies the inclusion of knowledge component of technology. Literary knowledge gets paid for in the shape of copyright, and technological knowledge in the form of patent rights. Thus, money becomes an indirect standard of measuring value of knowledge.

What one could say about a given knowledge text is whether it is significant or not in a given context; whether it is useful or not; whether it is repetitive or new; whether it represents a concept, a theory, an ideology and so on, all of which are judgmental. In the absence of quantitative methods, expert judgment, benefit analysis, and indirect relationship studies are employed for assessing the utility of knowledge and its impact. On the other hand, effects of knowledge and the results of application of knowledge can be ascertained by studying the resulting change.

One can recognize the impact of a particular item of knowledge in a specified sphere or on an individual's actions, behaviour, and value system. Similarly, the health of a nation can be related to its medical research, pharmaceutical industry, public health policies, level of education, state of economy, and so on. These factors when put together reflect that nation's state of knowledge. Assessment of the results of knowledge found in a society enables one to identify that society as educated, culturally advanced, permissive, conservative, and so on. Such assessments may help in formulating developmental policies on knowledge or taking corrective actions where necessary. Immeasurability of knowledge makes it difficult to set managerial objectives in terms of specific cognitive units of meaning.

REPRODUCIBILITY OF MENTAL TEXT

A knowledge text in the mind and the same text in its explicit form will not be identical in all respects and exactness to a comma and a full stop. Shannon's theory of communication discussed in chapter 10 shows that there is always a transmission loss in any information transfer process, but this loss pertains to the physical aspects of messages. Of greater concern to knowledge study is the loss in terms of cognitive value. Loss in the process of transferring of knowledge from one person to another person occurs primarily due to two reasons - a) when communication mode employed by an individual is unable to convey completely and accurately one's mental text ; and b) that no two human minds are endowed with the same capabilities. If two persons can think or perceive all things in exactly the same way- time wise, space wise, meaning wise, and minute detail wise, then those two minds cease to be different cognitively. There will always be some difference between knowledge in the mind of the transferor and the same expressed in its language form, and between the communicated knowledge in the form of language and in its perceived form in the mind of the transferee.

In any knowledge transfer encounter it is almost impossible to transmit completely and accurately the exact knowledge text in the mind of the transferor to a recipient. This anomaly does not seriously affect the value and utility of the transferred knowledge, so long as the additions and deletions occurring during transfer process are small and are not of critical nature. The anomaly occurs because of the problems inherent to communication and language, because of the variations in the mental ability to express and grasp, and due to differing social, cultural, experiential and environmental backgrounds of the participating parties. So long as the loss occurring is very small and is not of critical nature, it does not affect the utility of such knowledge to the recipient.

The unintended changes taking place in a knowledge text will be more in indirect transmission, and transmission through records. As a corollary, it means that the transfer of knowledge from one mind to another mind in a knowledge transfer encounter depends on the cognitive and communicative abilities, and the environmental background of the participants in the encounter. A consequence of this characteristic is the ability or inability of two parties in a knowledge transaction to interact at the same wavelength of understanding. The inability of the mind to transmit knowledge accurately and exactly as intended may result in a gap between what one "knows", "says" and "records". This gap could also be the result of a willful act on the part of the participants. Exact and complete reproducibility of knowledge frames in the mind without loss of integrity has practical importance to individuals and professions involved in communication, transmission and dissemination of knowledge as they are required to ensure that the original text of knowledge remains the same throughout. This factor becomes more critical when knowledge passes through an intermediary who processes and services the texts for others. Equally important is the language employed to represent and convey the mental text. Development of the art of communication, creation of technical terminology, training of the mind in the use of cognitive skills are likely to reduce the adverse effects of this characteristic.

KNOWLEDGE IS NOT LOST THROUGH TRANSFER

Unlike a true commodity, knowledge is not destroyed or lost by use or consumption; in fact knowledge is not a consumable item. In the act of transfer of knowledge, either directly or indirectly, from one person to another person or to a group of persons the transferor is not deprived of the knowledge transferred by him. For instance, in a teacher-student situation, the teacher continues to hold the knowledge even after the act of passing on the knowledge to the students. Similarly, in the action of reading a book by some one, the author of the book is not deprived of the knowledge he has transmitted while the reader gains. If it is not for this characteristic knowledge would not have survived so long, and the story of civilizations would have been different. It is tempting to imagine the state of man and society, if knowledge were to get destroyed by use. Even death can not destroy knowledge, if it is recorded and stored or transmitted to another person. This is how the thoughts, epics and other mental texts from ancient times have survived and is available to us. Knowledge can only be suppressed by social and political acts of man. By exploiting this property of knowledge technology, beginning with the invention of writing, paper and printing to the present-day computers, has enabled maximizing the use and dispersal of knowledge overcoming the barriers of time and space. Nondestructive nature of knowledge and information has economic implications in the form of intellectual property rights discussed in chapter 15. Education exploits this property of knowledge fully.

In the act of transferring knowledge the transferor may enrich his own store of knowledge in the course of interaction. When the interaction is between two or more minds of more or less intellectually balanced, then the stock of knowledge is likely to get enriched in both the minds. The concept of conferences and discussion groups are based on this characteristic of knowledge. In reality, it is sharing rather than transfer of knowledge. This unique characteristic facilitates the growth and spread of knowledge in society. The instant any knowledge is transferred, its exclusive association with the person possessing that knowledge ceases. It also means that a given knowledge may be held by several persons at the same time, thus it becoming public knowledge. Since the transfer results in the loss of exclusive control over private knowledge, the decision to transfer or withhold it is governed by considerations of when, to whom, and how much of knowledge to transfer. There is no way of knowing whether the transferor has transferred all the knowledge he has agreed or meant to transfer or only a portion of it. Hence ownership and transfer rights become pertinent aspects of a transfer. Orderly transfer is made possible by giving property rights, such as copyright, patent right, and trademark right. Transfer characteristic of knowledge in contrast to the characteristic of material goods, where the seller is deprived of the goods sold does not deprive the transferor of his knowledge. Transfer of a given item of knowledge any number of times does not deprive the transferor of the knowledge thus transferred.

KNOWLEDGE — A FUNDAMENTAL CONSTITUENT OF NATURE ?

The concept of knowledge has attracted numerous interpretations. Consciousness, awareness, reality, perception, response to a stimulus are some of the terms used to describe knowledge. These terms are often used synonymously. Knowledge is the direct object of inquiry of epistemology, a branch of philosophy. The problem of establishing the nature of objective knowledge in its information format also falls within the domain of science, especially physics and communication engineering. Any attempt to go into the nature and form of knowledge has to begin with the origin of knowledge. The origin of knowledge is brain and mind. Brain is a physical entity, where as mind is an abstract conceived concept. Knowledge is an unique gift of nature to human species. Some sort of awareness exists in other organisms too. But, such awareness is not called knowledge. Animals recognize danger, sense sources of food, and engage in reproductive process. For these and other acts organisms communicate with other members of the community. With a few exceptions, like apes which display limited learning abilities, such acts are in the nature of instinct, rather than thinking. Philosophers and psychologists draw a distinction between the physical and the mental- the brain and the mind. The neural part of knowledge (the preferable term is information) at the physical level consists of converting stimulus into signals carrying meaning. Mental aspect of knowledge deals with consciousness, formation of thoughts, perception, cognitive characteristics and the like connected with understanding and meaning (Ryle, 1949; Wittgenstein, 1973). Knowledge will not have any significance unless one can make meaning out of it individually or socially. The characteristic of transferability vests knowledge with use value, exception being self use of self-created knowledge stored in one's memory.

Knowledge, other than our knowing that it is a phenomenon of the human brain, as such has no characteristics or properties of its own. Whatever properties we attribute to knowledge are the properties of brain and mind. Knowledge creation is a process of the central nervous system, and knowledge may be considered as a phenomenon — something directly apprehended by the senses; that our consciousness makes out, as distinguished from what it is in itself (Chambers Dictionary, 1993). Knowledge is a phenomenon of nature occurring in human beings. Physical sciences try to explain all natural phenomena, but knowledge has not been on its prime agenda of exploration may be due to the abstract nature of knowledge, and having no physical form (see chapter 10).

Going by science, all things and phenomena in nature must belong to any one of the fundamental constituents- time, space, matter, and energy. Knowledge phenomenon seems to be related to energy. It has the complexities and quirks similar to that of quantum mechanics. Biology and neural science, physics and engineering treat information in its physical form of electrical or electrochemical state of energy (see chapters 9 and 10). However, there is a growing school of thought within the physical sciences community that is inclined to consider information (which may be extended to cover knowledge) as the fifth fundamental constituent of nature besides matter, energy, time and space (Sigfried, 2000). If it turns out to be true, it opens up a new vista of scientific enquiry beckoning the attention of brilliant scientific as well as philosophic minds.

CLOSURE

Use of knowledge is determined by its characteristics. These characteristics are of two types: a) characteristics that are domain specific, related to particular cognitive skills, and are context bound; and b) characteristics that are fundamental in nature and applicable to the entire universe of knowledge. These characteristic are stated below.

1. Knowledge constitutes a basic human need; it is a psychological necessity. This need is conditioned by genetic and environmental factors and works through brain and mind. The brain has been designed by nature to serve some intended purposes. By making Knowledge a basic need, nature seems to keep brain active and support other objectives like survival.
2. Man is surrounded by human world and natural environment. Natural environment is made-up of components like time, space, gravity, geography, climate, flora, and fauna. Human created environment is evolved through social, cultural, political, economic, and other such factors. The two environments together shape an individual's and societies' knowledge behavior.
3. Knowledge by itself is incomplete and provisional in character. This limitation is due to continuous growth in knowledge, and constant invalidation of some knowledge

caused by change. Other limitations are imposed by the quality of mind, range limitations of human sense organs, characteristics of language, and other communication modes employed to express knowledge. The negative effects of most of these limitations can be overcome or reduced.

4. Knowledge is not measurable by quantitative means. One can only observe its impact and also say whether a given knowledge text is significant or not in a given context. By observing the development of knowledge in different domains in a given society, one can say how progressive that society is, and devise development plans based on the assessment.

5. Mental knowledge texts cannot be transferred completely and accurately from one mind to another mind or reproduced identically in all respects. Effectiveness of transfer depends on the mental and communicative abilities, and the environmental background of the participants in the transfer.

6. Transferring knowledge from one mind to another does not involve any destruction of knowledge, and the transferor is not deprived of the knowledge thus transferred.

Deciphering the mystic characteristic of knowledge phenomenon, as of now, has remained beyond human comprehension. The key to breaking the enigma may lie in treating information as a fundamental constituent of nature like space, time, energy and matter.

A challenging task before scholars, researchers and educationists is how to overcome or at least reduce the adverse effects of many of the limitations of knowledge. These limitations impede the growth of knowledge, affect its quality, hampers providing access to knowledge, and its optimal utilization. Some of these limitations can be overcome. One example is that by exploiting computer, telemetry, and artificial satellite technologies it has become possible to overcome a few of the time and space imposed limitations on information transmission. Similarly, the progress in scientific instrumentation has reduced naturally imposed human perceptional range limitations by extending the operational range of the sense organs. There are many unexplored areas of brain and mind-caused limitations affecting knowledge processing as a general phenomena and causing cognitive variations in individuals. This is a challenge to scientists and scholars working in areas, such as cognitive psychology, brain research, Artificial intelligence, linguistics, and education to study these limitations and find ways of reducing them. Of all the challenges, the greatest challenge is to know how neuron assemblies in the cortex become consciousness in mind.

REFERENCES

Arbib, Michael A. Ed. The Handbook of Brain Theory and Neural Networks. Cambridge (Mass.), The MIT Press, 1995.

Boulding, K.E. Knowledge as a Commodity. *In* Beyond Economics: Essays on Society, Religion and Ethics. Ann Arbor, University of Michigan Press, 1970.

Bourne, L. E. et al. The Psychology of Thinking, Englewood Cliffs (NJ), Prentice- Hall, 1970.

Castello, T.M. and Zalkind, S. S. Psychology in Administration. Englewood Cliffs (NJ), Prentice-Hall, 1963.

Chambers Dictionary 1993. Edinburgh, Chambers Harrap, 1993. (Indian Ed. Allied Chambers India, 2000).

Diener, R. A. V. Conflicting social visions on the nature of information: Social, cultural, economic and political perspectives. Pp. 3-6. In Flood, Barbara et al. Comp. Challenges to an information society. (Proceedings of the 47th ASIS Annual Meeting. Vol. 21). New York, Knowledge Industry, 1984.

Jones, P.C. The Nature of Knowledge. New York, Scarecrow Press, 1964.

Lewis, M.A. The Theory of Economic Growth. London, Allen and Unwin, 1985.

Neelameghan, A. Expressions of Time in Information Sience and Their

Implications. Pp. 103-117. *In* Greenway, Frank. Ed. Time and the Sciences. Paris, Unesco, 1979.

O'Connor, D.J. and Carr, Brian. Introduction to the Theory of Knowledge. Brighton (Sussex), Harvester Press, 1982.

Perry, J.W. The Characteristics of Recorded Information. *In*, Shera, J.H. et al. Documentation in Action. New York, Reinhold, 1956.

Platt, J. R. The fifth need of man. *Horizon*, Vol. 1, July 1959. P.106.

Poggio, Tomaso and Koch, Chrstoff. Synapses that compute motion. *Scientific American* 256: 42-48, 1987.

Read, J.L., 1998. http://www.enchantedmind.com/html/science/brain_capacity.html

Russell, Bertrand. Human Knowledge: Its Scope and Limits. London, Allen and Unwin, 1948.

Ryle, Silbert. The Concept of Mind. Chicago, University of Chicago Press, 1949. Sousa, David A. How the Brain Learns. Ed.3. Thousand Oaks (Calif.), Corwin Press, 2006.

Shera, J.H. The Foundations of Education for Libralrianship. New York , Wiley- Becker and Hayes, 1972.

Sigfried, Tom. The Bit and the Pendulum: From Quantum Computing to M. Theory- The Physics of Information. New York, Wiley, 2000,

Wittgenstein, Ludwig. Philosophical Investigations. Ed.3. London, Macmillan, 1973.

4
Cognitive and Intellectual Processes

In the creation, processing, and application of knowledge the brain employs different cognitive methods like thinking, conceptualization, analysis, correlation, classification, reasoning and comparison. This chapter explains these cognitive processes and their impact on knowledge, and knowledge driven actions.

THINKING

To think is the foremost mental characteristic of human beings. Rene Descartes, the French philosopher, declared "cogito ergo sum", which in English means "I think, therefore I am". Holyoak and Morrison define thinking as "*the systematic transformation of mental representations of knowledge to characterize actual or possible states of the world, often in service of goals*" (Holyoak and Morrison, 2005, p.2). They also conclude that a mental representation of knowledge is an internal description that can be manipulated to form other descriptions. To count as thinking, the manipulations must be *systematic* transformations governed by certain constraints. Thinking often appears to be a conscious activity of which the thinker is aware. Thinking includes the elements of belief, foresight and judgement. It is interrelated to other sub-forms of cognitive processes like reasoning, decision-making, and problem solving. Thinking need not be orderly, constructive and correct, as it could be imaginative. Thinking field need not be factual. We use concepts to identify and express an item, which is the object covered by thinking.

CONCEPTUALIZATION

The process of forming concepts is *conceptualization*. A concept is any identifiable mental image. Conceptualization is basic to all human thinking and knowledge processing activities. Of the many definitions of a concept given in the Webster's dictionary, the following are relevant here: a) something conceived in the mind: thought, notion, idea (in a general sense); b) the resultant of a generalizing mental operation: a general mental image abstracted from percepts; a directly intuited object of thought; a theoretical construct (in philosophy); and c) an idea comprehending the essential attributes of a class or logical species; and d) an idea that includes all that is characteristically associated with or suggested by a term (in logic). Conceptualization is the act or process of conceptualizing (Webster's, 1993). From these definitions, we can infer that conceptualization is a characteristic of the human mind to form a total picture or an image through a small number of percepts or attributes, and the ability to identify and distinguish one concept from another. A concept evolves from "schema". A schema is a structured representation that divides up the properties of an image of a thing into dimensions and values on those dimensions (Murphy, 2002). Concept formation may start from reacting to signals conveyed by stimuli, followed by analysis, visualization and correlation of the details leading to the identification or formation of the concept, or it may follow the reverse route. Concepts carry out two broad functions: categorization and communication. Category is the class of objects in the world. Categorization is the process by which mental representations, i.e., concepts (meaning a set of entities or category), determine whether a given entity is a member of a category. This allows us to understand more about a new entity so categorized by virtues of the knowledge we already know about the category — a learning function. Addition of a new novel entity to a category is likely to enlarge or limit the boundaries of that concept. Communication part of concepts is largely taken care of by language. Further, to understand concepts and conceptualization we need to understand the functioning of memory. Memory organization corresponds to meaningful relations between concepts and how they are structured in memory (Medin and Rips, 2005). Different aspects of memory are further dealt with in chapter 9.

Language enables a speaker to transform configurations of ideas into configurations of sounds, and it enables a listener within his own mind to transform these sounds back into a reasonable facsimile of the ideas with which the speaker began (Chafe, 1970). A concept is expressed through language. Semantics (i.e., meaning) is the branch of language that deals with meaning, particularly of words. *Referential semantics* — popular with linguists, but refuted by psychologists — is the theory that explains how the language and the world are connected. Some psychologists view that the meaning is built out of the concepts, and "concepts are our representation of our word meaning" (Murphy, 2002). According to psychologists, in learning word meanings initial concepts are already there in the mind, and it is only naming them. New concepts are formed building on the initial word learning. Most of the concepts one perceives in life are already formalized through words and symbols. Context of the situation participates in the modulation of meaning. Meaning of a word in a set of words is also related to its association with other words in the set. The study of this property i.e., recognizing patterns in the representation of words having similar meaning and its exploitation has led to the development of *semantic analysis* — a computational method used in processing of large texts. An unresolved issue between linguists and cognitive psychologists is whether concepts are determined by the language or language determines concepts. The role of language in conceptualization is not fully resolved.

Knowledge Approach to Concepts. Concepts and knowledge are closely linked to each other. It is reasoned that concept generation and use begins with some prior knowledge held in the mind. One of the main functions of concepts is induction, and induction is one of the methods used in knowledge derivation. The current knowledge approach to the study of concepts is based on empiricism, and in empirical phenomenon there is no place for prior knowledge (Murphy, 2002). This brings us back to the argument of rationalism versus empiricism discussed in chapter 8. It is hypothesized that knowledge might affect categorization of concepts in two different ways: a) indirectly by changing the concept representation during learning (i.e., before categorization); and b) directly by activating the knowledge during category judgment (Murphy, 2002). A concept-driven cognition could turn out to be erroneous because of factors such as dominance of one concept leading us to ignore other factors relevant to the situation being considered (Stillings et al., 1995).

Though there is a view that there is no scientific basis for the existence of concepts, the idea of conceptualization helps us in understanding, thinking, and using of knowledge.

To think and comprehend, to denote and connote about the inner and the outer world take thousands and thousands of concepts. Concepts help in knowing the cause and effect relationship, in reducing the strain on memory, in identifying objects, and in lessening the need for constant learning (Bruner, 1956). An examination of the following statements shows some of the functional aspects of concepts.

1. "The mother earth is ever merciful". This statement shows the correlation feature of concepts. It shows the

relationship between mother and earth, time and mercy, and earth and mercy. It also expresses a connotative relationship in the form of metaphor.

2. "Yes, it is a mobile phone of foreign make". The concepts embodied in the words "yes", "mobile", "phone", "foreign" and "make", show several characteristics/ categories of concepts. "Yes" shows the property of confirmation. "Mobile phone" and "foreign make" include the characteristic of classification, besides bringing in spatial and temporal relationships behind these concepts. There is also the indication of the idea of local make, though not specifically mentioned.

3. "Mr. Fancy was absolved of the crime for lack of evidence". In this case, the concepts behind the words "absolved", and "lack of evidence" exhibit a cause and effect relationship, besides showing the role of reasoning.

4. "Mumbai is the commercial capital of India". Here, the concept contains an inter-domain relationship by way of linking a specific concept/domain (Mumbai city) to a broader concept/domain (India, a country). Concepts have the property of relating one concept to another concept in the same knowledge domain or in other domains. Recall of a seemingly unrelated experience or idea at the sight of a particular object or hearing a sound is an example for intra-knowledge domain correlating feature of concepts. Correlation may yield new concepts or modify a known knowledge structure.

ANALYSIS, INTEGRATION, CORRELATION AND INTERPRETATION

Analysis, integration, and correlation are fundamental processes employed by mind in thinking. In the context of cognition, knowledge and information, the following definitions selected from the Webster's dictionary are relevant. Analysis is taken to mean: a) separation or breaking of a whole into its fundamental elements or component parts, b) detailed examination of anything complex made in order to understand its nature or determine its essential features, c) the resolution of knowledge into its fundamental factors or original parts, and d) the elucidation, clarification, and explication of expressions and statements through determination of their meaning or logical use. All these features come into play in analyzing thinking process, understanding and applying knowledge, and in processing information.

Analysis. It is the first basic step in cognitive processes like reasoning, problem solving, judgment, decision-making and planning. Analysis involves identifying the constituent parts in a given problem or a knowledge text, and segregating them so that each part can be studied for its role, composition, value, position, effects, properties and characteristics in relation to the composite whole. Before one starts analyzing, one has to know the purpose of making an analysis. Then only it is possible to know or determine, what, when, and how of analysis. The purpose is indicated by why the activity is studied. Purpose of analysis differs from knowledge domain to knowledge domain. In chemistry, the purpose may be to identify the composition of a chemical compound; in grammar it may be to identify the type of words, phrases, and clauses in a given sentence and establish the role of each part; in industry it may be to study a given problem situation and find appropriate solution to it; and in information analysis, the purpose may be to identify the various concepts in a text, study their interrelationships, and evaluate them for use.

The methods employed to analyze depend on the purpose of analysis, the nature of the situation to be analyzed, and the knowledge domain. The methods used are mental processes and instrumental techniques applied individually or in combination. While mental analysis is done through thinking, instrumental analysis is done through the use of various types of instruments. These methods and techniques may be further subdivided based on specialization. For example, in cognitive analysis one may employ the process of analogy, in optics one may use diffraction grating, and information processing may employ both intellectual processes and computers.

Integration. Integration is the opposite process of analysis. According to Webster's dictionary, integration is the act or process or an instance of integrating: the condition of being formed into whole by addition or combination of parts or elements. It may also be defined as the process of combining and coordinating separate and diverse elements into more complete or harmonious whole. All the features of analysis appear in integration, but the main point is that integration proceeds after analysis. In integration, the elements, relationships, and roles found from analysis are studied, and then combined in such a way, that it results in achieving the set purpose or goal. Integration may involve interpolation and extrapolation of parts and features, and also structuring and restructuring the situation or the system by employing various options. An eminently successful integration displays the property that the whole is greater than the sum of its parts.

Correlation. Correlation is the mental process of establishing the interrelationships that are obvious and not so obvious among phenomena in nature, and in the actions of man. Examples for correlations, inter-knowledge correlation, and intra-knowledge correlation have been cited while explaining conceptualization. Correlation may give rise to new knowledge or modify the existing knowledge structure. Establishment of relationship between cause and effect, experience and conclusion, association and recognition are some of the essential steps involved in correlating process.

Interpretation. Used in a general sense, interpretation refers to explaining the contents of a text in a simple manner. In the cognitive sense, interpretation is a particular way of thinking. Where a text contains a concept which is amenable to different explanations, to interpret is to bring out those explanations to give a better or a new insight of the text. A given text or a phenomenon can be interpreted in different ways so as to show its features and properties that hitherto had remained unexplored or ignored by the interpreter. To arrive at conclusions in research and in many other activities, the given set of data need to be first analyzed, and then interpreted. An interpreter may employ different modes of interpretation depending upon the context or the goal in mind of the interpreter. An item, text or phenomenon may be interpreted in different ways to get different views or perceptions of the same text. In interpreting, the interpreter brings to bear on his subject his expertise and past experience in the field. Interpretation makes use of different attributes, such as rational, scientific, sociological, legal, moral, artistic, philosophic, ontological, psychological, and so on. How we interpret a text also depends on the use of language, selection of words and the construction of the sentences in the text. Interpretation has the property of showing an existing knowledge text in a new light, and creating new knowledge.

Reasoning

Reasoning is a particular way of thinking, and thinking leads to knowledge. Reasoning in a limited sense is thinking aided by logic. Logic was a highly developed branch of ancient Indian philosophic tradition. Its roots in the West go back to the ancient Greek philosophy. A broader interpretation of reasoning includes critical thinking, decision-making, and problem solving. Intuition, imagination, and trial-and-error methods of thinking, irrespective of their usefulness have no place in reasoning. For many western philosophers/ psychologists of the nineteenth century, logic provided the laws of thought as idealized statements of how people reason. Subsequently, philosophers restricted reasoning to the study of formal relations between propositions, but not with the thinking processes that produce them, which became central theme of research in the hands of cognitive psychologists (Johnson, 1968). Our emphasis here is on the broader sense of the term, and not on logic in the sense preferred by philosophers.

The two principal strands of reasoning are inductive reasoning and deductive reasoning. Inferencing is a key element in both the strands. In deductive reasoning the process of inferencing proceeds from the general to the specific, and it is reversed in inductive reasoning, i.e., inferencing process proceeds from the specific to the general. While deductive reasoning yields absolute certainty, induction results in probability (Overton, 1990, xv). (see also chapter 13).

Critical Reasoning. Critical reasoning is making an analysis aimed at finding the reason behind one's beliefs and actions. Included in it is evaluation of other people's reasoning. It is to help come up with better reasoning. Main skills in critical reasoning are: a) recognizing the reasons behind the action and the conclusions drawn, b) recognizing unstated assumptions behind the reason, c) drawing conclusions, d) appraising evidence and evaluating statements, and e) judging whether conclusions drawn are warranted. Underlying these skills is the ability to use language with clarity and discrimination. One employs reasoning by presenting reasons or evidence in support of his statement to persuade others to accept his or her viewpoint. This is the essence of argument. In arguments, clear and precise use of language plays a critical role since evaluation of reasoning depends upon the clarification of the exact meaning of word or phrase; and on the ability to summarize another person's reasoning, which affects understanding (Thomson, 2002). Reasoning skills are transferable.

Analogical Reasoning. Reasoning by analogy rests on the principle that the conclusions drawn in one context or problem will be useful in another similar context when the contexts/ problems are comparable. Analogical method of reasoning is particularly useful when the objective is to explain and to persuade in arguments. It is a mental ability, which the mind frequently employs in daily encounters, research and discourses (Diestler, 2005). Kekule's discovery of the benzene ring is seen as an example, where analogical reasoning helped him to grasp the idea of a ring made of closed strings from the similarity he saw in the tail-biting snakes in his dream.

People often use analogy for explaining things in teaching, in speech and writing, as analogy helps in reinforcement of conviction. Metaphors and related forms of symbolic expressions are employed in everyday use of language, in the arts and in cultural practices like ceremonies, because of their similarity relationship. When we reason analogically, we retrieve structured images from memory; do the mapping; draw inferences; and make relational generalizations (Holyoak, 2005).

Domain-specific Reasoning. (Legal Reasoning). The nature of reasoning can shift from general or absolute to specific or bound depending on the domain, as could be seen in legal reasoning. In legal reasoning, information is selected or rejected so long as it results in a coherent story; an example is the role of circumstantial evidence in criminal cases. Legal reasoning differs from general reasoning because: a) it involves impartial reasoning applied by judges, and motivated reasoning used by lawyers to obtain verdicts in favor of their clients, although the facts of the case are same to all the three parties- prosecution, defense and the judge; b) it employs deductive method, i.e., rule-based reasoning as well as analogical method, i.e., case-based reasoning. Deductive reasoning is used for drawing conclusions by applying or non-applying various statutes. Analogical reasoning is employed for deciding analogical relevance of applicability of previously decided cases to the case on hand (precedents); c) legal reasoning is final and is decided on the basis of information and material placed before a judge- there is no question of waiting for further confirmation as in science- even if the information presented is incomplete or ambiguous or both; and d) the idea of free will is preserved (Ellsworth, 2005).

Fallacies. Errors in reasoning are called fallacies. Causes of fallacies can be traced to faulty analogy, false cause, hasty conclusion, red herring, appeal to tradition, equivocation, appeal to pity, ad homonym, and begging the question (Diestler, 2005). Recognition of fallacies helps us in analyzing the quality of reason backing the conclusions.

Classification

Classification is a cognitive process of differentiating. The neural system of the brain distinguishes all incoming sensations before converting them into awareness or responses *vis-à-vis* knowledge items already stored in the memory. The process of classification theoretically rests on identification of attributes and differentiating members on the basis of chosen attributes. Items having same or similar attributes are ordered together to form categories. Categories are linked through relationship; the most common ordering is hierarchical from generic to specific. Choice of classification principles depends on the nature of objects to be classified and the purpose of classification. Criteria of selection of attributes for differentiation are critical.

Attributes may be selected on the basis of perceptible characteristics like physical features of objects to be classified; genetic and morphological characteristics; kind and degree of differences in a characteristic; quantitative characteristics, such as frequency and probability of distribution of members; and many others. When classification takes a formal shape, it becomes a scheme of classification. Language plays an essential role in classification.

Impact on Knowledge

The cognitive processes discussed above are identified processes, which have received considerable attention in the form of study and research. Besides these, the brain employs many other complex processes particularly in the creation of 'new' knowledge that still remain a mystery. As noted by Shera "... the brain can do more than process or manipulate information telegraphed to it by the senses, more than conceptualize, distinguish, and group— it can generate 'new' information from stimuli received through clues and analogies; it can solve problems, apparently by fragmenting them into manageable parts having familiar connotations and then bringing all of its resources (such as memory) to bear on each fragment in turn; it can remember sights, sounds, tastes, smells, and physical contacts, and it can be trained to remember them better than it might be naturally inclined to do; it can 'imagine', and direct the creation of things which have never before existed, by applying or relating some of its stored knowledge in new ways; it can retain, on a subconscious level, information which it is not aware of remembering; it can fill in information gaps created by the absence of sensory evidence, reaching conclusions or formulating concepts by intuition or postulation..."(Shera, 1972, p.12).

The impact of cognitive processes is on the significance of knowledge at the output and outcome stage. They also indicate the mental ability of individuals. Applying the same cognitive methods to a given knowledge situation different persons may draw different conclusions or the same person may perceive the situation differently at different times. When a person's perceptual behaviour deviates from that of the commonly accepted pattern, society generally tends to associate such deviations with either creativity or mental aberration. Perceiving things uniquely is considered to be a characteristic of creative minds. Variation in perception seems to be caused by the quality of the mind, the type of cognitive method employed, past experience, and the environment. Often, this quality of perceiving differently is the cause of differences of opinions and conflicts, aided and abetted by other psychological factors. On the other hand, the growth and progress of knowledge depend on this characteristic.

The cognitive methods shape the type and the nature of knowledge produced. Cognitive processes lead to the discovery of new concepts and patterns from out of observations of the external environment and experimentation as in science, and also to rearrangement of known patterns and relationships to create new forms as in arts (Shera, 1972). The cognitive processes also affect directly the quality, reliability and quantity of knowledge generated, and indirectly the amount of resources like time, efforts, and money spent on knowledge activities. Society invests considerable resources to equip individuals in the use of these processes. In fact, an objective of research is to develop such techniques, and that of education is to train persons in the selection and use of appropriate cognitive process.

Cognitive Skills

Cognitive processes are also developed and applied in an expert way to specific areas of action. When the objective of such an application has a clear practical goal, then those cognitive processes appear as skills. Three such skills - creativity, problem solving, and decision-making are further explained.

Creativity. It is a cognitive process that is distinct from general thinking process, and occurs unusually. Following a general approach, creativity is defined as the ability to generate new ideas or perceive things in a unique way. Creativity and intelligence seem to be two distinct forms of mental ability. A related process is innovation (creativity of lower order) which means improving upon an existing idea, product or process. The genesis of creativity is traced to complicated mental processes involving: a) logical thinking; b) cross-fertilization of ideas and relationships; c) problem solving; and d) a free flash of ideas from conscious and subconscious levels of the mind. Creativity is a product of imagination, intelligence, curiosity and often agonizing involvement.

One can discern different textures in creativity, such as:

managerial creativity, scientific creativity, artistic creativity, computational creativity, and many others. Managerial or organizational creativity is mostly associated with problem solving, ability to see opportunities for growth which is not apparent, and enriching managerial processes. The organizational management needs to keep in mind certain traits sometimes associated with highly creative persons, such as aversion to strict discipline, high sensitiveness in certain aspects of personality and even eccentricity (Narayana, 1991). Scientific creativity has to work within the constraints of scientific method, scientific laws, objectivity and rationality. If the creativity crosses these limits, then such a creativity will be of revolutionary import or unworthy of being considered as scientific. In artistic creativity, it is imagination, emotional and aesthetic values and not rational rigidity that count. Computational creativity, a product of computer thinking is dealt with in chapter 10.

Creativity is described by Margaret Boden in her book *The Creative Mind* as the ability to come up with ideas or artifacts that are *new, surprising and valuable*. 'Ideas' here refers to intangible items like concepts, scientific theories, and chorography. Artifacts refer to material constructions like paintings, sculptures, toys, and furniture. Creativity is not a special 'faculty', but an aspect of human intelligence, i.e., finding its expression through conceptual thinking, perception, memory and reflectivity. Creativity is of two types: 'psychological' creativity, and 'historical' creativity. Psychological creativity means that the creative idea is new to the person creating it. Historical creativity refers to creativity of the first order, where the idea generated is of original inventive type, i.e., not known to anybody. Creativity has two elements, "surprise" and "newness". An idea may be surprising because it is unfamiliar or unlikely, though the idea was before you all the time, but you had not grasped it, and is new because no one could have even dreamt of it as it was impossible, yet it did occur to you. The creativity act may be the result of: a) combining of ideas, b) exploring conceptual spaces, and c) transforming the space.

Combination of Ideas. In this, surprise is caused by making unfamiliar combination of familiar ideas. For a novel combination to emanate, the person must be acquainted with a large repository of knowledge about the idea, and the mind must be engaged in manipulating knowledge around the idea. Further, for the combination of ideas to make sense there must be some intelligible conceptual relationship among them.

Exploring Conceptual Space. Conceptual spaces are structural styles of thought. Generally, these are already there enclosed in one's background of culture or peer group. It is disciplined way of thinking in space belonging to the particular social group with which the person is familiar. The characteristics of the spaces surrounding ideas are distinct to each domain. Exploratory creativity enables the creative person to see the possibilities in the structured space they had not thought of it before.

Transforming the Space. In this type, the thinking process involves change in the mental map of the person caused by abrupt change in the style of thinking. The supposedly impossible idea can come about only, if the creator changes the preexisting style in some way (Boden, 2004).

Knowledge and Creativity. There is a school of thought that thinks creative thinking and knowledge coexist in a state of tension. It is argued that a creative thinker needs the knowledge of the domain to initiate the thought process, but overwhelming quantum of knowledge will only lead to stereotyped thinking and cannot yield novel ideas or creative thoughts. This perception is known as "tension view". However, there is an opposite view called "foundation view" which holds that creativity builds on knowledge, and there need to be no tension between the two (Weisberg, 1999).

Problem Solving. A problem may be perceived as the

discrepancy or dissonance existing in a situation's current state of affairs and some desired state of affairs. Problem solving is the process of finding solutions to remove or counter the dissonance factors, so that the desired state of affair is reached. The desired state becomes the goal. Problem solving, thus, is a cognitive method employed to achieve the goal. It is generally recognized that problem solving are of two types: "general" or "domain-free" problem solving, and "expert" problem solving. How the problem is represented makes the difference between the two types. In general problem solving, the problem solver begins with understanding the problem, identifying the elements or factors obstructing the path leading to goal achievement, finding possible solutions to counter the effects of negative factors, and test the solution to confirm its suitability for adoption. Gestalt view holds that problem solving involves thinking at unconscious level; it is a discontinuous process having an incubation period, which is followed by a sudden appearance of insight leading to an instant flash of solution. However, the current thinking suggests that problem solving is a continuous and accumulative process (Best,1999). It is generally accepted that creativity plays a role in problem solving. Problem solving is also treated as an information processing exercise (Newell, 1966; Newell and Simon, 1972).

A problem can appear as either well-defined or ill-defined. A well-defined problem will have a clearly defined start state, and clearly defined goals; selection of solutions and their testing are easy. Ill-defined problems are those where beginning state and goal state are not fully defined, and some elements may be missing. One reason for this is that the goal is not easily specifiable and changing, as in the goal "achieving success in life". A method followed in solving ill-defined problems is to restructure the problem by breaking it down into easily solvable subunits. Breaking-down into subunits helps focused thinking on the subunit goal (Best, 1999).

Classifying problems will facilitate in the selection of

appropriate problem solving method for a given problem. Cited by Best, Greeno groups problems into: a) problems in inducing structures, categorized by determining the relationship among several elements in the problem; b) problems in transformation whose solution lies in finding the sequence of operations that transform the initial situation into a goal state; and c) problems in arrangement, wherein the solver is guided towards the solution by rearranging the elements in the problem according to some criteria. This way of grouping is said to help adopt relevant and particular skills suitable to solve a particular group of problems. It is also likely that the problem itself may suggest the analogy that fits into the problem. The grouping may also point out to the solver to find explicitly the type of suitable analogy (Greeno, 1978; Best, 1999).

Expert Problem Solving. Expert problem solving is domain specific. In expert problem solving, the problem solver applies his knowledge of basic principles of the domain, and makes use of the insights acquired through experience. In expert problem solving, the problem space exhibits the distinctive features of the domain (Stillings, 1995). Selection of problem solving methods differs from domain to domain. For instance, management problem solving has to take into account the human component, which is not the case in scientific research. In expert problem solving, semantic memory plays a vital role. Another feature of expert problem solving is the increasing use of collective expertise.

Problem Solving Methods. Reasoning is one of the basic cognitive processes employed in problem solving. How the question is framed can influence our reasoning. In general problem solving, heuristics is the most commonly used methods, particularly in solving everyday problems. It is a rule of thumb method, which is fast and easy to apply. However, the solution is not guaranteed. Algorithms and simulation are most frequently used techniques in solving problems, particularly in complex problems. Algorithms may not always be efficient, but they always work. In solving ill-defined problems algorithms may not be of much help, as parameters of the problem can not be completely specified (Best, 1999).

Decision-making. In everyday life and in managing organizations, we are frequently confronted with problems and situations requiring us to make a choice among several possible solutions that may be available. Choosing from among the options is decision-making. Decision-making is a specific type of mental ability. The classical thinking on decision-making is based on "rational theory of choice" or "standard economic model". According to these models, the person making the choice is guided by his or her perceived "subjective utility" of each alternative. Final selection will be the one that offers the maximum expected utility. Subsequent research has shown that a number of factors, not necessarily rational enter into shaping ones preferences. Some of the factors are: one's perception of risk and value; tendency to avoid decisional conflicts; need to accommodate influences of salient identities and emotions; ignoring to take into account factors that appear to be inconsequential, but not so in reality; and acceptance of the decisional situations without applying critical evaluation. A critical evaluation of the situation by applying different frames may lead to unbiased decisions (Le Boeuf and Shafir, 2005). Past experience becomes an important influence on the individual's decision-making.

The objective and the nature of the decision, factors involved in the decision, and effects of the decision vary from decision domain to decision domain. The decision domain may be broadly grouped into: individuals and their personal living, science and academic research, industry and economics, and governance. Barring scientific research, other domains affect and get affected to varying degrees of impact by social and other external influences. Corporate decision-making (also called management decision-making) differs from personal decision-making, and both differ from that of a scientist's decision-making. In a scientist's decision-making there is no place for irrational imagination, subjectivity, social, cultural, and human factors. Collective decision-making is one of the methods frequently employed to supplement or overcome the cognitive as well as domain knowledge limitations of individuals in arriving at wise decisions. Collective decision-making takes different forms like a committee's decision, expert advice-based decisions or open forum decisions.

The process of managerial decision-making begins with studying the decision situation or the problem, premising, identifying and evaluating the alternatives, and the final selection of the alternative. Different decision models are constructed to evaluate the effectiveness of each option by varying the variables in the model. Operational research, system analysis, and decision theory are some of the methods used in constructing the model and their evaluation.

Statistical Patterns in Knowledge Texts

Distribution of information carrying items in certain knowledge and information related activities and effects, like literary output of authors, occurrence of words in long texts, a small percentage of items in a large collection of documents in a given knowledge domain accounting for an extremely high percentage of usefulness, are found to follow distinctive patterns. Study of these distribution patterns, which are mostly hyperbolic, has led to the formulation of many empirical laws which are examined in "bibliometrics", "infometrics", and "scientiometrics". These sub-disciplines are engaged in the development and use of a variety of measures to study and analyze several properties of information and documents, productivity of research, growth and obsolescence, citation studies, and scattering (Ravichandra Rao,1991). The phenomena in its simplest discrete manifestation may be stated as input increasing geometrically produces an yield arithmetically (Fairthorne, 1969), Hyperbolic distribution is also found in a number of other areas of human activities, and the distributions are named after the discoverers, namely Weber-Fechner laws (stimulus-response relationship), Pareto distribution (distribution of wealth in different communities), Willis' law (distribution of family, genera and species in taxonomy), Berger-Mendelbrot law (genera-species distribution, variations in market prices, and communication systems). Lotka's law, Bradford law, and Zipf's law are the important laws in bibliometrics.

S.C. Bradford found that a small number of journals account for the bulk of articles pertaining to a given topic, and to cover the same number of articles in subsequent groups of journals, the number of journals to be covered is in the order of a geometrical progression (Bradford, 1948).

Alfred Lotka discovered that the number of authors making *n* contributions is about 1/ *n* of those making one contribution, and the proportion of all contributors making a single contribution is about 60 percent (Lotka, 1926).

G.K. Zipf noted that if words in a large text are ranked on the basis of the frequency of their occurrence in a long text in decreasing order, then the frequency of occurrence of a word is the reciprocal of its rank (Zipf, 1949). Zipf attributes the rationale behind the rank-frequency phenomenon to the "principle of least effort". In other words, the words which have a high frequency of occurrence in any language are those that cost less in usage or require less effort in communication. Zipf also observed that once, by chance, a group has achieved a dominant position it retains that position for a long time, indeed is more likely to be promoted than the less fortunate groups (Scarrot, 1974). This is a phenomenon of success breeds success. Based on the study of the relationship between the frequencies of use of books in libraries, their arrangement on the shelves, and the time taken to access them Booth suggests that human memory has some mechanism that recalls most frequently used items more readily than less used items (Booth, 1969).

Unlike the laws of nature, the truth of which are not subjected to human manipulation, distribution laws are arbitrary and the results can be altered by changing the social arrangement under which the laws operate (Fairthorne, 1969). Hyperbolic distributions are the "inevitable result of combinatorial necessity and a tendency to short-term rational behaviour whenever a group of people have to use a repertory of given elements to form compounds and when one aspect of the 'cost' or inconvenience of these elements is dominant...... . Usually the elements and their use arise from the way people choose to observe, arrange, or talk about things, not from the nature of the things themselves. Therefore designers and administrators can cheat these laws by changing the elements, their costs, and the rules for using them..." (Fairthorne, 1969 [2005, p.190]).

The h-index. Publication of *Science Citation Index* provided a method for studying the pattern of citation of scientific papers by scientists, i.e., to find how many times a particular paper by a given scientist has been cited by others in their papers. From this, one could assess the relative influence of the cited paper (and the author) on other authors in the field (impact factor). The field of study came to be called "Scientiometrics"- the science of measuring and analyzing science largely based on bibliometric methods. In the year 2005, J.E. Hirsch, a physicist developed an index to measure the impact of theoretical physicists' relative quality (Hirsch, 2005). The index is popularly called h-index or Hirsch number. It is based on a scientist's most cited paper, and the number of citations it has received in others' publications. The h- index application has spread to other disciplines. It is now used by some for assessing a scientist's worth for job-related purposes. Since then, a few other indexes have also appeared (Wikipedia, 2009). Hirsch's technique has received a lot of appreciation and some criticism. Critics say, besides other perceived drawbacks, the index gives only the number of citations and it does not consider the context of citations. It can be said that the index enables to find the relative scientific worth of a particular scientist, a scientific group or an institution solely based on citations. A citation-based criterion forms only one of the criteria for assessing a scientist's scientific worth. There are many other factors such as psychological, organizational and scientific which the index cannot probe.

Bibliometric laws are derived from the empirical study of data to arrive at the laws mostly relating quantity to yield. What is needed is the basic research on finding out the cognitive basis for the occurrence of such patterns, that is, to find out why and how the mind adheres to the distribution phenomena. Nature seems to have evolved the principle that to create one or a few unique items there has to be thousands or even millions of items of ordinary or relatively less important items. Evolutionary theory shows that the arrival of Homo sapiens had to be preceded by creation of several other forms of life. To fertilize one egg a female body needs a single sperm, but the male injects over a million sperms. Similarly, to create a Buddha or an Einstein nature creates millions and millions of people of far lesser uniqueness. The same principle seems to act in certain areas of knowledge phenomena and accounts for the operation of the laws of distribution.

Receptivity of Mind to External Knowledge

Human mind is often receptive to thoughts originating from external people's thoughts. An individual's receptivity to thoughts coming from outside agencies is conditioned by: a) genetic factors characterized by genotype, b) environmental influences corresponding to phenotype, and c) the existing state and stock of knowledge in the individual. It is not that every person is receptive to all types of knowledge all the time and from all sources. Receptivity is a selective process of the mind. Receptivity of mind to external sources of thoughts fall into two categories: a) passive receptivity, and b) active receptivity.

Passive Receptivity. In passive receptivity, a person interacts with an information source indirectly as in reading a book or in self-learning. There will not be any direct participation of other persons in the knowledge encounter. It is strictly a single party phenomenon, the party being the seeker himself. On the other hand, in active receptivity there is direct participation of other persons.

Active Receptivity. In active receptivity, the personality of the influencing party does have an impact on the receiving mind. More charismatic the influencing party, greater is the capacity to enhance receptivity in the recipient. Receptivity also depends on the level of confidence the recipient has in the external party sharing his or her knowledge. Ability to enthuse confidence in the mind of the receiving party depends upon the receiver's assessment of the deliverer's repository of relevant knowledge and its reliability. The receptivity of the mind to external source of knowledge is thus, influenced by three factors: a) charismatic personality of the deliverer; b) level of confidence existing between the receiver and the deliverer; and c) receiver's perception of the deliverer's stock of relevant knowledge, its reliability and suitability in relation to the problem. Mind's receptivity to new ideas and new knowledge differs from person to person. Generally, most human minds are not readily receptive to new ideas and knew knowledge. Receptivity to new ideas and putting them to action means an openness to accept change, and willingness to bear the consequence of change. A major reason hindering receptivity to new ideas seems to be the fear of risk associated with change following the application of new knowledge.

Social psychologists see receptivity of mind in a slightly different angle. They equate receptivity with persuasion and attitude change, the study of which was a part of learning theory in earlier days. Kruglanski sees it as an individual's attitude towards his or her information encounter, and names it as "ascribed epistemic authority". In interpersonal relations and problem situations one encounters a continuous flow of information in the form of advice, plans and briefs from various sources. Such encounters take place in the background of social influences, and the decisions made under such influences is called "social judgment". The most common problem associated with social judgment is deciding about whom to trust (informationally), and whose statements to discount or regard with suspicion. Such judgments affect not only an individual's affairs, but also the larger society. The communicator derives his influence from his epistemic authority, which is based on the characteristics, such as his or her expertise, trustworthiness, similarity or likeability. These characteristics are assessed by the receiver through perceiving the consequences of accepting or rejecting a given source's influence, and are generalized to other similar sources. Here, epistemic authority denotes " a source on whom an individual may rely in her or his attempts to acquire knowledge on various topics..., and it addresses the extent to which an individual is prepared to rely on a source's information and to accept it" (Kruglanski et al. 2005, p.351). In identifying a source as an epistemic authority, a person may be guided by characteristics such as seniority (e.g., an elder), a role (e.g., a priest, a teacher) or level of education (e.g., a doctorate degree), an appearance in print (e.g., published in a journal), specialist knowledge in the desired knowledge domain (e.g., consumer protection law, neurosurgery). Thus, epistemic authority ascription is conceived as meta-cognitive beliefs about a source of knowledge. It is also possible that one may believe in one's own epistemic authority by virtue of having acquired knowledge in a given knowledge domain (Kruglanski et al, 2005). Persuasion is one of the important methods used by people to make others receptive to their ideas and knowledge.

Persuasion. One of the traits of man is to influence other persons to accept his or her viewpoint on any issue. Persuasion is one of the methods employed to convince others, more so in a competitive situation. Main elements in persuasion are: a) person or persons to be persuaded, b) persuader, c) message carrying the persuasive agenda, and d) communication of message. Candidates canvassing for votes in an election, arguments of lawyers before a judge in an arbitration case, influencing customers through single or repeated messages about a product or service to be sold in marketing are some examples of persuasion. Environment, affect, motivation and belief, prior knowledge, and past behavioural attitude are some of the other factors that impact on the cognitive processing of persuasive messages. A successful persuasion not only convinces the persuaded, but also leads to favorable action towards fulfilling the objective of persuasion. In group persuasion, once the leaders and opinion-makers in the group are made to accept your viewpoint then persuading others becomes easy. Study of group psychology will be of added help.

Persuasion research has generally followed the line of analyzing and surmising how a persuasive message acts on the recipient of the message, and the consequential change in the behaviour of the persuaded. Cognitive social psychologists have come up with a few persuasion models. One such model presented by Albarracin on the effects of persuasive communication on cognition makes seven postulates as follows:

1. The processing of communication received by the recipient proceeds in stages that involve information interpretation; retrieval of prior knowledge from memory; and identification, selection, and use of information as basis for judgment.
2. The receiver interprets the arguments of persuasive message as well as other information that is available at the time. Decrease in ability and motivation are likely to first affect the processing of information that is more difficult, but easier to interpret.
3. In processing messages, the recipient recalls information

from prior knowledge from memory primarily to validate or refute the new information contained in the messages.

4. The recipient identifies potential bases for judgment and then chooses information on the basis of relevance. The receiver's ability and motivation reduces or strengthens the influence of the arguments contained in the message.
5. The receiver may form beliefs from the evaluations of the content of the message, then integrate this and other information into attitudes. He may then develop intentions to engage in the action implied in the message. However, these stages can be bypassed and their sequence altered.
6. If conflicts are detected at the time of processing the persuasive communication, then the analysis of information contained in the message will be done more carefully. Detection of conflicts, if any, appearing later, affects the relevant information and gets integrated. This may impact on the attitude development.
7. Communications that have a direct impact on a stage closer to the behaviour lead to greater change maintenance than communications that have an impact on an early stage (Albarracin, 2002).

Persuasive Methods and Techniques. The most widespread and effective channels of persuasion in use are the print and the electronic media including TV, audio, radio, telephone and the Internet. By employing brain-washing techniques people may be persuaded to think and act against their own better judgment, and such a persuasion is called *subliminal* persuasion. Subliminal persuasion acts at the unconscious level.

A principle used in persuasive advertisements is based on the Gestalt psychology that the whole is greater than the sum of the parts (Diestler, 2005). An example is the "Complan" TV advertisement in which questions (slogans), which are whole and complete in the initial stage are continued in subsequent stages with the effective words deliberately left out, which are automatically filled out by the viewer as the mind makes out the whole slogan even in the latter absence of the critical message carrying words.

When receptivity to knowledge is enlarged to include knowledge held by more than one person it uses "collective knowledge". The term collective knowledge is used here in a limited sense, unlike in "sociology of knowledge" where it stands for collective awareness of a society (see chapter 11).

Collective Thinking. Knowledge is studied as a phenomenon occurring in individual agents in epistemology. Knowledge also occurs in group activities and in multi-person encounters, where according to Fagin, it takes the characteristic of distributed knowledge. The study of distributed knowledge helps us understand and analyze complicated agents involving groups. Reasoning about distributed knowledge has a key place in disciplines ranging from game theory and computer science to linguistics and social psychology (Fagin,1995). Since this knowledge is distributed among many persons, the appropriate term to use seems to be collective thinking.

Collective thinking process, in which individuals pool their knowledge and experiences in dealing with a given problem or issue, is one of the most common and widespread means that people follow in processing knowledge for action. Collective thinking helps shape and reshape existing knowledge resource in individuals and organizations. It is in vogue from time immemorial in all societies, ranging from aboriginal tribes to modern societies. The need for collective thinking arises because of the limitations of an individual mind to grasp fully all intricacies in a given problem or situation. A psychological aspect of collective thinking is that it diffuses the responsibility for the consequences of the decision. Collective thinking works through different vehicles. In democratic governance structures, the chosen representatives of the people provide the benefits of collective thinking for shaping and executing state actions. In industrial organizations, it takes the forms of board of directors, advisory and executive committees; and in research and academics the purpose of collective thinking is served by conferences, seminars and meetings; and in individuals it takes the form of consultation or seeking advice from others.

Intelligence. Intelligence may be defined as the capacity for learning, reasoning, understanding, and similar mental activity. The word "capacity" also implies that intelligence differs among people (Grigorenko, 2008). There are other definitions too. However, all definitions seem to agree that the concept of intelligence includes elementary cognitive processes like perception, attention, and sensation; and higher order processes like abstraction, reasoning, problem solving, decision-making, and processing of knowledge. Intelligence is also defined as the ability to adapt to one's environmental, biological and physiological states. Emotional and motivational factors do influence the development of intelligence. Intelligence seems to involve three basic processes, namely, the ability to come up with novel ideas (synthetic feature), evaluating the quality of these ideas (analytical part), and convincing the suitability of the idea for adoption (practical aspect) (Sternberg and O'Hara, 1999). These components of intelligence are also involved in creativity.

The etiology (the study of the source of origin) of variation in intelligence is attributed to the consequences of the inter-play of genotype (nature) and phenotype (nurture) elements characterizing the individual. The study of group differences in intelligence takes upon gender differences, ethnic and racial differences, cultural differences, and differences in special groups, such as physically challenged (Grigorenko, 2008). Development of intelligence and its decline are age related phenomena. Another aspect of intelligence study is testing of intelligence, which has led to the development of IQ (intelligent quotient). IQ is employed to assess applicants for admission in schools and colleges, recruitment of personnel in the defence services, and so on. Intelligence test results do vary depending on the intelligence criteria, such as skill, primary judgment, adopted for testing of Intelligence. A negative use of intelligence testing is that it has become handy to vested interests and bigots to denigrate particular sections of society on the lines of race and gender.

Closure

The formation of human knowledge is based on cognitive processes acting upon the newly received messages by the brain through sense organs and the knowledge previously formed and stored in memory. The cognitive processes impart distinctive characteristics to knowledge, each characteristic serving a particular purpose. The important cognitive processes are : conceptualization, analysis, integration, correlating, reasoning, classifying, creative thinking, problem solving, and decision-making. At the centre of these processes are conceptualization and reasoning. Conceptualization is the picture drawn by the mind, i.e., concept about anything and everything a human being feels and perceives. Concepts fulfill two functions- categorization and communication. Categorization is the process of ascertaining whether an incoming picture received through senses belongs to an existing category of concepts in mind or a new one. Communication function is served by transforming a concept into sound, which is largely done by language. Concepts are held in memory as neural structures.

Reasoning is thinking in a particular way, and that thinking when identified becomes knowledge. In philosophy, thinking based on logic is reasoning. In a broader sense, reasoning includes critical thinking, decision-making, and problem solving. Critical reasoning is making analysis aimed at finding the reasons behind one's beliefs and actions. Critical reasoning employs a number of skills such as: analyzing the causes behind an action, collecting evidence and evaluating them, and drawing conclusions. Inductive reasoning and deductive reasoning are the most commonly employed types of reasoning. Analogical reasoning is applying conclusions drawn from one context to another similar context. When reasoning is modeled on the basis of distinctive features of a knowledge domain and its requirements, it is called domain specific reasoning, examples : legal reasoning, and scientific reasoning.

Classification is a cognitive process of differentiating one item from another in a collection on the basis of selected attributes. The brain employs classification to distinguish one sensation or concept from another for storing them in memory and subsequent recall. Classification brings order and is employed in activities ranging from daily routines to identifying stars in galaxies.

Creativity is a mental process of conceiving things uniquely. It is a sub-conscious process involving logical thinking, cross-fertilization of ideas and relationships, problem solving, and sudden flash of ideas. Involved in it are imagination, intelligence, curiosity, and often agonizing time. Creativity is of different types, e.g., managerial creativity, artistic creativity. It being a skill can be developed. While the "tension view" of creativity holds that beyond a certain quantitative level, knowledge leads only to stereotyped thinking; the "foundation view" holds that there need be no conflict between the two, as creativity builds on knowledge

Problem solving is a cognitive method used to overcome obstacles standing between a goal and its achievement. Problem solving is of two types: general problem solving and expert problem solving. Gestalt view of problem solving implies thinking at the unconscious level, and that it is a discontinuous process. After an incubation period, the solver suddenly gets the insight of the problem, and the solution appears in a flash. Classifying problems helps in choosing the method most suited to tackle a given type of problem. Heuristic is the most common method used in general problem solving. In expert problem solving, the problem and the solution are field specific. The expert discovers the solution by applying his expert knowledge of the field, and his experience. For complex problems algorithms, and simulation methods are frequently used.

We are confronted with taking decisions at every stage of life. Decision-making is choosing among the options available to steer a course. It is a specific type of mental ability. "Rational theory of choice" explains the theory of decision making in the classical way. In this the person making a choice is guided by the perceived "subjective utility" of each option. Current thinking shows that there are other factors like—perception of risk and value, tendency to avoid decisional conflicts, need to accommodate identities and emotions, inclination to opt for easy options, and ignoring to take into account seemingly trivial factors, but apparently not. The pattern of decision-making varies from field to field, and hence we find managerial decision-making, political decision-making, and so on. Rational decision-making is not possible without information, its analysis and evaluation pertaining to the decision situation.

Apart from the cognitive processes described so far, the human mind exhibits other unique properties like— display of distinct statistical features, receptivity to knowledge held by external human agents, which takes the forms of persuasion, collective thinking, and the like. By training our mind to learn these cognitive skills one will be better equipped to handle a given knowledge situation. At present, we do not fully know the intricacies of the working of these processes in terms of their distinguishing synaptic characteristics, neural configurations, and the elusive mind. When we succeed in resolving this puzzle, it may be possible to order and control these processes.

REFERENCES

Albarracin, Dolores. Cognition in persuasion: An analysis of information processing in response to persuasive communications. Pp. 61-130. *In* Zanna, Mark P. Ed. *Advances in Experimental Social Psychology.* Vol. 34, 2002.

Best, John B. Cognitive Psychology. Ed. 5. Belmont (CA), Wadsworth Publishing, 1999.

Boden, Margaret A. The Creative Mind. Myths and Mechanisms. Ed.2. London, Routledge, 2004. (Indian reprint).

Booth, A.D. On the geometry of libraries. *Journal of Documentation* 25(1): 28-42, 1969.

Bradford, S.C. Documentation. London, Crosby Lockwood, 1948.

Bruner, J.S. et al. A Study of Thinking. New York, Wiley, 1956.

Chafe, W.L. Meaning and the Structure of Language. Chicago, University of Chicago Press, 1970.

Diestler, Sherry. Becoming a Critical Thinker: A User Friendly Manual. Ed.4. Upper Saddle River (NJ), Pearson-Prentice-Hall, 2005.

Ellesworth, Phoebe. Legal Reasoning. Pp. 685-703. *In* Holyoak, Keith J. and Morrison, Robert G. Ed. The Cambridge Handbook of Thinking and Reasoning. Cambridge (Mass.), Cambridge University Press, 2005.

Fagin, Ronald. et. al. Reasoning about Knowledge. MIT Press, 1995.

Fairthorne, Robert A. Empirical hyperbolic distributions (Bradford-Zipf-Mandelbrot) for bibliometric description and prediction. *Journal of Documentation* 25(4):319-343, 1969. (Republished as 60 years of the Best in Information Research Progress in Documentation. *Journal of Documentation* 61(2):171-193, 2005).

Cf. Greeno, J.G. Natures of Problem–Solving Abilities. Pp. 239-270. *In* Estes, W.K. Ed. Handbook of Learning and Cognitive Processes. Hillsdale (NJ), Erlbaum, 1978.

Grigorenko, Elena L. Intelligence. Pp.70-74. Vol. 4. *In* Darity, William A. Jr. Ed. International Encyclopedia of the Social Science. Ed. 2. Farmington Hills (MI.), Gale, 2008.

Hirsch, J.E. An index to qualify an individual's scientific research output. Preprint. http://arxiv.org/pdf/physics1050825. 2005.

Holyoak, Keith. J. Analogy. Pp.117-142. *In* Holyoak, Keith J. and Morrison, Robert G. Ed. Loc. cit.

Holyoak, Keith J. and Morrison, Robert G. Ed. The Cambridge Handbook of Thinking and Reasoning. Cambridge (Mass.), Cambridge University Press, 2005.

Johnson, Donald M. Reasoning and Logic. Pp. 344-50. *In* Sills, David L. Ed. International Encyclopaedia of the Social Sciences. Vol. 13. London, Macmillan & Free Press, 1968.

Kruglanski, Arie W. et al. Says Who?: Epistemic authority effects in social judgment. Pp.345-392. *In* Zanna, Mark P. Ed. *Advances in Experimental Social Psychology*, Vol.37. San Diego (CA.), Elsevier/ Academic Press, 2005.

Le Boeuf, Robyn A. and Shafir, Eldar B. Decision Making. Pp. 243-265. *In* Holyoak, Keith J. and Morrison, Robert J. Ed. Loc. cit.

Lotka, A. J. Frequency distribution of scientific productivity. *Journal of Washington Academy of Sciences 16 : 317- 323, 1926.*

Medin, Douglas L. and Rips, Lance J. Concepts and Categories: Memory, Meaning and Metaphysics. Pp. 37-72. *In* Holyoak, Keith J. and Morrison, Robert G. Ed. Loc. cit.

Murphy, Gregoy L. The Book of Concepts. Cambridge (Mass.), MIT Press, 2002. (Paperback Edn. 2004).

Narayana, G.J. Library and Information Management. New Delhi, Prentice-Hall of India, 1991.

Cf. Newell, Allen. On the representations of problems. *Computer Research review, p.*18-33, 1966.

Cf. Newell, Allen and Simon, Herbert A. Human Problem Solving. Englewood Cliffs (NJ), Prentice-Hall, 1972.

Overton, Willis F. Reasoning, Necessity, and Logic: Developmental Perspectives. Hillsdale, Laurence Erlbaum, 1990.

Ravichandra Rao, I.K. Ed. Informatics- 91. Selected papers from the third International Conference on Informatics. 9-12 August, 1991, Bangalore. Bangalore, Sarada Ranganathan Endowment for Library Science, 1992.

Scarrott, G. Will Zipf Join Gauss. *New Scientist* 62: 402-404, 1974.

Shera, J.H. The Foundations of Education for Librarianship. New York, Wiley-Becker & Hayes, 1972.

Sternberg, Robert J. and O'Hara, Linda A. Creativity and Intelligence. Pp.251-272. *In* Sternberg, Robert J. Ed. Handbook of Creativity. Cambridge (U.K.), Cambridge University Press, 1999.

Stillings, Neil A. et al. Cognitive Science: An Introduction. Ed. 2. Cambridge (Mass), MIT Press, 1995.

Thomson, Anne. Critical Reasoning: A Practical Introduction. Ed.2. London, Routledge, 2002.

Webster's Third New International Dictionary of English Language. Cologne, Merriam-Webster, 1993.

Weisberg, Robert W. Creativity and Knowledge: A Challenge to the Theories. Pp.226-249. *In* Sternberg, Robert J. Ed. Handbook of Creativity. Cambridge (U.K.), Cambridge University Press, 1999.

Wikipedia. http://en.wikipedia.org/wiki/Bibliometrics.

Zipf, G.K. Human Behavior and the Principle of Least Effort. Reading (Mass.), Addison-Wesley, 1949.

5

Utilization and Growth of Knowledge

Knowledge and information are the engines that are driving the twenty-first century world. Knowledge derives its energy from its characteristic that it has potential for use. To put knowledge to use, first it has to be created and then it needs to be transmitted to reach the actual and potential users. The three phases of knowledge phenomenon– creation, transmission, and utilization decide the role and impact of knowledge in society. Creation of knowledge and utilization of knowledge are so interlinked that one leads to the other. Higher the rate of creation of knowledge and its dispersal greater will be the utilization of knowledge and vice versa. We begin with the utility function of knowledge.

UTILIZATION OF KNOWLEDGE

Knowledge has utility. The term 'utility' is used here in its ordinary usage to mean usefulness. Utility of knowledge is subject to different interpretations depending on the context and approach. For a philosopher knowledge has use, if it fulfils the standard criteria of epistemology; for a librarian, if a record embodying knowledge is referred to by his patrons; for a common man, if it helps him in his interactions.

Knowledge and user are interlinked. Utility of knowledge is use and user dependent. For example, knowledge of taxation law is of use to lawmakers, legal interpreters, students of law, tax consultants, taxpayers, and generally not of direct interest to others.

The term 'use' has different connotations. The example of librarian stated above shows that he collects knowledge (in its surrogate forms) for the use of others. The basis for acquiring documents by a library is that the items acquired will be consulted or borrowed. There is no certainty that all the collected items will be consulted. They may be used immediately or in future or not at all. What is true of the librarian is also true of the actual user. The use thus becomes a function of probability, unless the seeker identifies specifically the exact item of knowledge he needs. Given a few exceptions, it is reasonable to conclude that in general a given knowledge item becomes useful either immediately or later to some one, somewhere. Thus, knowledge has "potential for value" (Taylor, 1986). The utility of knowledge is established only when the potential for use is converted into actual use. To ascertain the conditions under which actual use takes place one has to define what is meant by use. The following analysis of use provided by Machlup, taking a letter as an example illustrates the issues involved:

> "...the recipient of a letter can decide to throw it unread into the wastebasket. Has he 'used' the information service in question? Does use of information— the process of transmission and reception, say, of a letter— mean (a) receiving it and thus getting a chance to read it; (b) receiving it and actually reading it; (c) receiving, reading, and understanding it; (d) receiving, reading, understanding, and appreciating it; (e) receiving, reading, understanding, and appreciating it, plus making it the basis of decision; or (f) receiving,

> reading, understanding, and appreciating it, plus letting it help you in making a decision and taking an action (or refusing to act) in line with the decision reached with the help of the knowledge obtained?" (Machlup, 1980, p. 203).

This analysis does not provide a direct answer to the question what really constitutes use. However, the analysis shows the two most important stages in the use of knowledge: a) acquiring knowledge, and b) making the acquired knowledge an instrument of action or satisfaction. Knowledge is likened to electricity or money, which is a form of energy that exists only when doing work (Drucker, 1975). This corresponds to stages (e) and (f) in the Machlup's analysis. The issue of what constitutes utility of a given item of knowledge can be conveniently resolved if one takes utility, as in economics, to mean "the power to satisfy a human want". The want may be spiritual, material or recreational in character. This criterion establishes the use of knowledge by linking it with the stage at which the recipient feels that his desire has been fulfilled. By fulfilling the want, knowledge could be taken to have served its purpose for that particular user. Therefore, utility is not something intrinsic to knowledge, but derived when knowledge is put to use. Putting knowledge to use implies satisfying two conditions: a) the user must already have or acquired the knowledge to be used, and b) the user must make the knowledge an instrument of action or satisfaction.

Satisfying the above conditions of use depends on many factors. Important among them are: a) the user must have the necessary cognitive skills; and b) the mind of the user must be receptive to knowledge. These two conditions imply that knowledge has no utility in itself unless it comes in contact with a receptive mind having the necessary cognitive skills and is put to use. From the utility functions of knowledge its further characteristics are inferred. These include:

1. Knowledge once acquired, if found not useful to the

acquirer it cannot be thrown as waste, unlike material wastes. Knowledge remains with the acquirer.

2. Knowledge can be put to repeated use. Knowledge that is useful to a person at a given point of time may be useful to another person in the same or different context or may not be of any use to anybody, anywhere in the foreseeable future.

3. Evaluation and selection of knowledge for its potential for use facilitates in putting knowledge to actual use. Many of the cognitive processes and post-information processes described in chapters 4 and 18 are involved in making evaluation.

Multiple Uses of a Given Item of Knowledge. Differentiating knowledge application-wise helps, to some extent, in specifying its utility or relevance. A reasonably sound scheme of classifying knowledge based on the criterion of end use provided by Machlup is covered in chapter 2. Such a classification makes an assessment of potential for use comparatively easy. Fig. 1 shows an example for how a given item of knowledge finds diverse applications and falls under different types of uses.

Knowledge item: Rape

Type of User	User interest	Type of application
Psychologist	Psychology of crime	Practical
Doctor	Medical examination	Practical
Lawyer/ lawmaker	Statutes on rape	Practical
Criminologist/ police	Crime detection/prevention	Practical
Linguist	Study of the word	Intellectual
Reader	Thrill/curiosity	Pastime
Literary author	Literary theme	Intellectual
Moralist	Conduct	Spiritual/ethical
Sociologist	Social order/reformation	Intellectual/Practical
Others	Uncertain/ephemeral	Unknown

Fig. 1. Diverse ways in which the knowledge item on rape finds use

Evaluation. Knowledge needs evaluation before use. The criteria of evaluation depend on the purpose for which knowledge is sought. One cannot assess the utility of a given knowledge without acquiring some of it during the process of assessment. Evaluation criteria also vary from discipline to discipline. For example, in evaluating a music album tonal aesthetics of the song becomes a critical evaluation criterion. Ultimately, evaluation always rests with the end user.

A serious problem in knowledge utilization is motivating people to use knowledge. For servers of knowledge the problem is to recognize the needs, tastes, values, and environment of seekers of knowledge, which enable them to collect and package appropriate knowledge texts to meet the requirements of the user or user segment. Knowledge providers are beset with the task of deciding the limits to which they can go in meeting these requirements and deciding the appropriate technology. Also, in some cases where it is considered that providing access to certain knowledge items is prejudicial to the interest of the community, society and\ or the state, restrictions are imposed.

Indefiniteness of Knowledge. There is no sure way of establishing definitely what knowledge item is useful to whom? when? and how? Use of knowledge gets confirmed only when the potential for use is converted into actual use. The utility of knowledge is not always completely and precisely predictable; it is one of probability. As every human mind is unique, it is impossible for any one individual to know or state precisely, definitely and completely what knowledge will be useful, when, where, and to what extent. The only thing one can possibly be sure of, is the utility of a given knowledge text assessed in the context of the user at a given time. We cannot "determine *a priory* the value of an individual message. We must work at the system level..." by estimating the probable utility of certain kinds of knowledge to probable strata of users remains valid (Taylor, 1986, p. 4). This is one of the reasons for creating records of knowledge, i.e., the knowledge thus recorded may become useful to someone (including the originator), sometime, someplace. This problem becomes more complex in the context of formal organized collections of knowledge records and providing access to the multitude of users.

A precondition for using knowledge is that its existence should be known. Searching for the existence of knowledge is beset with difficulties, such as : the required knowledge may not exist; it may exist but may not be readily available; if available he may not be sure of whether the available knowledge exactly fits his need; and it is also possible that the user may not be equipped to utilize it at that particular point of time; and at the worst, he may not be sure of what knowledge he is seeking. To alleviate these difficulties, to some extent, knowledge and its records are organized. To meet this end techniques, such as cataloguing, classification, indexing, abstracting, and information retrieval methods have been devised. If digitalization of knowledge record has solved to a great extent the problem of physical access to the enormous volumes of information presently generated, this advantage is compromised to some extent by the exploding growth of new knowledge. The intellectual efforts needed to cope up with the current knowledge explosion have only aggravated the problem of putting knowledge to use.

Development of services, such as the staff function in defence; consultancy services in business, medicine, engineering, law and government; information dissemination services by libraries and information centres; Knowledge Management functions in industry; and even advising by well-wishers have become important because of the uncertainty and other such factors associated with knowledge flow and knowledge use. It is also possible that knowledge acquired earlier with no particular need in mind may later become useful. The unpredictable nature of the utility of knowledge affects the growth of knowledge particularly in organized sector. The unpredictable nature of outcome of knowledge application influences the decisions relating to investment on research as well as on providing information support services. These aspects of the problem are further dealt with in subsequent chapters.

Effects of Passage of Time on Knowledge. Knowledge has a dimension of time. Utility of knowledge is related to time. Knowledge does not deteriorate with age, but its validity and utility may. With passage of time, knowledge *per se* does not change. Earlier knowledge pertaining to a topic may get superseded by later day knowledge, thus affecting its use, which could be seen from the following examples:

1. Aristotle's comprehension of motion of a body in space states that no inanimate body can move without a motive force; unless it belonged to four natural elements from which the universe is made of – fire, air water and earth (Narayana, 1977).

In this case, the knowledge on the cause of motion of bodies reasoned out by Aristotle remained valid in use until the fourteenth century when it was discarded. In other words, this knowledge has last its validity and thereby it's utility now.

2. Knowledge conveyed by the announcement that "a cyclonic storm will lash the East coast at 1600 hrs. tomorrow" will have only a short-time utility for the concerned parties (other than weather researchers and record keepers), if the incident does not occur.

Unlike material objects, a knowledge item neither changes nor deteriorates with the passage of time. The particular knowledge text may get superseded, outdated, extended, modified, contradicted or discarded by subsequent changes yet the original knowledge account remains the same. Knowledge of alchemy of the past remains the same even today, but not its validity and utility. When the utility of a given knowledge decreases with time, then it is said to be getting "obsolete". Obsolescence is defined as "the decline over time in validity or utility of information" (Line and Sandison, 1974, p. 283). The consequences of using obsolete knowledge can be very serious.

The application of any item of knowledge generally results in an outcome. In many cases, the age of the item of knowledge used is likely to influence the outcome. The age of knowledge therefore is an important factor to be taken into account in all knowledge application situations, such as decision-making and research. The impact of age factor varies from knowledge field to knowledge field. For example, the validity of factual knowledge in science is relatively more stable than in social sciences. Knowledge in fields like philosophy, ethics, morals, religion and literature retain their utility over a fairly long period of time.

Older knowledge and its records are of most significant value to historians, anthropologists and archaeologists because of the insight they provide on the circumstances and environment prevailing at the time of occurrence of the event. In contrast, latest knowledge takes precedence over pre-dated knowledge in sciences, technology, medicine, and law. Here, the importance of age does not relate to time *per se*, but to the contents of the text. Later the text, it is expected to incorporate subsequent findings, which make the text more relevant. Study of trends in the usage of records in specific knowledge fields provides general guidance to the management of records and their utilization. This is where tools and techniques like citation analysis, market research, and expert guidance are expected to help the user of information.

INCREASE AND SPREAD OF KNOWLEDGE

The phenomena of increase and spread of knowledge is understood better by the study of the universe of knowledge, its organization and development. In dynamic societies, the stock of knowledge (totality of knowledge) keeps on expanding.

The expansion of knowledge is of two types: a) increase in knowledge, and b) spread or diffusion of knowledge. The increase in knowledge is accounted by the creation of new knowledge, and the spread of knowledge refers to making available existing knowledge to more number of people or putting existing knowledge to new use or repeat use. The following examples of knowledge use make the distinction clear:

1. In developing light-activated drugs for treatment of cancer, Edelson made use of a drug known as 8-MOP, whose history extends back to the ancient Egyptians, in treating cutaneous T-cell lymphoma. The first modern studies on 8-MOP were taken up by El Mofty in the 1940's. His results greatly interested A. B. Lerner. Research by W. L. Morison at Harvard University had reveled that T lymphocytes are quite sensitive to the damaging effects of 8-MOP and ultraviolet radiation. These findings suggested the tantalizing possibility of removing the malignant cells from the body subjecting them directly to the toxic pairing of drug and light. What Edelson could not have foreseen was that this would turn out to be the key to the therapy (Edelson, 1988). This work by Edelson represents creation of new knowledge.
2. Sheila learnt the art of cooking from her mother, and is now writing a book based on it.
3. Building a house by Sharma. For this, he learnt all about building layouts and plans, building by-laws, building materials, construction methods, cost, sources of financing, service connections among others. At each stage of the activity, he had options and had to make decisions. Finally, the knowledge applied results in the building of a house.

These examples show that Edelson, Sheila and Sharma begin with using already existing knowledge as base. In the case of Edelson, his subsequent research has resulted in the creation of new knowledge. In the other two cases, there is only spread or diffusion of already existing knowledge to new persons or repeat use, and not in the creation of new knowledge. In the latter two examples, the existing knowledge has resulted in action and not in the creation of any new knowledge even though there has been evaluation of already known knowledge, and decision-making leading to action.

Machlup uses the phrases "subjectively new knowledge" meaning "a process resulting in one or more persons knowing what he or they had not known before", i.e., diffusion, and "socially new knowledge" to mean " a process resulting in a person (or persons) knowing what neither he (or they) nor anybody else had known before" (Machlup, 1980, p. 158). Boulding prefers the terms "growth in knowledge" for diffusion and "increase in knowledge" for new knowledge (Boulding, 1970, p.143). It is more appropriate to use the term "spread" to denote transmission/dissemination of existing knowledge and "increase" for new knowledge. Popper observes that from the viewpoint of epistemology, growth of knowledge is split into *common-sense knowledge* and *scientific knowledge.* And, the *"growth of knowledge can be studied best by studying the growth of scientific knowledge"* (Popper, 1972, p. 15). He further adds that common-sense knowledge grows by turning into scientific knowledge. The growth of scientific knowledge is the most important and interesting case of the growth of knowledge. Language analysis is one of the methods employed in studying the growth of knowledge for "the growth of scientific knowledge may be said to be the growth of ordinary human language writ large" (Popper, 1973, p.216).

Increase in Knowledge. Increase in knowledge is a phenomenon of "knowledge breeds knowledge". Universe of knowledge expands by the processes of cumulation, fission, fusion, and evolution.

Cumulation. A further examination of Edelson's invention mentioned earlier shows that the process underlying the creation of new knowledge also involves the use of cumulated knowledge from the time of ancient Egypt to the work of Morison. However, the new knowledge created by Edelson is not the result of mere aggregation; it involved experimentation, observation and application of cognitive processes and scientific methods. In this case, the phenomenon of "knowledge breeds knowledge" has taken the route of cumulation of knowledge. The cumulation effect of knowledge directly affects the world of records. One of the benefits of cumulation effect, particularly in the fields of research and academics, is that later knowledge texts generally incorporate the relevant results of earlier research, thereby provides the requisite knowledge background and indicates the takeoff stage from where further work proceeds. The creation of knowledge through research accounts for only a portion of the total knowledge generated in the world. Enormous amounts of knowledge are generated outside research— in daily engagements of individuals, in management, in arts, crafts, literatures, in political processes, in commerce and industry, tourism, and many others, which do not follow the rigorous methods of science.

Cumulation leads to the creation of new knowledge and adds to the stock of knowledge. The process of aggregation could make the knowledge item more powerful than the original due to its synergetic effect. Baruch attributes this to the nonlinear effect of aggregation of knowledge. By collecting and fusing pieces of already existing knowledge, one can impart additional value or power to the collection (Baruch, 1985). Cumulation in this form is largely a case of information reprocessing and repackaging for dispersion of existing knowledge units to meet the requirements of specific users or purposes.

Fission and Fusion. Fission is the bursting of an existing subject field giving rise to an entirely new area of investigation, as is the case with laser which resulted from narrow intensification of research in optics. Expansion by fission also takes place by division of a field into two or more narrow fields of study or specializations, e.g., artificial intelligence separating from cybernetics. Fusion is the merger of two or more subjects or application of the theories, techniques, and results of one or more disciplines to another area of study giving rise to new branches (Ranganathan, 1967), e.g., bioinformatics.

Evolution. An important causal force in the expansion of knowledge is the process of evolution. This is particularly true in the case of humanities, art and literature. Expansion of knowledge in these fields is greatly influenced by the impact of evolutionary factors on the social conditions, values and the system of organization of society at the time (Kemp, 1976).

Spread of Knowledge. Sustenance of society depends among other factors on the effective use of existing knowledge stock. A society's progress depends on the creation and application of new knowledge or by finding new uses for existing knowledge items. Either way, it means extending the frontiers of knowledge. Spread of knowledge promotes the use of existing knowledge by providing opportunities to know. Knowing can trigger off action, and action can lead to the creation of new knowledge. Though the term "diffusion" is a synonym of "spread", it is more often referred to spread of innovative knowledge produced by science and technology research (technology transfer), and market related information. Spread of knowledge also fulfills another important function, namely, replenishing the stock of knowledge in society otherwise lost by death, old age or incapacity. Primarily, knowledge is spread through the vehicle of education, a major portion of which goes into providing every new generation with the knowledge of the past and the present. The other vehicle of spreading knowledge is through social and cultural acclimatization. Knowledge breeds knowledge when there is effective information infrastructure, and an environment conducive for creation of new knowledge. Spread of knowledge is facilitated by large-scale production of knowledge texts in various types of formats, physical forms, and standards to suit the requirements of different segments of users; and by the provision of access facilities at affordable cost. Internet, the World Wide Web, and the telephone systems have become the most important instruments in that infrastructure.

Diffusion. In relation to knowledge, diffusion may be defined as the process by which an innovation is communicated through certain channels over time among the members of a social system (Rogers, 1995). An insight of the diffusion mechanism enables us to know how the mechanism works in different domains and environments, and helps in the selection and development of appropriate diffusion strategies. To derive maximum results from innovative knowledge, it must reach all those persons, professions, and organizations that can apply and exploit it for improving their working, creating wealth and well-being. Diffusion generally takes the form of transfer of knowledge/information from:

1. Research laboratories and development institutions to industry and other economic production agents, including agriculture and farming;
2. Trade, industry, and business to consumers and markets;
3. Government and its agencies, legislature bodies, and judiciary to citizens; and
4. Social, political and non-governmental forums to targeted audiences.

Diffusion of information, particularly technological information, is more pronounced in the field of industry. Some of the agencies entrusted with the task of diffusion are: extension services and field agencies set up by governments and by industries; specially created bodies for diffusing specific types of information, e.g., National Research and Development Corporation of India entrusted with the work of diffusing research and patient information developed by state sponsored R&D establishments; information "Gate Keepers" in industry; market research and product promotion units in trade and commerce; in-house information units; and library services. The need for diffusion of information is greater in the case of new ideas, innovations, and R&D findings than in already existing knowledge. In the latter case, the objective is to extend the reach of knowledge to hitherto uncovered segments of economy. A vital element in successful diffusion is "reverse diffusion", i.e., getting the feedback from the clients.

Diffusion Research. The main elements in diffusion are innovation, communication channels, time, and the social system in which diffusion takes place. The communication part of diffusion displays two special features, in that, the messages conveyed are concerned with new ideas, and it involves sharing of knowledge between the diffuser and the recipient to arrive at mutual understanding. In the classical version of diffusion, the source of innovation, such as an R&D agent, packages the innovative knowledge in a standard form and dispenses it to the potential beneficiaries who may accept or reject the innovation. This centralized mode of dispersion has been most successful in diffusing agricultural knowledge to farmers. The alternative model is decentralized diffusion, where participants converge to create and share information with one another, and decide how the diffusion process should be managed. One of the shortcomings of diffusion research is the implied expectation that an innovation should be diffused and adopted by all members of a social system, and that the innovation should neither be re-invented nor rejected (Rogers, 1995). Diffusion research is more active in the areas of industry, economics, and markets than in other fields. The focus of research has included the study of the types of diffusion, factors affecting diffusion, and the role and efficacy of diffusion agents. Diffusion research has produced a number of models. Some of the well-known models are: Roger's model on adoption of innovation, Epidemic Model, Economic Theory Model, Stock Adjustment Model, and Vintage Model (IGNOU, 2005).

Diffusion Characteristics and Knowledge as Practice.

Stickiness and slipperiness are seen as inherent properties of knowledge, meaning that the diffusion process needs directed efforts to give momentum to the flow of knowledge. Push is needed, when the relationship between the knowledge item and the context or medium through which it flows is conducive for sharing, and a pull, where it is opposite (parties don't want to share). Diffusion context was earlier explained through types of communication structure, i.e., "radial" or "wheel" type. With the social, economic and political power shaping social systems, the structure of knowledge flow is deemed to take either a hierarchical form or horizontal form. With diffusion study shifting to social systems and social capital, it must consider the heterogeneity of the modes of knowing and of the contexts of that knowing. Diffusion of knowledge in industry has to include the "practice" dimension which gives uniqueness to the knowledge embedded in practice, if it is the best. Here, diffusion means creating a new practice, guided rather than determined by prior practice (Spender, 2008).

There is a close relationship between growth of knowledge and spread of knowledge, which in turn is closely related to the type of society, and the socio-economic culture in which the knowledge operates. A traditional society is static "largely because the effort which is required to transmit the culture takes almost all of the available energy of the society which can be released for this purpose. Most of the energy of the society goes into simply keeping it alive......It is only as resources become available over and above what might be called knowledge subsistence— that is, a minimum necessary to transmit an existing culture— that a culture is likely to change. Once the change is begun, however, it has to take place at an accelerating rate, for every increase in knowledge permits the release of resources to develop a further increase in knowledge. When the increase of knowledge becomes specialized, as it does in a scientific society, the acceleration is all the greater. Thus, the most crucial knowledge of all is that which leads to the release of resources for the pursuit of knowledge" (Boulding, 1970, p. 145). However, the growth of knowledge brings in its wake numerous problems with serious consequences for the wellbeing of society which are discussed in a later chapter.

OVERGROWTH OF INFORMATION

Because of increasing developmental activities, population growth, leaping rate of science and technology advances, and the Information and Computer Technology revolution there is an information explosion. This has become an irreversible phenomenon. We are reaching the stage of over abundance of information. This growth is bound to aggravate the information scene, which is already complex, by creating new problems and by exacerbating existing problems. As Peter Drucker says, given the current rate of knowledge growth, information will not be the factor limiting our actions, but it is our ability to process available information (Edersheim, 2007). The effects of the exponential growth of information will be more pronounced in the following areas: a) quality and value of information; b) credibility of information; c) effects on individuals and organizations; d) decision-making; e) managing information; f) information asymmetry; g) growth of knowledge and wisdom; and h) optimal use of information.

Quality of Information. There is an inverse relationship between quantity and quality in all creative phenomena, including knowledge creation. As the volume and rate of information production increases, maintaining content-wise high quality in records gets affected. This has already lead to enormous output of information with lower density value per document, duplication of information, creation of more texts of ephemeral value, and increased competition. With the availability of enormous volumes of information, assessing the quality of information and keeping track of fraudulent and dubious information will become difficult.

Credibility. The decreasing quality will affect credibility of information. The consequences of relying on information of doubtful credibility could be serious. This will be more so in the fields of medicine, military, and in interpersonal relationships. It will be difficult to identify information of doubtful credibility before use. Source of origin of information and reputation of the source will become major criteria in establishing the credibility of information accessed. Information in the public domain has greater chances of coming under scrutiny due to its public exposure than private information. For the credibility of privately generated information one has to depend on the integrity of the source and on cross-verification.

Oral information passing through several agents will be more susceptible to credibility gap than visual texts. The consequences of using information of doubtful credibility in the spheres of political, social, economic, and inter-personal relations may lead to loss of confidence in the system, misuse, misunderstanding, and monetary loss; in the sphere of research and learning waste of time and resources. It may become necessary to enact laws against the creation and circulation of doubtful information in public domain. Such a situation may give rise to a new profession of information verifiers, similar to patent regimes.

Effects on Individuals. The study of the effects of information on individuals and in domain specific knowledge will receive greater emphasis. At present, the focus of research is on the information behaviour of knowledge players as scientists, engineers, decision-makers and others, and how information functions in individual knowledge domains. Knowledge and information have become predominant factors that influence behaviour, interpersonal relations, and one's philosophy of life, value system, mode of thinking, decision-making, and other facets of life. What motivates one to seek information, how does one acquire information, what does one do with it, what effects it has on others, what information to use in a situation of information overexposure, how governments tackle the problems arising out of information overgrowth will become the themes calling for enormous research efforts. Society may turn more towards sociologists, psychologists, religious leaders and philosophers for guidance.

Decision-making. A decision made without taking into consideration all the relevant information is faulty. Information used in making a decision must also be reliable. Decision-making becomes difficult in situations of both plenty and scanty information. The problem will become exceedingly complex because of the difficulties in quickly assessing the impact of each item of information out of the large mass of information. At the same time in the competitive world, partly caused by abundance of information, any delay in decision-making may entail huge risk. A general tendency of the human mind is to seek options whose implementation needs the least effort. This is equally true of information use. Excess of information thus makes decision-making difficult, strenuous, and time consuming. It is also possible that with excess of information in hand, one may miss some information item which may be small but vital. With so much information around, their analysis and evaluation in relation to the decision situation become difficult. With the ever increasing complexity of life which creates and demands enormous quantities of information, the problem of dealing with over production of information cannot be avoided. The adverse effects of information surplus could be minimized by employing quality checks in the production, evaluation, and transmission of information.

Managing Information. Overgrowth of information makes information management quite complex and more difficult. The existing problems in the following areas will become more acute, and new issues may crop up:

1. Public and private domains of information.

2. Flow of information across national and trans-national borders.
3. Intellectual property rights.
4. Individual's right to secrecy and public's right to access.
5. Developments relating to Internet, web sites and other technology based instruments and their impact on individuals and society.
6. Organization, resource allocation, and other related management issues.
7. Utilizing information.

Information Substituting for Knowledge and Wisdom. Fruitful use of information is complete when it ultimately leads to knowledge, and knowledge to wisdom. It is not that increased intake of information results in more knowledge, and abundance of knowledge to greater wisdom. Because of this, there is the danger of information surplus leading to an information culture rather than seeking knowledge and wisdom. In such a situation, society will trade on information devoid of fullness and the inner meaning of life. Education could become mastering of skills and manipulating with computer keys. The faculty of thinking may get reduced to mere operation of computers and cell phones. Instead of exploiting the tremendous potential of information for improving the standard of living, the growth of culture and enrichment of society; its misuse could become a heavy drag in the form of social cost and relegation of human values. Further, control of information may pass on to the hands of a vested few or the state which could have very serious consequences.

Specialization is the cause for and also the consequence of the growth of knowledge. If the positive aspect of specialization is division of labour which leads to efficient ways of applying knowledge, its negative effect is the fragmentation of knowledge. Fragmentation of knowledge inhibits cross fertilization of ideas. Further, fragmentation of specialties and therefore the relative isolation of specialized literatures from one another suggests that "there may exist numerous unintended and unnoticed relationships among these isolated literatures. If that is so, then a systematic search for such connections ought to be a worthwhile pursuit- a pursuit that goes beyond information retrieval, and may resemble the correlation and synthesis functions of intelligence analysis" (Swanson, 1988, p. 96).

Optimal Use of Information. Creation, processing, disseminating and utilization of information consume resources and involve heavy investment. Underutilization or non-utilization of information stock will be wasting of resources. Marginal utility of information becomes more pronounced in a situation of information abundance. Application of cost-effective methods in information-centered activities, sharing of information, charging high volume users of specialized information, finding additional uses for information, enlarging the area of user population, relegating unwanted stock of information, co-operation between private and public information sectors, taking advantage of technological advances are some of the steps that could lead to greater and more effective use of information. The use of information must result in benefits commensurate with the resources expended. This is the only way of justifying expenditure incurred on information whether in the private or the public sector.

Information Gap. An individual's attitude and capacity to acquire information and more so, knowledge is shaped by genetic factors and the environment. Because of this, there is wide variation in the information level of individuals and societies causing information gap. Since it is possible to control the environment to a large extent, it should be possible to reduce the gap by providing increased and easy facilities of access to all, opportunity to use, and motivation to absorb information. Parents, schools, organizations, government and society have a role to play in reducing the gap. However, education and information services have a special responsibility in this. It is not the lack of availability of information, but its identification, distribution and providing access become the key issues. Providing equal opportunity of access to information to every one will be one major step in reducing information gap. This is linked with the overall policy of managing information as a resource. It raises many policy issues, such as free access to information, investing in information related activities, locating, selecting, processing and providing access through information services, networks policies, development of information strategies and techniques, sound education policy, infrastructure development including provision of computer connections to remote rural areas, and optimization of use of information records.

Abundance of information will further increase information gap that exists not only between individuals, and in different segments of the society but also between nations. A huge information gap exists between industrially advanced countries and developing countries. It is in the interest of world peace and harmony that such gaps are bridged. The work of world bodies like the UNESCO, and the WHO in this area is commendable, but crucial issues concerning free flow of information in signatory countries is governed by WTO treaties, which involves hard bargaining.

TRANSMISSION OF KNOWLEDGE

Knowledge held in the mind of a person if not transmitted to a receptive mind or recorded is lost. Some of the lost knowledge may be recreated later by the same person or by someone else, but that is not relevant here. Knowledge received or generated by an individual is stored in the memory part of the brain. The life span of human beings is limited and memory may deteriorate even earlier. The only way of retaining that knowledge is either by communicating it to others or storing it in the form of records. If either of this is not dome, the knowledge held in the memory of that person is lost for ever. The invention of speech made possible the oral transmission of knowledge (and also history) from one person to another, from one generation to another, and from one place to another. However, it is writing that created records of knowledge and made access to knowledge independent of the individual and time. It is neither worthwhile nor practicable to record every bit of knowledge that is generated.

Private and Public Knowledge. Recording of knowledge has many implications. In the earlier example, the knowledge about the drug created by Edelson was available only to him until its publication, and thus remained as *private knowledge* of Edelson. After its publication, it is available to all and has thus become *public* or *social knowledge*, i.e., socially accessible knowledge. In the second case, the art of cooking is still the private knowledge of Sheila and becomes public when brought out as a publication or broadcast. In the case of Sharma, the acquired knowledge remains his private knowledge. When the knowledge in the mind of an individual is available only to him, then it is considered as personal knowledge (or private knowledge). Personal knowledge becomes social knowledge (or public knowledge) when it comes under the collective possession of society or social system in the form of records and is available without discrimination to all members of that society (Kemp, 1976). Some social knowledge could become personal knowledge and vice versa. As such, in some cases their precise demarcation is difficult. In between there is semi-social knowledge- like medical and educational records, and property records of citizens held by government agencies. However, in epistemology the term "public knowledge" is used to mean objective knowledge, i.e., our knowledge of the external world derived from perception; and "private knowledge" to mean knowledge about self obtained through apperceptions. Polanyi observes that "true knowledge which is deemed to be impersonal, universally established and objective becomes personal knowledge of the knower by his personal participation, the intellectual commitment to comprehend and establish contact with a hidden reality. Personal knowledge is neither subjective nor objective, but transcends the disjunction between subjective and objective" (Polyani, 1985, p.30). The significance of this attributed characteristic is that it serves the cause of promoting knowledge heritage and transmission of culture in society. It also enables linking of the past with the present and the future; near with remote; inanimate with animate. Loss of knowledge is a loss to society. Replication of lost knowledge may not always be possible, and even if it is possible it involves duplication of efforts and miss-utilization of human talent. Libraries (public), Internet and networks exist for servicing public knowledge.

TYPES OF TRANSFER

Transfer of knowledge may take place between two or more persons or through records. When the transfer is between two or more persons through direct communication it becomes *interpersonal transfer*, and when the transfer is through a record or its other forms it is *impersonal transfer*.

Interpersonal and Impersonal Transfer. The transfer of knowledge from one person to another person or groups of persons has the following features:

1. An essential condition for transfer of knowledge is that there must be a knower or a source of knowledge and a recipient or a receiver of knowledge.
2. If the transfer involves interaction between the knower and the knowee, then the transfer becomes *interpersonal* and *direct.*
3. Interpersonal transfer need not be direct face-to-face. One may use a telephone, teleconferencing or other direct communication channels.

4. If the knower is substituted by a surrogate, such as a record, then the transfer becomes impersonal and indirect.
5. When the transfer of knowledge is exclusive and the participants are limited, then the transfer may be deemed to be *private.*
6. When the transfer of knowledge is open to all and the transferee participants are many, then the transfer may be deemed to be *public.*
7. When the transferor happens to be a recoding instrument, then the transfer becomes instrumental transmitting only signals. This falls outside the realm of human transfer of knowledge till the time the signal becomes information.

Acquiring knowledge generally involves both interpersonal and impersonal transfer of knowledge. Impersonal transmission is indirect, without the presence of the knower, and necessarily involving either a mediator or a record. A doctor who acquires knowledge through a medical school, professional colleagues, published literature, observations and study of patients' case histories maintained by him uses all the three types of knowledge — personal, interpersonal and impersonal. Indirect transfer of knowledge is facilitated by the mediatory role of organizations such as libraries.

When the transmission is truly impersonal, the transmitted knowledge will be free from the emotions and personal nuances of the knower — a characteristic of objective communication. In impersonal transmission the transit loss will be minimum, and the transmitted knowledge remains unalloyed. Transmission of knowledge through electronic media, unless it is in interactive mode, is devoid of human touch. Effectiveness and efficiency of impersonal transfer of knowledge on the knowee is both positive and negative. Communication, by establishing direct relationship between the

parties, creates a receptive human environment more conducive for faster understanding and more effective absorption of knowledge. The interaction may result in modification of the original text. It may also affect the knowledge content of communication (Drucker, 1975). Deciding the extent of operation of these two interwoven components - knowledge and communication constitutes a dilemma. Providing knowledge services devoid of communication as in an exclusively man-machine information system may create psychological problems for the user, although the system ensures a high content of knowledge and faster transmission. The type of transfer of knowledge impinges on the psychology of communication. Understanding the different types of transfer, their characteristics and effects on the users of knowledge is an essential requirement to knowledge dispensers in various forms and information professionals.

Transfer Through Records. Records may be considered as surrogates of knowledge and information. Impersonal and indirect transfer of knowledge plays a crucial role in the functioning of modern society. Indirect transmission of knowledge necessarily involves a record and a means of representing knowledge in a record. Features of recording and records need further elaboration in view of their being instruments of impersonal and indirect transfer of knowledge. Records to convey knowledge or information have to fulfill certain conditions and they are: a) existence and selection of knowledge to be recorded, b) physical media for recording, and c) a perceptual mode for representing knowledge.

The source of knowledge is the human mind. The physical medium currently used for recording includes paper, magnetic tape and computer chips. The media employed for conveying knowledge are language, sign (e.g., a cross) or by commonly accepted convention (e.g., a red signal in traffic means stop), and sound. The concept of an information representation may be explained in terms of carrier, container and convey functions of a sentence (Fox, 1983). Before the invention of writing, memorizing and oral transmission of texts (though limited to a select few) gave the ancient scriptures, epics and other texts the characteristic of personal and direct transmission. But for this, these knowledge treasures would have been lost to the world.

CLOSURE

Creation of knowledge, its transfer, and its utilization are the three basic features of knowledge phenomenon. "Use" of knowledge has different interpretations. Utility characteristic of knowledge is fulfilled only when knowledge is actually put to use; otherwise, knowledge has only potential for use. Same item of knowledge may find different uses depending upon the users and their fields of interest. Utilizing knowledge is influenced by several factors, such as: relevancy of the knowledge item to the intended application, indefiniteness associated with knowledge, and current competitive validity of knowledge. Knowledge is also a growing phenomenon. The growth of knowledge is accounted by increase in knowledge (i.e., new knowledge), and spread of knowledge. Knowledge increases through accumulation, i.e., by the operation of "knowledge breeds knowledge" phenomenon. The other processes through which knowledge increases are fission, fusion, and evolution. Information-computer-communication technology has opened up a new channel of creating information by analyzing, interpreting and interpolating already known data as in gene manipulation. Spread of knowledge takes place through: the institution of education; libraries and other information service agencies; social and cultural inheritance; and now through the medium of Internet, web sites, and mobile phones.

Though the expanding growth of knowledge and information are the engines driving the modern society towards progress, they are also generating negative forces having harmful impact on individuals' and society's well being. The effects of growth will be more pronounced in the areas of: a) quality, value and worth of knowledge; b) credibility of information; c) growth of knowledge and wisdom; d) effects on individuals, institutions, and society; e) decision-making; f) information disparity and asymmetry of information in society; and g) optimizing use of knowledge.

Distinguishing between public knowledge and private knowledge has consequences for ordinary citizens, industry and trade, and governments. Transfer of knowledge from the creator of knowledge to others is broadly categorized into impersonal transfer and interpersonal transfer. Transfer of information through records is next only in importance to transfer through voice. Understanding the utilization and growth aspects of knowledge have major implications for individuals and society.

REFERENCES

Baruch, J. J. Comments. *On* "Branscomb, A. W. Property rights in information." Pp. 121- 122. *In* Guile, B. R. Ed. Information technologies and social transformations. (Proceedings of the Second Symposium on Technology and Science Priorities, Oct. 4, 1984. Organized by the National Academy of Engineering). Washington (DC), National Academy Press, 1985.

Boulding, K.E. Knowledge as a Commodity. *In* Beyond Economics: Essays on Society, Religion and Ethics. Ann Arbor, University of Michign Press, 1970.

Drucker, P. F. Management: Tasks, Responsibilities, Practices. Bombay, Allied Publishers, 1975. (Indian edition).

Edelson, R. L. Light-activated drugs. *Scientific American* 259: 50-57, 1988.

Edersheim, Elizabeth Has. The Definitive Drucker. New Delhi, Tata McGraw-Hill, 2007.

Fox, C.J. Information and Misinformation: An Investigation of the Notions of Information, Misinformation, Informing and Misinforming. Westport (Ct.), Greenwood, 1983.

IGNOU (Indira Gandhi National Open University), New Delhi. Master's Degree in Library and Information Science. MLI-101: Information, Communication and Society. New Delhi, IGNOU, 2005.

Kemp, D. A. The Nature of Knowledge: An Introduction for Librarians. London, Clive Bingley, 1976.

Line, M. B. and Sandison, A. 'Obsolescence" and changes in the use of literature with time. *Journal of Documentation*_30: 283-350, 1974.

Machlup, Fritz. Knowledge: Its Creation, Distribution, and Economic Significance, vol. 1: Knowledge and Knowledge Production. Princeton, Princeton University Pres, 1980.

Narayana, G. J. Ballistics: A Biblioview. Pune, Institution of Armament Technologists (India), 1977.

Polyani, Michael. Personal Knowledge: Towards a Post-critical Philosophy. Chicago, Chicago University Press, 1985.

Popper, K. R. Conjunctures and Refutations: The Growth of Scientific Knowledge. Ed 2. New York, Harper & Row, 1973.

Popper, K. R. The Logic of Scientific Discovery. London, Hutchinson, 1972,

Ranganathan, S. R. Kinds of bonds between two subjects including fusion bond. Pp. 35-41. *In* Annual Seminar 5, 1967. Bangalore, Documentation Research and Training Centre, 1967. (Mimeographed).

Rogers, Everett M. Diffusion of Innovations. Ed. 4. New York, Free Press, 1995.

Spender, J.C. Knowledge, Diffusion of. Pp.281-282. Vol. 4. *In* Darity, William A. Jr. Ed. International Encyclopedia of the Social Science. Ed. 2. Farmington Hills (MI.), Gale, 2008

Swanson, D.R. Information retrieval and the future of an illusion. *Journal of the American Society for Information Science* 39: 92-98, 1988.

Taylor, R. S. Value-added Processes in Information Systems. Norwood (N.J.), Ablex Publishing, 1986.

Dimensions

6

TIME, SPACE AND KNOWLEDGE

Human life and living is governed- from birth to death- by time and place. Asleep or awake, stationary or mobile, at work or at rest, we are bound to a time and space axis. Seasons of the year and the landscape mainly decide the agricultural practices; time and place dictate the functioning of industry, trade and service; and the hour and location indicate our eating, mating and sporting activities (Griffiths, 1999). Since knowledge is a mirror image of human life and activities, it cannot be divorced from time and space. In fact, research has shown that the human brain has a separate domain in the right half of the brain to process spatial and temporal aspects of knowledge. Hence the study of knowledge phenomena will be incomplete, and in some cases impossible, without taking into account the time and space dimensions.

NOTIONS ABOUT TIME AND SPACE

At the ordinary phase of living, everyone is aware of 'time' and 'space' and has some notion about what they mean to him or her. Notions of time and space exist in their various preferred forms in the context of an individual's mental disposition and attendant environment. The sense of time and space is also influenced by culture. Thus we have feminine time as well as feminizing time (Forman, 1989), festival time and funeral time, linear time, cyclic time, historic time, machine time, tea time, bed time, lost time, gained time, and so on. Similarly, we have cosmic space, mind space, exterior space, functional space, living space, and so on, all of which signify some attributed or inherent characteristics of knowledge. But going beyond the ordinary comprehension of time and place, one reaches a position full of complexity, indeterminacy and even confusion. Further insight into the properties of time and space will add to our increased understanding of at least some aspects of knowledge. Our notions of time and space, and their roles vary from knowledge domain to knowledge domain— for example, in science time and space along with matter and energy constitute the four fundamental constituents of nature which run the universe; in astrophysics/cosmology, there is the theory that the universe is running down, and consequently there is energy loss or increase in entropy, which corresponds to the positive direction of time. Thus, "time's arrow, or probability vector, affects the physical, biological, and communicative patterns in the universe" (Neelameghan, 1979, p. 105). In cosmology, time and space explained in its simplest form to the benefit of laymen by Norman Wheeler is that "matter tells space-time how to curve, and space-time tells matter how to move" (Von Baeyer, 2003, p. 139); in politics and economics, time and space\place are strategic elements to achieve goals; and in sociology and psychology, time is "a dimension of our experience and our activity, but this dimension does not correspond to a simple physical reality. The concept of time is imposed on us by our experience of changes: the physicist and the biologist must introduce a parameter *t* to account for the evolution of natural phenomena" (Fraisse, 1968, p.25).

The requirements of social living necessitate organization of time. Any organization of time has to provide for:

1. Systems of time measurement;
2. The allocation and scheduling of time by individuals; and

3. A set of attitude toward time past, time present, and time future (Goody, 1968).

To the 'process philosophers' such as Alfred North Whitehead, the flow of time or human advance through it is a metaphysical fact. In contrast, to the 'philosophers of the manifold', the flow of time or human advance through it is a mere illusion. To the contemporary philosophers of time like Herman Minkowski, the renowned mathematician influenced by Einstein's special theory of relativity, space and time constitute a unitary entity of time-space having distinguishable time-like and space-like directions. To the modern philosophers of language learning to handle the word *time* "involves a multiplicity of verbal skills, including the ability to handle such connected words as *earlier, later, now, second and hour...*"(Encyclopaedia Britannica, 2007. Vol.28, p. 662). Between time and space, the latter is comparatively easier to comprehend than the former. Space is "a boundless, three-dimensional extent in which objects and events occur and have relative position and direction." (Encyclopaedia Britannica, 2007, Vol. 11, p. 61). In human context, to understand better the notions of time and space, one has also to take into account three other attendant elements, namely matter or material, actor or identity, and action.

TIME, SPACE AND REALITY

Knowledge is about human comprehension of entities and phenomena embedded in a space-time structure of the universe. On the other hand, Emmanuel Kant, the philosopher asserts that time and space are *a priori* forms of intuition and are conditions to which all appearances must conform (Kant, 1929). A marvelous characteristic of human mind is its ability to traverse through space and time in any direction of past, present and future. The fruits of this wandering across the chartered and the un-chartered world of space and time by means of observation, experimentation, thinking, imagination, dreaming, and other mental abilities is the creation of a vast ocean of human awareness. This journey through time and space may be acts of conscious efforts or casual encounters, and is only limited by the capacity of the individual mind and that of human experiencing. A second limitation is that human intellect cannot conceive beings and things say in another unknown planet of a far-away star in a remote galaxy in terms of concepts other than human. A third limitation is that the sensing capacity of human sense organs has definite range of reach and limited sensitivity.

Our understanding of time and space varies from the ordinary, common sense perception to that of most abstract mathematical form as in Einstein's special relativity theory. One is ordinarily familiar with the concepts place or position, time, distance, size or measurement, and their combination called motion. Motion, in turn, involves the concept of identity: one and the same object is thought to occupy different places at different times. Thus, as in Zeno's paradox, our most simple, common sense beliefs about ordinary objects moving from one place to another involves our most complex and deepest concepts: space, time and identity. This means that they are concepts as opposed to realities that exist "out there" (Kolak and Martin, 2002). All physical objects and phenomena in the universe are either matter and/or energy, encapsulated in a space-time framework. Thus, understanding reality also means encountering time and space.

Perception and Reality. Understanding the relationship between knowledge and perception has been a principle concern of many philosophers. Sense-data theory, realism and phenomenalism are the main perception theories in epistemology. The focus of all the three approaches has been that of establishing reality of things in nature, and also explaining the perceptual anomalies, such as optical and other types of illusions- a space/time/sense phenomenon. For example, how is one to explain the phenomenon of a straight rod submerged in a glass of water that looks bent when seen from outside. Sense-data theory, and realism explain this by distinguishing an object in the universe in terms of reality or objective reality. Bertrand Russell explains these anomalies in terms of 'physical space' or space as defined in science; 'real space', that is public; and 'apparent space', that is private to the perceptionist (Russell, 1912). Phenomenalism approaches the problem in terms of perceived properties of objects in a given space-time framework. For our ordinary purposes, the common-sense understanding of time and space is sufficient.

Science is concerned with reality, social sciences and humanities are also concerned with reality, but there is a fundamental difference in their approaches. While science deals with absolute reality, the latter two by their very nature deal with subjective reality. Thus, time and space dimensions of knowledge are involved in both objective reality and subjective reality.

TIME, SPACE AND FORMS OF ART

The main forms of art- music, dance, painting and sculpture are one's articulation of emotions or mental visions in time and space. Music is a form of emotion expressed through modulation of sound/acoustics along the time axis. Dance is patterned movement of human body and body parts in space; and in group dance, there is the additional feature of synchronization of one's movement with that of other actors in the group- a time element. Painting is depiction of reality, as visualized by the artist, in the medium of physical space. Sculpture is a three dimensional presentation of an artist's perception of reality of things in space. Thus, all art forms are intimately linked with time and space.

KNOWLEDGE: PAST, PRESENT AND FUTURE

In any discussion or presentation of knowledge, the time dimension often gets associated with the labels 'future' 'present' and 'past'. This distinctive part of experiencing characterizes a knowledge item time-wise or period-wise and indicates its relevance and significance to the user of that knowledge.

Past knowledge. It is the knowledge created prior to a given time or period as the reference point. The past part of past knowledge may range from nanosecond to light years.

Present knowledge. It is the knowledge created in the present, and knowledge that is presently available. It is difficult to precisely demarcate present knowledge from that of past knowledge, which task belongs to the domain of philosophy. Relatively speaking, an event like holding a seminar on knowledge at Bangalore, India at 12 noon (local time) is a future event for someone in Cleveland in US, and a past event to some other in Auckland, New Zealand because of the zonal time differences. More glaring is the time difference when it comes to inter-planetary travel and inter-stellar space communication. For practical purposes, one may treat all knowledge as present knowledge until it is superseded by a later one. Another way, though logically incorrect, is to go by the current validity status of a given knowledge domain.

Future knowledge. Unlike future time, there is no future knowledge; all knowledge is either past knowledge or present knowledge. According to the theory of psychological arrow of time we feel the direction in which time passes, the direction in which we remember the past but not the future (Hawking, 1988). Any future knowledge has to be created only in future. Though the concept of future knowledge is cognitively valid, its field is empty. By peeping forward in time, one does predict or hypothesize the occurrence or behaviour of a given knowledge domain in the future. The content of the knowledge domain, in this case, belongs to the realm of the future, its origin or generation is in the present.

MEASUREMENT OF TIME AND SPACE

Ever since man related time and space with various aspects of daily life, religious beliefs and festivals, measuring became an inescapable requirement. To measure one needs a standard scale or a measuring unit. In antiquity the units of measurement were determined on a local basis. Later, the development of trade and commerce across the borders and overseas created the further need for measurement standards. The standard is set with reference to a recurring phenomenon of nature occurring with certain regularity or some permanent event. of political or religious significance. This has provided choice in the selection of the reference point. The time taken by earth to complete one orbit around the sun became the basis for measurement of time, and the invention of solar calendar (the Julian and the Gregorian calendar). The most accurate and internationally accepted standard for time is the second determined by the pulse rate of the element cesium (9,192, 631, 770 oscillations per second) in the International System of Units. The standard unit of length is the distance traveled by light in a vacuum in 1/299,792,458 second. Even in our age "of measuring femtoseconds and star clusters 11 billion light-years away, time defies true objective measurement. It can be seen to go slow and even stall out at certain moments only to brashly and breathlessly rush forward at others. Time can be wasted, kept, saved, spent, killed, lost and longed for" (Duncan, 1998, p.xvi). This only shows how incomplete our knowledge is. Measurement serves two purposes in science: a) testing, and b) seeking of knowledge as in scientific research. Knowledge thus gained, in turn, assists new forms of measurement to be conducted (Sydenham, 1979).

TIME AND SPACE COORDINATES OF KNOWLEDGE

While knowledge cannot be divorced from its time and space relationship, the reverse is not true. The importance of time/ period, and space/place dimensions of knowledge varies depending upon the knowledge domain, meaning a specific item of knowledge or a given subject field and the intended use. What it means is that in using or specifying a particular knowledge domain one may ignore its time and /or place dimension, if they are considered not relevant to the context or conditionality of use, though both the components are present in the knowledge domain.

The temporal dimension of knowledge may be further divided into: a) general time, and b) time of tense. General time refers to the time in seconds, hours, days, years, centuries, light years, and so on. Tense refers to past, present and future periods of time. This division of time helps in understanding better a knowledge domain and its context, as the use of knowledge is context driven.

The time (general) and the space dimensions of knowledge exhibit two further subdivisions- one relating to the knowledge domain itself, and the other pertaining to the time of disclosure of the content in a given domain. Thus, knowledge has four subsets of time and space dimensions, besides the time of tense, as follows: a) domain time or event time (i.e., knowledge domain time); b) domain space or event space (i.e., knowledge domain space); c) disclosure time (i.e., knowledge disclosure time); and c) d) disclosure place (i.e., knowledge disclosure place), which are further explained.

Domain time. It is the time (and in some cases period), when the event or action contained in a given knowledge domain takes place. The domain time is an integral part of the domain and it impacts on the subject content of the domain.

Domain space. It is the space or place where the event or action contained in a given knowledge domain takes place. The domain space impacts on the content of the domain.

Disclosure time. It is the time (and in some cases date or year) when the text or information about the content of the knowledge domain is disclosed or made known or put to use. The content of the knowledge domain is the resultant of research, learning, discovery, development, experience, and other knowledge creation processes.

Disclosure space. It is the space or place from where the information about the content of the domain is disclosed or put to use.

The following knowledge domains, given as examples, make clear the distinctions between the four different identities of time and space:

1. The regime (1279-13 BC.) of Ramses II, the 3rd king of the 19th dynasty of the ancient Egypt. The knowledge domain in this example has the time element of 1279 - 13 BC. This is the domain time. The other part of time dimension is the year of deciphering hieroglyphic script in the year 1822 AD, when the account of the regime was made known to the world, which is the disclosure time. The domain space is the Nile River Basin in Egypt, and the disclosure place is London where the account of the regime was published or made known. Similar distinctions of time and place apply to the accounts of subsequent knowledge on the subject by later studies.
2. The origin of the universe: Our present understanding. In this case, the domain time is 1500 million years in the past, when the universe originated, according to Big Bang theory. Disclosure time refers to the years 1922 and 1927, when Alexander Friedmann and Abbe Georges Lemaitre first proposed the theory. The modern version of the theory was propounded by George Gamow and others during 1940, which is also a disclosure time.
3. Legal registration of a crime that has taken place. Here, the domain time refers to the time or the period when the crime was committed, while the disclosure time is the date and time when the crime was reported to the police and the "First Information Report" was registered. The domain place is the place where the crime occurred, and the disclosure place is the place of the police station where it was recorded.

TIME IN CULTURAL AND SOCIAL PHENOMENA

Cultural Time. Viewed from a cultural perspective time appears as progressive and evolutionary, recurrent and reversible (cyclic) or linear and irreversible. While, traditional culture is rested on the perception of time as cyclic phenomena, from which the theme of destruction and recreation of the cosmos through great deluge is born; modern culture rests on linear and irreversible conception of time.

In Social Context. Hectic nature of modern day life has become one of time and place scheduling. Time has become one of the scarcest items. With the increasing emphasis on achievement, and the impact of information driven industrial economy social realities of life and vision is subjected to a good deal of fear and hope. Setting goals and their pursuit within time frames has become an important objective to most individuals and organizations. Time frames are governed by past experiences, present considerations, and future expectations. Decision-making is guided by these time frames (Cemalcilar and Tarcan, 2008). Choosing a time frame involves an economic factor called "time preference" which is explained later in this chapter.

Time-Space in Social Relations. Time/space distanciation and disembedding of social relations from space are the two distinguishing features of the late twentieth century life (post-industrial society?) at least in the advanced western societies. Time-space distenciation is defined by Anthony Giddens as "the separation of time from space and their recombination in forms which permit the precise time-space "zoning of social life" (Giddens, 1990).

Social life is embedded in a time-space matrix and social knowledge is a reflection of social life. Giddens observes that for all ordinary actions of daily life, time was linked to space via place, and in turn both time and place to the contents of the actions. Devices like calendars and maps helped in the calculations of time and ordering space. The inventions and the wide use of mechanical clock enabled social actors to separate time from space. In traditional societies separation of time and space played a limited role, as the impact of time and place embedment of social actions remained comparatively stable. But, in modern social life separation of time and space takes on a dynamic role. Giddens asserts that "besides its institutional reflexivity, modern social life is characterized by profound processes of the reorganization of time and space, coupled to the expansion of dismbedding mechanisms-mechanisms which prise social relations free from the hold of specific locales, recombining them across wide time-space distances. The reorganization of time and space, plus the disembedding mechanisms, radicalize and globalize pre-established institutional traits of modernity; and they act to transform the content and nature of day-to-day social life" (Giddens,1991, p.2). Because of the disembedment of identity from time and space "many forms of 'lived time' are possible in social settings structured through the separation of time and space... it provides the very basis for their recombination in ways that coordinate social activities without necessary references to the particularities of place..." (Giddens, 1991, p.17). Disembedding serves several purposes, which include:

1. To serve as a research method in social sciences.
2. To transform a three-dimensional system into a two-dimensional system of information in bioinformatics, where the three dimensional molecules of DNA and RNA are reduced to two dimensional linear symbols which serve as a common language to the international community of molecular biologists.
3. To provide flexibility in approach to recombination of disembedded information as in the production of recombinant genetic molecules (McNally and Wheale, 2001).

Related to disembedding is sharing of knowledge. Sharing of knowledge is "an effective means of reducing and bridging the gaps- spatial, temporal, and cultural- in and between societies" (Neelameghan, 1979, p.116). It may be interesting to ponder over whether the abstract concepts of distenciation and disembedding be applied to the fields other than social sciences. It has applications in biological sciences, and may not be valid when applied to the study of natural phenomena belonging to inanimate world. Disembedding social knowledge of social actions from time and space matrix is an abstract concept which enables us to see social actions in a different perspective.

USES OF TIME AND SPACE COMPONENTS OF KNOWLEDGE

By making use of time and space dimensions of knowledge many benefits can be derived. Some of them are explained here:

A Definition of Knowledge. The time dimension of knowledge, consisting of the past, the present and the future coupled with the space dimension does provide a means of defining knowledge in its historical and developmental context. Following this, knowledge is defined as the accumulated awareness of the thoughts and deeds of man over the past, the present and the future that is available to humankind.

Reconstruction of Past Knowledge. All creations have a past, a present, a future, and a location. But, only the human race has been endowed with the ability to think back through time and space, and ponder over the future. The application of this gift of nature has resulted in a vast body of knowledge about the past events and the path of development the mankind has traversed. It has also enabled man to relate himself meaningfully to his environment, to the larger cosmos and observe its play. The time/period characteristic of knowledge enables us to reconstruct the evolution of man as a social being and his world from prehistoric times to the present, encompassing various human civilizations and cultures, and relate himself to nature. The period studies are not limited to prehistoric and animate world alone, but go beyond that to the times of the origin of life on the planet earth and further. With reconstruction of past knowledge, "....the past begins to acquire an independent existence of its own. To-day an individual's cultural equipment is no longer limited to what is handed down orally from one generation to the next but includes, potentially at least, the entire contents of the libraries, the written records of the past ages and dead societies, and the thoughts of distant scholars. The cultural heritage is vastly extended and with it the whole conceptualization of space and time. Change and duration become more concrete parts of one's existence" (Goody, 1968, p. 39).

Some portions of this universe of knowledge are bound to be imperfect and incomplete due to the finite life span of man and the natural constraints on his span of reach to renegotiate the past. Due to a priori and speculative nature of research involved in understanding the past and the future phases of knowledge, it is inevitable that many gaps, inaccuracies and uncertainties occur in these reconstructions. These limitations and gaps are bound to be addressed as research advances, which is a continuous process.

Universe of Knowledge and its Mapping. With the help of domain time and disclosure times one can charter the course of development of knowledge through the ages and arrive at the universe of knowledge. The domain time supplies individual entities of knowledge. These entities when put together and arranged relationally form the map of universe of knowledge. Such a map enables us to trace the contours and boundaries of different knowledge domains. Such maps can be drawn for individual knowledge domains, if a domain is sufficiently large in breadth, composition and depth.

As Division Characteristics in Taxonomy. To classify has been an inherent characteristic of human mind. To classify, in the primitive sense, is to divide the entities in the universe into groups. With the progress of time, the idea of division slowly led to thinking of classification as a method for not only making many groups, but also for ranking the groups to serve the purpose in hand. This "inherent tendency to rank, i.e., to arrange in a specific sequence in space, or in time, or in space-time mesh— is a result of the finiteness of the speed of nervous impulse within the human body. Finite speed gives rise to rank, sequence and structure. To classify, then, in the second sense is probably a neural necessity" (Ranganathan, 1957, p. 391). With the growth of knowledge and knowledge records there arose the practical necessity of classifying and arranging the physical records by subject. This is the purpose of all library classification schemes. The universe of knowledge arrived at by ordering of all known knowledge entities forms the basis of building general schemes of classification of knowledge. It is on this foundation that all major schemes of library classification by subject— Brown's Subject Classification, Bibliographic Classification by Bliss, Dewey Decimal Classification, Universal Decimal Classification, Library of Congress Classification and Ranganathan's Colon Classification have been designed. Time and space are two important characteristics used for ranking and grouping wherever they are relevant. However, what is of interest is how the different schemes apply time and space characteristics for bringing division/ groups. This follows the basic structure underlying each scheme, whether enumerative, faceted or hybrid. A faceted scheme like Colon Classification uses time and space as common isolates forming separate schedules in the scheme. This overcomes the most serious weakness found in every "general system apart from Colon, and that is the failure to observe strictly the fundamental rule of classification, which is to apply one principle of division only at a time and exhaust it before applying another. The modern name for this is, of course facet analysis" (Mills, 2003, p. 277). Time and space added in the form of chronological and space devices as in Colon Classification brings scientific order in the arrangement of classes such as later in evolution / time (Ranganathan, 1967).

Bibliographic Elements /Meta Documents. Disclosure time and disclosure place of a knowledge item are two important bibliographic/ meta document elements. These correspond to the date and place of publication of documents (both in print and non-print form), filing of patents and other items claiming intellectual property rights. Disclosure time and disclosure place also serve as identification factors in disputes over a knowledge domain and its ownership.

Identification and Proof of Priority. Disclosure time establishes ownership/authorship of a given knowledge domain as in a research paper, a monograph, a patent, a software programme and others. It decides the priority of right in the case of intellectual property when more than one body claims priority for the same item. Disclosure time acts as a proof in establishing truth or facts in matters involving legal disputes.

Inter-Relating Knowledge Texts, Authors and Usage. The elements of time are also used to correlate different information records, if they have a time relationship. Similarly, time element is used to correlate the works of different authors, if they are cited. This function is achieved by following the "systems of authority" in a discipline like religion; and by the practice of referencing, i.e. citing previous works, especially in the fields of knowledge that are fully developed and well organized. Passage of time has an important bearing on the utility of information texts, the study of which is a part of "bibloiometrics" a branch of information science.

Reference Point. Reminder. Domain time and domain place serve as reference points in history, archaeology and anthropology. Studies in these fields, in general, pertain to a particular date or period, and place. In social transactions and personal life noting down or remembering of time and place associated with certain event or action serves as a reminder to the person to follow it up. For example, date and time of a scheduled meeting recorded in a personal diary also serves as a reminder to attend. So are the birth dates, journey dates and time, and many others that are part of every day life.

Age of a Publication as an Evaluation Criterion. The value of a given item of knowledge or an item of information to an user is also related to its age. The age of a particular item of information is the time gap between the time of its creation or its disclosure time and the time of its intended use. Age affects the value of a given item of information because the world of knowledge is dynamic, and therefore any item of knowledge in a given domain is always subject to further advancement, modification or even invalidation by the findings of subsequent studies. As a result, the value of a given item of information generally decreases with time, and particularly so in the area of science and technology; in other words, a given item of knowledge/information may become obsolescent in the context of particular users. Obsolescence is defined as the "decline over time in validity or utility of information" (Line and Sandison, 1974). Another concept derived from the relationship between time/age of publications in large collections and use/user value is "half-life" of literature.

Communication. Human communication is a 'time-binding' act. The 'time-binding' function of social communication connects through space and times the ideas and experiences of the past with the present. This is mainly done through symbolic language, numbers, gestures and other linguistic artifacts (Neelameghan, 1979, p.103). Communication in all its forms - oral, print, audio-visual, and electronic, personal and impersonal, formal and informal- has two sides, namely: a) knowledge content of the message with time and space as environment in which the content is embedded, and b) the physical medium. Communicating a message involves, besides language, not only what knowledge or information is delivered, but also how much of it, where and when, which are functions of space and time.

A mental text can be expanded or compressed depending upon the intended audience to whom the knowledge is meant and also the expectations of the author of the text or communicator. Expansion and compression of texts are related to time and space, which in turn impinge on cost. In print and visual presentations, space factor influences the design of page/ frame/ format, and the physical form of presentation. In digital communication the volume of data (space relationship) in bits and qbits, which the system can store, handle comfortably, and transmit speedily (a time relationship) are of vital importance.

From times immemorial, time and space/distance acted as the biggest barriers in human communication. Because of this barrier, transfer and spread of knowledge and information suffered the most. Advances in communication technology, which introduced radio, telephone, telex and the TV bridged the gap to some extent. The time and space gap between the knowledge producer and the knowledge seeker has been now bridged almost completely by the Internet and the mobile phone. Today, the main impediments in the way of providing universal access to information come not from time and distance factors but from mental, educational, managerial and resource barriers.

ECONOMIC SIGNIFICANCE

Time and space play a pivotal role in economics. This is evident from the fact that land (a part of space), labour, and organization constitute three of the four factors of production. Labour as well as organization are inseparably connected to time. Labour is measured in units of time or in physical quantity, i.e. in volume space. Time is one of the organizational factors in optimizing results and achieving objectives. Similarly, time is a key factor in measuring productivity. Knowledge is a part of organization and together with information and communication it binds the other three factors of production. A critical aspect of modern day economics and industry is how to cope-up with the rapid changes occurring in the environment and keep ahead of competition. To put it in other words is how to deal with time and space.

In Planning and Business Contracts. In all premeditated actions of men and women, planning features in their thinking process that precedes action. Given the complexities of the modern day world the need for planning and the areas of planning are ever enlarging. A timeframe is an essential part of any plan. A plan is a knowledge document incorporating a timeframe and usually geographic area/ location within which the plan is to operate. Like reasoning, planning too seems to be an independently recognizable part of thinking. The timeframe of a plan may range from years, as in the case of economic plans to hours, minutes and seconds in the case of precision works and critical operations. In material contracts inclusion of time and place clauses is a part of normal legal practice. Any breech of time and place terms of a contract may result in escalation of cost, dislocation work, payment of damages or even termination of the contract itself.

Flexible Working. One of the great achievements of information technology is its enabling people to override the time honoured pattern of following vocational activities during daytime hours, sleep and other activities in the evenings and nights. Similarly, it has helped abridge the separation of workplace from home. Both these features have given place to a new found flexibility in the choice of working hours and place of work, especially in the service sector of many advanced, as well as, developing economies. Such workers have come to be known as "teleworkers"- those employees who work outside the offices and factories, from the comfort of their homes either full-time or part-time, and the practice is named "telecommuting". Telecommuting is said to increase productivity by 30%, but creates many managerial problems like managerial control, communication, and security of information. This flexibility has become possible because any person located in any corner of the universe is able to have 24 hour access to information and knowledge sources worldwide, provided the requisite infrastructure is in place.

Billing Information/Communication Access. Charging information, in certain cases, according to the time spent or the space required to communicate/display information is a viable option. Time and space are also used as standards to measure information. In all such cases, pricing is related solely to the amount of time and space required for the physical transmission of information and has nothing do with the cognitive content and quality of information accessed by the user. A few examples are:

1. Advertisements in news papers are charged by the column space required to display the item.
2. Commercial displays in television programmes and radio broadcasts are charged according to time in seconds and minutes, the display lasts.
3. Information stored and communicated via computer terminals is measured in physical quantities of bytes and k-bytes.
4. Editing of texts, and preparing of index portion of a text are sometimes paid on a page basis. In fact, an approximate price of a newly published monograph can be determined by multiplying the number of pages the book has by the prevailing average cost per page.

In certain knowledge-based services, such as legal service and medical consultation, the amount of time the service provider spends on the consulter is accounted in arriving at the fee. In education, a purely knowledge transferring profession, paying per hour/lecture to ad hoc teachers is not uncommon.

Value Addition. Time and space have attributes of adding economic value to goods in certain conditions. The value addition in those cases is due to rarity or scarcity imparted to the material goods by time or space. Take the example of soil of the moon brought to earth by the explorers of the moon. A gram of the moon dust would be priced unimaginably high, if the same is put to sale. The high price is due to the money value added to the soil by the knowledge and fact that it is from the moon; whereas the intrinsic material worth of it is negligible outside research. Until the time planetary travel becomes common, the scarcity value will remain. Ordinarily, a buyer of the soil would go by the knowledge and belief that the dust is from the moon, fortified by certification, and not by actual scientific assaying. An example for value addition to goods by time is that of rare coins, paintings, artifacts and books that become rare items by virtue of passage of time and scarcity. It is the time and the knowledge of that time that adds to the value more than the physical characteristics or content of the rare item. In contrast, in the case of vintage vine the value addition is caused not only by the time factor, but also by the change in quality brought about by ageing.

Time Preference. It is an economic choice, where one prefers to forgo the present wants to future benefits that will follow the present sacrifice. Implied in this decision is the assumption that the future benefits will be larger than what is sacrificed. It is a tradeoff between foregoing immediate benefit or enjoyment and anticipated future benefit. The essence of time preference is clearly conveyed by the adapted proverb "a bird in the hand may be worth two or more in the future". Time preference amounts to discounting the value of future goods. Future trading in commodities, taking a life insurance policy are examples for time preference. Opting for time preference contains the element of risk due to uncertainty. Philosophers and economists are divided on the issue of rationality of time preference (Weirich, 2008).

Intellectual Property Rights: Time and Place. If binding of knowledge with time and space is an inherent characteristic of knowledge, modern societies through the agency of the state have bestowed certain types of knowledge with intellectual property right, a man-imparted characteristic. These rights are: copyright, patent right, trademarks, designs right, and right to the use of brand name of certain types of geographically associated goods. Time enters copyright and patent right by being incorporated into law, a time limit up to which the exclusive private ownership right is valid. Space, i.e. place factor participates through "Geographical Indications of Goods" law granting the right to the exclusive use of brand names of goods that are specific and special to certain geographical areas, e.g., the brand name "Mysore Silk" (Taraporevala, 2006).

Outsourcing of Knowledge-based Activities. Business Process Outsourcing (BPO), Knowledge Process Outsourcing (KPO) and Call Centre activities are based on the direct exploitation of the time and space dimensions of knowledge/ information. These functions are based on the principle of making use of the time difference between the different time zones of the world. For example, the time in India is ahead of the time in USA by 8 to 10 hours and behind New Zealand time by about 10 hours. A number of business houses in the U.S. and the U.K. have transferred their client enquiry and answering functions to Call Centres /BPOs in India. A query on the scheduled departure of a flight from say, New York to San Francisco by an American client in Florida to an American airlines service is answered may be by a lady based at Bangalore or Gurgao, India Call Centre. Similarly, many of the information based activities like composing and editing, content generation and processing of texts are outsourced from one country to another, if it is economically and technically advantageous. But for the time and the space dimensions of knowledge and the availability of requisite computer and communication infrastructures this would not have been possible. Besides time and space factors, in any decision to outsource an activity many other considerations, such as competitiveness, state policy, and legal implications are also involved.

Time and Space Instrumentation. Need for measuring time and space necessitated building of instruments that laid the foundation of instrumentation industry. The needs of time measurement led to the development of horology. Though the era of mechanical clock has ended with the advent of electrically/electronically operated clocks and watches, the watch industry is flourishing with the continuous development and introduction of newer styles of watches, as well as time mechanisms embedded in jewelry, cell phones and other gadgets. Building of special purpose clocks like industrial clocks, stop watches, and space condensing and space enlarging instruments like microscope and telescope, and recording instruments like photographic camera have become inevitable tools in extending the reach of man and expanding the frontiers of knowledge. It is only because of advanced scientific instruments employing infrared technology, Doppler effect, charge-coupled devices, and many others that man could land on moon; satellites could relay data and pictures; and biologists could splice genes. Specialized instrumentation has provided man the power to override nature's limits on the reach of his sense organs, the main means of acquiring perceptional knowledge of the outer world.

All intended human ventures are conducted in a time-space enclosure. How efficiently these activities are accomplished determines the progress of the economy as a whole. Efficient economies are lead by shortening, i.e. compression of time, and in inefficient economies the time is stretched. For example, a road construction work with a target time of 3 years, if finished before the scheduled time there is compression of time; and stretching of time, if it crosses the limit of 3 years. Shortening of time means more compression of information per unit of time and higher the tempo of economic progress. Compression of space also saves time. In normal situations, shortening of time leads to higher profit. However, there are exceptions where elongation of time leads to more profit as in the entertainment industry. In a TV serial programme stretching the contents over time increases the number of episodes and thereby profit.

In a competitive world, how each country uses time—whether it compresses time or stretches— will decide its ability to compete successfully in the international market. Internally, by shrinking time and space the economy advances faster leading to all-round welfare. In this sense, time is a resource, like land and capital, which nations use to build their economies. Some use it more efficiently than others and become leaders, and those who do not remain laggards (Roy, 2008).

Emotive Aspects. Time and place elements bestow an emotive edge to certain types of knowledge. Emotionally charged knowledge can change the mental state of millions of people across the world. A specific knowledge item associated with space/ place such as Ayodhya in India, believed by the Hindus to be the birth place of Rama; and an item linked to a date, such as September, 11, 2002, the day on which the twin towers of New York was attacked by terrorists exemplify the emotive aspects of time and place dimensions of knowledge. Hence, this feature of knowledge can also be exploited by governments, politicians, religious heads, society leaders, and many others either for the good or for the bad. Other time and space related incidents, like a birth day, a wedding anniversary day play important emotional roles in the personal lives of individuals.

DOMAINS OF SPACE AND TIME

Space is studied generally under three divisions: a) the *physical* cosmic space; b) the *mental* space dealing with thinking, including logical and formal abstractions; and c) the *social* space encompassing social behaviour and practices. Of course, people treat space in any number of contexts, such as- public space, private space, literary space, kitchen space, and so on. To the Western thinkers, in the beginning space came under the orbit of philosophy, later space occupied the minds of mathematicians. The mathematicians developed the science of space under geometry and topology, and thus, space became mathematical space. Once again space came under the domain of philosophy, especially epistemology. The reason for this is that the relationship between mathematics and reality (physical or social) was not obvious, and the mathematician's natural disinclination towards social or physical reality, that is subjective reality. Thus, mental space got resurrected. Today mental space connotes a wide range of meaning, such as- logical coherence, practical consistency, self-regulation and the relations of the parts to the whole, the engendering of like by like in a set of places, the logic of container *versus* contents, and so on (Lefebvre, 1993). Space as a discipline is well developed in the form of geometry. It is also an important dimension in other disciplines like cartography, geography, geology, architecture, painting and sculpture. In contrast, time as a discipline is largely bound with cosmology, time and motion studies, calendar making, and horometry.

CLOSURE

Knowledge is bound by time and space. Every normal human being is not only aware of their existence, but also has some notions about them. Time and space affect lives of individuals and their pattern of living. In the new order of society, for most people time has become the single scarcest item.

In Kantian philosophy, time and space are *a priori* forms of intuition and conditions to which all appearances must conform. Sense-data theory, realism and phenomenolism are the main perception theories that seek to explain reality of things in nature, which is governed by time-space frame-work. Time and space are relevant factors in arriving at both objective reality, as in science, and subjective reality as in social sciences. Knowledge is bound by past, present and future concepts of time. Measurement of time is determined on the basis of orbital time of earth around the sun on which solar calendar is devised. Scientific measurement of time is based on the pulse rate of element cesium.

Time coordinates of knowledge consist of *domain time or event time* referring to the time or period when the event or action contained in a given knowledge item/domain took place; and the *disclosure time* meaning the time or date when the information about the contents of the said knowledge domain was disclosed or made known to others or recorded. Similarly, space coordinates of knowledge are made-up of *domain space*, which is the space or place where the event or action contained in the knowledge item/domain took place; and *disclosure space/place* showing from where the information about the said knowledge item is disclosed or put to use. Time and space coordinates are important elements in research and in communication of information.

Social life is embedded in time and place. By disembedding social activities from time and place pattern of living can be reordered, and social norms and formats can be shifted to different places. History is calibrated against time/period and space/place. History is the knowledge of the events and the descriptions of how human society has evolved in the past ferreted out of time and place structure.

Time and space components of knowledge have numerous uses. The uses include: mapping the universe of knowledge; serves as a division characteristic in taxonomy; establishes priority in research; interrelates different knowledge texts; becomes a reference point in history, archaeology and anthropology; serves as an evaluation criteria in determining the relevance of a given knowledge item to a given application; compressing or expanding texts. Time and space are involved in a number of economic activities like: scheduling of activities, flexible working, in determining price of a service or labour; adding value to a commodity; in limiting intellectual property rights; in outsourcing of activities; in the development of time and space measuring instruments; and in measuring efficiency. Time and space has the characteristic of becoming critical factors in certain cases. In human affairs, time and space has the ability to change the psychological potency of knowledge items, which can affect the mind.

For men and women in business, factories and offices time and space is all but schedules; for ordinary folks time can be wasted, kept, saved, spent, killed, lost and longed for; for sociologists time-space are constituents of social life; for physicists and cosmologists time/space can move backwards or even come to a naught in singularity; for mathematicians, space can appear in more number of dimensions than the Euclidean dictum of three; for library, information, and Knowledge Management theorists, time and space are characteristics applied for ordering and arranging of entities in the universe of knowledge; and finally, time and space shift and shape reality to the seekers and users of knowledge. Unlike other organisms in nature which respond instinctively, it is only the human mind that can perceive and act thoughtfully upon space and time. Time and space give knowledge its relational characteristic, significance and dimensionality or coordinates, which help us in identifying, processing and applying knowledge. How we manage time and space in our daily lives and in organizations is one of the factors that determines success or failure, progress or status quo. Time and space enclose change, which is the topic of next chapter.

REFERENCES

Cemalcilar, Zeynep and Tarcan, Kumkal G. Time Orientation. Pp. 368-369. *In* Darity, William A. Jr. Ed. International Encyclopedia of the Social Sciences. Ed. 2. Farmington Hills (MI), Gale, 2008.

Duncan, David Ewing. The Calendar. The 500-Year Struggle to Align the Clock and the Heaven and What Happened to the Missing Ten Days. London, Fourth Estate, 1998.

Encyclopaedia Britannica, The New. Ed.15. Chicago, Encyclopaedia Britinica, 2007. Vol. 28. Pp.662-673: Time.

Ibid. Micropaedia. Vol.11. Pp.61:Space.

Forman, Frieda. Feminizing Time: An Introduction. Pp. 1-9. *In* Forman, Frieda Johles and Sowton, Caorran. Eds. Taking Our Time. Feminist Perspectives on Temporality. Oxford, Pergamon, 1989.

Fraisse, Paul. Time-1: Psychological Aspects, pp.25-30. *In* Sills, David L. Ed. International Encyclopaedia of the Social Sciences. Vol. 16 London, Macmillan & Free Press, 1968.

Giddens, Anthony. Modernity and Self-Identity: Self and Society in the Late Modern Age. Stanford, Stanford University Press, 1991.

Giddens. Anthony. The Consequences of Modernity. Cambridge (Mass.), Polity Press; Palo Alta (Ca), Stanford University Press, 1990.

Goody, Jack. Time 11: Social Organization. *In* International Encyclopaedia of Social Sciences. Ed. David L. Sills. Vol. 16. Macamillan and Free Press, 1968.

Griffiths, Jay. Pip Pip. London, Flamingo, 1999.

Hawking, Stephen. A Brief History of Time: From Big Bang to Black Holes. London, Bantam Press, 1988.

Cf. Kant, Emmanuel. Critique of Pure Reason. N. K. Smith. Tr. London, 1929.

Kolak, Daniel and Martin, Raymond. The Incredible Shrinking Zeno. Pp. 57-70. In Kolak, Daniel and Martin, Raymond. The Experience of Philosophy. Ed. 5. Belmont (Cal.), Wadsworth/ Thomson Learning, 2002.

Lefebvre, Henri. The Production of Space. Nicholson-Smith, Donald. Tr. Oxford (U.K.), Blackwell,1993, (Originally publication 1974, 1984).

Line, M.B. and Sandison, A. 'Obsolescence' and changes in the use of literature with time. *Journal of Documentation* 30: 283-350, 1974.

McNally, Ruth and Wheale, Peter. Environmental and Medical Bioethics in Late Modernity: Anthony Giddens, Genetic Engineering and the Post Modern State. Pp. 97-114. In Bryant, Christopher, G.A. and Jary,

David. Ed. The Contemporary Giddens: Social Theory in Globalizing Age. Hampshire, Palgrave, 2001.

Mills, Jack. Bibliographic Classification. *In* Drake, Miriam A. Ed. Encyclopaedia of Library and Information Science.Ed.2. Vol.1. New York, Marcel Deckker, 2003.

Neelameghan, A. Expressions of Time in Information Science and Their Implications. Pp.103-117. *In* Greenway, Frank. Ed. Time and the Sciences. Paris, Unesco, 1979.

Ranganathan, S.R. Prolegomena to Library Classification. Ed.2. London, The Library Association, 1957. Ed.3. Bombay, Asia Publishing, 1967.

Roy, Barun. The time divide. *Business Standard* (Bangalore), April, 2008.

Rusell, Bertrand. Perception, Knowledge and Induction. In Kolak, Daniel and Martin, Raymond. Loc.cit. Pp.268-282. (Originally published in The Problems of Philosophy. Oxford University Press, 1912).

Sydenham, P.H. Measuring Instruments: Tools of Knowledge and Control. Stevenage, Peter Pergrinus, 1979.

Taraporevala, V.J. Law of Intellectual Property. Mumbsi, The Author, 2006.

Von Baeyer, Hans Christian. Information: The New Language of Science. London, Weidenfeld and Nicolson, 2003.

Weirich, Paul. Time Preference, Pp.369-370. *In* Darity, William A. Jr. Ed. International Encyclopedia of the Social Sciences. Ed. 2. Farmington Hills (MI), Gale, 2008.

7

CHANGE: A PRECURSOR OF KNOWLEDGE

Change is a natural phenomenon. One of the important features of change is its un-detachable association with time and space, which in turn has consequences on the creation and utilization of knowledge. In nature, change is caused by the interaction of matter and energy in a time-space envelope. In human affairs, a change occurs when an individual interacts with other individuals or with the environment in a time and space or place embrace. Nothing is permanent in the universe. Living organisms, and non-living objects of this earth and that of a far away galaxy, particles inside the matter and the genes ordering of life in cells—all undergo change, but their difference is in the nature, magnitude, frequency and duration of change over time and space. A change can take place in less than a microsecond to that of billions of light-years and may happen in micro-space or at the order of galactic space depending upon the item. What has change to do with knowledge? The study of change indicates that change is a precursor of knowledge. If there are no changes taking place in the universe, human life and society, and if everything is constant all the time and allover space then there would be no growth of knowledge. Webster's dictionary lists several meanings to the word "change", but a constant feature underlying these meanings in the context of action or phenomena is the sense of "*different*" or "*to make different*", and the synonyms given are *alter*, *modify*, and *vary* (Webster's 1993). These dictionary meanings miss the factors of time and space, which are inseparable parts of change. A more satisfactory technical explanation is that a change occurs in an existing order or system whenever there is:

1. A break followed by variation or difference in the functioning of a system or behaviour over time.
2. A modification, however imperceptible it may be, in an existing mode of functioning.
3. A disruption affecting continuity, orderliness, regularity, harmony or equilibrium of a system.

A change is always with reference to an existing state of functioning giving place to a different order and is contingent on time and space. From the study of change taking place in animate and inanimate universe and its impact knowledge is extracted. Gained knowledge when applied as an input may lead to further change creating a cycle: knowledge → change → knowledge → change → knowledge... Thus, the phenomena of change in the universe bound by time and space are an inexhaustive source of new knowledge.

CHARACTERISTICS OF CHANGE

Changes are of three types, namely:

1. A change that occurs with certain regularity and having ascertainable time and space interval, e.g., orbital movement of the earth around the sun is a change of position and time in relation to the sun occurring with certain regularity. The earth takes 365/366 days for one complete orbit, and forms a basis for measurement of time and invention of calendar.
2. A change same as in 1 above, but with minor deviation

from the normal or predicted behaviour of the system, e.g., menstrual cycle in women.

3. A change that occurs randomly, e.g., transfer of power to the people of India by the British in 1947 is a change of great consequences to the future of India, Great Britain and the world. This change is also instrumental in shaping knowledge on India in the post-independent era brought about by a time/space divide. Prediction of Sir Winston Churchill, the War-time prime minister of Britain and many others that transfer of power to Indians will lead to disintegration of the country has not only been belied, but the nation has become a leading democracy in the world with a strong economy, which exemplifies a property of predicted knowledge. Another example is an abrupt change caused by the abandonment of a regularly followed practice of greeting one's beloved before going to sleep, which is a sure sign of an emerging conflict.

The significance and effects of each type of change varies from knowledge domain to knowledge domain. There are easily discernable qualitative differences between changes occurring in inanimate world and those occurring in the organic and social world of man, the latter is invariably affective and value laden in nature.

Effects of Change. A change may affect the system or the attainment of the set objective positively, negatively or with zero effect. An intended change must result in positive gain as the person introducing the change is clear about the end objective, and will have worked out the change strategy in advance. It is possible that the intended change may affect the subject negatively because of faulty strategy or improper implementation of "change" plan or due to the entry of unforeseen changes in the environment. This necessitates course correction action during implementation. Occurrence of natural noncyclical change, i.e., unintended and unforeseen change may impact the system positively or negatively or with nil impact, which will be known only after the occurrence of the event.

PHENOMENA OF CHANGE

In the natural world we live, the pre-change state of matter or phenomenon undergoing change, other than in physical and dynamical systems, will either be destroyed or modified giving place to a different matter or different phenomenon. Destruction and new creation occurs, if it is a chemical change and modification, if it is a physical change. In either case the original state of the matter or phenomena ceases to exist, except in temporary changes. In the emotional and social worlds change takes on a complex form as human events and actions are linked to the larger dynamics of social, economic, political and psychological forces, which are conditioned by time and place. A change could occur as an one time event, as successive events or as intermittent events. After a change, the body undergoing the change can be reconstructed, at least theoretically, but outside its original special-temporal framework of the past. The effects of the reconstructed change - good or bad, can neither carry the original experience nor they can be retrieved. A changed organic relationship can be restored to its pre-change state, a new political system can be reversed to its earlier form, but outside the original timeframe. In impersonal systems of organizations effects of change may have a cascading effect spread across time and space, for example - a change in the corporate taxation policy may effect even the smallest household; a change in the socially sanctioned marriage norms may affect the whole community and the offspring of such a marriage. How does knowledge respond to change?

Controlling Change. Effects of change in a system and its environment may vary from inconsequential to that of extreme impact — positive or negative, including the very survival of the system. This raises the question whether change can be controlled? The answer is both yes and no. A change is caused either by forces of nature or from actions of man. A change brought about by social actors and organized activities is amenable to control, at least theoretically, as they are the results of human initiation; and therefore can be started, stopped or directed to follow an intended path. Precisely because of the self-initiated nature of change, mankind has advanced to the stage of post-modernism. On the other hand, of the changes caused by forces of nature some can be controlled or prevented from taking place and some cannot. For example, dams are built across natural flow of water in rivers to irrigate lands, generate power, and control floods. But, many a change caused by nature, such as movement of planets, stars and galaxies or causing of earthquakes, and eruption of volcanoes are beyond the control of man. What is possible is to address the harmful effects of uncontrollable change through precautionary actions, and also derive benefits from change wherever nature allows. Change has great impact on the quality, magnitude and the direction of growth of knowledge and its utilization. In fact, large segments of change that are taking place in human affairs are the result of planned changes utilizing existing knowledge that help in the birth of new knowledge, with time and space acting as midwives.

Critical-time, Critical-space and Critical-knowledge. All human affairs and actions of nature move along time and space with certain momentum. When this momentum is disturbed by actions of human agents or by nature, to bring it back to normalcy or overcome the adverse effects of the change, if any, or to achieve an intended goal often necessitates certain counter-action. The selection of time and place of execution of intended action plays a critical role in determining the outcome, which in many cases may not have severe repercussions. But, there are many situations where the choice of time and space/place of action makes all the difference between life and death, success and failure. In such cases, time and space/place take the characteristic of criticality; for example, in a delicate neurosurgical brain operation, the operational place and space become critical; another example is the criticality of time element in a missile attack. In the case of a heart attack, the first one hour, it is called "golden hour", is critical to the survival of the patient. Similar to time and space, knowledge too has a dimension of criticalness. In the case of knowledge, the most difficult part is ascertaining what knowledge and information is critical to a particular action or situation and when. A special feature of knowledge and information, unlike in most other fields, is that any item of knowledge or information has the potential to become critical. For example, in the interpretation of legal texts, certain words and phrases carry critical-effect. Unaware of the requisite critical knowledge, a medical man can cause the death of a patient instead of saving life.

Identification of critical-time, critical-space, and critical-knowledge in any action is one of subjective assessment. Accurate identification of items and parameters that impart criticality and also their proper assessment affects the outcome of action. No action in nature or human affairs takes place until the system reaches the critical point — a volcano will not erupt until the internal dynamics of the earth below reaches the critical point. It is not that in every incident of change critical-time, critical-space, and critical-knowledge are *sine qua non*. As most of the events and actions occurring in the daily world are so routine and ordinary that they do not involve critical-time, critical-space and critical knowledge. In research, in quality assessment, in cost control, in *Critical Path Method*- a management technique, and in a large number of events affecting life and living criticalness of events account for radical change.

In business, industry and in many individual human activities, a change generally creates either a challenge or an opportunity to the parties concerned. Dealing with challenge or opportunity often involves application of knowledge/ information. A laissez-faire culture reacts to the change on the basis of feedback, whereas an aggressive and creative individual or organization tries to change the environment for its benefit following a feedforward approach. Whatever be the approach, knowledge/ information form a critical resource. It is the strategy marked by vision and organizational culture that decides how knowledge resource is utilized to achieve the all important competitive edge. But strategies and tactics are also functions of time and space. Having designed the right strategy based on sound knowledge is not of much use unless appropriate time/space factors are built into the execution framework.

SECTORAL CHANGE

The word "change" taken alone does not convey anything more than that it means difference and is in some way related to time and space. To know and understand change beyond its fundamental characteristics of difference and time-space relationship one has to consider the context of change. The context is supplied by the relevant field, subject or knowledge domain with which the particular change is associated. Study of change, in a way, forms a sector study. As examples, change in three sectors - science, sociology and economics are treated here.

Science. The universe is not static. Things in nature are constantly undergoing changes- small or large, slow or fast, observable or hidden. Discovering the nature of change occurring in the physical universe is one of the objectives of science. A scientific interpretation of change is that the natural world seems to be undergoing progressive non-cyclic change within which are woven countless number of cyclic processes. From cyclic changes, constant in their frequency ratios, one can measure stages of progressive change. Our time concept implies: a going-on change of the world and a presence of equivalent units of time for measuring any process of change. There is also a contrary view that the origin of time rests on the existence of causal relationship among all physical events (Schlegel, 1967). The characteristics of change in inanimate physical world differ from that of organic world, and both differ from that of human world. The theory of change in the physical sciences is to account for happenings in the physical universe with forces of nature acting as the agents of change (Meadows, 1971). Change in physical technologies is methods and designs for transferring matter, energy, and information from one state into another in pursuit of a goal or goals (Beinhocker, 2006). Within science there is a separate branch of study - "dynamical systems", whose objective is to describe how natural systems change over the course of time.

Dynamical Systems. A basic tenet of science is that the principles of nature can be expressed in terms of mathematics, and physical events can be predicted and designed with mathematical certainty. The natural world consists of different systems made of parts such as particles, atoms, molecules, planets and stars which move around different paths governed by the equations describing motion. The mathematical study of long-term behaviour in systems that evolve in time, usually under unchanging times is named *dynamical systems* (Hasselblatt and Kotak, 2002).

The principal idea behind dynamical systems is to describe how a system changes over time. Dynamical systems involve a space, time, and a time evolution law. The space part is set with structures, whose elements represent possible states of the system. The time part may take discrete or continuous form, and reversible or irreversible state; and the time evolution law, in general settings, is a rule that allow us to determine the state of the system at each moment of time ***t*** from its states at all previous times (Kotak and Hasselblatt, 1995). Even a continuous-time system can be made to appear like discrete-time system. The study of dynamical systems is the study of long-term asymptotic behaviour, and especially that of its qualitative aspects, which require direct methods that do not relay on prior explicit calculation of solutions. Seeking probabilistic solutions is a part of dynamical systems study, since finding the relation between determinism and probability is a central mission of dynamical systems (Hasselblatt and Kotak, 2002).

The discipline of dynamical systems evolved from classical mechanics, and celestial mechanics founded largely on the works of Galileo and Newton. Later, the field extended its boundary by including problems drawn from mathematics, electricity, magnetism, thermodynamics, other natural sciences, and from biological world. The phenomenon of change occurring in the world of nature is not limited to dynamical systems alone, but also includes those innumerable changes taking place as individual and independent items also form the topics of scientific enquiry. Besides the field of science, a vast portion of the world of change is accounted by human agents acting through historical, social, economic, political and other types of percepts exhibiting characteristics that are specific to them. Knowledge domain of change is very vast and touches upon every aspect of human life.

It is said that mathematics is the queen of all sciences. If it is so, then statistics is the hand maiden of all sciences. Change research depends heavily on observations of the phenomena in all its facets over time. Observations and experimentation yield large amounts of data. Collection, organization, analysis and interpretation of data, which is the function of statistics, help us understand change phenomena and also predict the future course of a change.

Social Change. Social change is the significant alteration of social structures, that is, of patterns of social action and interaction (Moore, 1968). No society remains static all the time. But, from the very early period of social history of man stability has been not only the social ideal, but also the normal social condition. In Western societies, it is in the last three hundred years change is accepted not only as inevitable, but also desirable (La Piere, 1965). With a few exceptions, most major social changes evolve slowly, at an even pace, and their impact is visible only after the completion of the transition. However, the significant social, economic, and cultural changes that are becoming visible in the knowledge society seems to indicate that they are of extraordinary present and future significance (Stehr and Meja,2005). Oriental societies, including India are no exception to the stability motto, and in fact the feudal system of societies that prevailed till recently had all the reasons to oppose change.

Process of Social Change. All socially significant changes occur through time under the conditions prevailing at a given period of time. Special processes and relationships of the period are central to social life. The centrality manifests itself at numerous conceptual levels— from mundane to higher, but still basic levels of abstraction, where special processes and patterns serve as useful indicators of technological and organizational adaptation of human groups to their natural and social environment (Frisbie and Kasarda, 1988). This means that social change is a product of time, space and social- historical environment of the period which is represented by the prevailing state of social, political, economic, and technological knowledge. There are several theories of social change and prominent among them are evolutionism, and cyclic theory.

Prior to modernism(and globalization), social change appeared in two modes— revolution and reform. The mid-twentieth century saw the appearance of a third mode of change prompted by social forums and "progressive groups" acting as "pockets of resistance". The resistance come from heterogeneous groups made up of citizens organizations, ecological movements, feminist groups, human rights activists, and many more (Rioufol, 2004). Invariably, the pockets of resistance mode will have an inbuilt ideological tilt or limited agendas, the success of which depends to some extent on the tactical use of information to spread their cause and influence people in favor of their cause.

Economic Change. Fundamentally, economics is all about creating wealth and its distribution; and this basic truth has not changed much even in the latest era of modernism. What has changed is the complexity surrounding the process of creating wealth in a competitive world, particularly due to the severe impact of rapidly changing technological and social environment, and changing value systems. Industrialization is seen as the key process of creating wealth, and is generally equated with progress or development, particularly in the context of developing countries. Bert Hoselitz observes that economic development, especially if it involves industrialization, implies " a rapid, and in a sense, revolutionary process which, if it is to take root in a society, must penetrate widely and deeply and hence affects social structural and cultural facets of a society. In other words, economic development consists not merely in a change of production techniques, but also, in the last resort, in a reorientation of social norms and values" (Hoselitz, 1995, p. 17).

Development and developmental transformation of society involve a change in the way people think and act, and in the way the society's institutions function. In this new interpretation of development, change is not only accepted, but promoted and routinized. In the knowledge-based economics it is ultimately the information and knowledge of one's own resources, institutions, social and economic organizations, and reforms will form the engines of development. Any asymmetry in information leads to an equilibrium in which resources are less efficiently allocated. Information flow in the system has a bearing on development. A weak information flow is caused by and results in poor institutional arrangements. Since, information is imperfect in developing countries including India, markets work imperfectly. Any under investment in the production and dissemination of knowledge, in the transfer and adaptation of new technology, will retard the process of developmental transformation. It is for the governments of developing countries to remove the existing bottlenecks, namely, lack of information, lack of a way to convert information into knowledge, lack of capacity to analyze, and lack of capacity to policy design (Lakshmanasamy, 2003).

REVOLUTIONARY CHANGE

Change occurs in different modes—gradual, abrupt, small-scale, large-scale, visible, hidden, discrete, continuous, cyclic, revolutionary, and many more whose measure is relative and often subjective. As against revolutionary change is evolutionary change, where things happen gradually under the influence of evolutionary forces created by nature as well as man. Creation of knowledge has followed both evolutionary and revolutionary styles. Because of its pervasive nature and extreme impact, revolutionary change has been the subject of many studies. Revolutionary change has enormous impact on the creation of knowledge.

The theoretical base of a revolution is always the creation of a few extraordinary minds supported by a small number of foundational knowledge texts. The works of Galileo Galilee and Sir Isaac Newton on mechanics, Max Plank on quantum physics, and Albert Einstein on relativity in the physical sciences; decoding of DNA structure by James D Watson and Francis Crick in the biological sciences; and Karl Marx's work on capitalism in political science are examples of such knowledge texts. Theoretical works, always small in number, become the intellectual foundation of a revolution. Once a revolution finds its first acceptance at least by a few, who matter, there will be a rush of further research and the knowledge in that field moves forward. It is followed by a mushroom like growth of knowledge in that particular field attracting several participants from the same or related fields of study contributing and sustaining the revolution. The development of knowledge in the new area will continue until another revolution in some other field begins attracting attention or the existing paradigm has exhausted its potential for growth or is replaced by a new paradigm.

Some criticism of and opposition to any revolution and its rationale, at least in the beginning, is a normal reaction. Hence the repository of knowledge on revolution will also comprise of opposing theories. Following sectoral approach, revolutionary change representing three knowledge domains - natural science, sociology and economics are considered here.

Scientific revolutions are "non-cumulative developmental episodes in which an older paradigm is replaced in whole or in part by an incompatible new one..." (Khun, 1970, p. 92). A paradigm represents the entire constellation of beliefs, values, techniques, laws, theories, instrumentation etc. shared by the members of a given scientific community. Khun reasons out that scientific revolutions occur when an existing paradigm ceases to function adequately in the exploration of an aspect of nature to which that paradigm itself had previously led the way. A scientific revolution changes our world-view of science. Such revolutions impact on the world of scientific knowledge, its direction of growth, and contribute towards knowledge revolution.

Social revolutions are rapid and their impact is pervasive to the whole society affecting its state and class structure in fundamental ways. It is a bottom up phenomena caused by the oppressed and deprived strata of society. Social revolutions combine two coincidences of social structural change with class upheaval and the coincidence of political and social transformation. A unique feature of social revolutions is that the basic changes in social structure occur together in a mutually reinforcing fashion with class struggle playing a predominant role (Skocpol, 1979). Social revolutions in India has an additional dimension of cast, and in most Islamic societies that of religion. The cause of all social revolutions may be traced to large scale social and power imbalances in the structure of a society caused by factors, such as race, language, gender, education, and sharing of resources and power. A society's inability or unwillingness to share equally educational (particularly professional and job-oriented), economic and political opportunities with the backward and the discriminated sections of society constitutes the most important cause of social revolutions. In other words, the main cause of social upheaval may be identified with the distribution of social, political and material knowledge in society.

Land, labour, capital and organization are the four factors of production, which go into creation of wealth. Any large-scale rapid change in the mode of use of any of these factors of production in an economy results in an economic revolution. Though not expressed explicitly, knowledge and information are included under organization and they act decisively in economic revolution.

Information Revolution. When a change radically alters an existing order of things and replaces it by a new order that is incompatible with the earlier is termed a revolution. In politics, the change relates to the system of ruling; in sociology, it is the social and cultural order; and in science, it is the scientific order constituting a paradigm. The revolution may be total or affecting only a major segment of the existing order. Information too has seen a few revolutions. The causal agent of the first information revolution was the invention of spoken language, which was followed by a supplementary revolution caused by the invention of writing. The world of information had to wait for a couple of millenniums to see the next revolution brought about by the invention of printing. The most recent and all pervasive information revolution is only three decades old and is caused by information technology — coming together of computer and communication technologies which created the Internet, the World Wide Web, and the mobile phone. Cybernetics and artificial intelligence have played an important role in the information revolution. The impact of information revolution is clearly seen in e-governance and in the "New Economy". In the new economy the myriad of wealth-creating systems is nothing else, but communication devices that do not directly handle matter, but instead facilitate the movements of bits of information in *cyberspace* and not place (Kefalas, 2003). It seems another information revolution is not too far off.

Unlike most other types of revolutions, information revolutions are the results of technological inventions, such as printing, and the Internet. The major effects of technological inventions have been on the instant spread of knowledge, its intensive use and raising of human spirit. Any revolution in any of the major disciplines impacts on the growth and application of knowledge.

KNOWLEDGE AND CHANGE

Change is a universal phenomenon and knowledge is a human phenomenon. Change and knowledge are closely inter-linked, and both exist and operate in a time and space enclosure. While change is a phenomenon of action, knowledge is a phenomenon of awareness or representation or comprehension. Change is a prime source of knowledge, and knowledge when applied under right conditions leads to change. Occurrence of change and the phenomenon of knowledge are bound to a particular activity or field. Thus we have political change, economic change, change in colour, and so on; and we have knowledge of physics, of heredity, of history, of management, of sports, of taboos, and so on.

To understand the impact of change on knowledge one needs to examine: a) the nature of change and its dynamics, b) the knowledge domain pertaining to the change, and c) the cognitive working mechanism of the brain. Neither science nor philosophy have so far been able to fully decode the mental process and more specifically the process of how sense input is actually transformed into awareness. Knowledge is considered by many to exist in two forms - tacit knowledge formed and stored in human memory and information, the external form of knowledge. The problem of awareness raises several questions for which we do not have definite answers yet. Some of the questions are: a) Does knowledge creation process involves change? If items of thought constituting a concept of knowledge exist independently and continue to do so then the change becomes only an integrating process. b) How an existing item of knowledge changes into new knowledge over time and space? c) What happens to the original item of knowledge that has given place to the new item of knowledge? d) Is the pre-change unit of knowledge destroyed in the change process or still retained in memory? Since one can recall and remember an item of knowledge in its pre-change state, it is reasonable to conclude that no destruction takes place. Regarding information there are no such problems. The pre-change state information continues to exist as long as it is recorded and stored either in an oral form or in a physical medium. If pre-state change events and phenomena enable one to interpret and draw useful conclusions, then such knowledge becomes a part of historical process.

Individuals and Change. Every human life is a string of changes occurring from the stage of conception till death within the structure of time and space flow. The string of changes is due to several causes, such as – physical, organic, psychological, religious, social, economic, material, and many others. Change appears in two forms: changes that are common to the entire human species, and those that are unique to an individual. Examples of the former are ageing, feelings of pain and pleasure; and examples for the latter are quality and intensity of pain and pleasure felt, and one's degree of understanding a given situation. The environment of change is made-up of factors dictated by nature, and the ones created by man in the form of social, cultural, economic and other practices. The process of socialization is intended to equip an individual to face the effects of change. Experience, education, social organization and knowledge are among the main actors that prepare an individual to cope-up with the changes, and also effect changes to achieve desired goals in life.

Experience. Experience, according to dictionary meaning (relevant to this topic) is something personally undergone, or lived through; direct observation of or participation in events; the act or process of perceiving; knowledge, skill or practice derived from direct observation of or practical participation in events; practical wisdom resulting from what one has encountered, undergone, or lived through (Webster's, 1993). Our understanding the reality of a thing or event and formulating our response to it, if called for, is directly influenced by experience. When confronted with a change, our mind enables us to compare it with our previous experiences and draw suitable conclusions. A major portion of change affecting individuals is accounted by the relationships the individual has with other individuals, groups and institutions. Cooperation, conflict, support, rights, and responsibilities flow from the relationships depending on the type of relationship. Assessment of the nature and effects of change combined with knowledge form a critical input for devising our response to a change. The act of human perception of change involves an inter-play of context and situation in which experience plays an active role. Contexts are "frameworks of meaning, and situations are the dynamic environments within which interpretive processes unfold, become ratified, change and solidify" (Cool, 2002, p.8). Contexts and situations are relational factors that participate in the process of perceiving reality and in the formation of one's information-seeking behaviour. Study of information-seeking behaviour has practical implications for information science. Our perception of a change or situation, and the formation of our response to the change are part reflective act of mind based on experience, and human organism (i.e., an individual's personality composed by physiological, psychological and other mental abilities) and knowledge. The reflective phenomenon is an ongoing process of the mind.

Reflectivity. Reflectivity, according to Anthony Giddens, a renowned sociologist, refers to the reflexive monitoring of action intrinsic to all human activity. In modern social life social practices are constantly examined and re-formed in the light of incoming information about those very practices, thus constitutively altering their character (Giddens, 1990, 1991). The role of reflectivity in the formation of our perception, and in the formulation of our response to change is negligible in changes happening in the natural physical world not involving human actors as participants. Where human actors are participants in the acts of change, then in the formation of our social knowledge about the change "the apprehension of meaning will be an act of the *whole* personality including the specifically social sector of the mind; indeed, it is not absurd to claim that the specifically social sector of the mind will have a larger say in the matter than either the sensual apparatus or the formal intellect" (Stark, 1958, p.15).

Initiation to Knowledge World. Growth in organisms is a process of change. From the time of conception of a child to its birth, growth, decline and death are all different stages of a change process, i.e., the aging process. As a child grows up, its behaviour formation, recognition of objects in the environment, and acquiring knowledge of the external world constitute a part of temporal phenomena. Physical growth and mental growth are interrelated. A new born baby's cry for feed or attention is an instinctive act; where as a toddler's mumbling for food or attention is linked to awareness process involving perception and language. The stage of physical change or age tells when the brain is ready for schooling, the range and depth of curriculum it can process (part of socialization process). The chronological stage of biological and mental changes is universal, but the rate of change varies from person to person. The study of age related mental changes in humans form a part of developmental psychology, cognitive psychology, and educational theories. The effects of time, space/ place on change involving human agents are influenced by cultural and geographic factors. Cognitive aging relates mental abilities to age. Measure of variability in speed of performance serves as an indicator of cognitive aging (Fultsch et. al., 2005). Time serves as a standard in measuring performance of time dependent changes.

CLOSURE

In human affairs, a change occurs when an individual interacts with other individuals or with the environment within a time/ space enclosure. In a technical sense, a change is a break in functioning of a system followed by variation or difference in its functioning. A change may appear as: recurring phenomena having certain period regularity; a regular phenomenon, but with minor variations; and a phenomenon that occurs randomly. The effects of change depend on the type of system undergoing the change- physical, chemical or human. A change may affect the system positively, negatively or with nil impact. While human caused changes can be controlled, at least in theory, not all nature caused changes can be controlled by man. There is an element of criticality surrounding the phenomenon of change made up of critical time, critical space, and critical knowledge in the occurrence of, or in effecting major changes. Many items of knowledge have the potential to become critical knowledge or critical resource.

Change is context bound. The context is indicated by the knowledge domain in which the change occurs. Apart from the theoretical fundamentals of change, the study of change becomes a sectoral study. Science considers change in terms of dynamical systems. Sociology treats change as a causal agent that alters social structures, social attitude, and social behavior in a given time-space zone. In economics, change is accounted by change of production techniques, social norms and values. Change in production techniques is intimately linked with technical knowledge and information. Occurrence of change may take different modes, such as: gradual, sudden, small-scale, hidden, discrete, cyclic, and revolutionary. Revolutionary changes are caused by a paradigm change in an existing system, and knowledge plays a crucial role in shaping the paradigm. The latest information revolution is powered by computer and communication technologies. Change and knowledge are two sides of the same coin—one leads to the other.

Change in human life takes two forms: changes that are common to all individuals, and changes whose effects are person dependent. Culture, social norms, education, experience, environment, and genetics are the major elements that determine the nature of change in individuals and society.

Change has a past, a present, and a future; and so is knowledge. We know (though not fully) how change has affected the destiny of man in the past, and how it is affecting him in the present. How it is going to shape the future remains a matter of conjecture. In today's world changes are occurring so fast, and their effects are so widespread and intense it is difficult for anyone to predict precisely what the future holds for humanity. However, the vision of the future drawn by Rifkin in the context of information seems within the realm of reality. He sees that "in our nanosecond culture everything changes so fast that it is necessary to construct a cosmology in which change itself is honored as the only timeless truth. By reinterpreting nature as the evolution of information, humanity achieves this end. Nature is no longer seen as a set of restrains, but rather as process of 'creative advance'. Knowledge gathering is now information gathering, and information gathering is the processing of changing conditions over time. With this linguistic metamorphosis, the door is opened to a thorough reinterpretation of existence as pure process devoid of any kind of ultimate, unchanging frame of reference" (Rifkin, 1998, p.220).

REFERENCES

Beinhocker, Eric D. The Origin of Wealth. Boston, Harvard University Press, 2006.

Cool, Collen. The Concept of situation in information Science. *Annual Review of Information Science and Technology 35:* 5-42, 2002.

Frisbie, W. Parker and Kasarda, John D. Special Process. Pp. 629-666. *In* Smelser, Neil J. Ed. Handbook of Sociology. Newburg Park (Calif.), Sage Publications, 1988.

Fultsch, David F. et al. Inconsistency in Response Time as an Indicator of Cognitive Aging. Pp. 33-58. *In* Duncan, John; Phillips, Louise and McLeod, Peter. Eds. Measuring the Mind: Speed, Control, and Age. Oxford, Oxford University Press, 2005.

Giddens, Anthony. The Consequences of Modernity. Stanford (Calif.), Stanford University Press, 1990.

Giddens, Anthony, Modernity and Self-Identity. Stanford (Calif.), Stanford University Press, 1991.

Hasselblatt, B. and Kotak, A. Handbook of Dynamical Systems. Vol. 1A. Amsterdam, Elsevier, 2002.

Hoselitz, Bert F. Non-Economic Barriers to Economic Development. Pp.17-27. *In* Corbridge, Stuart. Ed. Development Studies: A Reader. London, Arnold, 1995.

Kefalas, Asterios G. Cybernetics. Pp. 365-378. *In* Bidgoli, Hussain. Ed. Encyclopedia of Information Systems. Vol. 1. San Diego (Calif.), Academic Press, 2003.

Kotak, Anatole and Hasselblatt, Boris. Introduction to the Modern Theory of Dynamical Systems. Cambridge (U.K.), Cambridge University Press, 1995.

Khun, Thomas S. The Structure of Scientific Revolutions, Ed.2. Chicago, University of Chicago Press, 1970.

La Piere, Richard T. Social Change. Tokyo, McGraw-Hill, 1965. (International Student Edition).

Lakshmanasamy, T. New information, new institutions and economic development. *The Asian Economic Review* 45: 425-439, Dec. 2003.

Meadows, Paul. The Many Faces of Change: Explorations in the Theory of Social Change. Cambridge (Mass.), Schenkman, 1971.

Moore, Wilbert E. Social Change. Pp. 365-375. *In* Sills, David L. Ed. International Encyclopaedia of the Social Sciences. Vol. 14. London, Macmillan & Free Press, 1968.

Rifkin, Jeremy, The Biotech Century: Harnessing the Gene. New York, Jeremy P. Tarcher (Putnam), 1998.

Rioufol, Veronique. Approaches to social change in social forums: Snapshots of recompositions in progress. *International Social Science Journal* 56: 551-563, Dec. 2004.

Schlegel, Richard. Time and Physical Process, Pp. 37-48. *In* Moore, Wilbert E. and Cook, Robert M. Readings on Social Change. Engelwood Cliffs (NJ.), Prentice-Hall, 1967.

Skocpol, Theda. States and Social Revolutions: A Comparative Analysis of France, Russia and China. Cambridge (U.K.), Cambridge University Press, 1979.

Stark, W. The Sociology of Knowledge: An Essay in Aid of a Deeper Understanding of the History of Ideas. London, Routledge & Kegan Paul, 1958. (Reprint 1971).

Stehr, Nico and Meja, Volker. Introduction: The Development of the Sociology of Knowledge and Science. Pp.1-27. *In* Stehr, Nico and Meja, Volker. Society & Knowledge: Contemporary Perspectives in the Sociology of Knowledge & Science. Ed.2. New Brunswick (NJ), Transaction Publications, 2005.

Webster's Third New International Dictionary of the English Language. Unabridged. Cologne, Konemann Verlagsgesellschaft, 1993.

8

Knowledge in Philosophy

The study of knowledge has interested philosophers both in the East and the West from ancient times. In India, the study goes back to the Vedic period (1500 BC), and in China it is traced to *Yi Jing* (the Book of Changes), an ancient compendium of divination belonging to the period of king Wen around 1000 years BC (Wikipedia). In the West it predates Pythagoras (569-475 BC) of the ancient Greece. The coverage here is limited to the developments in the West. The study of knowledge, its origin, nature and limits has been the concern of epistemology, a branch of philosophy, and its object is to explain what knowledge is; and how human beings know what they claim to know. Recent advances in physics, mathematics, biology, psychology, neurosciences, artificial intelligence, cybernetics, linguistics, and sociology have contributed significantly to our further understanding of the functioning of human brain, mind, and society, which are contributing to the advancement of the study of knowledge phenomena. A few highly practically oriented thinkers are somewhat skeptic about the relevance of epistemological discourses to practical life. Skepticism is itself a topic of study in philosophy. Lately, there have been a few attempts to apply some of the theories of epistemology to provide a theoretical base to the organization of knowledge, user studies, and certain other areas of information science, and Knowledge Management (Hjörland, 2005). This makes it necessary for people studying and applying knowledge and information to know, at least, the broad contours of epistemology. Epistemology evolved out of philosophy, and hence it is appropriate to begin with the philosophers' perspectives of knowledge. Further, epistemology is so interlinked with many of the doctrines of philosophy that the latter enters in some way or other in any discussions on epistemology.

HISTORICAL PERSPECTIVE

The Greek philosophic tradition began much earlier than Socrates. It is traced to those thinkers who were called by Aristotle the First Philosophers, and their philosophy as "natural philosophy". From Pythagoras (569-475 BC), Socrates (469-399 BC), Plato (428-348 BC) and Aristotle (384-322 BC) to Archimedes (287-212 BC), the study of the natural world was a part of their primary or secondary philosophical enterprises. Their discourses formed the foundation on which the theories of knowledge were built. Plato made a distinction between knowledge derived from the sensory world and the knowledge formed from the world of "ideas" or "forms". For him, sensory world is only "trope" or conjectures, and not real knowledge; where as knowledge derived from ideas (rational knowledge) is the true knowledge (Tavakol, 1990). His pupil, Aristotle's work *Organon* on logic and language covers the theory of knowledge. They are in six parts: *Categories, On Interpretation, Prior Analytics, Posterior Analytics, Topics, and Sophistical Refutations. Prior Analytics* is about logical inference also called *syllogistic*. Syllogism suggests a logical relationship of one statement following the other leading to a logical consequence. A syllogism consists of three different categorical statements, two premises, and a conclusion. The *Prior Analytics* tells us which pairs of categoricals logically yield a third. *Posterior Analytics* extends syllogistic to science and scientific explanation. In his view, a science is a deductively ordered body of knowledge about a genus or domain of knowledge. Scientific knowledge (*episteme*) consists not in knowing *that*, but rather in knowing *why* (Audi, 1995). This heritage from ancient Greece underwent radical reevaluation during the period of European Renaissance. New facts derived from scientific discoveries and scientific thinking by philosophers and discoverers, such as Nicholas Copernicus (1473-1543) and Johannes Kepler (1571-1630) led to the formulation of the laws of planetary motion; Galileo Galilee's (1564-1642) work in dynamics, and his discovery of the moons of Jupiter orbiting around it, rather than the earth; and Andreas Vesalius (1514-1564) scientifically describing the human anatomy were instrumental in shattering the earth-centered cosmology that had prevailed from the days of Aristotle. However, the final break with the past came with the publication of *Philosophiae Naturalis Principia Mathematica* by Sir Isaac Newton (1643-1727) in 1687. The impact of Newton's work on the mechanism of nature's functioning was so profound that it left everlasting influence on the latter-day philosophers of the Enlightenment— from Locke to Kant of the 18th century.

By late 15th century, the then existing philosophic tradition was captured and presented by Leonardo da Vinci (1452-1519), in the form of three fundamental propositions that were based on experience, instrumental or mechanical science, and mathematical sciences. Further examination and study of these propositions led to: a) the development of empiricism by Francis Bacon (1561-1626) based on the principle of experience; b) materialism by Thomas Hobbes (1588-1626) built on instrumental and mechanical science; and c) rationalism by Rene Descartes (1596-1650). Descartes was largely influenced by mathematical principles though he used the other two themes. These three developments made deep impact on the course of epistemology and are the forerunners of the modern day versions of empiricism, materialism and rationalism (Encyclopaedia Britannnica, 2007, Vol. 25).

Empiricism. Francis Bacon besides his deep interest in advancing scientific research by applying scientific method, built his position in philosophy on the basis of empiricism developed by applying a new technique or type of reasoning. The new type of reasoning is to be derived from experience. For him experiencing was the sole means of arriving at valid knowledge. Hence drawing conclusions and formulation of general principles are to be based on observations, experimentation, and experiencing. Knowledge is not a priori, but empirical. His experience-dependent stand on knowledge and his new approach to the study of natural sciences inspired a number of thinkers and continue to influence even today.

In the Enlightenment, the pendulum swung back from metaphysical and rationalistic hold on philosophy evident at the Renaissance period to that of epistemological and empiricist. The main authors of the new movement, in what is called the "British Empiricism", were John Locke (1632-1704), George Berkeley (1685-1753), and David Hume (1711-76). Locke established that ideas belong to two distinct types: the ideas of sensation, and the ideas of reflection. The idea of sensation is the one where the idea is the object of the understanding of what one thinks; and the idea of reflection is reasoning. His fundamental stand is that reasoning is secondary to sensation. Locke's empiricist epistemology may be summed up as: a) sensation is the ultimate source of knowledge, i.e., ideas; and b) all knowledge phenomena are compounding of simple sensory materials into an integrated set of concepts and ideas in the mind. Locke recognized the distinction between "primary qualities" like solidity, figure, and motion which emanate from the object itself, and "secondary qualities", e.g., smell and colour which are the creation of the mind only. It was Berkeley who tackled the issue of primary and secondary qualities raised by Locke by stating that primary qualities are reducible to secondary qualities. He asserted that sense-data can be considered as "objects for the mind" rather than as "qualities adhering in a substance." Thus, he resolved the duality of substance and quality, i.e., reduction of substance to quality which is the essence of "phenomenolism". Hume pursued the problem of origin of knowledge tracing it to sense impressions. He held that knowledge or the perceptual experience of man is an associative characteristic of the mind. And in the formation of sense perception, factors like cause and effect are not bound with the things, but are caused by an inexplicable nature of the mind. His denial of causal phenomena as an intrinsic principle governing nature, and the idea of a mind without cohesiveness created a philosophical crisis or skepticism, which was reconciled later by Kant.

Seen from knowledge perspective, it can be concluded that empiricists believe that the real world can be known only by observation or experiencing, and any claim to knowledge by other means like thinking are only reflections of our ways of using words (Barrow, 1988). However, empiricism exempts mathematical and logical knowledge from the test of experience as they employ analytical methods, symbolism and syntax, which make them true and valid. Empiricists do concede the existence of some a priori knowledge in the mind, but regard it as insignificant. Empiricism has certain limitations. Empiricism, if applied vigorously many of the physical concepts like 'entropy' have to be abandoned either because they cannot be experienced or can be fully verified. Further, for example, it is not possible to experience the concepts like "humanity" and certain colour differentiations though the edifice of empiricism rests on experiencing.

Materialism. Hobbes shared Bacon's philosophical method and Galileo's mechanics. For Hobbes all knowledge has its origin in sense impressions and all sensations are caused by the action of external bodies upon the organs of sense. The content of philosophy, according to Hobbes, is made up of: a) physics, b) moral philosophy, and c) civil philosophy. Physics is the science of the motions and actions of natural bodies conceived in terms of cause and effect. Moral philosophy (in effect psychology) is the psychological world of man. And civil philosophy is the social world, i.e., how society is to be managed. (Encyclopaedia Britanica, 2007, Vol. 25). He stressed that the study of cause and effect relationship helps in revealing the materialistic facts of nature.

Rationalism. Rene Descartes is considered the father of modern rationalism, popularly called "Cartesian rationalism". Descartes stands irrevocably on 'thinking' the criterion of being. His famous pronouncement "cogito ergo sum", "I think, therefore I am" sums it all. He asserted that knowledge of the external world is the preserve of the mind and not of senses. Rationalism rejects the theory of sense- experience as the basis of all knowledge. It is the antithesis of empiricism. On the whole, the then philosophical world stood in a state of confusion with irreconcilable philosophical stands. This state of affairs prepared the ground for creative thinking in the field of knowledge, which resulted in the modern theories of knowledge. Two continental philosophers, the Dutch Jew Benedict Spinoza (1632-77) and Gottfried Wilhelm Leibniz (1646-1716) continued with the tradition of rationalism. Leibniz was the first to distinguish "truth of reason" from "truth of facts", and to contrast the "necessary" propositions of logic and mathematics (which express identities and are universally valid) with the "contingent" (or empirical) propositions of science, which hold good only for certain existential conditions. Strong rationalism was the common feature shared by Descartes, Spinoza, and Leibniz. From an epistemological view, it is seen that rationalists insist that only reason can apprehend reality. By applying reason in the form of deductive and mathematical methods to a subject body in the external world, one arrives at true knowledge.

Origin of Knowledge and Language. Tracing the source of origin of knowledge has been an important issue in both philosophy and epistemology. There are two principle views on the issue, namely, a) that knowledge is innate to human beings, and b) it is acquired. Innate theory insists that knowledge is already seeded in the mind at birth. This view is supported by some of the modern day linguists. According to Noam Chomsky, language is a mirror of mind in a deep and significant sense. It is a product of human intelligence created anew in each individual by operations that lie far beyond the reach of will or consciousness (Chomsky, 1976). He observes that with relatively minor differences, it looks plausible to claim that the structure of sentences is overwhelmingly similar to the structure of thoughts, taking it for granted that thoughts have structure (Smith, 1999). There is no consensus on the existence of 'language of thought'. Chomsky's work establishes that language faculty constitutes a separate module with precise internal structure. On the contrary, behavioural psychologists contend that all knowledge is acquired through experience.

Synthesis. As far as knowledge part of philosophy is concerned, it fell on Immanuel Kant (1724-1804) of Prussia to reconcile Leibniz's extreme rationalism and Hume's extreme empiricism, i.e., the gulf between a priori origin of knowledge and sensory basis of knowledge. This he did by what he called "transcendental method", which is also known as "critical method". The critical method consisted of a critical examination of the powers of a priori reason and to enquire what reason can achieve sans experience. He dealt with critical reasoning in natural philosophy (science) in his 1781 (2nd ed. 1987) work *Critique of Pure Reason*.

Kant in his Critique condemns both dogmatism and skepticism in very strong terms. On empiricism he holds a dual view. While he rejected the certain claim of empiricism as universal and necessary knowledge (a priori status), because no knowledge derived from any particular experience (a posteriori status) could justify it; and at the same time, he defends its scientific character. Similarly, he concedes the possibility of a priori cognition of the fundamental principles of natural science (a posteriori status) (Guyer and Wood, 1998). Kant's a *priori* and a *posteriori* conception of thought/ knowledge lies between extreme rationalism and extreme empiricism. He draws three distinctions among propositions/ knowledge: a priori vs. empirical, necessary vs. contingent, and analytic vs. synthetic. Knowledge is a priori, if it is already in the mind and not caused by experience; and empirical, if it is based on experience. A true proposition is necessary, if it is true in all possible situations; otherwise it is contingent. In an analytic proposition, the predicate belongs to the concept of the subject; in a synthetic judgment, the predicate lies outside the subject concept. However, Kant agrees that there are important class of propositions that are both a priori and synthetic, which are found in arithmetic and geometry (Dancy and Sosa, 2003).

19TH AND 20TH CENTURY DEVELOPMENTS

The philosophy of Bacon's Empiricism, Hobbs' Materialism, and Descartes' Rationalism, and the later works of Locke, Leibnitz, and Kant have continued to serve as reference points to the 19th and 20th century philosophers. Keeping these as source principles and influenced by the changing world, the new thinkers have tried to search for fresh philosophical insights and develop doctrines based on them. Beginning with the late 19th century philosophic endeavor in the West developed on the lines of two separate traditions: Analytic philosophy and Continental philosophy. Epistemology has followed the same pattern. Analytic philosophy was largely swayed by the tradition of Locke and Hume. The pursuit of analytic philosophy by Anglo-American philosophers led to the development of logical positivism, realism, phenomenalism, revival of sense-data theory, and skepticism. On the other hand, the Continental philosophers were swayed by speculative and historical tradition, and followed descriptive approach giving rise to phenomenology.

Positivism. Mainly influenced by Bacon, the British Empiricism, and a few others, the French philosopher Auguste Comte (1798-1857) developed the philosophy of Positivism, a later form of empiricism. The main thrust of positivism is on ordinary observation of phenomena, and principles of particular science to comprehend reality. In comprehending knowledge, one encounters instances or facts and not universal reality. To arrive at the universal reality one has to bring together all the particular instances that share certain common features and name it. The features by themselves are of no existence other than residing in our collection of particulars (Barrow, 1988). Further, it states that knowledge of phenomena is relative and not absolute. It rejects all metaphysical propositions.

ANALYTIC EPISTEMOLOGY

Analytic philosophers' epistemological interest in the 20th century is based on the philosophic strands of symbolic logic and the British Empiricism. Within this strand there have been two approaches: a) those that have followed a formal style originating from logic; and b) others following the informal style based on ordinary language. This has led to three schools: common sense realism, Logical Positivism, and Naturalized Epistemology.

Common Sense Realism. G.E. Moore (1873-1958) is credited with the finding of this school. According to him, analysis is to clarify thought. The methods of analysis include the creation of symbolic language, and the close examination of everyday speech. The analysis of objects in the world makes use of both formal logical techniques and informal language in use. Moore called this "the common sense view of the world" which is made up of propositions about the world known to be true, e.g., "The earth has existed for many years". In his view, all knowledge is the common sense view of the world. He says that all notions about the world are made up of a number of propositions, which are accepted by all to be true with certainty, e.g., the earth exists and people live on it. Hence any view contrary to this common sense view can be rejected. He also rejects all forms of skepticism and idealism. Ludwig Wittgenstein (1889-1951) also rejects skepticism and idealism, which arise due to simplistic misunderstanding of epistemic concepts like "belief", "knowledge", "certainty", and "justification" expressed through everyday language.

Logical Positivism. Logical positivism (also called logical empiricism) was developed originally by a group of Austrian thinkers, mostly scientists and mathematicians, known as the Vienna Circle under the leadership of Moritz Schlick (1882-1936) in the 1920s and 1930s, and included among others Rudolf Carnap, Herbert Feigl, Philipp Frank, and Gustav Bergmann. To logical positivists knowledge in its original and purest form is a complex intellectual structure sustained by a linguistic or conceptual framework to express what is to be categorized and predicted. The structure receives its content from sense experience. The positivistic theory of knowledge presents the structure, content, and basis of human knowledge derived from empirical principles. Science is regarded as the repository of all genuine knowledge, and as such, the aim of logical positivism is to present the structure, i.e., the 'logic' of science. Thus, the theory of knowledge becomes the philosophy of science. Its task is to: a) analyze the meanings of the statements of science empirically, and only empirically, i.e., by observation or experience; b) show how certain observations or experiences serve to confirm a given statement in the sense of making it more warranted or reasonable; and c) show how non-empirical or a priori knowledge of the necessary truths of logic and mathematics is possible even though the fact can be intelligibly thought or known is empirically verifiable or falsifiable (Dancy and Sosa, 2003). Logical positivists make a clear distinction between scientific propositions and propositions derived metaphysically. *Language, Truth, and Logic* by A.J. Ayer (1910-89) published in 1936 had a good deal of influence on establishing British Empiricism.

Naturalized Epistemology. It is the doctrine developed by W.V.O. Quine (1908-2000), which states that epistemology has no normative function, i.e., belief function, but only to describe how knowledge, especially scientific knowledge is actually arrived at, i.e., scientific communities' belief system.

PERCEPTION AND KNOWLEDGE

The interest of analytic philosophers in the first half of the 20th century centered on the relationship between perception and knowledge. The prominent thinkers to follow this line were Bertrand Russell (1872-1970), G.E. Moore, H. H. Price (1899-1984), C.D. Broad (1887-1971), A. J. Ayer, and H. Paul Grice (1913-88). Though they differed considerably in their positions, all of them subscribed to "sense-data" theory. It also led to the development of realism and phenomenalism.

Sense-Data Theory. According to this theory, "sense-data" is the input to knowledge by perception. This input is relayed to mind by sense organs. The sense organs capture things in the external world in the form of sense-data. The perception or the awareness produced in the mind out of the sensory data is called "sense datum". The derivation of sense datum is direct and does not depend either on inferencing or judgment. However, sense datum theory is unable to explain beyond doubt some of the perceptual deviations like a straight rod appearing bent when partially immersed in water. Attempts to overcome these limitations of the theory lead to phenomenalism and realism..

Phenomenalism. Passing the test of perceptual experience is central to phenomenalism. All objects have perceivable features or properties. Any entity to claim the status of knowledge must pass the test of perceptual experience, meaning that the properties of things must be perceivable. According to phenomenalists, all objects are made up of a set of perceivable properties or features (e.g., size, colour, mass, etc.), which when perceived as a coherent whole constitute the knowledge of that object. Hence they reject the idea of mind-dependent and mind-independent concepts of realism. Phenomenalism explains perceptual errors, raised in realism, in terms of coherence and predictability. Erroneous perception occurs when there is a mismatch between the present perceptual experience held in the mind about an item and its unspecified future experience. Private and public notions of knowledge are explained by means of coherence of perception. In phenomenalism, if the perception of an entity of knowledge by one person is same as with others, then it is known as public, (e.g., a table, a motor car), and if the perception (e.g., feeling of pain, joy) differs it is private.

Realism. It is an offshoot of empiricism. Realism, as is the case with many other concepts in epistemology, appears both as philosophy and epistemology, the former constituting the source base for the latter. Realism as an epistemological theory is based on perception. Realism distinguishes all our notions into mental and physical. Mental notions refer mostly to sensations like pain, fear and desire; whereas physical notions refer to physical objects and phenomena. Mental items are thus "private" to an individual, in the sense, that each item is to be experienced individually and that experience is not same in all people. Physical entities, on the other hand, are "public" in the sense that the existence of the entity — say a computer or a chair does not change from person to person, and to prove their existence need no experiencing. In other words, mental notions are mind-dependent and physical objects are mind-independent. It is assumed that mental phenomena being mind-dependent do not have to prove its existence. Epistemology is concerned with mind-independent aspects of realism. The main drawback in the doctrine of realism and its extended forms— direct realism which relies on the mode of direct perception of the physical objects perceived, and representative realism which incorporates the notions of indirect perception by the mind— is their inability to explain satisfactorily the perceptual errors like visual aberrations and distortions. The important proponents of realism included Ayer, Moore, and James J.Gibson (1904-79).

Idealism, Solipsism and Intuitionism. The proponents of idealism consider that what one claims as knowledge is merely an idea. Since the knowledge one claims to have is a product of the human mind, we "can never be sure that there exists any direct correlation between reality and our ideas about it. The entities in our theories do not really exist in the universe; they are entirely imposed upon the chaos of sense data by our minds" (Barrow, 1988, p.12). Solipsism, an extension of idealism takes the extreme position that knowledge of the external world perceived by an individual is nothing but a product of one's own imagination. Believers of intuitionism assert that knowledge is the result of intuition rather than reason or observation; what is self-evident is taken as true.

CONTINENTAL EPISTEMOLOGY

In the early part of the 20th century, the Continental philosophers were engaged with the problem of discrepancy between the knower and the known. At that time, the German philosopher Edmund Husserl (1859-1938) thought that the main reason for the anomaly was the investigators not focusing on the object of knowledge as they are actually experienced. Based on this conviction Husserl came out with the philosophy of phenomenology.

Phenomenology. The philosophy of phenomenology propounded by Husserl states that knowledge is the result of description of experiential phenomena, i.e., the pure intentional content of consciousness or 'noema'. Such descriptions must be devoid of all preconceptions. He prescribes a number of phenomenological 'reductions' (methods) to arrive at noema. The core reductions are 'eidetic' reduction and 'transcendental' reduction (also called "epoche"). In the transcendental reduction one sets aside all objects transcendent to consciousness, and instead focuses on the intentional content immanent within it. According to him an object is 'transcendent', if only one aspect of it can immediately present before us at a given time, e.g., redness of tomato. Such a revelation of the object is 'immanent', and is given all at once transparently so that no perspective variation mediates our apprehension of it, i.e., the noema of the object under consideration. The eidetic reduction gives the ideal internal structure and contents of the mental world, i.e., the noema of the mental state. Transcendental reduction and noema together is supposed to isolate and project the pure consciousness (Carman, 2003).

Martin Heidegger (1889-1976), a follower of Husserl, discarded transcendental reductions and followed a new path by emphasizing the importance of milieu on human cognition. The American pragmatist philosopher John Dewey (1859-1952), influenced by the philosophy of phenomenology, developed the theory that knowledge is the resultant of a dynamic process of interaction between a living being and his or her environment.

EPISTEMOLOGY (CENTRAL THEME)

Among the chief questions epistemology attempts to answer are: What is knowledge? How do we get it? Can our means of getting it be defended against skeptical challenge? (Grayling, 2003). This takes us to three basic concepts, namely, truth, belief, and justification with which the classical theory of knowledge starts. Generally, epistemologists begin to address the first question "What is knowledge?" with "belief". The standard definition reads that knowledge is *justified true belief.*

Justified True Belief (JTB). The prime focus of epistemology in its classical form is to establish or certify the claim by a person that he knows, what he says he knows. Knowledge in the JTB context is focused on *propositional* knowledge. A proposition is something which can be expressed by a declarative sentence (e.g., "The fort is to the left of the road"), which purports to describe a fact or a state of affairs. The statements of propositional knowledge are expressed using "that" clauses (e.g., Raman knows that the fort is to the left of the road). Propositional knowledge to be called knowledge must satisfy certain conditions that are based on the criteria of belief, truth and justification. According to the traditional analysis, followed from the time of Plato, knowledge is *justified true belief*. In other words, it means that a person 'S' has the knowledge of the proposition 'p' that something is the case when, and only when the following three conditions are met:

A person, S, knows that p if and only if:

1. p is true;
2. S believes that p; and
3. S's belief that p is justified.

Because of what is known as Gettier's problem, it is shown that compliance with the criteria of truth, belief, and justification alone are not sufficient for 'p' to become knowledge, and it must satisfy further conditions (Gettier, 2003). The additional condition so needed is explained by "Causal Theory of Knowing" by Alvin Goldman. The other theories which have addressed this problem are. "Knowledge: Undefeated Justified True Belief" theory by Keith Lehrer and Thomas Paxson; and "Contextualism and Knowledge Attributions" by Keith DeRose (Steup, 2008). It is suggested by some scholars that the cause of Gettier problem is due to insufficient analysis of justification. Newly proposed elements to be taken into account in justification include: a) internalism, meaning that justification depends solely on factors internal to the believer's mind; b) foundationalism which states that there is an asymmetrical relationship between any two beliefs; and c) coherentism, meaning that a belief gets its justification by virtue of its membership in a set of beliefs that all fit together in the right way; and d) externalism, which states that at least some factors external to the believer's mind determine whether or not one is justified (Internet Encyclopedia of Philosophy, 2009; Hamilton and Cairns, 1961; Kleiman, 1990). There are two other fundamental issues connected with certifying knowledge, and they are certainty and skepticism.

Knowledge and Certainty. The concept of certainty is one of the associated criteria for knowledge, the others being belief, justification and truth. Certainties are of different types. There are three different lines of thought on the relationship between knowledge and certainty, and they are:

1. One knows something, if that person is certain of the thing he or she claims to know. A belief to be accepted as knowledge must pass the test of certainty.
2. One can be certain of a thing, if one knows it. A thing that nobody knows may be true, but not necessarily be certain, the view held by Moore.
3. Knowledge and certainty are not interdependent according to Wittgenstein.

Skepticism. Skepticism has been a fundamental issue confronting philosophers in their attempts to establish the existence of knowledge. Skepticism refers to limits, or scope of human knowledge. Among epistemologists there are two different views on skepticism. One view is that skepticism is not to be refuted as it is the inevitable result of epistemological reflection. Holders of this view stress the point that skepticism with its imperfectly justified beliefs is always open to revision. The other view is that it is not a practical option to establish the existence of knowledge. It holds that nothing is known or can be known, and hence it is worth ignoring it altogether (Grayling, 2003). Some divide skepticism into *knowledge skepticism* and *justification skepticism*. Both are further divided into: unrestricted and restricted skepticism. Unrestricted knowledge skepticism implies that no one knows anything, and that no one is even justified in believing anything. Restricted skepticism refers to skepticism applied to a particular domain of supposed knowledge, e.g., knowledge of the external world. One of the most difficult problems in skepticism is *the problem of the criterion*. This is because whatever criterion we try to think of to specify skepticism we will be using one unspecified or undefined criterion to specify another unspecified criterion, like one blind man leading another blind man. The birth of modern epistemology and modern philosophy at the hands of Descartes owes it to skepticism. It has been a crucial force in determining the course of Western philosophy (Audi, 1995). It may be said in general that skepticism takes the form of a request for the justification, of those knowledge claims, together with a statement of the reasons motivating that result (Grayling, 2003).

NATURE OF KNOWLEDGE

Philosophers have followed differrent approaches to understand the nature of knowledge and to specify it. These include: a) linguistic/behavioural psychological approach, b) sense-data theory, c) commonsense epistemology, d) analysis of the concept of knowledge from "to know", and e) differentiating knowledge by type. The last two are explained now (Encyclopaedia Britannica, 2007, Vol. 18) as the others have already been covered.

By Analysis of the Concept "To Know". A simple approach to explain the nature of knowledge is to go by analyzing the expression "to know" in the concept "knowledge" occurring in daily usage. The idea is that such an examination gives one type of insight of the phenomena associated with the concept. Hence analyzing what is meant by "know how", "know what", "know that", "know when" and "know where" sheds light on our understanding the nature of knowledge. Since "know when" and "know where" refer to time and place, one must refer to "know how", "know what" and "know that" to understand the nature of knowledge.

Practical Knowledge. "Know how" implies how to do things. It refers to human skill or ability, and hence this type of knowledge is called *practical* knowledge or *procedural* knowledge. When one says that he knows swimming, what it means is that he has the knowledge of swimming without having to convey to others the ability of swimming. "Know what" has the same property as "know how" in this regard.

Propositional or Descriptive Knowledge. In contrast to "know how", "know that" denotes the possession of specific items of information or facts, which can be expressed in the form of propositions or declarations describing the facts. Hence it is called *propositional* knowledge or *descriptive* knowledge. It means that one has the knowledge that something is the case or that it is so. For example, when one says that he knows that "alcohol is a byproduct of sugar manufacturing", he is stating what he thinks he knows. It is expressed information, the content of which is what a person thinks that he or she knows. This knowledge is formed out of one's reflection or expression. They are mostly in the form of propositions, beliefs or statements. Most of our knowledge about the external world is propositional knowledge. Propositional knowledge could be of either *a priori* origin or *a posteriori* origin. Propositional knowledge is the subject of a number of epistemological interpretations in the analysis of knowledge discussed under the head "justified true belief." Propositional knowledge is further divided into— inferential and non-inferential.

Inferential propositional knowledge is the result of inferences. Most of scientific knowledge is inferential. The source of non-inferential propositional knowledge is intuition. One understands institutively what the abstract concepts like "love", "god" or "mercy" means, and hence is an example for non-inferential propositional knowledge.

DIFFERENTIATING KNOWLEDGE BY TYPE

Philosophers have also tried to explain the nature of knowledge by categorizing them into different types by their distinctive characteristics. They are categorized into mental and non-mental, occurrent and dispositional, a priori and a posteriori, and descriptive and justificatory.

Mental and Non-mental Knowledge. The Greek philosopher Plato stated that knowing is a mental state, but it is different from believing. Contemporary philosophers subscribing to state of mind theory think that knowing is one member of a group of mental states that can be arranged in a series according to increasing certitude in the order of guessing and conjecturing, thinking, believing, and feeling sure, and knowing, the most certain of all these states. Thus, they conclude that knowledge is a form of consciousness. The state of mind theory is rejected by many philosophers. Wittgenstein rejects it on the ground that knowledge and certainty are not mental states like say surmising and being sure. Another view is that an item claiming the status of knowledge rests on it fulfilling certain behavioural and other complex conditions. Many concede that mental states may be involved in the formation of knowledge, but knowledge itself is not a state of mind. Similar view was expressed by J.L.Austin (1911-1960).

Occurrent and Dispositional Knowledge. According to this model, a distinction is made between knowledge of which one is currently aware of, i.e., occurrent knowledge, and knowledge which has a disposition or propensity to behave in certain conditions, i. e., dispositional knowledge. The distinction between these two types seems to rely on the ability of the mind to recall. In dispositional knowledge one can have knowledge of things that he or she is not aware of at a given moment, but the same becomes available later by recalling from mind.

A Priori and A Posteriori Knowledge. An item of knowledge where establishing the truth of it does not call for any factual or empirical proof is called a priori knowledge and by definition it is true. For example, the statement "crows are black in colour" does not need any inquiry or observation to establish its truth; by definition crows are black, and it denotes a priori knowledge. On the other hand, the truth of the statement "this road leads to Delhi" needs to be established by factual means. The knowledge conveyed by the later statement is a posteriori knowledge. A posteriori knowledge is obtained only through experience. All empirical knowledge is a posteriori. Propositions representing a priori and a posteriori knowledge are further distinguished into: necessary and contingent, analytic and synthetic, tautological and significant, and logical and factual propositions.

Descriptive and Justificatory Knowledge. How one gets the knowledge of the external world? The philosophers including Husserl, Moore, Bertrand Russell, A. J. Ayer, and H. H. Price maintain that knowledge is derived by description of items in the external world. Hence this type of knowledge is referred to as descriptive knowledge. It is contended that knowledge is formed by apprehending through description the objects in external world and also the contents of the human mind. A descriptive statement merely states facts without expressing any value judgment. Opposed to the descriptive school of thought is the theory that knowledge is formed by explanation, a function of rational justification (of beliefs) of the items in the external world. The knowledge so recognized is called justificatory or normative knowledge. A normative statement expresses a value assessment.

SOCIAL EPISTEMOLOGY

Social epistemology is emerging as a new branch of epistemology. Its focus is on the shared aspect of knowledge as well as the social situatedness of the knower. It overrides the Cartesian paradigm of individual knowledge and the associated challenge of skepticism, and instead views knowledge as being a shared product of groups of individuals

(Aarons, 2006). The origin of social epistemology is credited to Margaret Elizabeth Egan and Jesse H. Shera from the field of librarianship. The beginnings of social epistemology are traced to the seminal paper on bibliographic organization published by Egan and Shera in 1952 (Egan and Shera, 1952). Stressing the need for a new epistemological discipline for library science, in his book *The Foundations of Education for Librarianship,* Shera lays-down the outline for the new discipline of social epistemology. The contents of the new discipline, extracted from his book are given below (Shera, 1972):

1. Social epistemology must develop an ordered and comprehensive body of knowledge about intellectual differentiation and integration of knowledge within a complex social organization.
2. It must study how intellectual forces shape social structures and institutions.
3. The new discipline must provide a frame-work for the investigation of the complex problem of the nature of the intellectual process in society— a study of the ways in which society as a whole achieves a perceptive relation to its total environment.
4. Social epistemology must focus upon the production, flow, integration, and consumption of communicated thought throughout the social fabric.
5. The new field of study has to be interdisciplinary in its heavy dependence upon many fields— sociology, anthropology, linguistics, economics, the physiology of the human nervous system, psychology, mathematics, and information theory, to name a few.
6. Social epistemology is expected to have practical results, and one of the most practical applications will be in librarianship.

In fact, some work on social epistemology was under way within the field of philosophy in the nineteeneighties, but at a low key. With the publication of the paper *On Regulating What is Known: A Way to Social Epistemology* by Steve Fuller in 1987 in the journal *Synthese*, the term was fully established (Zandonade, 2004). Fuller wrote in that paper that social organization of knowledge was an important concern of epistemology of Comte and Stuart Mill, but its significance was later lost under the sway of logical positivism. In describing our cognitive pursuits the function of "epistemology" in social epistemology is only to facilitate our prescribing them. The key features of Fuller's account of social epistemology are stated here (Fuller, 1987):

1. The fundamental question in social epistemology is to decide "*How should the pursuit of knowledge be organized, given that under normal circumstances knowledge is pursued by many human beings, each working on a more or less well defined body of knowledge and each equipped with roughly the same imperfect cognitive capacities, albeit with varying degrees of access to one another's activities?*" (p.145, italics is original author's).
2. Our cognitive pursuits— different ways of pursuing knowledge and creation of a variety of intellectual products— must be accounted following normative principles, and not by isolating them from social world and social judgments. In describing our cognitive pursuits the function of "epistemology" in social epistemology is only to facilitate our prescribing them.
3. The ultimate goal of social epistemology is "to map out the structure of cognitive authority among all the disciplines as a means of providing direction for research" (p.149). The study of how knowledge claims are established and how granting of epistemic warrants lead to the distribution of power in a covert manner in society

is an important assignment in social epistemology.

4. A prime concern of social epistemology is to determine how social organization of knowledge can be optimized, i.e., establishing division of cognitive labour in society. Production of knowledge is an "economic process" and the key issue in regulating knowledge production is a problem of redistribution of production processes and not of accumulation.

The formulation of social epistemology based on truth and belief-centric classical epistemology is generally traced to Alvin Goldman's work during 1970s and 1980s. Goldman divided epistemology into: individual epistemology, and social epistemology (or "epistemics"). While individual epistemology examines the psychological processes underlying the epistemic subject, the social epistemology tries to identify and evaluate social processes by which epistemic subjects interact with other agents, and how the subject's belief system gets influenced, i.e., social-episteme practice. One example of this practice is the study of the communicational acts of the second and third party agents in the association, and the institutional structures that guide or frame such communicational acts. The theme is further explained by him in terms of "veritistic value." Veritistic value is the value placed on having true beliefs rather than false beliefs or no opinion (uncertainty). Goldman sees this principle working in everyday life, and in science, law, education, and others. Veritistic approach gives social epistemology an evaluative or normative quality, and not it remaining a purely descriptive or explanatory discipline (Goldman, 1987, 1999; Stanford Encyclopedia, 2009).

The field of social epistemology is getting broadened by inclusion of topics like: feminine phenomena explained by applying the principles of truth, belief, and justification; Case study-based research on historical development of specific domains like science (i.e., sociology of science), of technology and so on; study of collaborative research phenomena; group belief and group knowledge (e.g., community knowledge). Current thinking in social epistemology is proceeding on the twin lines of : a) theoretical issues taking up individual's knowledge behavior, and social branches of epistemology; and b) applied issues commonly involving truth acquisition and error avoidance (Stanford Encyclopedia, 2009). However, there is one question that has not been satisfactorily and completely answered till now is how social epistemology and sociology of knowledge are distinct?

CLOSURE

Every philosophical tradition has given a high place for knowledge. Epistemology draws its support and inspiration from philosophy. Hence, to study knowledge, one has to begin with the study of knowledge portion of philosophy. Western organization of philosophy has a separate branch called epistemology allocated to the study of knowledge. Epistemology is set with the task of explaining what knowledge is, its origin and nature. The roots of Western philosophy are to be found in the ancient Greek philosophy from Pythagoras to Archimedes, and of epistemology in the works of Plato and Aristotle. Modern philosophy and epistemology were shaped by the European Renaissance, the Scientific revolution and the Enlightenment. By late 16th century Bacon, Hobbs and Descartes had given clear and compact form to empiricism, materialism and rationalism, respectively. It is on these three schools, the modern Western philosophy and also epistemology have further developed. However, it needed the intellectual craftsmanship of Locke, Leibnitz, and Kant to fine tune them and give further focus. In the late 19th century Western philosophy split into two traditions- Continental (European) and Analytic (British). Continental tradition gave birth to Husserl's phenomenology. Analytic philosophy engaged in symbolic logic and empiricism blossomed into commonsense philosophy, logical positivism, perception and knowledge, realism, and phenomenalism; each of which has its counterpart in epistemology.

On the central themes of epistemology the attention concentrated on finding out what constitutes knowledge. The classical view is represented by the proposition "knowledge is justified true belief" and the Gettier's problem. Later it was discovered that any claim to the status of knowledge has to satisfy not only the classical conditions of justification, truth and belief, but more than that. Associated with defining knowledge and theories of knowledge are certainty and skepticism. Of practical interest to practitioners of knowledge besides theorists are: the nature of knowledge examined by analyzing the activity or description indicated by the term "to know" in the concept knowledge (leading to practical knowledge and propositional knowledge); differentiating knowledge by type (giving rise to mental and non-mental, occurrent and dispositional, a priori and a posteriori, descriptive and justificatory knowledge). Epistemology began as a field of study of knowledge phenomena as it operates in individuals and continues to be so. However, the study of knowledge phenomenon as a group or social act opened up a new field called "social epistemology" as a branch of epistemology whose origin is traced to J.H. Shera, a librarian.

Epistemological concepts and theories enter in many of the discussions on the foundations of knowledge, organization of knowledge, and applications of knowledge in real life. Further, they supply the theoretical concepts on which library science, information science, and Knowledge Management are developed. There are two major criticisms against epistemological exposition of knowledge, and they are: a) it is too theoretical and abstract to be of much help in facing real life situations, and b) it is individual centered, and thus ignores social situatedness of knowledge. These objections are tried to be met by social epistemology by extending its scope by including the needs of developmental knowledge and its applications with particular attention paid to social dimension of knowledge. The study of epistemology provides the requisite background for those engaged in knowledge related activities; and for others it is likely to broaden their horizon.

Treatment of knowledge in epistemology differs from that of natural sciences and social sciences. In epistemology and in humanities, knowledge is viewed as "the result of cognitive and cultural processes, which enable an individual to act within his or her personal world. Here, personal experience and abilities are central issues when it comes to having knowledge about something (Thellefsen and Thellefsen, 2004). This in a way sets the limits of epistemology in the present context. Moving away from the tenacious adherence to the tenets of truth, belief and justification centered classical epistemology, and with current emphasis on empiricism, social and economic characteristics of knowledge epistemology holds promise to further our understanding of knowledge in its societal, economic and daily living contexts, and in suggesting solutions to some of the knowledge related problems of the 21st century, the century of knowledge society. Already it has contributed towards laying the theoretical foundation for librarianship, information science, and knowledge management.

REFERENCES

Aarons, Jeremy. Epistemology and Knowledge Management. Pp.166-172. *In* Schwartz, David G. Ed. Encyclopedia of Management. Singapore, Idea Group Reference, 2006.

Audi, Robert. The Cambridge Dictionary of Philosophy. Cambridge (NY), Cambridge University Press, 1995.

Barrow, John D. The World Within the World. Oxford, Clarendon Press, 1988.

Carman, Taylor. Husserl and Heidigger. Pp.842-859. *In* Bunnin, Nicholas and Tsui-James, E.P. Ed. The Blackwell Companion to Philosophy. Ed.2. Malden (MA), Blackwell Publishing, 2003.

Chomsky, Noam. Reflections on Language, 1976. *In* Chomsky, Noam. On Language. Chomsky's Classic Works: Language and responsibility and

Reflections on Language in one volume. New Delhi, Penguin Books, 2003. (Originally published by Fontana/Collins, 1976)

Dancy, Jonathan and Sosa, Ernest. Ed. A Companion to Epistemology. Malden (MA), Blckwell Publishing, 2003. (Blackwell Companions to Philosophy).

Egan, M. E. and Shera, J. H. Foundations of a theory of bibliography. *Library Quarterly* 22 (2) : 125-137, 1952.

Encyclopaedia Britannica, The New. Chicago, Encyclopaedia Britanica, 2007. Ed. 15. Vol.18. Epistemology. Pp. 472-488.

Encyclopaedia Britannica, The New. Chicago, Encyclopaedia Britanica, 2007. Ed. 15. Vol.25. Philosophy, The History of Western. Pp. 733-760.

Fuller, Steve. On regulating what is known: A way to social epistemology. *Synthese* 73 (1-2):145- 183, 1987.

Gettier, Edmund. Is Justified True Belief Knowledge? Pp. 306-307. *In* Moser, Paul K. and vander Nat Arnold. Ed. Human Knowledge: Classical and Contemporary Approaches. New York, Oxford University Press, 2003.

Goldman, Alvin. Foundations of social epistemics. *Synthese* 73:109-144, 1987.

Goldman, Alvin. Knowledge in a Social World. Oxford (U.K.), Oxford University Press, 1999.

Grayling, A.C. Epistemology. Pp. 37-60. *In* Bunnin, Nicholas and Tsui-James, E.P. Ed. The Blackwell Companion to Philosophy. Ed.2. Malden (MA), Blackwell Publishing, 2003.

Guyer, Paul and Wood, Allen W. Tr. and Ed. Immanuel Kant. Critique of Pure Reason. New York, Cambridge University Press, 1998.

Hamilton, Edith and Cairns, Huntington. Knowledge as Justified True Belief. Pp.907-917. *In* The Collected Dialogues of Plato. Routledge and Methuen, 1961. (Also reprinted in Kleiman, Lowell and Lewis, Stephen. Loc.cit.).

Hjörland, Birger. Library and information science and the philosophy of science. (Introduction to the special issue). *Journal of Documentation* 61 (1) : 5-10, 2005.

Inrernet Encyclopedia of Philosophy: Epistemology. http://www..iep.utm.edu/e/epistemo.htm (Accssed February 2009).

Kleiman, Lowell and Lewis, Stephen. Philosophical Discussion: What is Knowledge. Pp.10-17. *In* Kleiman, Lowell and Lewis, Stephen. Philosophy: An Introduction Through Literature. St. Paul, Minnesota, Pargon House, 1990. (Paperback ed. 1992).

Shera, J.H. The Foundations of Education for Librarianship. New York, Becker and Hayes, 1972

Smith, Neil. Chomsky: Ideas and Ideals. Cambridge University Press, 1999.

Steup, Matthias. Epistemology. *In* Zalta, Edward N. Ed. The Stanford Encyclopedia of Philosophy. 2008. http://plato.stanford.edu/archives/win2008/entries/epistemology/

Stanford Encyclopedia of Philosophy. Social Epistemology. 2001. Revised Aug.2006. http://plato.stanford.edu/entries/epistemology-soicial/ (Accessed 9th April, 2009).

Tavakol, M. Sociology of Knowledge. Theoretical Probems. New Delhi, Sterling Publishers, 1990.

Thellefsen, T. L. and Thellefsen, M. M. Pragmatic semiotics and knowledge organization. *Knowledge Organization* 31 (3), 177-187, 2004.

Wikipedia, Chinese philosophy. http.//en.wikipedia.org/wki/chinese_philosophy.

Zandonade, Tarcisio. Social epistemology from Jesse Shera to Steve Fuller. *Library Trends* 22 (4) : 810-832, 2004. (Spring issue).

9

Biological Basis of Information

Biological information is of two types: a) genetic information encoded in genes which are transmitted from one generation to the next generation in all biological species, and b) information relating to changes in the internal and external environment to which an organism has to adapt to survive. An organism's ability to cope up with the environmental changes depends on neural phenomena. Nature has assigned the task of processing information to brain and neurons.

Just as a computer is an information processing machine the human brain too is an information processing mechanism, but with a major difference. While a computer is an artifact, human brain is a live organ created by nature. Survival of biological species, including humans, depends on their adapting to the environment. Adaptation is built around continuous receipt of information in the form of stimulus (including internal signals) from the surroundings by the brain and responding to those signals. Unlike other biological creations human beings have mind, which can think and express through speech and signs. It is the brain that processes information and stores it in memory. The phenomenon of transformation of information into awareness or knowledge is yet to be understood. The biological basis of information processing has two aspects: a) physiological, and b) mental or psychological. In contrast to the physical basis of information studied in terms of bits and bytes in chapter 10, the biological and psychological approach tries to examine information in its physical (stimulus/data) and mental (perception and meaning) forms, and their relationships, which is central to knowledge phenomena.

NEURAL TRANSMISSION

In order to survive in their environment biological species depend upon processing of information relating to their environment. The mechanism of information processing in higher organisms, such as human beings and other vertebrates are highly advanced and complex. An insight into how the nervous system senses changes in the external and internal environment, process information thus gathered, and frame appropriate responses has helped us in developing artificial intelligence, control systems, and advanced computer brain. The basic units in the nervous system are *neurons*, i.e., the nerve cells. Similar to the functioning of a computer, neural processing of information in organisms consists of input functions carried out by *receptor neurons* carrying incoming signals; central processing looked after by the *central nervous system* (CNS) comprising of the brain and spinal cord; and output functions delivered by neurons named *effectors*. The CNS located in the brain controls and coordinates the activities of the entire nervous system. CNS is a vast neural network handling billions of messages. This vast network consists of a number of sub-networks made up of neurons with distinctive properties. Each subsystem discharges well-defined functions, such as sense perception, reflex action, body immunity and others. The intricate network of neurons in the CNS continually combines the signals from the receptor neurons including from those which provide feedback on the state of the effectors. These neurons with past experience encoded barge the motor neurons with signals which will yield adaptive interactions with the environment (Arbib, 1995). Each neuron functions as an information processor and to know how neuron network works it is necessary to know about the structure and functioning of neurons.

Neurons are the basic units in the nervous system. Neurons, numbering in billions, are joined together to form cord-like fibers called nerves and nerve tissues. Neurons are of different types. Nerves form a network of pathways (circuits) that carry electrochemical impulses (charge, signal, information, pulse, and message) to all parts of the body. Neurons are coupled to receptors and effectors neurons, which are special types of neurons designed to carryout specified functions.

Receptors continuously monitor changes in the environment which act as stimulus (e.g., hearing the word say "Taj Mahal") and convert the stimulus into neural messages called impulses, which in turn are transmitted to the CNS. The neurons in the central system interpret the incoming impulses and decide the response (perceiving the monument Taj Mahal). The responses from the CNS in the form of impulses are transmitted to *sensory neurons*, i.e., neurons carrying sensory information or to *motor neurons* which control *muscles* and glands or to *interneurons* which transmit impulses between sensory and motor neurons.

Working of a Neuron. A neuron is made up of *cell body or soma*, i.e., the central portion, *dendrites and axons* as shown in Fig. 1. The cell body acts as a station for receiving stimulus from dendrites and passes it on to the next neuron as impulses *via* axons. The cell body is filled with a fluid having sodium, potassium and other ions; and is surrounded by a semi-permeable membrane which is sensitive to electro-chemical changes.

Dendrites. Dendrites, which number about six to a neuron, are tube like protrusions from the cell body. A dendrite receives impulses about a change in the environment (stimulus) from an axon of another neuron or sense receptors and carry them into the cell body. A change in the electrical potential between inside and outside the cell membrane induced by a change in the concentration of sodium and potassium ions inside the cell body enables the dendrite to isolate and transmit the incoming impulse to the cell body. Dendrites along with the cell body, thus provide the input. If the difference in electrical potential across the membrane at the *axon hillock*, a point on the cell body from where axon starts, exceeds the threshold point it triggers what is called an *action potential*. An action potential yields a pulse (minute electrical discharge) that propagates along the length of the axon. If the potential difference is small then the pulse generated moves only a short distance and subsides before reaching synaptic terminal, except in sensory cells like rods, cones and bipolar cells of the retina.

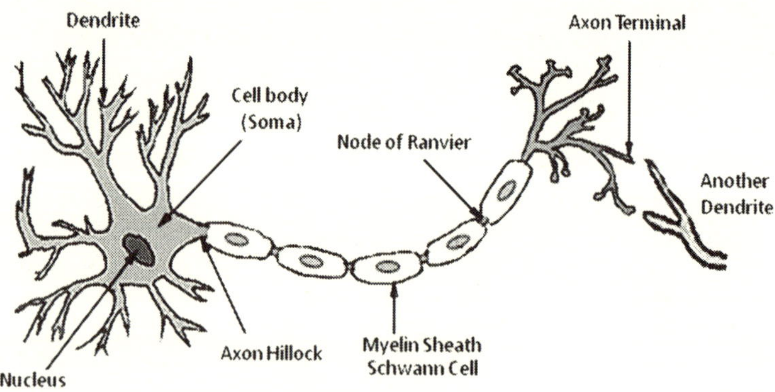

Fig. 1. Structure of a neuron

Axon. Synapse. Plasticity. An axon is a long nerve fiber sprouting out of the cell body at axon hillock. Axon branches out into a number of fine nerve lines, whose terminal is called a *bouton*. A dendrite makes its connection with a bouton separated by a small space known as *synaptic cleft* and the process of transmission of impulse from one nerve-cell with another is called a *synapse*. Some axons have a myelin (an organic chemical) sheath. Transmission of a nerve impulse through an axon with myelin sheath can occur only at the *nodes of Ranvir*, the little gaps along the axon where the successive segments of the myelin sheaths join. On the other hand, transmission of impulses along an axon without the myelin sheath is passive. Schwann cells in the myelin sheaths enable impulses to move faster by by-passing the nodes of Ranvir. When an impulse reaches a bouton certain chemicals called neurotransmitters are released at the synoptic clefts. These neurotransmitters enable the impulse to move to the next neuron by a synapse. At the synapse communication takes place between neurons through the action of neurotransmitters, and the process is called *plasticity* of the synapse. The strength of the connections between nerve cells, and the ability to communicate chemically determine the characteristic of the synapse. Neurotransmitters "link neurons in a chain that can be retraced to evoke a certain movement or feeling or thought, a phenomenon captured in the oft quoted phrase 'neurons that fire together, wire together'. It is at the level of the synapse that neuroplasticity lives or dies" (Holloway, 2003, p. 18). However, the term plasticity is also used very loosely to describe any change taking place in the brain from the creation of new neurons to the remapping of the regions of the brain.

COMPUTATIONAL NEUROSCIENCE

The study of neural transmission of impulses in organisms has contributed to our understanding certain aspects of information phenomena, and has enabled us to create systems analogous to neural networks outside biology. The neural networks which meant prior to 1980s networks of biological neurons constituting the nervous systems in animals is now also used to refer to the technology of parallel computation having computing elements of "artificial neurons". The artificial neurons are loosely modeled on simple properties of biological neurons, usually with adaptive capability to change the strengths of connections between neurons (Arbib,1995). The brain theory has developed largely by the application of computational techniques to model biological neural networks and is named "computational neuroscience". Adaptive parallel computing style of the brain inspired scientists, engineers and physicists to analyze and apply artificial networks with a number of applications, such as artificial intelligence, simulation, control systems, and design of super computers. Neural networks and brain theory incorporate a number of interdisciplinary subjects with interesting results, and in the process both the host discipline and the brought-in disciplines have benefited.

PROCESSING OF GENETIC INFORMATION

James D. Watson and Francis C. Clark in their landmark discovery made in 1953 decoded the structure of deoxyribonucleic acid (DNA) molecule, a component of genes. Their findings have enabled us to understand how DNA initiates and controls the functioning of cells in organisms, including transmission of genetic information. From the structure of DNA molecules biologists established the critical role of DNA in organizing and ordering of life activities at the molecular level of cells. Cells are the basic processing units in all organisms. A cell consists of protein molecules, which serve as processors of all life activities. These proteins are encoded in each cell by genes. Proteins are made up of twenty different amino acids. DNA prescribes and controls the sequence of amino acids, which determine the genetic information of an organism. Ribonucleic acid (RNA) carries out the instructions encoded in a DNA. Another type of nucleic acid called tRNA (transfer RNA) helps in linking in the correct order the amino acids of a protein chain in several cellular structures. DNA is compared to a storehouse or cellular library that contains all the information required to build the cells and tissues of an organism. Replication of this information in any species ensures continuity of genetic traits from one generation to its next generation (Lodish, 2000).

Transmission of Genetic Information. Heredity is genetically acquired characteristics transmitted from parents to their offspring through genes. Mechanism of transmission of genetic traits is explained through the functional model of a gene.

Model of a Gene. Genes are made up of molecules of the nucleic acid DNA. DNA combined with proteins called histones, together makeup rod like bodies called chromosomes in the nuclei of a cell. DNA represents the hereditary material. Genes carry the genetic information codes to the next progeny through the synthesis of protein molecules. The total DNA in the chromosomes of an organism is referred to as its *genome.* DNA is a thin chainlike molecule made up of smaller chemical units known as nucleotides. A nucleotide contains deoxyribose (sugar), phosphate, and a nitrogenous base. Genetic message is made-up of the sequences of nitrogenous bases in the DNA. A DNA molecule is composed of two strands of nucleotides paired to each other in a twisted rope ladder like structure in the shape of a *double helix*. Each nucleotide contains one of four types of bases — adenine (A), cytosine (C), guanine (G) and thymine (T). A, C, G and T bases function as genetic alphabets encoded with genetic information. These bases pair with each other according to set rules to form rungs of the DNA ladder. The pattern of pairing of the bases is such that reading the sequence of bases along one side of the ladder is the complimentary sequence on the other side. The sequence of bases in a DNA determines the composition, structure and above all the function of the cellular protein. Before a cell divides the two strands of a DNA gets split lengthwise separating the base pairs. Each of the split strand picks up free nucleotides from the cell nucleus and pair with the matching bases, thus replicating the sequence of bases found in the mother DNA strands. This results in two double strands DNA. Each daughter DNA receives all the characteristics of the parent DNA molecules, thus replication of gene takes place. The transfer process involves the synthesis of polypeptide protein chains using the information present in the gene by employing the genetic code that relates nucleotide sequence to amino acid sequence.

Synthesis of protein takes place according to instructions carried by a gene, which is called *gene expression*. Protein synthesis takes place in two steps - *transcription* and *translation*. Transcription process generates different types of RNAs required for protein synthesis from genomic DNA. The nucleotide sequence which determines the genetic information is copied into mRNA (messenger RNA). The single strand of mRNA then leaves the nucleus and serves as a blueprint for the synthesis of protein, i.e. *protein translation*. In the translation process tRNA interprets the amino acid sequence in the mRNA. While the required energy for all chemical reactions, including protein synthesis, is supplied by adenosine triphosphate (ATP) molecules in the cell, the initiation and control of chemical reactions are regulated by catalytic proteins called *enzymes* (Lorkowski and Cullen, 2003; Encyclopaedia Britannica, 2007, Vol. 19).

DNA Data. Bioinformatics. Sequencing of genomes of each biological species generates extremely large volumes of DNA data, which has many applications. Without the use of computers collecting, analyzing and providing instant access to the data is impossible. Bioinformatics, a sub-branch of computer science is functioned to analyze DNA, structure and sequence other proteins, and make that information available. Applying bioinformatics techniques a number of databases covering specific topics, such as gene sequence, protein structure, genomic mapping, analyzed data on protein multiple sequence alignment have been created. Bioinformatics employs predictive techniques, sequence assembly and finishing methods, phylogenic analysis, and many more. The objective of bioinformatics is to assist in gene discovery, in the design of molecular modeling, site-directed mutagenesis, and other types of experiments that can potentially reveal hitherto unknown relationships with respect to the structure and function of genes and proteins, and in comparative genome analysis (Baxevanis and Quellette, 2002).

DNA Data. An exhaustive source for DNA data has been the Human Genome Project. The project was initiated by the U.S. government and carried out by the Human Genome Organization with the participation of the United Kingdom, Italy, France, Russia and Japan; and involving scientists from all over the world. The main task of the project was to carry out the complete sequencing of the entire human genome and identify the structure of each gene. The project began in 1987. The first phase was completed in 2000 and the results were published in 2001. There was also a private commercial initiative (J. Craig Venter's Celera Genomics) which too ventured to sequence the majority of human genome and announced the completion of the task simultaneously in 2000. The first DNA Data banks were established in USA at the Gen Bank of the National Institute of Health, Bethesda and in Germany at the EMBL Data Base at the European Molecular Biology Laboratory, Heidelberg. With the finding of complete genome of several organisms it is now possible to make comparative analysis of genomes, and the field of study is known as *genomics* (Lodish, 2000).

A more daunting task than that of genome mapping is that of *proteome* mapping. Proteome refers to the full set of proteins expressed in a given organism. The study of spatial-temporal harvesting, identification, and quantification of proteins in a given sample and their specific biochemical process is named *proteomics*. To research for proteome data and complete mapping of proteome by singular initiative is well beyond our present capabilities (Lambert and Schriemer, 2005).

GENOMIC RESEARCH, HUMAN GENOME PROJECT, AND APPLICATIONS

Human Genome Project is one of the outstanding

achievements of molecular biology with a number of possibilities for the future of mankind.

Genomic research has become a fertile field for the development of a number of novel applications and also gene based biotech industries (Das, 2000). The list of industries includes molecular medicine, microbial genomics, genetically modified seeds, and livestock breeding. The application areas include bio-archaeology, anthropology, evolution and human migration, Personal Genome mapping, DNA computing, and DNA forensics.

Personal Genome Map (PGM). PGM is an individual's biomedical identity card detailing how out of six billion base pairs of nucleotides, contributed equally from father and mother, the base pairs are sequenced in an individual. From the PGM one can get to know about an individual's generic data, such as health (like genetic defects and disease proneness), psychological behaviour pattern, genealogy, personal identification data, and the like. The PMG can be misused by insurance companies, law enforcement agencies, criminals, and even friends and neighbors (Church, 2006).

Genotype and Phenotype. The issue of heredity vs. environment (nature vs. nurture) has confronted biologists, psychologists, sociologists, and philosophers for a long time. An organism's hereditary make-up is shaped by genetic information transmitted by parents, which is called genotype; and the results of complex interaction of the organism with its environment, which is named phenotype. Transfer of hereditary information is accounted by gene expression, which describes the whole process of genetic mechanism, whereas in phenotypes the transfer of information is through neural mechanisms. In summary, a human being's total makeup is dictated by two types of information: hereditary and neural. Heredity is controlled by information transmitted by gene. Neural information which accounts for sensual and cognition, body's internal mechanism and external behavior are governed by neural phenomena. Thus, information forms a fundamental force governing all biological organisms.

DNA Computer. Similarities between Turing machine, the computing machine conceived by Alan Turing, the British mathematician and the functioning of DNA as an information processor in biological cells prompted scientists to think of using DNA molecules as a computing device. In 1994, Leonard M. Adleman of the University of Southern California solved traditional problems using a DNA computer. Though working DNA computers have been built in recent years (Weizmann Institute, Israel in 2001 and by others) and DNA chips are produced by some bioengineering enterprises, commercial introduction of DNA computers has to wait for some more years. Some biotechnology experts reckon the possibility of creating hybrid computers by combining the technologies of DNA computer and the silicon chip-based computer. Meanwhile research is also progressing to build RNA–based computer, which will be more powerful than the DNA. Presently, DNA computing has found applications in mathematical computing, and as a sensor to identify abnormalities in body functioning.

In a DNA computer, DNA is the "software" and the enzymes are the "hardware". The output is in the form of a DNA strand, which has to be interpreted by human beings, unlike the traditional computer where the output is displayed on screen or comes out as printout. DNA computer uses a four digit code made up of the four base pairs of A, T, C and G instead of the binary system of "0" and "I". The Boolean operation of "and" is done by separating the strands and "or" by mixing two DNA solutions together. Using enzymes DNA strands can be functionalized to do logical and mathematical manipulations. Storage density of information in DNA computer is trillion times more than that of a silicon chip-based computer and has immense parallel processing power. However, DNA computers have some limitations. In a DNA computer the functions of a silicon chip is carried out by collections of DNA spots denoting single genes in the form of an array on a material base, such as glass, plastic or silicon; and the purpose is to identify and/or calculate the large amount of genes simultaneously- considering this way it is not computing (Chellaiah, 2007)

PROCESSING OF SENSORY INFORMATION

To understand how the human brain processes information it is necessary to know the structure and functions of the nervous system. Life is controlled by the nervous system made up of the *central nervous system*(CNS), and the *peripheral nervous system.* The peripheral system acts as a messenger carrying stimulus from the outside environment and from within the body to the CNS and back. The central nervous system is made up of the brain and the spinal cord. While the brain constructs our mental life, the spinal cord controls the physical body functions. The spinal cord made up of nerve bundles connects the brain with all other parts of the body. The brain is the centre which receives stimuli and interprets them into cognitive functions like learning and knowledge formation. The parts of the central nervous system are shown in Fig. 2.

The brain consists of two parts - forebrain and brainstem. Brainstem is further divided into 'between brain' (diencephalon), midbrain (mesencephalon), and hindbrain (rhombencephalon). Diencephalon houses epithalamus, hypothalamus, thalamus and pituitary glands. Thalamus receives stimulus from sensory organs (except from nose) and transmits them to cortex. Some parts of diencephalon are involved in regulatory functions of the body and behaviour. Except *tactum* area of midbrain which receives visual and auditory signals other areas of midbrain are not directly involved in cognitive functions, and so is the hindbrain excepting *medulla oblongata* which passes impulses between the cortex and the spinal cord. However, cerebellum is now considered to play a part in learning and in higher cognitive functions.

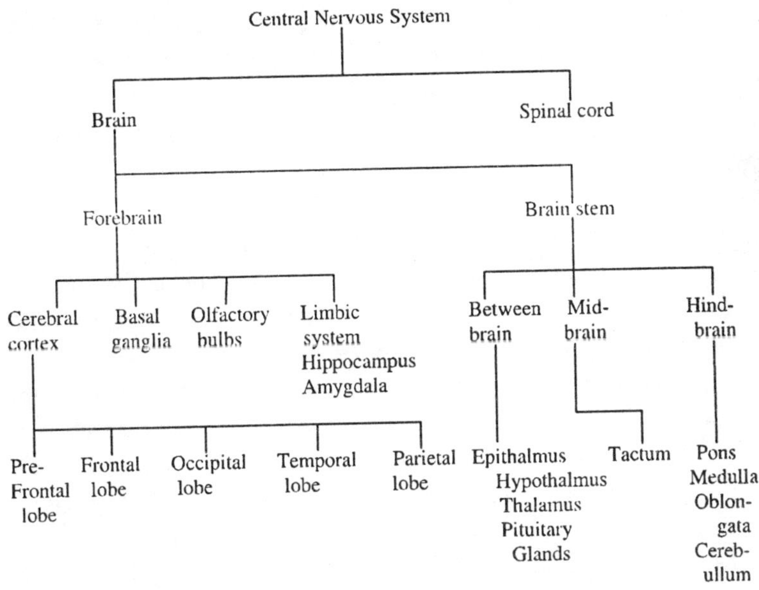

Fig. 2. Parts of central nervous system

The forebrain (*cerebrum*) is the area that specializes in cognitive functions, such as perception, learning and knowledge formation. The forebrain is divided into *cerebral cortex, basal ganglia, olfactory bulbs,* and *limbic system*. Of the limbic parts only *hippocampus* (seahorse) is thought to play a role in memory formation besides affection and spatial orientation.

Cerebral cortex located in the forebrain processes sensory signals, which accounts for perception and consciousness. The cerebral cortex occupies an area of 100,000 to 200,000 mm. Its wrinkled and folded structure embedded with an array of nerve tissues and neurons makes it a vast operational theatre. The cerebral cortex is divided into: a) the frontal lobe, b) occipital lobes, the area for visual perception, c) the temporal lobe, the location for primary and secondary processing of auditory signals, long-term storage of sensory information and emotional part of sensation, and d) parietal lobe, the portion that seems to integrate sensory information processed in the other three lobes participates in visualization process and in direction guidance. *Somatosensory* cortex, a part of *post central gyrus* of the parietal lobe processes signals of touch and pain. The frontal lobe made up of cortical tissues is connected to other cortical regions and subcortical tissues with numerous pathways. Earlier, the frontal lobe was considered to be the seat of intelligence, consciousness, ethical values, and similar mental faculties. Subsequent research has shown that the frontal lobe is also involved in complex cognitive functions like speech formulation, planning, problem solving besides motor control involving tactile or visual guidance. Thus, cerebral cortex forms the supreme operating area for producing perception and knowledge (Stillings, 1995). Memory is of different forms, e.g., immediate memory and short-term memory. Specific areas in the brain are associated with specific memories (Sadava et al., 2008). The structure of the brain is shown in Fig. 3.

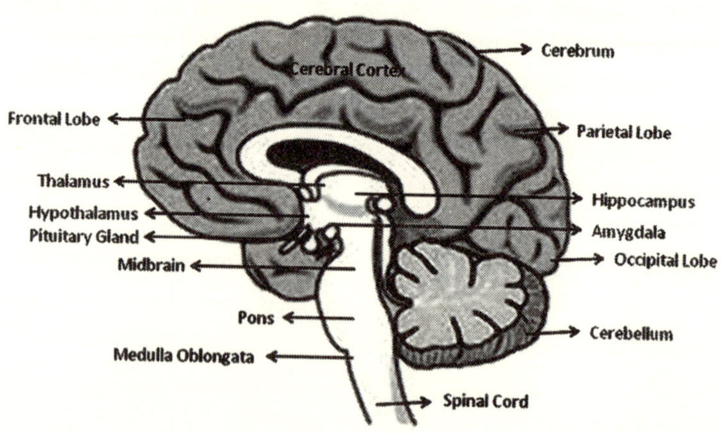

Fig. 3. The structure of the brain

NEURAL BASIS OF INFORMATION AND KNOWLEDGE

All biological species, including humans, process information for survival. Only human beings with their most advanced brain are capable of processing information in numerous ways and depths, and transform information into knowledge. A simple example is "cross-modal association", the unique ability of human mind/brain to transfer information received by one sense mode to that of another. This characteristic enables numerous associations of an idea derived from one sense organ with other sense modes, which in turn endows human beings with special creative ability to plan ahead and influence future (Neelameghan, 1979).

Human perception and knowledge are the results of information phenomena accomplished by neurons, and directed by the central nervous system. Cognitive scientists explore information phenomenon as an information processing mechanism or as a connectionist phenomenon. The connectionist approach is also known as connectionism, distributed processing or neural networks. A system's information–processing capabilities and the mechanism through which information is processed together constitute the system's *cognitive architecture*. Sometimes, the information-processing approach is referred to as the classical version of cognitive architecture (Stillings, 1995). Information-processing model is built on the principles of a computer, whereas connectionism follows the pattern of human brain functioning. The difference between the two approaches becomes clear when we consider the basic features of the two shown in Table-1.

Table 1. Distinguishing features of information processing by computer and brain

System's components/ functions	*Computer system*	*Human brain system*
1. Input	As electronic charges in binary code	Neural signals in analog form
2. Processing	Programs built artificially	Neural process of the brain
3. Commutation	Serially at incredible speed	Parallel at slow speed

4. Storage	Memory. Storing data in binary code	Memory. Storing as neural configurations
5. Output	In electronic digital form	Cognition/awareness in analog form
6. Role of language	Not relevant	Plays a unique role
7. Organism factors	No impact	Affects cognitively

Information-Processing Approach. Information-processing systems are presented as abstract models. Fig. 4 shows a basic model.

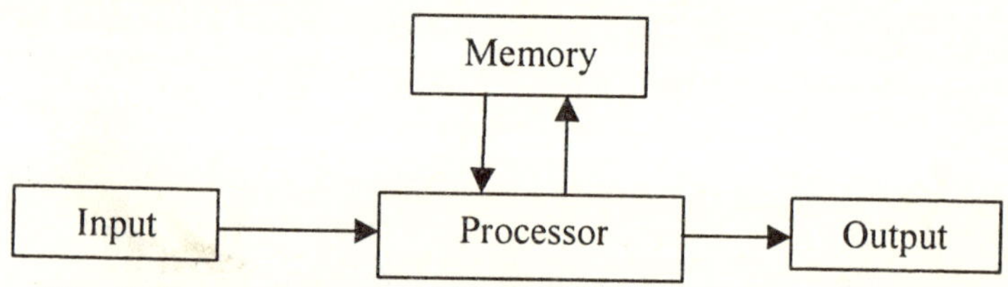

Fig. 4. Basic model of an information processing system

The components of the model and their basic characteristics are explained below:

Input. It is in the form of sensory signals conveyed by sense organs.

Output. It is in the form of consciousness, knowledge, and other cognitive mental features. Output includes appropriate neural signals conveyed to motor system to execute responses.

Processor. The processor transforms sensory signals into cognition, thoughts, and action instructions. The human processor works in two stages: input stage and cognitive stage. In the input stage, the receptor neurons transduces the incoming sense signals in the form of energy and matter (light, heat, force, and matter as in taste and smell) into neural electrochemical compositions representing information, which will be used at the cognitive stage.

Memory. It is the storage space where processed information is stored as representations or images. The representations are in the form of neural configurations. In the information-processing approach representation takes the form of a symbolic structure.

It is hypothesized that cognition is a formal physical symbol manipulation process with the functions of semantic interpretations that take care of meaning and "adaptiveness" to the environment. To carry out the cognitive functions the symbol system has to be flexible. The system's flexibility is attributed to its ability to access large amounts of representations, i.e., structured symbols stored in long-term memory. However, the validity of the physical symbol theory is disputed by many cognitive scientists. It seems that the human nervous system is a complete symbol system with enormous cognitive flexibility. Van Neumann's random access memory principle found in general purpose computer does not help explain the cognitive flexibility of the brain. Human memory does not seem to operate with discrete, numerically addressable locations (Stillings, 1995). At the same time, the nervous system functions in a dedicated manner in processing signals received from different sense organs. It is believed that cognitive processes are programmable, in the sense that the central processor has built-in facilities to accomplish an unlimited range of information processes (Stillings, 1995).

Language. According to present reckoning, language is represented in an unconscious propositional form that is later translated into natural language at the time of expressing the thought. A proposition is taken to be the simplest complete unit of thought (corresponding to "sign" in semiotics, the field of study of signs).

Connectionist model. The distinctive features of connectionist models relate to representation of information, cognitive/mental features, memory, and language. These models make use of data obtained from mapping the structure and different functions of brain using techniques such as electroencephalography (EEG) and functional magnetic resonance imaging (fMRI), cognitive experimentations, and reasoning.

Representation. Sensory information carried by stimulus in the form of physical energy is converted into patterns of neural compositions (a kind of neural energy), i.e., representations. The representations are the basic units that are used in all subsequent cognitive processes. Not all sensory input is converted into representations. These internal representations have their own characteristics, such as: transitory existence (short-term memory) and permanent existence (long-term memory). Formation of representations is a continually evolving process involving connecting of information units through reduction and elaboration. Elaborations play a key role in shaping what eventually is understood and remembered (Best, 1999). Classification of representations leads to categories, which assist higher level cognitive processes.

Cognition Has a Functional Value. An event (or a mental image) can be described as a neural phenomenon and also as a mental phenomenon. As a neural phenomenon, the event is explained in terms of neural activity. As a mentai event, it is explained in cognitive terms like schema, thinking and awareness. Though terminologically the two forms are independent, yet they are coterminous, i.e., two faces of the same coin. Not all cognitive events are mental events. There could be cognition without mentality (Best, 1999).

Consciousness occurs when stimuli is converted into electrical signals which the brain can understand. Earlier hypothesis was that sensory perception is caused by linear transmission of signals along discrete neural routes between stimulus receptors and higher processing centers like neurocortex in the brain. Later research on rats has shown that signals are encoded in the spatiotemporal activity patterns of entire neural ensembles. It is further surmised that mammalian brain, more likely, depends on highly distributed neural ensembles dynamically formed by broadly tuned cells in attaining perceptual capability (Nicolelis and Ribeiro, 2006).

Memory. All cognitive and mental productions are formed by neurons and groups of neurons acting upon the information stored in memory. Sensory information formed in the short-term memory is not sufficient by itself to achieve higher level mental functions like thinking, decision-making, and creativity. Such functions are possible only by acting upon representations drawn from long-term memory. The mechanism of semantics, awareness and other aspects of mind, and also of memory are further described in later sections.

Cognitive scientists divide knowledge (and also memory) into *procedural* and *declarative* knowledge. Procedural knowledge refers to knowledge involving skills, reasoning, problem solving, and the like; it is related to "knowing how", and is dynamic. Declarative knowledge pertains to facts and descriptions; it is related to "knowing what", and is static in nature. Memory is also categorized into *semantic memory* and *episodic memory*. Semantic memory refers to storing of items of knowledge about the world and happenings that is shared by many. Episodic memory is limited to items of knowledge belonging to one's own experience and is linked to a particular time or place. A third categorization makes a distinction between *implicit cognition/implicit memory and explicit cognition/explicit memory.* Implicit cognition works at the unconscious level and the explicit cognition works at the conscious level. It is generally accepted that most cognitive tasks including perception, memory, problem solving, and creativity involve both implicit and explicit processing. Processing of implicit and explicit thoughts is done separately by the memory. (Leitman, 2000). Implicit knowledge and explicit knowledge also have different meanings than the one stated here. The categorization of knowledge and memory has implications for our understanding the nature of knowledge, working of memory, and are useful in analyzing thinking process.

Sousa's Connectionist Model. The connectionist model developed by David A. Sousa, keeping in mind learning and higher order thinking, in his book *How the Brain Learns* (Sousa, 2006) is briefly described here.

The human brain is an open parallel-processing system continually interacting with the information from the external environment and internal signals conveyed by sensory receptors. Information from the senses passes through the sensory register (explained later) into immediate memory, and then to working memory for conscious processing.

Sensory stimuli enter the brain as a stream of electrical impulses. These impulses are generated by neuron firings in sequence and transmitted along specified sensory pathways. There is functional specialization with each type of neurons processing specific types of sensory impulses, and make the brain perceive them as vision, sound, touch, taste and smell as the case may be.

All input sensory information (other than smell) first reaches thalamus located in the limbic system. Thalamus in association with *reticular activation system* (SRS), a portion of the brainstem, first screens all the incoming bits of information and the process is known as *sensory register*. The sensory register screens the incoming data against the past experiences and retains only those impulses considered important, all happening in milliseconds. This screening is a continuous process and is known as *perceptual* or *sensory filtering*. The sensory register holds the retained information for a very brief span of time (in seconds) and is called *sensory memory*. The filtered data then move to cortex area through two short-duration temporary memories, namely *immediate* memory and *working* memory. Immediate memory and working memory together constitute short-term memory. The immediate memory processes incoming information on a priority basis in the order of survival or reflexive importance, emotional relevance, and finally of new learning. The information from the immediate memory is passed on to working memory located in frontal lobe, where conscious processing aided by representations drawn from long-term storage, if necessary, takes place. The working memory is a short-term memory with limited capacity to process an average of two to seven items of information, depending on the state of development of the brain. Information in the short-term memory is further assessed for its relevancy based on past experience before it is encoded for retention in long-term memory. The two important criteria that decide whether the information is to be encoded for long-term memory are sense and meaning. If the new item of information makes sense and/or meaning then the item is encoded by hypothalamus for retention in long-term memory storage. In the long-term memory neurons undergo change in structure. If the information is not stored within 24 hours of knowing then the chances are the item is not stored in the long-term memory, will not respond to recall. The term long-term memory refers to the process of storing and retrieving information, where as long-term storage means the storage location in the brain.

The contents of the long-term storage constitute our conscious world, the world of our consciousness, knowledge and belief. In other words, the long-term storage provides us our worldview of the self and the creation. The concept of self is shaped by our past experiences and forms the basis of our response to events.

Phenomenon of Memory. Memories are formed when a network of neurons fire together on activation. Memories are stored in small bits and are distributed in sites throughout cerebrum. Stimulus causes impulses which are carried to concerned sensory area in the brain. The impulses move along the axon to the synapse. At the synapse, the release of neurotransmitter chemicals transfer the signals as chemical messages to the dendrite of another neuron. As the messages enter the neighboring neurons, they initiate a series of electrochemical reactions that cause the second neuron to "fire", i.e., generate a signal. The process continues as a chain reaction exciting more neurons to fire. When this happens repeatedly the neurons form a network and fire together when activated at a later time, thus forming memory.

Until recently, neuroscientists had believed that neurons are the main communicators of messages in the functioning of brain. Learning and thinking processes were thought to be carried out and controlled solely by neuron networks. It is now established that non-neural *glial* cells, which outnumber neurons nine to one, influence the formation of synapses and help determine the strength and phase of neural connections over time; such changes are essential to learning and storing in long-term memory. Glial cells have their own networks parallel to neural networks facilitating communication between them. Recent advances have shown that glial cells have the power to alter neural signals at the synaptic gaps between neurons and can influence where synapses are formed. Interestingly, the beginning of this new insight is traced to the discovery of large number of glial cells in the dead brain of Albert Einstein by Marian C. Diamond of the University of California at Berkley (Fields, 2004).

Brain and Mind. From the viewpoint of knowledge, the vital issue is how impulses(electrical charge carrying information) become consciousness(knowledge). Brain theory seeks to analyze how the brain guides the behaving organism in its interaction with the dynamic world around it. Much of what is mental is sub-symbolic and /or unconscious. However, it seems to be clear that some mental activity (e.g., contemplation) need not result in overt "interactions with the dynamic real world," and much of the brain's activity (e.g., controlling normal breathing) is not mental. Face recognition seems to be a mental activity, which we do not carryout through symbol manipulation. Earlier, *cognitive psychology* tried to explain mind in terms of information theory and symbol manipulation, but now the emphasis is on *connectionism*, which model human thought and behaviour in terms of parallel distributed networks of neuron-like units, with learning mediated by changes in strength of the connections between these elements (Arbib, 1995).

Closure

Human brain transforms stimulus received through the sense organs in the form of signals representing the surrounding world into consciousness. In this process the main actor is neuron. Processing of signals is a neurobiological process and is of two types: transmission of genetic information from parents to their offsprings and processing of sensory information.

In genetic transmission, the principal actor is DNA. Genetic message is made up of the sequences of nitrogenous bases in the nucleotides of a DNA. A DNA molecule is composed of two chains of nucleotides arranged in the shape of a *double helix*. The process of transmitting genetic information in the form of combinations of four bases in a predetermined order is called protein synthesis. Protein synthesis takes place in two stages– *transcription* and *translation*. In transcription RNA molecules which carry the genetic information are generated from the gnomic DNA. In translation process newly generated RNAs recombine to form new baby DNAs. DNA research has thrown open a number of new areas of applications, including bioinformatics.

The study of sensory processing of information, which accounts for consciousness/knowledge, has followed either Information Processing approach or Connectionist model. The former is based on the principles of the working of a computer. It is hypothesized that cognition is a formal symbol manipulation process with the functions of semantic interpretations that take care of meaning and "adaptiveness" to the environment. In the Connectionist model stimulus conveying sensory information in the form of electrical impulses is converted into neural representations adopting parallel processing. These representations serve as the basic units in all subsequent acts like advanced cognition, memory formation, and initiation of language.

The study of the purely subjective phenomenon of consciousness, which belongs to the disciplines of philosophy and religion, is now also the concern of biologists, especially neuroscientists and cognitive psychologists. Consciousness is equated with the state of being aware or awake, knowing about the self and the world around us; and the feeling of how it feels to be me. Neuroscientists are hoping that brain imaging and electrical recording of neural changes will reveal the 'neural correlate of consciousnesses'. There is no single part of brain that switches on when conscious and switches off when quiet. Even if we find a pattern of brain activity that correlates with conscious experience it does not explain why should the activity of a mass of neurons feel like anything? Why does a rose appear red? One explanation is that consciousness is an emergent property of active networks of neurons, in other words, something that arises from the interaction between these neurons, but which is not found in the neurons by themselves. Another theory attributes consciousness to the weird quantum states; yet another tries to explain consciousness mathematically in terms of synchronous oscillating brain waves. On the extreme side are the views that our brains are ill-equipped to understand their own consciousness or that consciousness is just an illusion (New Scientist, 2004). The mystery of how the brain transforms tiny electrical discharges of billions of neurons circulating through complex neural networks (physical carriers of information) into consciousness (knowledge) remains unresolved.

REFERENCES

Arbib, Michael A. Ed. The Handbook of Brain Theory and Neural Networks. Cambridge (Mass.), The MIT Press, 1995.

Baxevanis, Andreas D. and Quellette, B.F. Francis. Eds. Bioinformatics: A PracticalGuide to the Analysis of Genes and Proteins. Ed.2. Singapore, John Wiley & Sons (ASIA), 2002.

Best, Johm B. Cognitive Psychology. Ed.5. Belmont (CA), Wadsworth Publishing, 1999.

Chellaiah, S. It is in the DNA too. *Business Line*, Monday, Nov.12, 2007. P. 3. (e World).

Chellaiah, S. Computing Differently: A look at the DNA computer: Features and applications. *Business Line*, Monday, Nov. 19, 2007. (e World).

Church, George M. Genomes for all. *Scientific American* 294 (1): 32-40, Jan. 2006.

Das, Somnath. Human Genome Project- The millennium gift to humankind. *Science and Culture* 66 (9-10): 328-330, Sept.-Oct., 2000.

Encyclopaedia Britannica, The New. Ed.15. Chicago, Encyclopaedia Britannica, 2007. Vol. 19. Pp. 699- 718: Genetics and Heredity, The Principles of

Fields, R. Douglas. The other half of the brain. *Scientific American* 290 (4): 26-33, April, 2004.

Holloway, Marguerite, The mutable brain. *Scientific American* 289 (3): 79-85, 2003.

Lambert, Sheena and Schriemer, David C. Proteomics and Mass-Spectrometry for the Biological Researcher. Pp. 181-209. *In* Sensen, Christoph W. Ed. Handbook of Genome Research. Vol.1: Genomics, Proteomics...Legal Issues. Weinheim, Wiley-VCH Verlag, 2005).

Leitman, Leib. Implicit Cognition and Thoughts. Pp. 431-453. *In* Holyoak, Lodish, Harvey et.al. Molecular Cell Biology. Ed. 4. New York, W.H. Freeman, 2000.

Lodish, Harvey et al. Molecular Cell Biology. Ed. 4. New York, W.H. Freeman, 2000.

Lorkowski, Stefan and Cullen, Paul. Eds. Analyzing Gene Expression: A Handbook of Methods and Pitfalls. Vol.1: Analyzing Gene Expression. Weinheim, Wiley-VCH, 2003.

Neelameghan, A. Expressions of Time in Information Sience and Their Implications. Pp,103-118. *In* Greenway, Frank. Ed. Time and the Sciences. Paris, Unesco, 1979.

New Scientist. 182(2463):24-33, September 04, 2004: 'The mysteries of life'.

Nicolelis, Miguel A.L. and Ribeiro, Sidarta. Seeking the neural code. *Scientific American* 295 (6); 48-55, Dec. 2006.

Sadava, David et al. Life: The Science of Biology. Ed. 8. Sundarland (MA), Sinauer Associates, 2008

Sousa, David A. How the Brain Learns. Ed. 3. Thousand Oaks (Calif.), Corwin Press, 2006.

Stillings, Neil A. et al. Cognitive Science: An Introduction. Ed.2. Cambridge (Mass.), MIT Press, 1995.

10
INFORMATION AS PHYSICAL REALITY

The term 'information' in common usage refers to externalized form of knowledge, i.e., a message conveying meaning, where as in communication engineering and physical usage information refers to a signal transmitting a coded message generally using binary code, such as "0" and "1". In science, particularly in physics, information is sought to be understood as a scientific concept with its underlying theories. Von Baeyer following etymology of the word *information* interprets information as transfer of form from one media to another. The term transfer means communication and form is about relationships. Transfer of form from one media to another necessitates coding (Von Baeyer, 2003). Thus, information is defined as the communication of messages, which is the focus of Shannon's theory of communication.

PHYSICAL THEORY OF INFORMATION

The foundations of the mechanistic study of information were laid by C.E. Shannon with the formulation of the theory of communication (also known as Shannon's information theory). Shannon explains the communication process (Shannon, 1948) in terms of: a) a source of message, b) an encoder, c) the message, d) a channel, e) a decoder, and f) a receiver of message. A message from the source is first coded into an artificial language (e.g., Morse code), and the coded message is transmitted through a channel (e.g., telephone cable). At the receiving end of the channel the coded message is decoded, which then reaches the receiver. Three factors that affect the reliability and efficiency of a communication system are: a) noise, b) entropy, and c) feedback.

Noise is the unwanted external interference that diminishes the accuracy of the communication and possibly distorts the message. Entropy is the property or the natural tendency of systems to be in a state of chaos, diffusion and distortion. Human society can be considered as a dynamic open system in constant interaction with information. The time-binding acts of man to control his environment create information. The continuous addition of information to the system increases negative entropy. Negative entropy helps reduce uncertainty, imposes order, and prevents the system from tending towards chaos (Neelameghan, 1979). A common practice followed, knowingly or unknowingly, to overcome the adverse effects of entropy in communication is the repetition of words, i.e., redundancy. A considerable portion of words used in writing and in normal conversation are redundant, but they serve the purpose of restoring loss of information or reducing misinterpretation that occurs due to distractions and other limitations of human mind to comprehend. Both redundancy and negative entropy act at different levels, and hence their impact on the receiver of the message varies. Feedback is the mechanism by which a system senses changes in the system and feeds back that information to the controller for evolving necessary responses. The response of one party to the message of the other party in an interpersonal encounter is often based on the feedback received on the reaction of the other party. The major drawback of Shannon's theory is that it interprets communication solely in statistical terms and ignores cognitive, emotional and aesthetic aspects. A computer receives its input message in the form of electrical impulses. The binary code "0" and "1" used for coding a message is generated by impulses by means of ON- OFF- ON- OFF- - - switching mode. This mechanism is carried out by semiconductors, also called *chips*, made of silicon. This is the basis of physical transmission of information in all computer and electronic communication systems. Crucial to the development of physical transmission of information are: a) increasing the speed of transmission, b) creation of storage medium capable of handling and storing mega volumes of information in the range of terabytes (= 1000^4 or 10^{12} bytes) which are problems of physical nature. Some of the enticing prospects that can have quantum impact on the growth of information include: a) development of new materials and technologies capable of storing very large volumes of data; b) use of optical signal transmission instead of the current mode of electronic frequency to create higher bandwidths for transmission; and c) replacing electrons by particles of light to enhance speed of transmission; d) and development of quantum computers to handle mega-volumes of computation (Von Baeyer, 2003). All these developments are on the physical aspects of information and do not address the mental aspects directly.

Physics of Information. Information, which has been the central focus of communication engineering, cybernetics and artificial intelligence (AI), is increasingly drawing the attention of natural science and more particularly physics. Computation of data by a computer is done with the real physical degrees of freedom, obeying the laws of physics, and using parts, such as bits and neurons. This interface of physics and computation, viewed from a very fundamental level, poses the question how do the laws restrict the processes of storing, changing one configuration of an array of bits (0s and 1s) into another configuration and transmitting that information. Rolf Landauer concludes that information handling is limited by the laws of physics, and the number of parts available in the universe; the laws of physics are, in turn, limited by the range of information processing available. This view is in contrast to the prevalent notion that laws of physics are independent of the contents and history of the physical universe (Landauer, 1991). Efficiency of information transmission is governed by the laws of thermodynamics, which impose a limit on the level of efficiency beyond which it can not go. Similarly, the speed of transmission is subjected to Einstein's Special Theory of Relativity which says that nothing can move faster than the speed of light which is 1,86,000 miles per second. This shows that the relativistic speed limits imposed by classical mechanics and the uncertainty principles of the quantum mechanics set by Heisenberg are also applicable to information. It is not surprising that information (physical) too shares the weird features of quantum mechanics when dealing with quantum information and teleportation. Quantum information is very fragile and any attempt to track its movement ends up in its destruction. At this level of analysis, information seems to follow "yes" and "no" principle in respect of knowledge analogous to wave and particle characteristics of motion in quantum physics (Sigfried, 2000). This could be interpreted to mean that information in a cognitive environment takes the form of knowledge and outside that environment information remains physical. Information is everywhere, it is distributed throughout the universe, and holding of information is an inherent characteristic of everything in the universe. Moreover, many scientists are now willing to concede that information belongs to the same fundamental category as that of time, space, matter, and energy. To physicists, all physical systems store information. Rocks, atom bombs, and galaxies too register and process information. Every electron, proton and other elementary particles store bits of data; and every time two such particles interact those bits are transformed. Physical existence and information are inextricably linked. In other words, as proclaimed by John Wheeler, it is "It from bit" (Lloyd and Jack Ng, 2004).

Quantum Computing. Next phase of information technology is expected to be engineered by quantum computing and nanotechnology. Quantum bits (*qubits*) harness the properties of elementary particles such as proton, neutron and electron, which exist in dual or multi states at the same time. For employing quantum mechanics to computation and quantum information capturing and controlling single quantum states is a prerequisite. In the last forty years many techniques to control single quantum systems have been developed, but it is a long way to go to fully harness the quantum power for complex and large-scale applications (Nielsen and Chung, 2002).

Quantum computing opens up enormous possibilities of quantum parallel processing, quantum entanglement, teleportation, and super dense coding. Presently, computers operate on the logic of serial processing. In this a task is divided into elementary operations, which are then carried out one at a time. Attempts so far to effect parallel processing by using two or more processors to work on the different aspects of a problem simultaneously have not been entirely successful. In contrast, quantum computers have simultaneity built into it. Compared to chip based computers the efficiency and power of quantum computers are extremely high. For example, to execute a classical algorithm using a terahertz (10^{12} Hz) would require 10^{24} steps which would take 1,50,000 years, where as a quantum computer would solve the same problem taking 10^{10} steps and complete the task in less than a second. Once technology succeeds in producing quantum neurons through quantum cellular automat employing nanotechnology, it will open the era of quantum computers (Murali and Padmanaban, 2007). At present, small quantum computers capable of doing a small number of operations have been successfully developed. In the area of cryptography, the technique of communicating secret messages over long distances and prototypes of quantum cryptography using qubits have been developed.

From quantum computer to black hole computers is an audacious jump of scientific thinking and speculation. Contrary to Einstein's General Theory of Relativity which says that a black hole only admits matter with no escape, latest speculation is that information can escape from a black hole. A black hole too computes. The size of its memory space is proportional to the square of its computation. The quantum-mechanical nature of information bestows computational property to a black hole by not destroying information that goes in. One theory is that entanglement mechanism which enables teleportation might work for black holes to make escape of photons at event horizon of a black hole (Lloyd and Jack Ng, 2004).

Given the universal existence of information and certain mysteriousness about information, there is a strong belief that an information (physical) approach to understand the deepest mysteries of the universe and the objects within it may have "the power to resolve many mysteries about quantum physics, life, and the universe. It is a new scientific view of science focused on the idea that information is the ultimate 'substance' from which all things are made" (Sigfried, 2000, p. 26). In fact, the agenda for the information approach was set by John Archibald Wheeler, an authority on quantum physics, when he said: "no element in the description of physics shows itself as closer to primordial than the elementary quantum phenomenon, that is, the elementary devise- intermediate act of posing a yes- no physical question and eliciting an answer... every physical quantity, every it, derives its ultimate significancé from bits"(Wheeler, 1999 cited by Sigfried, 2000, p.5).

AFFECTIVE AND NON-AFFECTIVE INFORMATION

The universe is made up of information- information about the contents and creations in the universe, their composition, properties and relationships. What science does is to study the universe, its constituent parts and different phenomena in nature, i.e., gathering and orderly presentation of information about the universe and its contents. All the time, earthlings are bombarded with information emanating not only from the planets, stars and distant galaxies, but also from the environment around us consisting of various life systems. Information hits us through various information carrying media, such as light rays, gamma rays, cosmic rays; and information reflecting phenomena, such as growth, death, movement and change. However, all these information bits are in the nature of raw signals, which need to be interpreted or decoded for significance and recorded for transmission. So, in a way, it seems that information is all about coding and decoding.

Information (physical) is of two types: a) responsive or active, and b) non-responsive or inert. Information emanating from inanimate objects on earth and from space are inert in the sense that the relationship between the observer and the object yielding information is one-sided, i.e. one-way traffic, as inanimate objects are incapable of participating with the observer. How would you describe the reaction of a machine to input from an external source say, when you put the switch on, start a car, or activate a computer? Could these be regarded as complex inanimate systems participating with observers? On the other hand, information projected by living beings, such as plants, virus, bacteria, animals, and human beings is animate; and has a responsive relationship with the observer. The responsive and inert characteristics of information seem to play an important role in information-knowledge conversion process. This characteristic of information impacts on the subjective –objective aspects of information. Information projected by inanimate objects and phenomena are relatively more objective compared to responsive type of information.

OBJECTIVE AND SUBJECTIVE NATURE OF INFORMATION

Scientists studying information treat it as a part of objective world, and hence apply the same tests of scientific objectivity. Information because of its esoteric relationship with knowledge scientific objectivity works only up to a point. Moreover, all observations, experimentations, and choice of research methodology are done by human beings as observers, which inject an element of subjectivity. Thus, "when nature is probed to its extremities the barrier between the observer and the observed dissolves in a most peculiar way that has observable consequences. It transpires that we can know that the act of knowing changes things in an unknowable way" (Barrow,1988, p.7). There exists a mystic relationship between information, a physical phenomenon and knowledge, a mental phenomenon. Understanding this relationship involves reconciliation of objectivity of science and subjectivity of mind. In other words, "....information mediates between the material and the abstract, between the real and the ideal. If we can understand the nature of information, and incorporate it into our model of the physical world, we will have taken the first step along the road that leads from objective reality to our understanding of it...." (Von Baeyer, 2003, p. 17).

AN INFORMATIONALLY STRETCHED UNIVERSE

The universe, including life, functions at three levels—mega, micro, and intermittent level, with the last one corresponding to human perceptional range. In the early phase of human history our concept of reality, i.e., our understanding of world and life, was limited strictly to the intermittent level, i.e., what our sense organs could mediate and the mind could think, beyond which it was empty. This limited worldview of creation began changing drastically following the impact of European Renaissance (14th century AD to 17th century AD) and the first Industrial Revolution (1760-1830). It resulted in new discoveries, inventions and scientific thinking; which in turn replaced orthodoxy, bigotry, and false convictions prevalent during the Middle Ages. The new vista showed that there is knowledge or reality beyond the intermittent level. It opened up the universe of the mega and the micro. Stretching the universe in the mega and the micro directions meant extending the boundaries of the world of information and also giving variety and depth to our vision of the universe. Two of the earliest instruments invented to probe into the nature of the universe at the mega and the micro- range were telescope and microscope, respectively. Development of various types of sophisticated optical, magnetic, acoustic and electronic instruments coupled with computer and communication capabilities have been responsible for most of our present-day knowledge, particularly relating to scientific, technical, medical, genetic, and space achievements. For example, spectrum analysis has enabled us to analyze the chemical and energy compositions of different stars, radio astronomy opened up the vista of distant galaxies and their stars, telecommunication systems have enabled earthlings to communicate with astronauts orbiting in space. Magnetic Resonance Imaging has made possible to map activities of the human brain at the level of neurons. By extending the reach of human sense organs beyond imagination, instrumentation coupled with human drive not only opened up the mega and the micro universe, but also extended the boundaries of information world.

COMPRESSIBILITY OF INFORMATION

Compressibility is a property of information that links closely information with physics, and indeed with all of science (Feynman, 1963). Deployment of brevity of expression and the use of command are the two most important means of imparting compressibility to information. Brevity retains cognitive links, which is an absolute requirement, and commands work as a mechanical device. The following examples make the distinction clear:

Newton's laws of motion and gravity are compressed forms of information about the orbits of all the planets known or yet to be discovered, and also the motions of their parent stars as well as those of footballs, tidal waves and other massive bodies in the universe. To give another example is

Einstein's relativistic field equation :

$R_{\mu\upsilon} - \frac{1}{2} g_{\mu\upsilon} + g_{\mu\upsilon} = 8\pi GT_{\mu\upsilon}$, condensed all the information contained in the original paper — fifty pages devoted to explain the symbols used, sixteen interlinked equations and several hundred entries needed to define a position and an instant in time-space besides infinity of relationships, descriptions of geometry of space-time, and distribution of sources of gravity covered by the equation. The amount of information in this one equation is so overwhelming that nobody can make use of it in full generality (Von Baeyer, 2003).

Compression of data is of critical importance in representing information in a compact form. Information is compressed by identifying and using structures that exist in the data. In transmission of information in digital form (in bytes) the number of bytes required to represent multimedia data can be very high. For example, to represent 2 minutes of uncompressed CD-quality music requires about 84 million bits. From this, one can gauge the time required to download all information from the Internet and web sites, the space required to store them, and the speed needed to handle all the data generated world over. Developing better transmission and storage techniques alone are not sufficient to meet the challenge. Morse code is an early example of data compression making use of sequences of (.) and (–) to represent letters that occur more frequently, e.g., e by (.) and a by (. -); and longer sequences to letters that occur less frequently, e.g., q by (—.-). Without compression of data it would not be possible to have Internet, cellular phone or digital TV (Sayood, 2001). Transmitting of coded information by binary digits 0101010101....... in the compressed form achieved by a single instruction "Repeat 01 without stopping" is an example of compressibility by command.

Compressibility of Sensory Data by Brain. It is estimated that our five sensory systems put together receive about 11 million bits of data per second, of which the eyes account for the maximum amount of 10 million bits, and taste the lowest of 1000 bits. Out of such a vast volume of incoming data per second the human brain in its active state, as in reading, processes a maximum of 50 bits of information per second. It means that the brain compresses 11 million bits it receives in a second into less than 50 bits of sensation. How does the brain find the time and the energy required to carryout this enormous compression? There is a time gap of half a second between the instant that the senses receive a stimulus and the instant the mind is conscious of a sensation (except in reflex action where the brain responds within one tenth of a second). The interval of half a second seems sufficient for the brain to process and compress the sensory input. The human brain contains nearly 100 billion neurons each of which acts as a processor and is connected to thousands of other processors. Utilizing this multibillion neuron powerhouse the brain can easily transact 100 billion operations per second (Encyclopaedia Britannica, 2007, Vol. 21). Thus, for the brain to process a mere 11 million bits per second looks a simple task. Understanding the process of compression seems to hold an important clue in unraveling the mystery of information, the physical becoming consciousness or knowledge, the mental.

Other examples of highly compressed information are 0 or "Shunya", elementary particles, genes and bits. Compressibility reduces space, time, effort and cost employed to record, transmit, and in using information. Probably, compressibility has something to do with the mystery behind information- knowledge conundrum. Von Baeyer notes: "It is the strange, compressible stuff that flows out of a tangible object, be it an atom, a DNA molecule, a book or a piano, and, after a complex series of transformations involving the senses, lodges in the conscious brain. Information mediates between the material and the abstract, between the real and the ideal. If we can understand the nature of information, and incorporate it into our model of the physical world, we will have taken the first step along the road that leads from objective reality to our understanding of it........." (Von Baeyer, 2003, p.17).

ARTIFICIAL INTELLIGENCE (AI)

Knowledge, whose principal characteristic is meaning, is the preserve of human mind and a prime concern of philosophy and psychology. Since knowledge is created in the brain — a physical entity, its study has also been a concern of science, particularly physiology and cognitive science. Information, the physical representation of knowledge, is the basis on which computers are designed. From the very beginning, the brain has been a model to the designers of computers, and their ultimate desire was to build systems capable of executing thinking functions of brain using artificial means, i.e., Artificial Intelligence (AI). Therefore, without the inclusion of artificial intelligence and its sister discipline *cybernetics*, whose ultimate objectives are to match or even better the intelligence function of the human mind, our understanding of the physical basis of information will be incomplete.

Artificial intelligence is a branch of computer science. Natural language comprehension and robotics are two major branches of artificial intelligence, and it is the former which is of special interest to designers of information systems. Natural language is distinct from that of computer language. It is 'understanding' that distinguishes human processing of language from that of a computer, which does not have the capacity to think. Programs have been successfully built by which computers can respond to natural language, but without knowing the meaning. For example, in a database query system natural language is to be first converted to some artificially constructed database query language designed for acceptance by computer. The ultimate goal of AI research is to create intelligent machines, i.e., computers which can think. In other words, the goal is to duplicate the mental faculties of "ordinary people". AI begins with the hypothesis that functioning of brain may be thought of at some level as a kind of computation. AI is also concerned with intelligence and towards that end makes use of information about how people do things (Charniak and McDermott, 1999). An important question is how to confirm whether an AI mechanism fully matches human intelligence in solving a given problem. Alan Mathison Turing, an English mathematician, developed a test in 1950, to differentiate between human intelligence and computer intelligence which is now called *Turing test*.

Design of artificial neural network is a key component in many of the applications of AI. These networks are actually based on the biological neural system implemented on an electronic device, such as a computer. They employ the basic features of biological neural networks, such as distributed computational mechanism, adaptability (trainability), non-linearity, and simplicity in the unit computation (Katagiri, 2000).

Computational Creativity. Scientific probing of mental processes by employing the methods of Artificial Intelligence (AI) and computer science has enabled scientists to frame hypotheses about the working of human mind in terms of neural networks and cognitive processes. An interesting question is whether artificial intelligence and computers can think as the human mind does? A more focused question is whether computers can come up with ideas that at least *appear* to be creative? The current state of research and development in the field has shown that computers can and do produce ideas by novel combinations. By putting together two or more ideas (data structures) and using connectionist methods computers are capable of creating new ideas by combination. Best example is the program called JAPE, which makes punning jokes of general type. Theoretically it is even possible to introduce more subtlety in moods to such programs by creating necessary database and link-making, and link evaluating (Boden, 2004).

Several computer built programs which explore creative space are already in use. One example is AARON, which creates thousands of painted drawings of appreciable quality. Such paintings are found displayed in galleries around the world. David Cope's Emmy system composes music in different styles. There are programs capable of analyzing experimental data and finding new ways of expressing scientific laws. AI-programs can even transform conceptual space by altering their own rules so that interesting ideas result. Evolutionary programs with inbuilt mechanisms which belonged to the human domain till now, are now used to design new molecules for use in basic research and /or medicine, and even evolve "brains" and "bodies" of robots (Boden, 2004).

Applications of AI. Artificial intelligence has entered many areas of activities involving human intelligence and knowledge. Currently artificial intelligence has found applications in areas ranging from information processing and information systems, such as pattern recognition, speech processing and function estimators, simulation, medical diagnosis, neural science, and cognitive psychology to the design of learning techniques.

Cybernetics. In 1948, Norbert Wiener chose the term "cybernetics" to describe the "entire field of control and communication theory whether in the machine or in the animal" (Wiener,1948, p.19). The theoretical base of cybernetics in Wiener's observations is that the functioning of both human system and machines are similar. The functioning is centered on problems of communication, control and statistical mechanics, which showed an essential unity of purpose and orderliness in both systems. Wiener considered that cybernetics should be able to accomplish "ideal or actual mechanization of thought" or reasoning machine. In setting this objective he was inspired by the closely related twin concepts of Leibniz — universal symbolism and calculus of reasoning from which the present-day theories of mathematical notation and the symbolic logic were developed. In fact, Weiner considered Leibniz as the patron saint of cybernetics. Leibniz's *calculus ratiocinator* contains the germs of the machine ratiocinator, the reasoning machine (Wiener, 1948). The concept of Turing machine capable of doing computation developed by Turing also aided his thinking. The objective of developing machines that can imitate human mind is common to both AI and cybernetics, the latter has additional dimensions of decision-making and control.

Cybernetic applications need conversion of and processing of enormous quantities of data, which can only be handled by computers. Shannon's theory of communication came handy in shaping communication part of cybernetics. The technique of converting a continuous information flow into discrete information units transmitted through coded signals via a channel became the processing part of cybernetics. The theory of encoding of information into input and output signals is called *automata*. To control a system is to control the unwanted effects of change for which feedback of information on the state of affairs of the system to the controller unit on a continuous basis is a must. Stimulus-response mechanism in animals and thermostat systems used to control temperature in buildings by "sensing" changes are examples of systems working on the principle of feedback.

The study of systems and in particular complex probabilistic systems is a major task in cybernetics. A system under study is analyzed, and the problem is translated into mathematical form and models to provide solutions. Once the analysis is complete and the problem is understood the requisite algorithms for processing on a computer are generated. An algorithm is a set of rules which gives a sequence of operations for solving a specific type of problem and must include the features of: a) finiteness (i.e., program steps must terminate at some point); b) definiteness (i.e., every statement in the programming language must be defined; c) input; d) output; and e) effectiveness (i.e., determining performance characteristics of a given algorithm (Knuth, 1977). Today cybernetics finds successful applications in areas, such as pattern recognition, automatic control devices, and automation. *Robotics*, a branch of cybernetics, specializes in machine handling of human tasks through remote control. There is a view that we are at the threshold of a cybernetic revolution deciding the future destiny of mankind.

A PERSPECTIVE FROM THE INFORMATION THEORY

The novelty of this perspective developed by V.V. Raman in his forthcoming publication *Truth and Tension from Faith and Framework* is integrating the element of "revelation" into a theory of knowledge from information. The perspective recognizes that there are three orders of information operating in the universe: 1. physical order of information, 2. biological order of information, and 3. "revelation" order of information.

1. Physical Order of Information. All matter is stirred or guided into ordered activity by encoding information. Encoding principles are evolved from the laws of physics— from gravitation and electromagnetism to those of elementary particle decay and gluon cementing. Everything in the universe runs on these laws. They are silent as the informational substratum of the universe.

2. Biological Order of Information. This order guides the transformation of sensory information into awareness by the complex cerebral processing. After all, awareness corresponds to accumulation of experiences derived from the senses — sight, sound, taste, feel and smell. Though our present state of knowledge limits the second order to the domain of human brain we cannot rule out the existence of other systems, possibly even more sophisticated, existing outside our world in the cosmos. At present we do not have tools and techniques to trace and analyze those systems.

3. Revelation Order of Information. It recognizes the phenomenon of "revelation", in which information is furnished

to the human brain with the knowledge about the world that is not directly derived from experience and carefully collected data. Third order information is given to, but to a few. The notion of revelation may be incorporated into the framework and terminology of current science and then to knowledge, which is explained further.

Consider the room in which we are. It is bathed in information-carrying electromagnetic waves from everywhere on earth, but of which none of us are ordinarily aware. However, if we are armed with appropriate electronic gadgetry we can decode all these million messages. That is what our radios and TVs, and cell phones do. It requires all the complexity of electrical circuits to decode the radiations from the antennas of the radio and television stations of the world. These *meaning-bits* may be crisscrossing the lengths and breadths of the universe, but if and when they encounter that highly evolved system called the brain they are deciphered. From this perspective we can understand why it took all these eons before the meaning component of the universe began to be recognized. But this to happen, the evolution of the human brain was a necessary pre-condition for the manifestation of an all-pervading consciousness in individual entities. This view explains revelation, insights, and the other discoveries made by human beings (Raman, with the permission of the author). The question is how far admitting the element of revelation is scientific?

INFORMATION-CENTRIC NEW COSMOLOGY

The formulation of the basic theories of evolutionary development in nature was greatly influenced by the philosophical thoughts of Alfred North Whitehead, the mathematician and philosopher of the early 20th century (Rifkin, 1998). Whitehead saw that all organisms in nature exhibit a purpose or "subjective aim", which is to survive and grow by adapting to the ongoing changes in the environment

(Whitehead, 1934). Taking cue from Whitehead's subjective aim which corresponds to the function of mind, Norbert Wiener built the theory of cybernetics. Cybernetics explains how systems maintain themselves over time through information feedback and processing of information reflecting the changing conditions in the environment over time. Wiener defines information as the "name for the content of what is exchanged with the outer world as we adjust to it, and make our adjustment felt upon it. The process of receiving and of using information is the process of our adjusting to the contingencies of the outer environment, and of our living effectively within that environment" (Wiener, 1954, p.26-27). Cybernetics has given a new meaning to our perception of evolution and ordering of life. Rifkin, in his book " *The Biotech Century*" depicts the main features of the new biological world order (Rifkin, 1998) and they are:

Cybernetic view of biological creations dictates that : a living organism is no longer to be seen as a permanent form but rather as a network of activity; in the new definition of life-the philosophy of being, life and mind become intricately bound to the notion of "processing" change; evolution is seen as efficient processing of information; as an evolution process negative feedback leads to stasis and positive feedback to transformation; ability to process complex and increasing quantities of information by individuals and organizations has become the standard of measuring their success; manipulation of genetic information to modify the future state of an organism and its environment represents the ultimate use of cybernetic principles and information processing skills; with every evolutionary advancement in the process of self organization of species, information feeds on further information to create more complex sets of relationships, which in turn increase the overall complexity of the system; the new matrix of evolution replaces the idea of life as a machinery with the idea of life as information; by resolving structures into functions and reducing function to information flows, the new cosmology all but eliminates the idea of species integrity. All living beings are drained of their substance and turned into genetic information. In the revised thinking about evolution everything is pure activity; information has become the primary object of our attention and evolution of life; with information's new exalted status, even knowledge itself is loosing its meaning and increasingly being subsumed under the category of information. Today, 'to be knowledgeable' and 'to be informed' have come to mean virtually the same thing, which means a revolution in the history of consciousness. Being informed is an ongoing process of anticipation and accommodation to changes going on in the environment, and knowledge is no more viewed as discovery of facts, but rather as an ongoing creative process.

Knowledge is created so fast that today's awareness is getting outmoded by tomorrow. Thus, we have far less toleration for timeless truths and ironclad laws of the earlier paradigm of science, which by their very nature, imposed boundaries and established limits. Boundary implies telling us what we can do and cannot do. Today, change itself is taken as the only truth. By reinterpreting nature as the evolution of information, a new information cum change-centric cosmology has born.

A THEORY OF KNOWLEDGE FROM INFORMATION

Stephen Hawking, the renowned physicist and cosmologist laments that "up to now, most scientists have been too occupied with the development of new theories that describe *what* the universe is to ask the question *why*. On the other hand, the people whose business it is to ask *why*, the philosophers, have not been able to keep up with the advance of scientific theories..." (Hawking, 1988, p. 184). This failure on the part of scientists and philosophers is one of the reasons why the confusion or mystery dogging knowledge and information remains unresolved. While philosophers stand by knowledge, physical scientists and biologists swear by information. The former conduct their studies employing analytical methods and assess knowledge by applying standards, such as belief, justification and certainty; the latter apply scientific objectivity dictated by physical laws, such as laws of thermodynamics and entropy, laws of motion, quantum mechanics, mathematical models and laboratory experiments. The lack of common meeting ground between the two approaches has prevented bridging the gap between knowledge and information divide. Fred I. Dretske from the field of philosophy presents in his book *Knowledge and the Flow of Information* an integrated theory of knowledge from information. He develops his thesis on the following lines:

The underlying structure of Shannon's theory of communication, when suitably supplemented, can be adapted to develop a semantic *theory* of information. Communication theory allows us to conceive information as an objective commodity, "as something defined in terms of the network of lawful relationships holding between distincts event and structures, one can,.... develop a plausible, and theoretically powerful, analysis of a signal's informational *content*"(Dretske, 1981, p. ***x***).

The traditional criterion of justification that accords knowledge its status (knowledge is justified true belief) is most unsatisfactory for resolving the problem of information-knowledge divide. Instead, one can begin with information as an objective commodity whose creation, transmission and reception do not require or presuppose interpretive processes, i.e., meaning. Given this freedom, one can develop out of lower order, purely physical, information-processing mechanisms, cognitive systems having the resources for interpreting signals, holding beliefs, and acquiring knowledge. Higher order information systems can then be seen as manifestations of progressive more efficient ways of handling and coding information. Meaning and mental attitudes that exhibit it are manufactured products using information as raw material. It is more fruitful to follow an information-theoretic analysis, which characterizes knowledge in terms of information and belief. This analysis seems to be in line with the cognitive psychologist view that cognition can be analyzed as formal symbol manipulation process (Stillings, 1995). This process can be given a semantic interpretation that accounts for their meaningfulness and adaptiveness to the environment. The symbol system is physical, and the formal processes are implemented in a particular physical medium, the brain.

Information qualifies as a *semantic* idea in virtue of intentional character. What information a signal carries is a reflection of the intentionality of our beliefs and knowledge. This suggests that "we may be able to understand the peculiar intentional structure of our cognitive states as symptoms of their underlying information-theoretic character" (Dretske, 1981, p. 76). Statements describing the information carried by a signal are intentional descriptions, and the phenomena they describe qualify as intentional phenomena. The ultimate source of the intentionality inherent in the transmission and receipt of information is of course, the nomic regularities on which the transmission of information depends. The logical next step is to apply the criteria of a signal's informational content to theory of knowledge. Knowledge is identified with information-caused belief.

Measuring and control instruments, like thermostats, may be regarded as information processing devices. These mechanical systems share some of the essential features of a perceptual-cognitive system. What distinguishes a genuine cognitive system from mere processors of information is that the former sustains belief, where as the latter does not sense belief in the information it receives. A tape recorder is incapable of knowing because the information it receives neither generates nor sustains an appropriate belief. The information-theoretic account of knowledge remains seriously incomplete as long as it lacks an account of belief.

It is the type of processing of signals by brain that distinguishes knowledge from information. Sensory analog processing of signals makes information a physical entity (e.g., seeing a duck) and cognitive digital processing of signals give information its cognitive character (e.g., identifying the seen physical item as duck) and makes it knowledge. In converting analog to digital form, there is always a loss of information corresponding to irrelevant portions in the input structure of information. Therefore, our perceptual experience can be identified with an information-carrying structure — a sensory structure in which incoming information about a source is coded in analog form, which is then subjected to the digitalizing process that accords conceptual or cognitive significance. Dretske's thesis attempts to bridge the existing information-knowledge divide and to arrive at a unified theory of knowledge. Though the theory is yet to be tested in real-time conditions, it serves as one of the excellent starting points for further research.

CLOSURE

Information as a physical phenomenon is explained through Shannon's theory of communication. Laws of physics impose certain limits on computations. Next phase of information processing technology is expected to be engineered by quantum computing and nanotechnology. Contrary to Einstein's General Theory of Relativity which says that a black hole only admits matter with no escape, latest speculation is that information can escape from a black hole. This leads to the inference that a black hole too computes. Analogous to quantum mechanics, one may hypothesize that information in a cognitive environment takes the form of knowledge, and outside that environment remains physical.

Information is embedded in all things and phenomena

in nature. Information seems to belong to the same fundamental categories of time, space, matter, and energy. The relationship between the observer and the source of information in nature could be either affective or non-affective. Information because of its esoteric relationship with knowledge is objective works up to a point, and beyond which the objectivity test fails. As stated earlier, information mediates between the material and the abstract.

Compressibility of information enables condensed representation of data as bits, or signals carried by neurons. Artificial intelligence and cybernetics in their present stage of development are capable of executing limited thinking functions of human brain. Information has become the harbinger of a new cosmology.

Any formulation of a unified theory of knowledge from information has to first discover the fundamental features and principles that characterize knowledge and information, and then proceed to establish their interrelationships as well as their intra- relationships with the other fundamental constituents of the universe - time, space, matter and energy. Any fruitful approach to the problem of information-knowledge dichotomy cannot ignore taking into account: a) philosopher's exploration of knowledge; b) the effects of compressibility of information, at the tiniest level- bit, qubit, neuron and DNA; c) linguistic phenomena of the brain; and d) weirdness of quantum mechanics and its possible relevance to information. At present, it seems that we are nowhere near the solution.

The central issue in the problem of information and knowledge is bridging the gap that exists between the physical and the mental approaches to the problem and decoding the mystic element inherent, but not apparent, in the information-knowledge dichotomy. Whatever be the approach, it has to elicit satisfactory answers to the questions that are similar to the one's put to Swethaketu of *Chandogya Upanishad* (Max Muller, 1900), on his return after completion of his studies, by his father, namely: " have you ever asked (your teacher) for that instruction by which we hear what cannot be heard, by which we perceive what cannot be perceived, by which we know what cannot be known?"

REFERENCES

Barrow, John D. The World Within the World. Oxford, Claranden Press, 1988.

Boden, Margaret A. The Creative Mind. Myths and Mechanisms. Ed. 2. London, Routledge, 2004. (Indian reprint).

Charniak, Eugene and McDermott, Drew. Introduction to Artifical Intelligence. Singapore, Longman, 1999. (First published by Addison-Wesley, 1985).

Dretske, Fred I. Knowledge and the Flow of Information. Stanford (Calif.), CSLI Publications, 1999. (Originally published: Cambridge(Mass), MIT Press, 1981).

Encyclopaedia Britannica, The New. Ed.15. Chicago, Encyclopaedia Britinica, 2007. Vol.21. Pp. 631-637: Information Theory.

Feynman, Richard. Lectures in Physics. Vol.1. Addison-Wesley, 1963.

Hawking, Stephen W. A Briefer History of Time. New York, Bantam Dell, 2005.

Katagiri, Shigeru. Ed. Handbook of Neural Networks for Speech Processing. Boston, Artech House, 2000.

Knuth, Donald E. The Art of Computer Programming. Ed.2. Vol.1: Fundamental Algorithms. Reading (Mass.), Addison-Wesley, 1977.

Landauer, Rolf. Information is physical. *Physics Today* 44(5): 23-29, May 1991.

Lloyd, Seth and Jack Ng, Y. Black hole computers. *Scientific American* 291 (5): 30-39, Nov. 2004

Max Muller, F. Tr. And Ed. The Upanishads: Part- 1. London, Oxford University Press, 1900. (Reprint: Delhi, Motilal Banarasidass, 2000). (The Sacred Books of the East Series. Vol.1).

Murali, D. and Padmanaban, G. " Quantum" jump. Quantum computing offers enormous potential that is waiting to be tapped, says the expert. *Business Line,* Monday, Dec. 10, 2007, p.4. (eWorld).

Neelameghan, A. Expressions of Time in Information Sience and Their Implications. Pp,103-117. *In* Greenway, Frank. Ed. Time and the Sciences. Paris, Unesco, 1979.

Nielsen, Michael A. and Chung, Isaac L. Quantum Computation and Quantum Information. Cambridge (U.K.), Cambridge University Press, 2002. (South Asian ed.).

Raman, V. V. Truth and Tension from Faith and Framework. To be published soon.

Rifkin, Jeremy. The Biotech Century: Harnessing the Gene and Remaking the World. New York, Jeremy P. Tarcher (Putnam), 1998.

Sayood, Khalid. Introduction to Data Compression. Ed.2. San Francisco (Calif.), Morgan Kaufmann, 2000. (Indian reprint. 2001).

Shannon, C.E. A Mathematical theory of communication. *Bell System Technical Journal* 27: 379-423, 623-656, 1948.

Sigfried, Tom. The Bit and the Pendulum: From Quantum Computing to M Theory- The Physics of Information. New York, Wiley & Sons, 2000.

Stillings, Neil A. Cognitive Science: An Introduction. Ed.2. Cambridge (Mass.), MIT Press, 1995.

Von Beayer, Hans Christian. Information: The New Language of Science. London, Weidenfeld & Nicolson, 2003.

Cf. Wheeler, John. Information, Physics, Quantum: The Search for Links. Pp. 354-368. *In* Hey, Anthony, J.G. Ed. Feynman and Computation. Reading (Mass.), Perseus Books, 1999. (Reproduced from the Proceedings of the Third International Symposium on the Foundations of Quantum Mechanics, Tokyo, 1989).

Cf. Whitehead, Alfred North. Nature and Life. Cambridge, Cambridge University Press, 1934.

Wiener, Norbert. Cybernetics or Control and Communication in the Animal and the Machine. New York, Technology Press (Wiley & Sons), 1948. (Ed.2, 1961).

Wiener, Norbert. The Human Use of Human Beings: Cybernetics and Society. New York, Avon Books, 1954.

11

Social Origin of Knowledge

Knowledge is sociologically significant because it is socially created, and social life is based on a shared sense of what is real and true. In general, sociologists perceive knowledge in all its forms as social products shaped by culture and structure of social systems (Johnson, 1995). Sociologists' approach to knowledge differs from that of natural scientists and humanities. They consider knowledge from a social point of view. In social sciences, "knowledge per *se* is not tied to the objective natural world or to the individual but is the result of social processes. Consequently, knowledge is tied to a discourse formed by social processes, and not to the individual. It is important to point out that the different forms and contents of knowledge occurring as a result of social processes within a given discourse cannot be transferred from one discourse to another. This is why the formal logic of the natural sciences is less successful when applied to the social sciences and the humanities; the epistemological foundations are different and the objects discovered are different;..." (Thellefsen and Thellefsen, 2004, p. 179). How this difference affects our understanding of knowledge representing socio-epistemological phenomena is explained by sociology of knowledge, the theme of this chapter. We begin with three preliminary observations on sociology of knowledge, and they are: validity, tradition, and approach.

VALIDITY, TRADITION, AND APPROACH

Validity. It is not that validity of sociology of knowledge is beyond questioning. Werner Stark cites two such contentions - one by Julius Kraft, and the other by Florian Znaniecki (Stark, 1971). He observes that Kraft has denied that there can be such a thing as the macrosociology of knowledge, and social reality is the source for social determination of thought-contents. For Kraft, knowledge is a psychical phenomenon; it is in people's heads, and cannot be explained by what goes on outside those heads. Social entities are not 'real' in any material sense, but they are only linguistic fictions, and hence have nothing to do with derivation of thought contents. However, there may be sociology of the organizations of knowledge (churches, schools etc.)— that there may be microsociolgy of knowledge as part of special and applied sociology (Kraft, 1934).

Florian Znaniecki, while asserting that there can be no sociology of knowledge, states that "systems of knowledge-viewed in their objective composition, structure, and validity-cannot be reduced to social facts, yet their historical existence within the empirical world of culture, in so far as it depends upon the men who construct them, maintain them by transmission and application, develop them or neglect them, must in a large measure be explained sociologically" (Znaniecki, 1982, p. 312).

Tradition. The pursuit of sociology of knowledge in each nation bears its own distinctive characteristic, thus giving rise to different national traditions, like German, French and American.

Approach. Any general observation of the field of sociology of knowledge leaves an impression that it is a set of theories stringed together and not a unified body of knowledge.

At the same time, a study of its statements, theories and traditions confirms that it is more than a recounting of its nature and scope. These two somewhat contradictory versions of sociology of knowledge lead to two distinct approaches to its study. Stark divides sociology of knowledge into: a) macro sociology of knowledge concentrating on the larger social cosmos, and b) microsociology operating in the limited area of scholarship and art (Stark, 1971). Doyle McCarthy also sees two approaches in the study of sociology of knowledge: a) the broad approach employing sociology and social theory to explain the social nature of mind and knowledge; and b) the particular approach that includes the works of theorists in the field identified as sociology of knowledge. The social theories of Marx, Durkheim, Weber, Simmel, and others which explain the relationship between society, mind, and knowledge help constitute the broad approach. Stark, Berger and Luckmann, and many others could construct their particular works from the basic material drawn from this broad approach (McCarthy, 2000).

HISTORY OF SOCIOLOGY OF KNOWLEDGE

Sociology of knowledge as a branch of sociology evolved out of the intellectual and philosophical turmoil of the late nineteenth century and early twentieth century Europe. German sociologists Max Scheler (1874-1928) and Karl Mannheim (1893-1947) were the first to call *Wissenssoziologie in 1924/1925.* Since epistemology concerns itself with the theory of knowledge from the standpoint of individual knower, it was left to social philosophers like Scheler and Mannheim to probe the social and group origins of knowledge to explain the then prevailing cultural/ philosophic "Worldview" born out of the ideologies of Karl Marx and Fredrich Nietzche. The aim of sociology of knowledge, they said, was to determine the relationship between thought and society, between knowledge and social structure. An early exposition of sociology of knowledge is traced to Augustus Comte's (1798-1857) sociological positivism, which states that " the objectivity of ideas lay in their social functions, all the sciences are reducible to the sociological" (Piepe, 1971, p.16).

The foundations of sociology of knowledge were laid by Scheler and Mannheim on the basis of two key concepts: social or existential determination of thought and historicism. The concept of social determination of knowledge has different interpretations depending on the version of sociology of knowledge under consideration. According to Mannheim, the existential determination of thought may be regarded as a demonstrated fact in those realms of thought in which we can show: a) that the process of knowing does not actually develop historically in accordance with immanent laws, b) that it does not follow only from the "nature of things" or from "pure logical possibilities", and c) that it is not driven by an "inner dialectic". On the contrary, the emergence and the crystallization of actual thought is influenced in many decisive points by extra-theoretical factors of the most diverse sort (Mannheim, 1952). Historicism is an intellectual approach through which we formulate our "Worldview" (Weltanschauung). All our observations of the socio-cultural reality are based on historicism (Mannheim, 1952). Stated simply, it means that all mental products are part and parcel of an ongoing process of historical process (Remmling, 1975).

Karl Marx on Ideas and Ideology. Karl Marx's thinking on sociology of knowledge is based on the premise that intellectual activity in any society is a product of historicity, economic factors, and class interests. Marx and Engels observed that the class ruling the society derives its power by controlling the means of material production and thereby also controls the means of mental production. The ruling ideas, i.e., the ideas of the ruling class, in every epoch of history are the ideal expression of the dominant material relationships. "The individuals composing the ruling class possess, among other things, consciousness, and therefore, think. In so far, therefore, as they rule as a class and determine the extent and compass of an epoch, it is self-evident that they do this in their whole range, hence, among other things, rule also as thinkers, as producers of ideas, and regulate the production and distribution of the ideas of their age" (Marx and Engels, 1982, p. 105). Once "the ruling ideas have been separated from the ruling individuals and, above all, from the relationships that result from a given stage of the mode of production, and in this way the conclusion has been reached that history is always under the sway of ideas 'the idea' 'die Idee,' etc. as the dominant force in history" (Marx and Engels, 1982, p. 107).

Max Scheler's Theory of Knowledge. Scheler was influenced by Edmund Husseler's phenomenology in formulating his thoughts on philosophy, philosophical anthropology, and sociology, the three issues on which his sociology of knowledge rests. The philosophic part states that human beings alone are able to grasp the essence, i.e., reality of the world from which ideas are formed. Reality can be realized only by studying living process in which an element of sacredness, i.e., an act of divine spirit, plays a part. The living process is made up of "spirit" and "drive", the central features of his theory of knowledge. Spirit determines only the particular "quality" of possible mental content, but the bringing of this possibility into existence is done only by drive conditioned factors of life. The former are "ideal factors" and the latter "real factors". Philosophical anthropology assigns important role to values in shaping human behaviour. Individuals are seen as both creatures of their environment and creators of their values. Society is made of different forms, i.e., types of social groups, which results in different forms of thinking (Tavakol, 1990; Becker and Dahlke, 1976). The content and the validity of knowledge are not determined sociologically, whereas "'the forms' of mental acts, through which knowledge is gained, are always, by necessity, co-conditioned sociologically, i.e. by the structure of society" (Scheler, 1924, p. 72 cited by Tavakol).

Karl Mannheim and Sociology of Knowledge. Mannheim's theory of sociology of knowledge has become the standard reference point for many of the later-day thinkers in the field. The theory of sociology of knowledge developed by Mannheim in his work *Ideology and Utopia* is in two parts : a) as an empirical investigation following description and structural analysis, and b) as an epistemological inquiry. In the empirical approach, thinking is a product of the process of social or existential determination. Formation of thought is influenced by existential factors of the most divorced sort rather than by immanent laws or by an inner dialectic. Existential connections of knowledge, i.e., the role actually played by existential factors in the history of thought, is a "correlation between types of knowledge and ideas, on the one hand, and the social groups and process of which they are characteristic", on the other (Mannheim, 1936, p. 243). The historic-social process is of essential significance as it accounts for when and where the human thoughts arose and more importantly asks *why* it took the form it did. At the same time, relating individual ideas to the total structure of a given historico-social subject, i.e., relationism clarifies in connection with what social structure did the thoughts arise and are they valid. The perspective we arrive at is not only a formal determination of thinking, but also goes into qualitative criteria employed in arriving at the structure of thought and its validity. The principal issue regarding perspectives is to ascertain how they are formed. Mannheim explains this through the theories of ideology and utopia.

The task of ideology is to unmask the conscious deceptions and disguises of human interest groups. Ideology, in its totality, refers to the subject's whole mode of conceiving things as determined by his or her historical and social setting, but devoid of any moral connotation. The ideologies lead to the formation of one's "perspective". Utopia is a state of mind "when it is incongruous with the state of reality within which it occurs" (Mannheim, 1936, p. 173). Incongruity is about objects which do not exist in the real world. The utopian incongruity, when it passes over into conduct tends to shatter wholly or partly the existing order at the time. There is a "dialectic" relationship between utopia and the existing order. When particular ideologies and particular utopias held by individuals translate into total ideologies and total utopias encompassing groups become the source of ideas and thoughts for the theorists to work upon the project of sociology of knowledge.

Other Contributions. Vilfredo Pareto, the social theorist from France regarded society as a social system with many subsystems. These social systems seek equilibrium when the system is disturbed by social attitudes. The disturbing factors are: physical, external, and internal in origin. His "theory of motivation" built on the twin concepts of "residues" and "derivatives" explains how the three factors affect human behaviour. He concluded that it is the internal factors like race, ethnicity, and especially class-based ideologies impact dominantly the social behaviour in society, which in turn affect the sociology of knowledge (Pareto, 1935).

Inspired by the pragmatic philosophy of Charles Sanders Pierce (1839-1914), William James (1842-1910), and John Dewey (1859-1952), American sociologists Thorstein Veblen and George Herbert Mead added American flavour to the study of sociology of knowledge. Veblen's work studies how habits of life, occupational role, social positions, community organization and norms shape one's formulation of thoughts and its mode of functioning. Mead draws upon social behaviourism to establish the social origin of mind, and stresses how important is the role of communication in understanding the nature of mind. Robert Merton contributed to the field through his "structural- functional theory" which fits into the broad tradition of social determination of ideas (Coser, 1968). Talcott Parsons' "general theory of action" calls for careful analysis of both cultural and social systems and their interactions, which in turn leads to the formation of perspective and ideology is an important addition to the theories of action. The problem of ideology involves fundamental relations to the values institutionalized in the social system. But neither values nor motivational commitments and their symbolization expressed in terms by themselves are forms of "knowledge". (Parsons, 1982). Werner Stark's work *The Sociology of Knowledge* audits the major theories in the sociology of knowledge and also discusses the role of "social determination of knowledge", meaning that mental life is shaped by prevalent social and historical conditions and not with the problem of ideology as theorized by Marx and Mannheim. His explanation of social determination of knowledge is more in line with cultural sociology.

THE NEW SOCIOLOGY OF KNOWLEDGE

In recent years, as a result of the demands of complex modern life and fast changing social realities, the pursuit of sociology of knowledge has taken a new turn. The emphasis has shifted away from the earlier philosophical, epistemological and ideological overtone to the study of knowledge in society at the pragmatic level. The new form has come to be known as "the new sociology of knowledge". The contours of the new sociology of knowledge were set by Peter Berger and Thomas Luckmann in their work *The Social Construction of Reality.* Their main assertions extracted from their book are stated below (Berger and Luckmann, 1966):

1. Human reality is socially constructed and the task of sociology of knowledge is to analyze this process.
2. Symbolism and symbolic language become "essential constituents of the reality of everyday life and of the common-sense apprehension of this reality" (p. 52).
3. The sociology of knowledge must concern itself with everything that passes for knowledge in society. It is this commonsense 'knowledge' that constitutes "the fabric of meanings without which no society could exist" (p. 27).

4. Emphasis should be on the use of empirical discipline in its concrete problems, i.e., sociological theory, and not the philosophical investigation of the foundations of the empirical discipline or the methodology of sociology.
5. Over emphasis on theoretical thought is not only unduly restrictive for the sociology of knowledge, but also "unsatisfactory because even this part of socially available 'knowledge' cannot be fully understood if it is not placed in the framework of a more general analysis of knowledge" (p. 27).
6. Any sociological theory of knowledge must address "how is it possible that subjective meanings become objective facticities?" (p. 27).
7. Sociologies of language and religion make essential contributions to social theory.
8. A comprehensive "theory of social action" derived by combing the social theories of Weber and Durkheim explains the problem of sociology of knowledge.

The essence of Berger and Luckmann's study is that knowledge and social reality exist in a reciprocal or dialectical relationship of mutual constitution. This new interpretation shifts focus of sociology of knowledge to the broad range of signifying systems that form and communicate the realm of social realities. This concept of social reality has influenced many researchers in humanities and sciences to follow a "constructed reality" approach, which sees the issue in sociology of knowledge as a "problem of meaning and the use of philosophical, literary, and historical approaches to study the social construction of meaning" (McCarthy, 2000, p. 2958). McCarthy makes the further point that this new interpretation has methodological implications in that Mannheim's theory of "social determination" gives place to semiotic study of culture.

Popper's Social Theory on Scientific Objectivity. The new sociology of knowledge is not only tolerant of criticism, but is also open to consider the principles and methods used to discover reality by other disciplines, such as natural sciences and economics. Commenting on the state of sociology, Karl Popper criticizes that the objectivity part of social theories on science is almost entirely neglected by sociologists of knowledge. He observes that the methods of natural sciences and particularly its "public character" enforce objectivity in science. Inbuilt into the public character of scientific method are: a) *free criticism*, a religion with the scientific community; and b) use of a common language (Popper, 1982).

The various social institutions like the laboratories, the scientific periodicals with their system of refereeing, and the congresses further scientific objectivity through criticism in natural sciences. This aspect of scientific method shows "what can be achieved by institutions designed to make public control possible, and by the open expression of public opinion, even if this is limited to a circle of specialists..." (Popper, 1982, p. 655). A common language based on experience followed by scientists in natural sciences serves as the impartial orbiter in resolving their controversies. "Experience" here is of a "public" character (meaning) like observations and experiments, as opposed to experiences in the sense of mere "private" aesthetic or religious experiences. An experience is "public", if everybody who takes the trouble can repeat it. Scientists try to express their theories in such a form that they can be tested, i.e., refuted (or else corroborated) by such experience. This is what constitutes scientific objectivity. Popper concludes : "what we call 'scientific objectivity' is not a product of the individual scientist's impartiality, but a product of the social or public character of scientific method; and the individual scientist's impartiality is, so far as it exists, not the source but rather the result of this socially or institutionally organized objectivity of science" (Popper, 1982, p. 650).

Another feature of the new sociology of knowledge is opening up its research front to the hitherto neglected areas of sociology, such as the influence of media, effects of information technology, newer theories of social power, environmental issues, feminist factors, and linguistic concerns to the creation, transmission, use and misuse of knowledge in various contexts. Sociology of knowledge which began as the study of competing and conflicting collective ideas and ideologies has now become more cultural and diffuse. Its subject matter today is both more differentiated and more diffuse, and includes the study of "informal knowledge", the knowledge of everyday life (McCarthy, 2000).

Social determination of knowledge is a foundational concept in the theory of sociology of knowledge. This determination is a group or class phenomenon shaped by the total perspective of a given epoch. However, it is the particular perspective, i.e., a product of the individual minds that leads to the formation of a total perspective. The role of social values in the formation of an individual's perspective is explained through the *Value System theory* by Werner Stark.

Value System Theory of Knowledge. Stark has proposed that social values held by an individual effectively shape his or her perception of a given knowledge situation. In most cases of knowledge encounters, there is a factual aspect and a perceptional aspect. The factual aspect is intellectually understood without the social mind entering into it. On the other hand, when it comes to perceiving of even physical facts and trying to find its meaning and relevancy one's social knowledge and previous social exposure do act upon the process of knowing. The process of socialization binds an individual to the social norms and cultural ethos of the society to which the individual belongs, which in turn shapes his or her value system. These values vary from society to society and are influenced by spacio-temporal conditions. Because of the differences in the social make up of individuals, the perception of a given fact or situation is likely to vary from person to person. Here, "the apprehension of meaning will be an act of the *whole* personality including the specifically social sector of the mind; ...will have a larger say in the matter than either the sensual apparatus or the formal intellect. Philosophically speaking, it is not a transcendental consciousness which takes in the meaning, i.e., the essence, of a social fact, but an immanent consciousness, a socially determined, socially specified, socially filled consciousness, the consciousness of a man who lives within a certain social order and apprehends all social events in terms of it" (Stark, 1971, p. 15). Stark observes that there could be an objection that the result of immanent consciousness is not knowledge, but *judgment* concerning meaning which corresponds to *valuation*. This objection is based on an invalid assumption that cognizance of facts, including social, precedes assessment of meaning which thus becomes an incidental or secondary act is the result of dogma, which needs to be corrected.

In social systems, unlike prejudice, valuation of a specific kind does not follow upon, but must *precede* the act of cognition. There exists a mental framework made up of social value systems through which one does judge what is of significance in any social fact. It is this grid that determines "on the one hand what will fall into our field of perception, and on the other will make it possible for us to co-ordinate our cognitions and form them into a coherent image, comparable, in its unity and clarity, to the picture which our categories or our senses enable our minds to form of the subhuman, material universe" (Stark, 1971, p. 16). Without the assistance of the framework, if one is to study the human social universe it would end up in a quasi-scientific picture of social happenings giving only the physical characteristics and formal dimensions, but not their social characteristics and historical dimensions.

The systems of values forming the framework are a *priori*. The "social *a priori* is as real and as basic to the functioning of the process of social knowing as the Kantian is to the process of physical and formal knowing" (Stark, 1971, p.16.) It is the *a priori* social judgments that enforce the cognitive focusing on social facts and impart coherence, unity, and meaning. Any social happening is a picture of innumerable, independent, disconnected and incoherent events and actions. It is the *a priori* social awareness that identifies significance and supplies co-significance to various elements to make it a meaningful whole picture. Hence without *a priori* notion of what is significant and what is co-significant "we could at best become aware of certain social facts, but we could not *know* any. For knowledge is clear and conscious, and, above all, structured knowledge. But the structuring of knowledge is dependent on a principle of selection and a principle of order, and both are to be seen exclusively in what we have called the 'grid'.... This does not mean, by itself, that everybody is for ever committed to the pre-judgments of the society which has made him; it does not mean either that the differences in their world-views and views of history which result from the underlying contrasting valuations of the different societies are something that we cannot conquer and overcome" (Stark, 1971, p. 17). In the formation of perspectives, there is another phenomenon involved and that is reflexivity.

REFLEXIVITY

Reflexivity is a mental socio-cognitive phenomenon that participates in the act of thinking and in shaping particular perspectives. It is also connected to ethnomethodology and epistemology. Reflexivity research has become a topic of increased interest among social scientists. In its general sense, reflexivity means an individual's reflexive monitoring of his or her actions, which may lead to course correction. Though reflexivity means different things to different people, one can discern three distinct meanings given to reflexivity: a) reflexivity having identity as its focus; b) reflectivity in research and writing; and c) reflexivity centred on reflexive knowledge, i.e., the knowledge equation between the observer and the observed.

Identity. Reflexivity in the sense of establishing identity is interpreting the underlying social currents to understand how they shape one's self–identity in late modernism or post-modernism world. Here, reflexivity works in its active form with pervasive conditioning of every aspect of active life, i.e., what Giddens calls "reflexive historicity of modernity" (Giddens, 1991, p. 76). Reflexivity of post-modernism which is different from reflexive monitoring of action seen in all human activity, pictures a society in which life-world undergoes drastic changes. In the post-modern society, identity is becoming increasingly reflexive as individuals make their own self-identity. The change involves transformation of the social institutions, wherein the traditional social values are being replaced by a fragmented social life dominated by individualization; and as a result the process of work, family, and class are getting restructured (Giddens, 1991; Scott, 2006). Alternative to the reflexive theory of identity, as pointed out by Sweetman, there is the habitus view presented by Bourdieu, which says that the 'embeddedness' of our dispositions and tastes suggest that identity may be less susceptible to reflexive intervention than Giddens and others have implied (Bourdieu, 1984; Sweetman, 2003).

Research and Writing. In social research programmes evidence leading to social insight of a problem is always analyzed against a personal background and personal beliefs, values, social and political commitment of the researcher. These traits are inevitably shaped by various factors like race, class, gender, language, and ability of the research worker. The conditioned subjectivity of the researcher interferes with all aspects of the person's research work — from selection of topic to the final presentation of the research findings. This way, reflexivity is "a performance that positions the author in relationship to the field, the act of research, writing and the production of knowledge more generally" (Haggerty, 2003, p. 158).

Reflexive Knowledge. In searching for reality in knowledge encounters by individuals one deals with objective knowledge inherent to the action domain or situation and subjective knowledge arising out of the reflexive part of the observer or participant. Reflexivity plays an important role in the formation of particular perspective, since formation of thought is always a phenomenon of the individual's mind. Reflexivity is one of the mental processes that explain how particular perspectives are shaped. Reflexivity acts on the objective reality and often reshapes it into subjective reality, which has consequences for the participants. A theoretical interpretation of the process of reflexive knowledge is given by George Soros.

George Soros on Reflexive Knowledge. A sociological aspect of knowledge phenomena is how an individual participant facing a given knowledge event or situation perceives, interacts, and formulates his or her response to it. Sociologists call this process "reflexivity". Much before the sociologists' interest in reflexivity, Norbert Wiener, the founder of "cybernetics" had studied this phenomenon and gave the concepts of feedback and feedforward mechanisms (Wiener, 1948). But, there is a fundamental difference between the two approaches. While reflexivity deals with knowledge as an organic cognitive process of the human mind, cybernetics deals with information in its purely physical format devoid of any cognitive element. Both the approaches involve adaptive response based on feedback. In fact, reflexivity as a feedback based response phenomenon is at work in cell biology ever since life originated on the planet earth.

Interpretation of Reflexivity. Soros explains that all human encounters with knowledge maintain equilibrium with facts or reality at one end and statement or thoughts at the other end. In natural science, the two sides of the equilibrium fully match or merge because there is no element of bias of the observer acting on the thought. In contrast, in events and situations involving thinking participants reality never gets truly reflected in the mind of the participant. The subjectivity of the observer's/ participant's thought invariably distorts the fact or reality behind the observed item, and hence what the participant perceives is not the reality, but a changed version of the reality. This implies that the participant is not dealing with knowledge *per se* but with the biased version of thinking. Any response based on this thinking affects the outcome in this unreal position. There are two types of relationship between thinking and reality: a) an active relationship referring to "participating function", and b) a passive relationship, i.e., "cognitive function". The interaction between the two functions is "reflexivity".

Reflexivity is a "two-way feedback mechanism in which reality helps shape the participants' thinking and the participants' thinking helps shape reality in an unending process in which thinking and reality may come to approach each other but can never become identical" (Soros, 1994: webpage). If thinking and reality are identical, then one's perception of reality corresponds to that of natural sciences. Complete identification does not happen in human situations because of the participants' perceptional bias in grasping reality. Hence there can neither be universally valid interpretation of reality nor certainty of outcome of decisions based on changing reality. In essence, reflexivity positions events and situations in a different way that has far reaching implications for epistemology, sociology, decision-making, interpersonal relationships, commerce, industry and finance. It affects our perception of the world itself, and more particularly so in the post-modernistic era. There exists equilibrium between the participants' perception of an event and the reality. Three different conditions of equilibrium are possible in reflexivity: a) "normal" in which the participants' view of a given event or situation and it's actual state of affairs do converge; b) far-from equilibrium conditions in which thinking and reality are very far apart with no tendency to converge; and c) one of revolutionary change where the participants' view cannot cope-up with change.

The fact that reflexivity occurs only intermittently provides us the insight of the events as they unfold, which enables us to formulate our response in the light of changes in the events and hence is of great significance. If reflexivity is non-intermittent, and it is so in most cases, we may look at it only from a different angle. Even then it could serve a useful purpose as we can draw general inferences by studying these normal, common standard situations. One has to distinguish "between humdrum, everyday events in which the element of indeterminacy introduced by the reflexive connection can be treated as mere noise, and historical events where the reflexive interaction brings about an irreversible change both in the participants' views and the actual state of affairs" (Soros, 1994). Reflective thinking is also influenced by *affect*.

Affect. Reflective thinking generally means pondering over an already perceived item of knowledge. In reflective thinking, the person debates within over the effects of one's action or the knowledge factors in the situation leading to action, which may also guide him in further thinking on the subject. A related process is *affect*. Affect is the positively or negatively valenced subjective reactions that a person experiences at a given point in time (Wyer, Clore and Isbell, 1999). An affect may be pleasant or unpleasant. In reflexivity, one's state of knowledge pertaining to a phenomenon or interpersonal encounters is the resultant of the interaction between the individual and the other participating persons or the changes caused. Whereas, in affect the state of feelings or knowledge in the individual is generally an internal response to the existing state of cognition or newly formed cognitions. Affective reactions are caused by one's perception of his immediate stimulus environment or by thoughts about past or future events. Narcotics and physical stimulations can also elicit affect reactions. Affect influences one's information processing mechanism in the brain, such as declarative knowledge, procedural knowledge, and judgments. Affect plays a role in behaviour and mood, memory and cognition (declarative, procedural, and episodic knowledge), judgment, motivation, creativity, communication, and persuasion.

KNOWLEDGE POLITICS

The impact of science and technology on modern society is overwhelming. Every new major scientific development results in a number of useful applications, which at the same time pose a number of problems needing society's immediate attention. Thus, knowledge particularly scientific and technical knowledge is becoming a co-determinant in shaping the political agenda. Knowledge politics is emerging as a new field of political activity in which deciding the social role of knowledge is a key issue. In this context, a number of new questions may be raised on the social role of knowledge. The questions raised by Stehr and Meja are: "What knowledge needs to be regulated and whose responsibility is this regulation? What knowledge do we require in the context of regulative knowledge politics? Do we need to regulate new scientific knowledge as closely or even more strictly as, say, traffic is regulated? If not, why not? If yes, for what reasons and protecting what interests? If strict restrictions apply, could absolute prohibitions (for example, outlawing human germline gene therapy) be enforced? Is knowledge about to become a private good (again)? What will be the identity of some of the major actors involved and how will knowledge politics be organized?" (Stehr and Meja, 2005, p.19). These questions fall into the domain of sociology of knowledge, and answers to these questions will shape a nation's knowledge policies.

SOCIAL EPISTEMOLOGY

In the early 1950s, a parallel development in the converging field of knowledge, social sciences and philosophy was initiated by two librarians - Margaret Egan and Jesse H.

Shera when they articulated a theory of "social epistemology" as a theoretical basis for bibliographic control. They defined social epistemology as "the study of those processes by which society *as a whole* seeks to achieve a perspective or understanding relation to the total environment- physical, psychological and intellectual" (Egan and Shera, 1952, p. 132). Clarifying the position of social epistemology in relation to other approaches to the problem of knowledge and society, they contend that social epistemology studies cognitive behaviour at the social level, whereas sociologists study goal-oriented and affective behaviour at the social level, psychologists study goal-directed and affective behaviour at the individual level, and classical epistemologists study cognitive behaviour at the individual level (Egan and Shera, 1952). Expressing in concrete terms, Egan and Shera state that epistemology is a theoretical framework for the study of the production, distribution, and utilization of intellectual products in society.

Fritz Machlup's major studies on the economics of information in America (Maclup, 1962, 1980, 1984) created further interest in the new field among select economists and sociologists.

There is near consonance between Shera's exposition of social epistemology and the "new sociology of knowledge". There can be no doubt that the theory of social epistemology propounded by Shera is a major contribution to the sociology of librarianship and information science.

Independent of the work of Egan and Shera, Steve Fuller from the discipline of philosophy announced "social epistemology" as a new branch of study within philosophy and gave its framework (Fuller, 1987). Fuller's brief is that social epistemology should supplant individual epistemology, and that it does not fit comfortably with naturalistic, psychological, or even historical approaches to epistemology (Schmitt, 1987, p. 1). Fuller's exposition has been detailed earlier in chapter 8.

CLOSURE

The branch of sociology dealing with the study of the social origin of knowledge and its characteristics is called "sociology of knowledge" (SOK). SOK developed on the twin concepts of social or existential determination of thought and historicism evolved by Max Scheler, and Karl Mannheim. Karl Marx's analysis of production of ideas was a significant contribution. Mannheim's theses interpret SOK in terms of ideology and utopia. Vilfredo Pareto of France stressed the dominance of factors like race, ethnicity, and class-based ideologies in shaping social behavior in society. American flavor was added by Thorstein Veblem, G.H.Mead, Robert Merton, and Talcott Parsons.

Sociology of knowledge interprets the role of social forces prevailing at any given historical period and critical social events on the generation of ideas and formation of ideologies, the characteristics of knowledge production, dissemination and use. While sociology of knowledge in its broader approach provides theoretical and philosophical perspectives of knowledge drawn from cultural, historical and geographical accounts; in its non-dogmatic approach called "new sociology of knowledge", it deals with knowledge of everyday life and related practical issues. The new sociology of knowledge, shorn of philosophical and ideological overtones, studies knowledge as it is shaped in everyday life and as practical problems, e.g., environmental issues. Werner Stark's value system theory of knowledge explains that social values held by an individual effectively shapes his or her perception of a given knowledge situation.

Reflexivity forms a part of social cognition studies. It explains certain aspects of cognitive processing of knowledge by participants in an action situation. Reflexivity affects knowledge in three ways: a) shapes one's self-identity, particularly so in post-modernism; b) impacts on social research programmes by reflexive transfer of research worker's personal traits and beliefs on the research work; and c) acts on the objective reality, and often reshapes it into subjective reality which has consequences for the participants. George Soros maintains that in all human encounters with knowledge the mind maintains equilibrium with reality at one end and thinking at the other end. Three different conditions of equilibrium are possible in reflexivity, namely: a) where one's perception of reality and the actual reality merge, as in science; b) where one's thinking and actual reality are far apart; and c) where the participant's view cannot cope up with change. According to Soros, reflectivity occurs only intermittently. A process related to reflective thinking is affect, i.e., feeling or the state of knowledge experienced by the individual at a given point of time. It is an internal response of an individual to the existing state of cognition or newly formed cognitions. Affect influences one's information processing mechanism by brain. It also plays a role in behaviour, mood, motivation, memory, and many cognitive and intellectual processes. Because of the acute implications of knowledge (particularly scientific and technical knowledge) on society, knowledge is becoming a co-determinant factor in shaping the political agenda of a society giving raise to what is called knowledge politics or social control of knowledge.

There is a counter part of SOK in philosophy, which is called "social epistemology." Social epistemology was described first by J. H. Shera, a librarian. His concept of social epistemology may be considered to be more in tune with SOK than epistemology. A number of disciplines like science, technology, religion, and education have also come under the scanner of sociological interpretation. Sociology of science has been enriched by the works of scholars like Karl Popper and Thomas Kuhn. The study of SOK can benefit by adapting some of the principles and methods used to discover reality by disciplines like sciences, and economics. Knowledge creators and information professionals operate within the boundaries of society. As such, a deeper understanding of the social dimension of knowledge helps them to examine their role in society.

REFERENCES

Becker, Howard and Dahlke, Helmut, Otto. Max Scheler's Sociology of Knowledge. Pp. 159-175. In Motwani, Kewal. Ed. Sociology of Knowledge. Bombay, Somaiya Publications, 1976. (Reprint from Philosophical and Phenomenological Research, 1940-41 Vol. Pp. 310-322).

Berger, Peter L. and Luckmann, Thomas. The Social Construction of Reality: A Treatise in the Sociology of Knowledge. Harmondsworth (England), Penguin Books, 1966.

Cf. Bourdieu, P. Distinction: A Social Critique of the Judgment of Taste. Richard Nice. Tr. London, Routledge & Kegan Paul, 1984.

Coser, Lewis A. Knowledge, Sociology of. Pp.428-34. In Sills, David L. Ed. International Encyclopaedia of the Social Sciences. Vol.8. London, Macmillan & Free Press, 1968.

Egan, M.E. and Shera, J.H. Foundations of a theory of bibliography. *Library Quarterly* 22: 125-137, 1952.

Fuller, Steve. On regulating what is known: A way to social epistemology. *Synthese 73: 145- 183, Oct. 1987.*

Giddens, Anthony. Modernity and Self- Identity. Stanford, Stanford University Press, 1991.

Haggerty, Kevin D. Review essay. Ruminations on reflexivity. *Current Sociology* 51: 153-169, March, 2003.

Johnson, Allan G. Ed. The Blackwell Dictionary of Socialogy: A Users Guide to Aociological Language. Oxford, Blackwell Publishers, 1995.

Cf. Kraft, J. In Grunwald, Ernst. Das Problem der Soziologie des Wissens. 1934.

McCarthy, E. Doyle. The Sociology of Knowledge. Pp. 2953-60. In Borgotta, Edgar F. and Montgomery, Rhonda, J. V. Eds. Encyclopaedia of Sociology. Ed.2, Vol. 5. New York, Macmillan Reference, 2000.

Machlup, Fritz. Knowledge: Its Creation, Distribution, and Economic Significance. 3 Vols. Princeton (MA), Princeton University Press, 1980, 1982, 1984.

Machlup, Fritz. The Production and Distribution of Knowledge in the United States. Prineton (MA), Princeton University Press, 1962.

Mannheim, Karl. Essays on the Sociology of Knowledge. Kecskemeti, Paul. Ed. London, Routledge & Kegan Paul, 1952. (Reprint 1972).

Mannheim, Karl. Ideology and Utopia. London, Routledge & Kegan Paul, 1936. (Reprint, 1972).

Marx, Karl and Engels, Friedrich. Concerning the Production of Consciousness. Pp. 97-108. In Curtis, James E. and Petras, John W. The Sociology of Knowledge: A Reader. London, Duckworth, 1982. (Reprint from German Ideology, edited by R. Pascal. New York, Internationnal Publishers, 1963. Pp. 27-43).

Pareto, Vilfredo. The Mind and Society. Translated by Andrew Bonigiorno. Livingstone, Arthur. Ed. New York, Bruce Harcourt, 1935. (Reprint, New York, Dover, 1963).

Parsons, Tolcott. An Approach to the Sociology of Knowledge. Pp. 282-306. In Curtis, James E. and Petras, John W. Eds. The Sociology of Knowledge: A Reader. London, Duckworth, 1982. (Reprint of Transactions of the Fourth World Congress of Sociology, IV. Louvian, International Sociological Association, 1959. Pp. 25-49).

Piepe, Anthony. Knowledge and Social Order: The Relationship between Human Knowledge and the Construction of Social Theory. London, Heinemann, 1971.

Popper, K. R., The Sociology of Knowledge. Pp. 649-660. In Curtis, James E. and Petras, John W. Eds. The Sociology of Knowledge: A Reader. London, Duckworth, 1982. (From The Open Society and Its Enemies. Ed.5. Routledge & Kegan Paul, 1966).

Remmling, Gunter W. The Sociology of Karl Mannheim: With a Bibliographical Guide to the Sociology of Knowledge, Ideological Analysis, and Social Planning. London, Routledge & Kegan Paul, 1975.

Cf. Scheler, Max. Problems of a Sociology of Knowledge. Tr. by M.S. Frings. Stikkers, K.W. Ed. With an Introduction. London, Routledge & Kegan Paul, 1924. (Reprint 1980).

Schmitt, Frederick F. Introduction (to the Issue on "Social Epistemology"). *Synthese 73: 1-2, 1987.*

Scott, John. Social Theory: Central Issues in Sociology. London, Sage Publications, 2006.

Shera, J.H. The Foundations of Education for Librarianship. New York, Wiley-Becker & Hayes, 1972. .

Soros, George. The Theory of Reflexivity. Lecture Delivered on April 26, 1994 to the MIT Department of Economics World Economy Conference, Washington, D.C. (http://WWW.geocites.com/ecocorner/intelarea/gs1html).

Stark, W. The Sociology of Knowledge: An Essay in Aid of a Deeper

Understanding of the History of Ideas. London, Routledge & Kegan Paul, 1971. (Original Print, 1958). Republished With a New Introduction by E. Doyle McCarthy. New Brunswick (NJ), Transaction, 1991.

Stehr,Nico and Meja, Volker. Introduction: The Development of the Sociology of Knowledge and Science. Pp.1-27. *In* Stehr, Nico and Meja, Volker. Society & Knowledge: Contemporary Perspectives in the Sociology of Knowledge & Science. Ed.2. New Brunswick (NJ), Transaction Publications, 2005.

Sweetman, Paul. Twenty-first century dis-ease? Habitual reflexivity or the reflexive habitus. *Sociological Review* 51(4): 528-549, Nov.2003.

Tavakol, M. Sociology of Knowledge. New Delhi, Sterling Publishers, 1990.

Thellefsen, T.L. and Thellefsen, M. M. Pragmatic semiotics and knowledge organization. *Knowledge Organization* 31 (3): *177-187, 2004.*

Wiener, Norbert. Cybernetics or Control and Communication in the Animal and the Machine. New York, Technology Press, 1948.

Wyer, Robert S. (Jr.), Clore, Gerald L. and Isbell, Linda M. Affect and information processing. Pp. 1-77. *In* Zanna, Mark P. Ed. *Advances in Experimental Psychology.* Vol. 31. San Diego, Academic Press, 1999.

Znaniecki, Florian. Sociology and Theory of Knowledge. Pp. 307-319. In Curtis, James E. and Petra, John W. The Sociology of Knowledge: A Reader. London, Duckworth, 1982. (Reprint of Znaniecki, Florian. The Social Role of the Man of Knowledge. New York, Columbia University Press, 1940. Pp.1-22).

Domains

12

SOCIAL KNOWLEDGE

Knowledge has many dimensions, and among them its social aspects constitute an important dimension. Social dimension of knowledge, in its broadest perspective, consists of knowledge of all known things in the universe that leaves a social impact on society, its actors, its structure, its components, and processes, i.e., the contents of "sociology". It does not exclude knowledge scientific, and knowledge humanistic to the extent they have social implications. Thus, social dimension of knowledge encompasses knowledge mirroring sociology, and sociology of knowledge corresponding to social origin of knowledge. In this chapter we consider the domain of social knowledge, its origin, development, and impact on individuals and society.

Sociology is a major branch of study within the broad domain of knowledge known as "social sciences". Social sciences together with humanities and the sciences constitute the universe of knowledge. A general definition of sociology is the "systematic formulation and testing of theoretical generalizations about the forms, processes, and consequences of the behaviour of human beings in relation to each other" (Lundberg et al., 1968, p. 14). Sociology studies "human societies, their interactions, and the processes that preserve and change them. It does this by examining the dynamics of constituent parts of societies such as institutions, communities, populations, and gender, racial, or age groups. Sociology also studies social status or stratification, social movements, and social change, as well as societal disorder in the form of crime, deviance, and revolution" (Encyclopaedia Britannica, 2007. Vol. 27, p. 331).

Social customs, norms, and organization, however rudimentary may be, have been a part of every culture on earth beginning from the days of cavemen venturing out to hunt or hug. Some features of what constitutes modern day sociology have been with us from the dawn of civilization and even earlier. All civilizations— whether Indus Valley civilization (Harappa and Mahonjedaro) of India, ancient civilization of Egypt or Inca civilization of Latin America had evolved their own social and material knowledge without which they could not have existed. *Manu Dharma Shastra* (200 BC/300 AD) is an example of a text on the sociology and religion of ancient India. Sociology in its modern sense could not have developed then as living was simple; the society was based on traditional agriculture and simple essential crafts. Further, religion and the authoritarian ruling pattern did not allow reasoning and thinking outside the set pattern. Sociology, in its modern sense, came into being in the eighteenth century Europe. Karl Marx (1818-1883), Emile Durkheim (1858-1917) and Max Weber (1864-1920) are considered the founding fathers of modern sociology, although the term "sociology" was coined by the French philosopher Auguste Comte (1798-1857).

WHAT IS SOCIAL KNOWLEDGE?

Social knowledge is any item of knowledge that has social consequences for society and its constituent parts, such as individuals, communities, institutions, and organizations. In other words, what all sociology represents is social knowledge. Even though social knowledge has been with us from the dawn of human history, its formal recognition, accumulation, interpretation and growth began from the late nineteenth century when the discipline of sociology got firmly established. With the social revolutions that have taken place since then, the stock of social knowledge has grown by leaps and bounds, and its boundaries have been extending fast. In the present context of modernity, Anthony Giddens, a renowned sociologist, observes that "... awareness of social rules, expressed first and foremost in practical consciousness, is the very core of that 'knowledegability' which specifically characterizes human agents. As social actors, all human beings are highly 'learned' in respect of knowledge which they possess, and apply, in the production and reproduction of day-to-day social encounters..." (Giddens, 1984, p. 21). In the same work Giddens draws a distinction between discursive consciousness and practical consciousness where "the former refers to knowledge the actors are able to articulate (what is said), and the latter refers to tacit knowledge, which actors are able to draw on in action but are unable to express (what is simply done)" (Orlikowski, 2001, p. 63).

Social knowledge differs from scientific knowledge in its selection of objects for investigation, in the subjective nature of all social phenomena, and in its methodology of approach to search for reality. In physical sciences, the object of investigation is natural phenomena, which are universal in nature and unchanging by themselves. Hence the scope for subjective interpretation is limited. In contrast, social knowledge deals with human actions and behaviours, which are determined by changing context and situation. Context and situation are characterized by the interaction of time, space, social environment, and the behaviour of individual actors and groups. Hence social research finding is never repeated in the universe, a truth that needs to be accounted in the development of social sciences research methodology. Since human nature is too subtle and elusive, in social science research the "assumptions about man and society often will have a decisive role in constructing the resultant pathways chosen for these pathways (model) really determine the research design. It is, therefore, not enough to pronounce the results; it is all the more important to spell out how it was obtained and under what assumptions" (Majumdar, 2005. p. 8). Scientific research follows scientific method in which repeatability and confirmation of a hypothesis by experimental proof is a fundamental requirement. On the other hand, social theories have to rely on subjective methodology, even though they may use some of the scientific procedures like statistical analysis and deductive inferencing. The importance of theories and laws in the development of scientific knowledge is an accepted fact. This is not the case with social sciences and humanities. Contemporary debates in philosophy of science on the role of laws in social sciences have thrown up opposing views. "Social science has no laws, it needs no laws" is the position taken by John Roberts. In support of his stand he cites that the nature of social science differs fundamentally from science and scientific laws, and hence any analogy with science is not relevant (Roberts, 2004). Opposed to this is the stand taken by Kincaid that while "the complex nature of social phenomena certainly presents difficulties, there is good reason to think that laws in social science are possible both in principle and practice" (Kincaid, 2004, p.183). He argues that complicating causes surrounding a social phenomenon can be handled in a way that allows reliable causal knowledge. Since humanities and arts are largely governed by emotions and taste there can be no laws governing them.

The Three Divisions of Social Knowledge. Sociologists classify sociology under three headings: a) *traditional* or *pre-modernity* corresponding to pre-Industrial Revolution era; b) *modernity* beginning from late nineteenth century and early twentieth century featured by industrial revolution, population dynamics, coming into existence of nation-states and secularization of social attitude; and c) *post-*

modernity characterized by urbanization, consumerism, impersonal relationship, increased encroachment of individuals' lives by governments, globalization and growth of transnational corporations, and the result of what Karl Polyani calls *the Great Transformation* (Bilton et al., *1996)*. There is no consensus among Western sociologists as to whether they are still in modernity or have entered post-modernity. These divisions seem relevant only to advanced countries of the West and possibly Japan, but not to the developing countries. The latter countries did not go through industrial revolution, were under colonial rule, and presently they are in different stages of development. The present state of development of these countries, at any rate, leaves them far behind post-modernity. A more helpful division of sociology appropriate to developing countries of Asia, Africa and Latin America is pre-colonial, colonial, and post-colonial. Since social knowledge is a mirror image of sociology, social knowledge may also be divided into: traditional or pre-modernity, modernity, and post-modernity; or pre-colonial, colonial, and post-colonial as applicable. The pre-modernity social systems have disappeared in the West, but they are still alive in many parts of developing countries like rural India. Their unique features, well advanced in certain respects, are represented by "community knowledge", which is discussed in the later part of this chapter.

EPISTEMOLOGICAL BASE OF SOCIOLOGY

A search for epistemological and ontological foundations of classical sociology takes us to Karl Marx, Emile Durkheim, and Max Weber, the founding fathers of sociology. The scenarios they present refer to large-scale holistic views of politico-social systems and not limited or individual threads of sociology. These views are presented below following McLennan's *Exploring Society* (McLennan, et al., 2000).

The Scientific Realism of Marx. Marx's philosophy of sociology consists of *scientific realism* in epistemology and *dialectical materialism* in ontology. He believed that both natural science and social science have some kind of 'objective reality' hidden behind them. By discovering and applying that reality, it is possible to control the forces of nature and society. While socially applied scientific knowledge generates productive forces, the analysis of social reality leads to identification of *socio-economic class* and *class struggle* that underpins capitalism. Unlike science which is experimental, social science has to develop systematic concepts including 'power of observation' to observe and capture concrete reality that shapes society. The discovery and analysis of reality behind dynamic forces acting in capitalistic societies, he believed, led to the formulation of his theory of capitalism. This reality of capitalist society consists of surface phenomena of events and actions, and deeply hidden structures of social life that are at variance with each other. Understanding the nature and force of this interplay between the surface and the hidden faces of society is of utmost importance to the study of sociology.

On the ontological front, Marx's view is expressed in terms of dialectical materialism. According to this, social world is dynamic and materialist in character. Things in the social world are concrete, contradictory, and dynamic. This materialistic relationship is an ongoing process that establishes the real concrete existences in the social world, which in turn forms a part of the larger universe.

Positivism of Durkheim. Durkheim's epistemological framework of sociology is 'positivism'. For him, sociology is a positive science since it deals with entities and realities in society, which he sees it as a *social organism*. Hence social reality and norms can be 'objectively' studied by discovering empirical facts through observation and scientific method, the two principle features of positivism as in scientific research. For example, scientifically collected data on suicide, its analysis and objective interpretation would give an accurate picture of one aspect of social reality in a given society. Thus, for him, to *think of social facts as 'things'* which when accurately observed and properly interpreted will show the distinctive nature of social conditions and how they change over time. However, his brand of positivism treats collective moral phenomena as an important object of social inquiry, though such a thing is not outwardly visible in society and also not in line with the spirit of science.

Ontologically, Durkheim leaned towards the theory that the nature of social life is conditioned more by moral facts than by material considerations. He believed in the bonding power of collective identity rather than in individual's social abstraction. According to him, all belief systems are about the power of the social bond; and even practice of science is an alternative form of worship.

Neo-Kantianism of Weber. Weber is convinced that it is impossible to get at the objective social reality. Reality does exist in social systems, but we cannot know it because whatever 'objective reality' we see behind social processes is a construct of our subjective mind. Since this view of social reality is similar to the one expounded by the German philosopher Immanuel Kant (1874-1904), about the nature of reality in external world, it is called 'neo-Kantian'. However, Weber believes that it is possible to get insights of social reality by studying society through the formulation and application of conceptual frameworks, such as capitalism, consumerism, and so on. But these conceptual frameworks are of 'ideal type' and are useful for research work or in explaining the social insights, but cannot capture social reality. Bureaucratic rationality with its brutal emphasis on efficiency, order, and administration determines the functioning of modern society, and this seems to be Weber's ontological perspective of sociology.

INTERPRETATION OF SOCIAL KNOWLEDGE

Social knowledge is context bound because social phenomena are context dependent. To get at the real meaning of knowledge representing a social phenomenon, one has to take into consideration the social framework of the period. For example, how one interprets the meaning of the U.S. Constitution which affirms "All men are created equal". Do we take that the institution of slavery, and rights of blacks and women were excluded from its purview. To interpret this properly, one has to consider the social conditions prevailing at that time and also what the framers of the constitution had in mind. The interpretation and the conclusions that follow will be subjective, as it depends on the choice of interpretation framework used. To arrive at reality, thus calls for the application of methods that are different from that of science. One such method is *hermeneutics*, the science of interpretation. Originally, the concept was applied to the interpretation of bible. Now its scope is widened to include interpretation of a wide range of forms and activities, such as works of art, writings, and acts of social and cultural significance. Hermeneutics is of particular importance to the study of social knowledge as its main concern is to study the subject matter on hand in its social context of the times. Hermeneutics enables one to find the true meaning or valid interpretation of knowledge of events and things. Because of the time gap and the changed social conditions arrival at truth is subjective, implying that "meaning is not fixed or predictable. This makes meaning and the social life on which meaning rests difficult to identify with any certainty" (Johnson, 1995, p.129).

Knowledge Cross-Check. In interpreting social life and social behaviour, sociologists do not stop just at coaxing meaning from out of social context and environment binding the phenomenon. In order to arrive at reality, sociologists make use of : a) the knowledge of how people make sense of their own lives and behaviour, i.e., what the individual thinks that he or she is doing and why, about how they make sense of their surroundings and other people; and b) the knowledge that sociologists bring to what they observe. The latter part is wider in scope and includes use of concepts like "role" and "social system" to understand social life. This method of interpreting social life and behaviour is named *double hermeneutics* by Giddens (Johnson, 1995).

Reality in Social Concepts. Concepts represent knowledge and knowledge represents reality. This is true of social sciences too. Knowledge of social life and behaviour are also represented by concepts. The meanings of terms that represent a social concept is not always permanent; it varies with the change in reality constituting the concept. The concept of "family", given as an example by Zins though not in the context of social knowledge, illustrates the change in reality constituting a concept and its consequences. In the past, the concept of "family" represented only heterosexual couples, with or without offspring, and that constituted reality. It is no more so now, at least in many Western cultures. Nowadays, unmarried couples, single-parent families, homosexual couples, and communal families also come under the ambit of "family"; in fact, the term 'partner' has almost replaced 'husband'/ 'wife'. An example from the Indian scenario is the term "harijans", earlier known has "untouchables". After independence and the "one man one vote" based democracy, the status of harijans has changed so significantly that the past reality behind the term does not match fully with the present. The consequence of the changing reality is the appearance of "cognitive dissonance when our concepts cease to represent the changing reality. This is the essence of the intellectual crisis that we commonly call "Post-modernism" (Zins, 2004, p. 52).

EFFECTS OF SOCIAL KNOWLEDGE

Social knowledge, apart from its main functions of describing social behaviour, offering solutions to social and socially related ills of a society, and help advancement of social progress, is also a source of power, agent of change, and an intellectual resource. Some of the other social effects of knowledge have been explained here.

Wisdom in Social Actions. Our actions and responses, both as individuals and as members of social groups, are the outcome of the decisions made in everyday life as individuals, and as constituents of social groups, institutions, corporate bodies, and governments. The situations calling for making decisions may range from inconsequential to that of life and death. A well thought out decision involves.

1. Assessing the situation in the light of existing information and tacit knowledge;
2. Study and evaluation of different available decision options and their likely consequences.
3. Selection of a particular action by applying wisdom.

A decision based on the application of wisdom differs from that of scientific or rational decision-making as in the latter, "imagination, positive subjectivity, social, cultural and human factors play only minor roles" (Narayana, 1991, p. 20). The seriousness of the consequences of a decision varies. The nature and the intensity of the outcome of a decision depend upon the situation and the actors involved. Decisions resulting in social repercussions are often made in a mental forum tinged by socio-psychological currents. Pride, prejudice, piety, loyalty, love, affection, revenge, jealousy, hatred, self-interest, and a host of other emotional factors invariably play a part in arriving at the decision. It is wisdom that keeps a check on the play of these emotional factors. The effects of a social decision will be felt individually and personally. In contrast, the effects of decisions required to be made by scientists, technologists, artists, linguists, and philosophers during the course of their vocation will be limited to the activity of their research, reworking of art, and the nature of discourse as the case may be. It is something like a course correction, which is an integral part of research and academics. In general, outside social sciences and medicine, such decisions will not have any serious physical and emotional consequences on others.

The fact that decisions which give rise to social actions affect individuals and/ or particular segments of society emphasizes the importance of knowledge and wisdom in the process of decision-making. Since final decision rests on the selection of one option among several others, application of wisdom in that process decides the good or bad of the outcome. An unwise decision on the part of a member of a family can destroy that household's harmony; an injudicious decision by a lawyer can ruin a client; an injurious decision by a public health authority can adversely affect the health of the community; a careless decision in business can result in loss, customer dissatisfaction, retrenchment of employees, and even the closure of the business itself. Wisdom-based decisions will minimize, if not eliminate, injurious consequences in areas of social interaction. If wisdom is so precious then what it is?

Wisdom is an abstract mental ability. It is generally accepted that wisdom is derived from knowledge, knowledge from information, and information from data. Wisdom involves judgment, and the action following a judgment must result in most good. While arriving at a judgment ethical and social considerations form part of the judgment process (Rowley, 2006). Wisdom which was earlier thought mainly as an individual's accomplishment is now being identified with organizations too. There is no precise way of telling when and how knowledge becomes wisdom. It appears that learning from experience, vision and mental maturity are some of the lead factors that go to shape wisdom. Still there is a current rhetoric in certain quarters of "Wisdom Management"; and it is difficult to imagine how one can manage wisdom and that too for others.

Knowledge as a Social Binder. The proverb "birds of the same feather flock together" underlines an important social characteristic of knowledge. Persons sharing the same knowledge or working in the same knowledge field when come together develop a natural affinity. This is a social phenomenon.

Knowledge establishes a natural bond between them by opening up further channels of communication to exchange knowledge about topics of common interest, and sharing of experiences. They come together to meet and discuss, exchange notes and views, debate and argue, and criticize constructively. This social interaction generally gets initiated by an individual or a small group of like-minded people with a common cause or interest. Later, it may get expanded to include a large number of people subscribing to the same objective. This is how social organizations like professional bodies, cultural organizations, business associations and unions, special groups, and alumni associations come into existence. These social organizations in the initial stages may be just small informal groups and later grow into large formal groups with written constitutions.

The objectives of such groups may vary from egalitarian to mundane. They may become pressure groups to influence decision-makers in favour of their exclusive interests. Some bodies may take up even advisory and executive functions. Their influence may extend from local level to that of national and international. With the enlargement of the group and increased specialization division of labour in the form of formation of committees and sub-committees dealing with specific knowledge or organizational functions takes place. Knowledge achieves a social function of binding different individuals working in the same area or having shared interests or common cause in a particular knowledge area. Binding characteristic of knowledge may take different forms and make use of different media of communication.

The social binding characteristic of knowledge discussed so far in general terms is technically explained by sociologists through the theory of social interactions. Social interaction involves many social processes and one of them is cooperation. Two or more persons or groups working for a common purpose in an enterprise are based on cooperation. Human interaction acquires some structure or organization to carry on its activity. When unacquainted individuals or groups come together to carry on complicated relationships to achieve the set goals, the association thus formed is a formal organization. There are three basic types of formal organizations: a) normative; b) coercive; and c) utilitarian. When formal organizations are based on voluntary cooperation with specific goals, they are called voluntary associations, which fall under normative type. For members of a voluntary association, as it is a love of labour for them, they work spare-time unlike paid professional employees.

A characteristic of voluntary associations is that the interest of the association and its members are not shared by the whole society. Voluntary associations are "often testing grounds for social programs that are still too controversial to be handled by institutional organizations. They also provide a channel through which the private citizen can share in the decision-making processes of society. This fact is particularly important to interest groups, political and social movements..." (Perry, 2000, p. 86). Professional associations are mostly voluntary associations. Some of them wield enormous influence in safeguarding and promoting the interests of the profession and its members. They act for the entire profession, if they are granted recognition to do so, examples being the American Medical Association, and the Institution of Chartered Accountants of India. In professional associations, knowledge takes upon the characteristic of group binding as well as representing the professional standards and presenting the social side of the profession to the society.

Digital Communities. In the world of cyberspace, social binding characteristic of knowledge has taken new forms like 'social networks' and 'digital communities'. The network phenomenon is an informal social interaction mostly conducted through Internet, web sites and mobile phone. Documents like books, journal articles, reports, and other forms of personal communications beside carrying information also help structure society, create social groups and maintain a sense of shared identity. In the promotion of digital communities and social networks information have long provided interesting social glue (Brown and Daguid, 2000). The practice of copying and circulating texts among religious communities and philosophical schools pre-dates the printing press. Sharing of information by exchanging preprints, circulation of letters is most common among scientists, which lead to the formation of what is called "invisible college". The sharing of information, and interests cutting across national boundaries, race, religion and language, has become more common and easier with the wide spread use of Internet enabled blogs, e-mail, chat, voice-mail, teleconferencing. Information sharing through Internet has created "Net communities" meeting the needs of persons seeking friendship, locating partners for marriage, getting tips on hobbies, and many other human desires. A negative side of digital communities is that they may be exploited by unscrupulous persons to carry out activities, which result in social evils, such as promotion of pornography, identity theft, and other cyber crimes.

Social networks are of two types: "Networks of Practice" and "Communities of Practice". In Networks of Practice, it is the common work-related practices followed by members that act as the glue. Practice and knowledge serve as the common factor among all members of the group, who are otherwise not familiar with one another. These networks mostly depend on indirect communication via websites, bulletin boards and the like; direct interaction between members is very limited. There is more of information diffusion and sharing than creation of knowledge. Communities of Practice, on the other hand, are a specific kind of community. They are focused on specific domains of knowledge, and over time accumulate expertise in those domains. They develop their shared practice by interacting around problems, solutions, and insights, and building a common store of knowledge (Wenger et al., 2001; Coakes and Clarke, 2006). In Communities of Practice, as the term implies, the members know each other more closely and work together as a community. Ideas and knowledge get distributed among the participants. It creates opportunities for development of highly productive and creative output by members. These social networks properly utilized by organizations and institutions will bring positive benefits to organizations and to society as a whole.

TRANSMISSION OF CULTURE IN SOCIETY

'Institutionalization' and 'socialization' are the two vital means of circulating knowledge in society. Sustainability of a society or a culture largely depends upon the processes of institutionalization and socialization.

Institutionalization. Knowledge in a society or a culture is in the minds of its people. Social and cultural knowledge are also entrenched in the customs and traditions, laws, rules and regulations, arts and artifacts, monuments, libraries, archives and web sites, and institutions of that particular society or culture. It is the circulation of knowledge that sustains societies and cultures. Through the process of institutionalization ideas and values, norms and motivation contribute either positively or negatively to the functioning of society. It conveys the collective customs, habits and expectations of man in society (Piepe, 1971).

Socialization. If institutionalization provides organizational base and body for enforcing the norms and values in society, the process of socialization introduces every new born child, over a period of time, to the social and cultural values, beliefs, norms and traditions of the culture or society to which the child belongs. Socialization takes place through several means, such as participation in community life beginning with home, imitation and personal observation, interpersonal relations, schooling, peer group influences, dictation from elders and community leaders, the media, and state intervention. In all socialization acts there is transmission or exchange of knowledge and information conveying social and cultural contents of the given society.

As a child grows into an adult, he or she becomes a trustee or guardian of the social and cultural norms and values of that particular society, and in turn passes on those values to the generation next. It is a continuous process in which knowledge gets recycled and also enriched. What knowledge is transmitted, and how much of it, and in what manner depends on the type of society and its dynamics. Sustainability of society depends as much on its knowledge resources as with other factors.

SOCIAL CONTEXT AND COGNITION

Study of knowledge has taken different approaches, such as epistemological/ philosophical, physical, sociological, and behaviourist psychological. It is also the focus of an interdisciplinary approach, namely social psychology. One definition of social psychology is that it is the study of social cognition, and social behaviour. Cognition is wider in scope than knowledge as the former includes sensation, perception etc. *Socially situated cognition* is a new approach that combines social psychology and *situated cognition*. Situated cognition is seen as an adaptive process formed by the interaction between an agent and the world, both physical and social (Smith and Semin, 2004).

After the initial hold of stimulus-response theories, social psychologists have generally favored mentally driven theories of classical style. Cognition is studied as a computational process of symbolic representation of thoughts with mental processes acting upon stored knowledge or images about the self and the external world. The operating mental processes include systematic or heuristic interpretation of persuasive message, effects of stereotypes, inferencing, and the like. How the thinking processes are influenced by the social factors and the environment, and their impact on the mental image is the central issue in social psychology. In contrast to the mental theory is *socially situated cognition* thesis, which holds that behaviour cannot be based merely on the individual's internal representations, i.e., knowledge, but on the interaction of the individual with the social and physical situations at the time of action. It is generally accepted by social psychologists that cognition, motivation and emotion function jointly as a part of a self-regulatory system sub-serving adaptive action; and mental representations are action oriented. Socially situated cognition thesis goes further and stresses that cognition is the resultant of an adaptive process of interaction between an agent and the world- both physical and social. The function of cognition is the control of adaptive action. Cognition is embodied; is dependent on, and intertwined with sensory motor processes. Cognition is distributed and preserved in the sense that it is encapsulated in our brains; it is also captured, extended and empowered by tools, such as language, physical instruments, and by social resources comprising of individuals and groups; and cognition becomes a socially shared phenomenon. Motivation and affect act as regulators of cognition. When information has no action relevance effect, it tends not to be remembered (Smith and Semin, 2004).

Since cognition is distributed in people, groups, and tools spread across time and space, it can be shared. The sharing property of cognition enables drawing expertise located in any single individual or a group to a wider section of ordinary people and tasks. Further, expertise from different disciplines can be pooled together to obtain solutions to cognitive-wise complex problems involving varied temporal zones and limits. Inherent in sharing of knowledge (*social coupling*) is communication.

Communication. While human bodies maintain their homeostasis, i.e., dynamic equilibrium through neural communication, it is cultural and social communication and co-operative behavioural patterns that maintains homeostasis in human societies. These behavioural patterns are based on the act of symbolic communication, which imparts a high survival value (Neelameghan, 1979).

Communication, apart from transmitting information, is intended to guide social action. Language and communication vitally influence shaping the cognitive content of messages exchanged between the communicators and their audiences. Language, signs, physical gestures and communicator's nuances do affect emotional state of audiences, and thereby the moods. Change in mood could occur in all members involved in sharing, which in turn affects the state of cognition in each member. Physical tools of cognition like books, maps, computers, and other such instruments promote actions leading to cognition. Cognition and its manifestations like the formation of attitudes, stereotypes, person impressions, and other inner representations are essentially for action (Smith and Semin, 2004). Social cognition, social knowledge, and sociology of knowledge are thus interrelated. Social knowledge differs from scientific and humanistic knowledge in its characteristics, research methods, and the nature of impact on individuals and groups.

Community Knowledge. Study of social knowledge in the West is mostly concentrated on social issues in modern societies centering on urban culture. This is because the social life of people there got transformed by Industrial Revolution. Scholars in developing countries have often followed the same trend though the realities are not same. One simple reality in a country like India is that 70% of its population lives in villages, and more than half of them are illiterate marginal farmers and agricultural labourers. They have plenty of knowledge about their natural environment, which no textbook explains. It is not that researchers have ignored rural culture and indigenous knowledge totally, but they are mostly guided by biased urban thinking and urban values in the selection of issues for study. Moreover, such studies have followed a piecemeal approach to the rural communities' issues. Research on indigenous people and their culture was more or less limited to the study of individual tribes or communities, their language, community structure, social lives and customs, and spiritual beliefs under what is generally known as tribal studies or ethnic studies. These studies were pursued initially, for the sake of knowledge itself or to get the background knowledge needed to facilitate proselytisation by Western Christian missionaries. For many of the "civilized" urbanites the general perception even today is that rural community knowledge represents mostly uncivilized/ undeveloped ways of living, and is not of much worth. But this is gradually changing in the light of research findings and changed perception that rural and indigenous knowledge have much to offer to the developed world, especially in areas like environmental protection, development of natural resources-flora, fauna, sand and clay; and in the production of many valuable chemicals and useful rural products.

It is difficult to define precisely "community knowledge". A simplistic definition is knowledge belonging to a community. This is true, but it does not convey fully the meaning of community knowledge in the sense it is used. Community knowledge is knowledge learnt and accumulated by a community over centuries of living intimately with nature, which are passed on from one generation to the generation next. It is not born out of laboratory experiments or academic research or school and college learning. It is evolved out of living amidst surrounding nature observing its impact on their daily living. Knowledge so acquired is mostly shared by word of mouth. Community knowledge is the core on which the community's culture, ways of living and belief systems are built and sustained. It is encased local wisdom. A distinction needs to be made between rural community in general and tribal / aboriginal communities.

Community knowledge possess valuable insights on the environment, the earth, climate, food, medicinal plants and animals, social and cultural value systems, ethnic music and the arts in relation to the community. Such knowledge is essentially locale specific, and may not even be found in modern textbook sources. This knowledge needs to be recorded (may even have to be recreated), processed, disseminated, and utilized (Neelameghan and Chester, 2007). In dealing with community knowledge and rural development one is faced with three critical issues: a) intellectual property rights, b) selection of appropriate information and communication technologies, and c) conflict between economic development and the indigenous way of life. The latter two issues need more exhaustive studies to do justice, and hence not covered here. Community knowledge is the property of the community, and hence it is public property. This calls for placing community knowledge outside the purview of private claims to intellectual property rights. The recent attempts by a private party to get a patent on turmeric whose medicinal value is well recognized for generations in the community knowledge in India is too well known. Fighting intellectual property right *(IPR)* cases on an item by item basis in several countries is difficult and time consuming. Therefore, there is an immediate need to arrive at a consensus at the international level to debar exploitation of community knowledge for economic benefit by private parties under IPR regime.

Some of the vital components of community knowledge are: a) languages/dialects of the local indigenous communities; b) cultures and cultural practice; c) histories; d) geography and local environment: for example ethnobotany; e) relation of the people to the local environments; f) interactions with plants, animals, and climate that promote wellness and productivity of all species in a bioregion; g) foods and raw materials they extract from their territory for use by themselves and for trade with other indigenous communities and the industrial world;

h) legal and historic relationships with their indigenous neighbors and with the nation state or states they reside within; and i) systems of governance and decision-making within the family, community, and nation (Neelameghan and Chester, 2007). Equally important is to recognize community knowledge as one of the natural systems of knowledge which holds promise to solve some of the intractable problems facing the world today, such as pollution, maintenance of natural food-chain, and environmental degradation.

CLOSURE

Any item of knowledge that has consequences for society, its constituent parts, and actors may be termed as social knowledge. Some features of what constitutes modern day sociology existed even in societies predating civilization.

Epistemological origin of sociology is traced to scientific realism of Karl Marx (1818-1883), positivism of Emile Durkheim (1858-1917), and Neo-Kantianism of Max Weber (1864-1920) although the term "sociology" was coined by the French philosopher Auguste Comte (1798-1857). Sociology (and hence social knowledge) is parceled into: a) *traditional* or *pre-modernity*, corresponding to pre-Industrial Revolution era; b) *modernity*, beginning from late nineteenth century and early twentieth century; and c) *post-modernity*. A more helpful division of sociology appropriate to developing countries of Asia, Africa and Latin America is pre-colonial, colonial, and post-colonial.

Social knowledge is context bound. To get at the real meaning of knowledge representing a social phenomenon, one has to take into consideration the social framework of the period. The methods of *hermeneutics* and *double hermeneutics* are employed in interpreting social life and social behaviour. Reality in social concepts keeps changing. Social effects of knowledge on social agents and groups are many, and the fields of impact include: a) decision-making, b) bonding social relations, and c) transmission of culture in society.

Social decision-making is largely influenced by social, cultural and psychological factors. Though the effects of social decisions will be felt individually, and personally; it may have a cascading effect on the whole society or segments of it. Hence decision-making should be guided by wisdom.

Knowledge has the characteristic of binding people through social interaction. One form interaction is cooperation between people. This often appears as formal organizations like trade unions and professional associations. What brings them together are the common interests and common goals of the members of such organizations. Sharing of knowledge and experiences, and circulation of information among members are essential features of such entities. "Digital Communities", "Networks of Practice", and "Communities of Practice" are some of the new forms of binding, which are dependent on the Internet and mobile phone. These fulfill a number of social needs, such as: seeking friendship, sharing interests like hobbies, and even in finding life-partners.

A vital social function of knowledge is transmission of culture in society. This is carried out by means of social instruments of *institutionalization*, and *socialization*. Institutionalization gives structure in the form of laws, rules and regulations, libraries, artifacts, monuments, archives, websites, etc. to the society's knowledge. Socialization is the process by which a society's values, customs, traditions, norms, and ways of living are imparted to every new member born into it. This takes place mostly through upbringing by parents, other social actors, learning and education.

Social psychology is the study of social cognition and social behaviour. The term cognition is wider in scope than knowledge as the former includes sensation, perception and a few others. *Socially situated cognition* view holds that cognition is for the adaptive regulation of action, and mental representations are action oriented; it is intertwined with sensory motor processes; it is distributed; it is also captured and powered by tools such as language, physical instruments, and social actors; and it is a socially shared phenomenon. Motivation and affect have a regulating effect on cognition.

Community knowledge is a segment of social knowledge evolved out of a community's continuous living amidst nature. The community knowledge is the core on which the community's culture, ways of living, and belief systems are built and sustained. It has the potential to offer solutions to many of the problems created by the urban culture.

Social phenomena, by its nature, is neither repeatable to get the same results nor has universal validity for all times. Hence the validity of social knowledge depends on the agents and the situation. This acts as a restriction on the application of social knowledge as a proactive instrument in solving social problems, and in progressing towards a more harmonious society, and a peaceful world. The challenge is how to make social knowledge a more potent force than it is now.

REFERENCES

Bilton, Tony et al. Introductory Sociology. Ed.3. London, Macmillan, 1996.

Brown, John Seely and Daguid, Paul. The Social Life of Information. Boston (Mass.), Harvard Business School Press , 2000.

Coakes, Elayne and Clarke, Steve. The Concept of Communities of Practice. Pp.92-96. *In* Coakes, Elayene and Clark, Steve. Ed. Encyclopaedia of Communities of Practice in Information and Knowledge Management. London. IDEA Group Reference, 2006.

Encyclopaedia Britannica, The New. Ed.15. Chicago, Encyclopaedia Britannica, 2007. Vol.27. Pp.316-364: Social Sciences.

Giddens, Anthony. The Constitution of Society. Cambridge (MA), Polity Press, 1984.

Johnson, Allan G. Ed. The Blackwell Dictionary of Sociology: A Users Guide to Sociological Language. Oxford , Blackwell Publishers, 1995.

Kincaid, Harold. There are Laws in the Social Sciences. Pp.168-184. *In* Hitchcock, Christopher. Ed. Contemporary Debates in Philosophy of Science. Malden (MA.), Blackwell Publishing, 2004.

Lundberg, George A; Schrag, Clarence C.; Larson, Otto N. and Catton, Willliam (Jr.). Sociology. Ed.4. New York, Harper & Row, 1968. (A Harper International Edition). Jr.

McLennan, Gregor; Ryan, Allanah and Spoonley, Paul. Exploring Society: Sociology for New Zealand Students. Auckland, Pearson Education New Zealand, 2000.

Majumdar, P.K. Research Methods in Social Science. New Delhi, Viva Books, 2005.

Narayana, G.J. Library and Information Management. New Delhi, Prentice-Hall of India, 1991.

Neelameghan, A. Expressions of Time in Information Sience and Their Implications. Pp. 103-117. *In* Greenway, Frank. Ed. Time and the Sciences. Paris, Unesco, 1979.

Neelameghan, A and Chester, Greg. Knowledge Management in Relation to Indigenous and Marginalized Communities in the Digital Era: National Conference on Library and Information Studies (NACLIN 2007). Colombo, Sri Lanka, 8-9 March 2007.[on CD]. Proceedings. html

Orlikowski, Wanda J. The Duality of Technology: Rethinking the Concept of Technology in Organizations. Pp. 62-96. *In* Bryant, Christopher G. A. and Jary, David. Eds. The Contemporary Giddens: Social Theory in a Global Age. London, Palgrave, 2001. (longer version appeared in *Organization Science*, 3: 398-427, 1992

Perry, John A. and Perry, Erna, K. Contemporary Society: An Introduction to Social Science. Ed. 9. Needham Heights (MA.), 2000.

Piepe, Anthony. Knowledge and Social Order: The Relationship between Human Knowledge and Construction of Social Theory. London, Heinemann, 1971.

Roberts, John T. There are no Laws of the Social Sciences. Pp.151-167. *In* Hitchcock, Christopher. Ed. Contemporary Debates in Philosophy of Science. Malden (MA.), Blackwell Publishing, 2004.

Rowley, Jennifer. Where is the wisdom that we have lost in knowledge ? *Journal of Documentation 62: 251-270, 2006.*

Smith, Eliot R. and Semin, Gun R. Socially situated cognition: Cognition in its social context. Pp.53-117. *In* Zanna, Mark P. Ed. *Advances in Experimental Social Psychology*, Vol.36, 2004.

Wenger, Etienne; Mc Dermott, Richard; and Snyder, W.M. Cultivating Communities of Practice : A Guide to Managing Knowledge. Boston (Mass.), Harvard Business School Press, 2002.

Zins, Chaim. Knowledge organization: An epistemological perspective. *Knowledge Organization* 31: 49-54, 2004.

13

Science and Scientific Knowledge. Technology

In the universe of knowledge, science occupies a unique position; it forms a major segment of knowledge; it has changed and is still changing the course of human civilization and along with technology, it affects the lives of individuals, their thinking mode and behaviour. The study of the growth of science and of scientific knowledge provide major clues to our understanding the development of specialized branches of science and the evolution of scientific knowledge.

DEVELOPMENT OF SCIENCE

Science is "ordered knowledge of natural phenomena and the rational study of the relations between the concepts in which these phenomena are expressed" (Dampier, 1982, p. xiii). Scientific research is continued search for scientific knowledge and understanding by scientific methods of observation and reasoning. It is through reasoning that the observed data is ascertained as to its nature, relationship with other data and significance. While science is knowledge, scientific research is the means by which scientific knowledge is created or modified. The most important attribute of science, notes Freedman, is its capacity for acquisition of knowledge

(Freedman, 1960). While, knowledge is enriched by science, science has benefited from the foundations of knowledge : logic, reasoning, language and communication.

The histories of both knowledge and science, in the Occident, have the same roots going back to early Greek period. While Socrates made definitions and reasoning a part of scientific method, Plato gave science a philosophic base. Pythagoras stressed the importance of hypothesis, experimentation and deductive logic in scientific research. Aristotle, among others, introduced classification of phenomena. Archimedes developed the scientific process that recognized the need for: a) combining mathematics with experimentation, b) unifying theory with practice, and c) seeking scientific insight through a succession of clearly defined, limited objectives. The Grecian era was followed by a period of darkness. It is only with the dawn of Renaissance when both science and knowledge were retrieved from the clutches of theology, astrology, magic, mythology, and superstition. This retrieval process began with Ibn Rashd (Averroes) followed by Francis Bacon, Copernicus, Galileo, Darwin and Huxley. Galileo is credited with laying the foundations of scientific research. His method of investigation stressed the need for: a) ascertaining the actual nature of phenomena and their relationships before attempting to formulate the causes for the phenomena; b) objectivity in observation; c) taking space and time factors in interpreting the observed and experimental data; and d) using instruments and devising simple experiments based on readily available experimental means (Freedman, 1960). This saw the rapid development of scientific research made possible by contributions from many sources. These included application of mathematical methods (John Napier, Isaac Newton, Renè Descartes, Gottfried Wilhelm von Leibniz, Joseph Louis Lagrange, C.F. Gauss, J. Clerk Maxwell, William Rowan Hamilton, and G. F. Bernhard Riemann) and statistical properties (Blaise Pascal and Pierre de Fermat) as tools of scientific investigation, use of laboratory and field experimentation (Michael Faraday), discovery through classification (Dimitry Ivanovich Mendeleev, Gregor Johann Mendel), experimental confirmation of a hypothesis (Louis Pasteur), use of binomial nomenclature in science communication (Carl von Linne Linnaeus) and use of accumulated mass of systematized information as a means of acquiring new knowledge as in psychological research (Francis Galton) (Freedman, 1960). More recently, computer aided research, observation from outer-space through artificial satellites, and development of remote sensing devices have become a part of scientific techniques. Survey methods, simulation and case studies have become the important means of research in disciplines outside science and technology. Scientific research and research methods have, apart from increasing the scope and tempo of science, given a new orientation to the study of knowledge. The phenomenon of scientific research has become an object of study. Such studies have focused their attention on the history, growth and structure of science, methodology of research, impact of science and technology on life and society, output of scientific literature, methods and effectiveness of communication of research findings, dissemination, and utilization of scientific knowledge.

Science Development in India. Physical sciences did exist in ancient India not by their own right, but as junior adjuncts to the study of religion and metaphysics. As early as 2,500 years ago ancient Hindus had interpreted matter through the theory of atomism. Mathematics and geometry were well developed. The modern system of numerals (Arabic numerals) in use today, which reached Europe via Arabs, is a unique gift from ancient India. Language study had so advanced in ancient India that the study of language structure and grammar had become central to Hindu science as mathematics and geometry were to Greek science. Ayurvedic system of medicine, based on the use of herbals for curing diseases, and surgical operations for treatment of injuries was in common use nearly 2900 years ago (Spangenburg and Moser, 2006). Then for over 1000 years from the time of the decline of Buddhism was the age of darkness in the history of physical sciences in India. A major explanation for this lies in the nature of Vedanta, the Hindu philosophy, which preached endlessly that physical existence of man is a myth. Sankara, the great exponent of Advaita philosophy, was unsparing in his criticism and denunciation of the atomic theory as propounded by the Vaiseshika philosophy, by ridiculing the author of the system itself as 'Kanada' or atom-eater (Ray, 1920). Authority of the Shastras ruled over reason to the detriment of the growth of natural philosophy. This is confirmed by no less a person than Rajah Ram Mohan Roy, the great reformer from Bengal, when he sought the British rulers to introduce progressive social and modern scientific ideas and practices in India. The new spirit in the pursuit of science began in the last quarter of the nineteenth century (Ray, 1920).

The dawn of an intense social change that could ensure the appearance of a new social form in place of the old order is at the heart of science taking roots in India. With the beginning of the nineteenth century, the Indian renaissance movement started in Bengal, which reached its zenith during the forties of the nineteenth century. This prepared the ground for the spurt of science in India in the beginning of twentieth century or a little earlier. In this saga, a few names stand out prominently, and they are: John Mack (who came to India in 1821), Professor of Natural Sciences in the newly founded college at Serampur introduced the teaching of chemistry, followed by O'Shaughnessy, Dr. F.N. Macnamara and Kanailal Dey (Ray, 1920). The other pioneers were: the teacher Henry Derozio, and Acharya P. C. Ray, Professor of chemistry, both from the Presidency College, Calcutta. Derozio exposed his students to the modern worldview as opposed to the then prevailing obscurantist ideas. Acharya Ray revived the ideas of renaissance in the minds of his students through his discourses on science, philosophy, economics and national liberation. Acharya Ray's students included Meghnad Saha, Satyendranath Bose, Jnan Chandra Ghosh, all of whom later became internationally famous (Bhattacharya, 2003). In the south of India, Srinivasa Ramanujan (1887-1920), the mathematical genius, and Sir C.V. Raman (1888-1970), the Nobel Laureate became the torch- bearers of science initiative. These pioneers of Indian science became not only the role models for the young scientists of the following generations, but also laid the firm foundation for science.

Establishment of research institutions in India is of British initiative, when the imperial government established the Survey of India (1767: maps), the Geological Survey of India (1851: minerals), the India Meteorological Department (1875: weather), the Botanical Survey of India (1890: plant resources), the Haffkine Institute, Bombay (1896: vaccines), the Agricultural Institute, Pusa (1903: agricultural research, which later became Indian Agricultural Research Institute), Forest Research Institute, Dehradun (1906: forests), the Indian Research Fund Association (1911: medical research), and the Council of Scientific and Industrial Research (CSIR) (1942). The first modern type universities were created by the British, when three universities were established at Calcutta, Bombay and Madras in 1857. The native initiative resulted in the finding of the Indian Institute of Science at Bangalore by J. N. Tata (1909), and the Benaras Hindu University, Benaras by Pandith Madan Mohan Malaviya (1916). On the other hand, the building of scientific forums is largely the initiative of indigenous pioneers like Mahendralal Sircar (the Indian Association for the Cultivation Science, 1876), Meghnad Saha (National Academy of Sciences, India, 1930), P.C. Mahalanobis (Indian Statistical Research, Calcutta, 1931), Sir C.V. Raman (the Indian Academy of Sciences, Bangalore, 1934), and the Indian National Science Academy, Delhi, 1935 (Rama Rao, 1998) superceeding National Institute of Sciences of India.

After independence, the Central government laid a strong foundation for the development of frontline disciplines having immediate impact on the national development by establishing separate Departments for Space, for Atomic Energy, for Science and Technology, for Ocean Technology, for Biotechnology, the Department of Scientific and Industrial Research (controlling CSIR), and the Defence Research and Development Organization. Under these departments, several research and development institutions came into being (Rama Rao, 1998). An industrial base was laid by the government by starting a number of public sector industrial undertakings. Judging how far these industrial units have fared in fulfilling the set objectives is beyond the scope of this book.

NATURE OF SCIENCE

Science is the objective study of nature, its contents and the laws governing natural phenomena. Science is "not merely thematic, that is the study of certain subjects. It is a study by certain method which emphasizes observation and experiment, reasoning and deduction, a method based on facts, their sequence and relative significance. The scientific method enjoins one to be critical of all things and accept only facts which are amenable to verification and test" (Thacker, 1958, p. 787). Nature of science shows certain distinctive features or themes, which are applicable to the whole of science. However, this view is not shared by all scholars. The distinctive features include: Unity of science, Cumulative character of science, Objectivity, Use of precise terminology, Basic and applied nature of research, Scientific method, and Scientific theories. The last two features of science are discussed later in this chapter.

Unity of Science. The concept of unity of science is derived from *reductionism.* Reductionism is an analytical method of explaining a complex system in terms of more elementary principles. Reductionism is of three types—ontological, methodological and epistemological. Ontological reductionism states that the entire material world can be ultimately reduced to elementary particles and forces enshrined in physics. Methodological reductionism asserts that science is deterministic and all theories must be capable of being explained by language of mathematical physics. Beginning with the lower level complexity, it should be possible to explain natural phenomena at the level of elementary particles, where the most general and powerful laws of nature disclose themselves. Epistemological reductionism means that 'laws' formulated in one area of science can always be reduced to special cases of laws in other areas of science. For example, the concept of entropy in physics has been applied to explain a number of phenomena in other fields like information science, and economics. Similarly, parallel processing of messages by brain has found application in artificial intelligence. It is claimed that all psychology can be reduced to biology, all biology to chemistry, and all chemistry to physics (Barrow, 1988). While Karl Popper, logical positivists and logical empiricists believe in unity of science there are many others including Thomas Kuhn, the noted philosopher of science, who are skeptical about reductionism, and the concept of unity of science (Ladyman, 2002). It is interesting to know that James C. Maxwell believed that science would be unified by methods of approach and not by any one theory; although his electromagnetic theory is one of the greatest unifying concepts of all times (Spangenburg and Moser, 2006).

Science is Cumulative. Supporters of cumulative nature of science assert that science builds on the preceding scientific work. There is continuity in science with organic linkages between different points of scientific activity and also with other branches of science. In contrast, art, literature, and philosophy are progressive in nature in a much looser and controversial sense. There is an opposite viewpoint aired by Kuhn that the "history of science does not consist in the steady accumulation of knowledge, but often involves the wholesale abandonment of past theories" (Ladyman, 2002, p. 97).

Objectivity in Scientific Research. In arriving at a scientific theory, the personal elements and situations of the experimenter are irrelevant. The evidence supporting the theory ought to be based solely on the facts observed from the experiment. Personal factors, such as who proposed the theory and when are not relevant; further, the researcher's own personal beliefs and scientific allegiance have no place in the formulation of an hypotheses (Ladyman, 2002).

Language of Science. From the beginning of modern science, its practitioners emphasized the need for adopting a distinct style of language for the presentation of scientific knowledge. In fact, the Royal Society of London founded in 1660 insisted that the style best suited to the needs of new sciences is not the Aristotelian style of verbose, but must be simple, direct and functional to the point of starkness (Purver, 1967). Science has evolved its own distinct style of expression based on a terminology having fixed and precise meanings. In scientific language there is no scope for confusion or its notation allows different interpretations.

Communication in Science. One of the hallmarks of science is its objective approach to scientific problems. Scientific truth, observes Heilprin, can be confirmed only by "communicating them openly and without restrictions, to all interested. This changes the meaning of science from an *individual* to a species enterprise" (Heilprin, 1995, p.57) The open system of communication followed by science ensures public scrutiny of the findings of a scientist by fellow scientists. Critical assessment carried out in science media forums in the form of open discussions, rebuttals, criticism or support gives science and a scientist's work the stamp of scientific integrity. Scientists adopt various modes of communication such, as publication of their findings in journals, participating in conferences and seminars, internal group meetings or colloquia where the findings are criticized, supported, modified or even discarded. System of "refereeing" is a unique procedure evolved by science by which process a research paper sent for publication by the author of a work is evaluated by peers in the concerned field applying the norms of originality of findings, methodology followed, relative merit of the research, supporting references, and the like. The advent of Internet, web sites, and other electronic modes has added a new dimension to scientific communication. It may be said that communication and information constitute the life blood of modern science. As it happens in all human affairs, even the best system can be abused by a miniscule of miscreants, but it is only a minor aberration in the progress of science.

Professional Associations. Science associations, academies, and higher institutions of learning like universities play an energizing role in promoting the cause of science. They help establish credibility of science in society. Science associations serve as forums for scientists to think together, share experiences, and work for the advancement of science in their respective fields, and may even sponsor research. Science professional bodies exert strong influence on science and its direction of growth. They have helped establish informal guidelines for settling of scientific disputes, in the development of methodology, and in setting the norms on communication with the outside world. For instance, the influence of the Royal Society of London established in 1660 extended far beyond the normal activities of a private society. Its influence was a causal force behind the scientific eruptions that occurred in the 2nd half of the 17th century. It was instrumental in laying a firm foundation for science by putting into action the vision of Francis Bacon, which called for replacing the then existing system of natural science by a new system best suited to the creation of new science (Purver, 1967).

Some of the other well known science associations that

have contributed immensely to the development of science include: Academie des Sciences, Paris (France) established in 1666; Deutsche Akademie der Naturforscher Leopoldina (the German Academy of Natural Sciences, Leopoldina, Germany) in 1652; the American Philosophical Society, Philadelphia in 1743, and the National Academy of Sciences, Washington (USA) in 1863; the Russian Academy of Sciences, Moscow (Russia) in1724; the Indian Science Congress Association, Kolkata in 1914, and the National Academy of Sciences, Allahabad (India) in 1930; and the Chinese Academy of Sciences, Beijing (China) in 1949 (World of Learning, 2008).

Basic and Applied Nature of Research. Scientific research is categorized into pure (or basic or fundamental) research and applied research. The fundamental difference between the two lies in motivation. Motivation in the case of pure research is the desire to know something; whereas in applied research, it is the desire to-do something. Basic research is concerned with the discovery of new knowledge and increasing our understanding of natural phenomena and the laws governing them. Its aim is not finding solutions of immediate practical problems. By definition, basic research "is at the frontiers of our knowledge; and the quality of work and achievements have to be judged by the entire international scientific community.... In contrast, applied research has very definite practical objectives" (Menon, 1982, p.1281). Design and development, on the other hand, "relates to the effective and economical execution of a task that has been shown to be feasible on the basis of applied research and past experience" (Menon, 1982, p.1281). Successful applied research leads to the generation of capital in the form of patents. Basic research has an essential place in higher education, and in the creation of requisite high-caliber manpower needed in different areas of research and industry.

An important question raised and answered by the late Homi Bhabha on basic research is whether it is possible to transform the economy of a country to one based on modern technology developed elsewhere without at the same time establishing modern science in the country as a live and vital force. The answer is no. This truth was firmly proved by Homi Bhabha himself. Bhabha was instrumental in establishing the Tata Institute of Fundamental Research (TIFR) at Bombay dedicated to conducting basic research in modern areas of science, like nuclear physics and high energy physics. TIFR set the pace for the growth of science and self-confidence. It ensured self-reliance in strategic areas of science and scientific manpower on which our entire nuclear programme was built indigenously. No foreign country either shares nuclear technology or supplies nuclear equipment except under extraordinary terms and conditions. On the importance of institutions like TIFR, Menon quotes Homi Bhabha's remarks: "The support of such (basic) research and, of an institution where such research can be carried out effectively, is of great importance to society for two reasons. First of all, and paradoxically, it has an immediate use, in that it helps to train and develop, in a manner in which no other mental discipline can, young men of the highest intellectual caliber in a society, into people who can think about and analyze problems with freshness of outlook and originality which is not generally found" (Menon, 1982, p.1280).

THEORIES, AXIOMS AND COMPUTER PROGRAMS

Theories are central to science. The term "theory" used in its broader sense is a statement or a set of statements about the relationships among variables. If the statements are about a single relationship between variables, then it becomes a law. Used in a restricted sense, a theory refers to a statement or a set of statements about relationships among variables that includes at least one concept that is not directly observed but that is necessary to explain these relationships (Mc Burney, 2001). According to deductive method of science, discussed later, a theory must be falsifiable. Theories contribute to science in three ways: a) unify unrelated concepts and laws about a phenomenon and through them explain the phenomenon, b) become useful in predicting new laws, and c) provide theoretical frameworks for further research (Mc Burney, 2001). Scientific laws are built on hypotheses. A hypothesis is a provisional statement that is assumed to be true for the purpose of testing its truth empirically. A scientific law is a hypothesis, whose validity is confirmed by empirical testing. One of the general principles of science is that if there is more than one theory that explains in all respects a phenomenon, then one must choose the simpler theory. This principle is often known as "Ockham's razor" and is credited to William of Ockham, the 14th century philosopher.

While science is structured on theories, mathematics is built on axioms. The general notion is that science, particularly physics, is different from mathematics; and yet, their common feature of compressibility makes the two look similar. In science, compression of experimental and observational data leads to scientific laws and theories, and in mathematics compression of computational experiments results in mathematical axioms and theorems. Theories and theorems display certain properties of simplicity, complexity, and randomness, which are also dealt with precisely in algorithmic information theory- a branch of modern mathematics (Chaitin, 2006).

Gottfried W. Leibniz, the German philosopher and mathematician in his essay *Discourse de metaphysique (Discourse on Metaphysics)* distinguishes between facts which can be explained by some law from irregular facts, which lie outside any law. A theory has to be simpler than the data it explains, otherwise it does not explain anything. Going by the algorithmic information theory, and a scientific theory is like a computer program that predicts our observations, the experimental data. Following Leibniz's differentiation, we conclude that if a theory is same size in bits as the data it explains, then it is worthless, because even the most random of data has a theory of that size. An useful theory is a compression of the data; and comprehension is compression, the principle underlying commuter programs and algorithmic descriptions. Contrary to Leibniz's observations that everything happens for a reason, and if something is true, it must be for a reason, the algorithmic information theory shows that certain mathematical laws are true for no reason. Hence, the only way to "prove" such facts is to take them as new axioms without using reasoning at all (Chaitin, 2006).

Axioms are mathematical facts which are taken as self-evident. All formal mathematical theorems are deduced properties of axioms. Mathematicians compress their computational experiments into axioms from which they then deduce theorems and supply proofs. Experimental mathematics, which studies new mathematical results discovered from problems run on computers, seems to stand methodologically midway between complete proof and quasi-empirical nature of computer calculations. Science, more particularly physics, depends on experiments and observations. Scientific data thus obtained is subjected to plausible reasoning instead of rigorous proof to make hypotheses. The hypotheses are merely verified by observing predictions. Computing works on the principle of programs, processing and output. Scientists compress their experimental observations into scientific laws, and then they show how their observations can be deduced from the laws. Thus, physics and experimental mathematics are in many ways similar to the execution of a program on a computer (Chaitin, 2006).

SCIENTIFIC METHOD

A scientist observes a phenomenon, collects data, develops hypotheses and subjects it to test by means of experimentation and observation. Analysis and description of this procedure is called 'scientific method'. The general view is that scientists apply either inductive logic or deductive logic.

Those favouring rational thinking applied to empirical facts as the basis of scientific achievements have greatly supported the process of *induction* as the main basis of science. However, the principle of induction as the basis of scientific method has been largely ignored by later day historians of science. The present consensus is in favor of deductive method.

Inductive Principle. An inference is called inductive, if universal statements are framed on the basis of singular statements (also called particular statements) evolved from the account of the findings of observations or experiments. In other words, inductive method refers to generalizations in the form of hypothesis or theories made on the basis of individual observations. The principle objections to the validity of inductive method in science are : it fails the test of *justification* and testability; and the principle of induction leads to inconsistencies (Popper, 1972). Supporters of inductive method believe that we cannot explain the scientific method and the justification of scientific knowledge without recourse to induction of some form or other. After all science is about confirmation as well as falsification (Ladyman, 2002).

Deductive Principle. The principle governing deductive method is that a hypothesis can only be empirically tested, and only after it has been advanced. Following deductive method a hypothesis is tentatively formulated and from it conclusions are drawn or predictions made by means of logical deduction. These conclusions or predictions are then tested by means of:

1. Comparing the conclusions with one another and with other relevant theories to find logical relations between them and also to find, if there are any inconsistencies.
2. Ensuring that the new hypothesis fulfills the characteristics of a scientific theory.
3. Establishing that the new theory constitutes a scientific advance, after satisfying various tests.

4. Testing the empirical applications of the conclusions which can be derived from the theory or predictions made.
5. Criterion of testing is either in terms of induction or by falsification. A scientific theory stands or falls by falsifying the truth of the hypotheses rather than by confirming.

If the hypothesis passes these tests then it is accepted tentatively. An empirical system should be capable of being tested by experience and must be possible to be refuted by experience.

The principle of scientific method espoused above as the norm of scientific discovery by Sir Karl Popper is known as "hypothetico-deductive system". Popper's postulation views a scientist's mind as alternating, sometimes rapidly, between imaginative and critical phases of thought. In the imaginative phase, the mind speculates about the problem and arrives at a hypothesis. Then, in the critical phase, the hypothesis is subjected to ruthless criticism. Only when the hypothesis passes all the tests it is temporarily accepted. After its general acceptance by the community of scientists, the hypothesis becomes an accepted theory. Hypothetico-deductive theory is criticized on two counts: a) that it is an elitist theory; and b) what goes on in average research, a scientist's involvement is far removed from both intuitive thinking and critical assessment (Dixon, 1973; Ladyman, 2002). Augmenting the field of scientific method is the work of cognitive scientists on 'scientific thinking' based on the principles of reasoning underlying the working of science.

Debate on the validity or otherwise of scientific method continues. One argument is that, on careful scrutiny, scientific method turns out to be little or no different from the analytical processes used in many other jobs and professions. The second argument is that scientific method is no more than scrupulously applied commonsense (Dixon, 1973). This argument attracts a caveat— nature itself has moulded human brain in a way that each half of the brain displays different, but distinctive traits, knowledge-wise. It is now established that people endowed with right brain characteristics display better aptitude for scientific work than the left brain. Quality science can flourish only when its practitioners are endowed with scientific temperament, questioning mind, and the ability to withstand periods of darkness before the dawn of truth.

SCIENTIFIC THINKING AND REASONING

How do scientists think and reason? Does scientific thinking and reasoning differ from general thinking or thinking of poets and artists are questions attended by cognitive scientists. Probing into the process of scientific thinking is likely to explain several key aspects of mind. Contemporary cognitive research has largely treated the problem of scientific thinking as that of: Problem solving; Analogical reasoning; Hypothesis testing; Conceptual change; Collaborative reasoning; Inductive reasoning; and Deductive reasoning (Dunbar and Fugelsang 2005), which are briefly described here.

1. Problem Solving. In this approach, scientific reasoning revolves around selection of research problem, setting experiments, collecting data, framing a hypothesis and testing the hypothesis. Here, a scientific research project is treated as a problem, and finding the correct solution to the problem completes the work of discovery or invention.
2. Analogical Reasoning. Confronted with a new scientific problem, the scientist looks for analogy by searching for theories or scientific findings with which the new problem or hypothesis can be explained, accepted or rejected. The analogy provides the means of confirming or modifying the analogy used as standard or the new findings, which results in a new concept or scientific relation.
3. Hypothesis Testing. It is the process of evaluating a

scientific proposition by collecting evidence to establish truth. The reasoning that goes into framing the hypothesis is critical because any biased inclination invariably shuts the scientist's open-mindedness to consider other hypotheses in the designing of experiments, and also in interpreting data.

4. Conceptual Change. Creation of new concepts or modification of existing concepts is a common occurrence in science as it is with any other energetic field of knowledge. A radical conceptual change necessitates restructuring of the pre-existing concept and the underlying conceptual knowledge. Restructuring or even discarding of existing conceptual structure arises when the existing structure can not explain the behaviour of a new scientific finding. When the conceptual change is the result of the efforts of a group of scientists working on a complex or a large scientific research program requiring a variety of specialties or involves division of labour, the concept becomes the product of collaborative reasoning.
5. Collaborative Reasoning. Scientific research has ceased to be a single individual's adventure. It is now a group activity, with inputs coming from different individuals and even from different disciplines. Collaborative approach energizes the creative talents of each collaborator towards the common problem. The reasoning or new insights of even a single member could trigger the path to the discovery of aimed results or throw up an entirely new line of thinking.
6. Inductive Reasoning; and
7. Deductive Reasoning. These two have been discussed earlier under Scientific Method.

Causal Thinking. Scientists use cause and effect reasoning in understanding and explaining a scientific phenomenon. While designing an experiment a scientist could incorporate a number of conclusions and controls to take care of any unexpected effects cropping up. Strictly speaking when one caters in advance for possible unexpected effects, it ceases to be an unexpected phenomenon.

Intuition. How scientists develop scientific theories, especially in empirical science, and what methodology they follow has interested both philosophers and historians of science for long. It is generally thought that science and scientific research are inspired by either creative imagination or critical empirical analysis. Sir Peter Medawar writes in *The Art of the Soluble* "truth takes shape in the mind of the observer: it is his imaginative grasp of *what might be true* that provides the incentive for finding out, so far as he can, what *is* true. Every advance in science is therefore the outcome of a speculative adventure, an excursion into unknown. According to the opposite view, truth resides in nature and is to be got at only through the evidence of the senses: apprehension leads by a direct pathway to comprehension, and the scientist's task is essentially one of *discernment*" (Medawar,1969, p.15, cited by Dixon, 1973). However, such rigid distinctions only reflect a perceptional difference over truth; each is valid up to a point. Scientific discovery is similar to an artist's creativity. Many great scientists like Sir Isaac Newton, the discoverer of the laws of motion, Friedrich Kekule, who unraveled the benzene ring, Dennis Gabor, the discoverer of holography have all acknowledged the sudden intuitive realization of truth. The intuitive part in their discoveries does not take away the importance of long hours spent over months or years in intellectual efforts, i.e., critical empirical analysis, needed to arrive near the intuitive point (Dixon, 1973).

There are many other factors associated with the successful working of science and scientific research such as: a) relationship between innovative research and resource (manpower and material) allocation; b) role of innovative methods and instruments; c) team research, d) chance observations, e) communication and information, and f) social and ethical accountability.

Classification. Citing from the book *Logic, Inductive and Deductive* by A. L. Jones, Heilprin observes that to make knowledge out of the data received from the senses, these data must be arranged and classified. The object of science is to get organized *knowledge*, and before knowledge can be organized it must be arranged as to enable us to see what facts (aggregates of direct sense impressions, patterns) are similar, and what are different (Jones, 1929, Heilprin, 1995). Progress of science has depended significantly on classification. Classification is a part of scientific thinking. Formulation of scientific laws presupposes some exercise of classificatory skills in examining all the relevant data, facts and relationships that form an input for propounding the laws. Taxonomy is central to the development of biological science. Ordering of organisms into phylum, family, genera and species and the use of binomial nomenclature are unique inventions. The study of stars, minerals and chemicals would be difficult without classification. Prediction of undiscovered elements from the gaps in Mandeleev's periodic table, and of stars and distant galaxies from classification is well-known. Classification into ideal types is predominant in social science.

SCIENTIFIC KNOWLEDGE

Of interest to the study of knowledge and its increase is the study of the pattern of development of science. Theoretically, knowledge encompasses the physiochemical universe which spans from our solar system and super clusters of galaxies about 15 billion years old and 10^{26} meters radius to that of electrons, quarks and other elementary particles of 10^{-18} meters. Further, it has to deal with the earliest forms of life, estimated between 3.8 to 4.5 billion years old, and including the history of the arrival of Homo sapiens somewhere in the past 1 to 2 million years ago. Ours is the World of Middle Dimensions between the two. A paradigm change has taken place in our understanding nature with the new scientific advances beginning with electromagnetic theory, the special and general theories of relativity, and the quantum mechanics. Thus, time and space are no longer separately absolute but form a space-time continuum; the concept of the field has come on stage and done away with the idea of action at a distance; the meaning of simultaneity has been altered and is no more absolute; the geometry of space-time can be non-Euclidean; quantum mechanics has an irreducible statistical core so that the earlier deterministic causality no longer remains valid; and in subnuclear phenomena matter can be created as well as destroyed (Mukunda, 2004).

Kuhn shows that science grows via the rise and fall of many "paradigms". A paradigm is the research consensus on the valid state of knowledge in any given scientific field at a given time. The state of knowledge or scientific research tradition comprises of laws, theories and their application, vocabulary and instrumentation which together provide the model for further research in that field. Discarding of a paradigm leads to a scientific revolution. Scientific revolutions are those non-cumulative developmental episodes in which an older paradigm is replaced in whole or in parts by an incompatible new one. The successive transition from one paradigm to another via revolution is the usual developmental pattern of mature science (Kuhn, 1962).

The study of knowledge is a branch of philosophy, and science was also known as natural philosophy. Science and philosophy can benefit from each other, and together enrich the knowledge world as a whole. Dampier observes that to the Greeks, philosophy and science were one, and in the middle Ages, both were bound up with theology. After Renaissance, philosophy and science separated, and now, one seeks the help of the other as both are involved in searching reality. Science is realizing "the fundamental concepts of physical science are abstractions, framed by our minds so as to bring order and simplicity into an apparent chaos of phenomena. The approach to reality through science, therefore, gives only aspects of reality, pictures drawn on simplified lines, but not reality itself. Nevertheless, even philosophers are coming to see that, in a metaphysical study of reality, the methods and results of science are the best available evidence, and that a new realism, if possible at all, must be built up by their means" (Dampier, 1982). The different philosophic stands on science and scientific knowledge may be summarized as follows: To David Hume (1711-1776), the philosopher, science is inductive and irrational; in the thinking of Karl Popper (1902-1994), the philosopher of science, it is non-inductive and rational; to Rudolff Karnap (1891-1970), the logical empiricist, science is inductive and rational; to Thomas Kuhn (1922-1996), the historian and philosopher of science, science seems to be both non-inductive and non-rational (Ladyman, 2002). Given the irreconcilable positions taken by the philosophers on the nature of science, it will be interesting to know what the scientific community itself feels about it.

Scientific and technological knowledge holds the key to material progress of mankind. Science and technology have become the main instruments of change. The impact of such changes is sometimes radical and at other times subtle. Its greatest impact is seen in the mode and style of living, belief systems and social relationships. Scientific and technological knowledge is a double-edged weapon. On the one hand, it is capable of alleviating poverty, illiteracy and disease resulting in the betterment of society and, on the other, capable of destroying mankind. At the practical plane, management of scientific knowledge is becoming increasingly complex. Decision-making on science matters and laying down science and technology policies now call for knowledge not only in the field of science and technology, but also in such diverse fields as economics, politics, government, education, military, industry, law, labour, and management.

Knowledge in any particular field presupposes a body of quite general principles into which it fits. The general principles are easily found in the discipline of science, which attained the highest level of generality. Propositions in natural sciences, particularly in exact sciences, posses the most general validity for the real world. The validity of the laws discovered through the methods of natural science is not confined to any individual domain of reality; it extends, in principle to the entire universe. Scientific knowledge everywhere is one; the most general principles are always the same (Schlick, 1974). Thus, scientific knowledge carries its validity when applied to other disciplines capable of receiving it. The essence of knowing absolutely requires that the participant betakes himself far away from things and to a height far above them, from which he can then view their relations to all other things. Further, "whoever comes close to things and participates in their ways and works, in engaged in living, not in knowing; to him, things display their value aspect, not their nature" (Schlick, 1974. p. 80). Pursuers of science become privy to knowing absolutely and also privy to knowing the nature of things rather than their value aspects as scientists view things dispassionately and are engaged in knowing and not in living. Scientific knowledge is thus characterized by knowing absolutely and knowing reality, i.e., the nature of things.

Scientific knowledge is expansive. Impact of scientific knowledge is felt even beyond science. Pervasive impact of science and technology is seen in varied human activities and enterprises, including arts and humanities, wherever it finds application. Scientific knowledge has its own distinctive form of growth. Knowledge pertaining to a problem under probe is made up of statement of research problem; review of previous work; experimental and observational details; methods, techniques and instrumentation used; collection of experimental data/results; formulation of hypothesis; drawing of conclusions, which constitute the distinct stages of scientific research. Scientific knowledge reflects vigor of science, objectivity, directness and clarity. Further, form of presentation of scientific results (scientific information and texts) too has its unique features, namely employment of scientific style with its precise terminology, use of standard form for presentation of research results with all references cited, and use of unique refereeing system. The norm of presentation and pattern of communication of research findings adopted by science has become a model for many other disciplines. The most important feature of scientific knowledge/information seems to be its influence on the mode of thinking by individuals and society.

Growth of Scientific Knowledge. The phenomenon of increase or growth of knowledge is more rapid in the fields of science and technology than in other fields. Popper observes that the study of the phenomenon of expansion of scientific knowledge has led to the recognition of the underlying principle of *cumulative effect* of science on the growth of science. Kuhn explains that the expansion of scientific research is through paradigms. A paradigm sets the guidelines for research and consists of a vocabulary, mathematical structures, preferred methodologies and examples. Science develops as a result of applying these methodological components to carefully chosen problems (Kuhn, 1970). Science and scientific knowledge are constantly evolving via the rise and fall of many research programmes or paradigms (Popper, 1973).

Growth of knowledge, maintains Popper, can best be studied by studying the growth of scientific knowledge. According to evolutionary epistemology, a branch of epistemology, the growth of scientific knowledge is the result of an evolutionary process. Evolutionary epistemology is founded on Darwin's theory of evolution through natural selection. Taking a post-Darwinian position, Popper sees that all organisms, including human beings are continually engaged in problem solving- problems taken in an objective sense.

Problem solving follows the method of trial and error of conjectures and refutations. New hypotheses are tentatively put forward and controlled by error-elimination. Critical arguments are an essential component in the method of error elimination. Thus, the growth of scientific knowledge is perceived as a non-cyclic, but continuous problem solving process in an evolutionary sequence (Popper, 1983) as shown below:

Problem → Tentative solution → Error elimination → New Problem

Criticism and *inventiveness* are the most critical elements in the evolutionary approach to the growth of scientific knowledge (Sengupta, 2000).

SCIENTIFIC DATA: THE BUILDING BLOCKS

Science and scientific research discover data pertaining to universe, its constituent entities and phenomena. The data, thus gathered make up the building blocks of knowledge. The importance of data is not limited to the growth of scientific knowledge, but also extends to other disciplines, including social sciences, philosophy, history, architecture, and even arts and fine arts. Science extracts data through observation and experimentation. This data when analyzed, evaluated, correlated, structured and connected to form concepts or meaningful entities by the application of cognitive processes results in knowledge and information. To give a few examples, data obtained by carbon-dating and chemical analysis of ancient monuments and artifacts enabled determination of historical facts pertaining to ancient civilizations; biological data of cells and genes have forced us to recast our notions of life and death; observed data from nature was the basis of Darwin's theory of evolution, which toppled the then prevailing religious dogma of God's creation of man, plants and animals.

Scientific research necessitated the invention and construction of instruments, which enable us to observe and measure phenomena in nature and extract data about the phenomena. The data thus collected constitute the building blocks on which theories are built, and phenomena are explained. The biggest limitation in observing and collecting data in science is the limited range of the human sense organs. Real scientific advances began only when scientists were able to observe phenomena which were beyond the reach of our sense organs. Microscope and orbital telescopes stretched the limits of human eyesight beyond imagination; infrared technology out shadowed human touch and sight; radar and sonar outbid the human ear and hand; powerful cyclotrons enabled nuclear scientists to see inside of an atom and collect data about the neutrons, protons and antiprotons; photography could take photos of Saturn rings furnishing new data.

Big Science......Massive Data. Today's big science is collaborative research generating mega volumes of information over a period of years, which can only be handled by high-powered computers with large data storage capacity. For example, in the Large Hadron Collider (LHC) facility at CERN, Geneva, each experiment is a collaboration of over 5000 physicists from hundreds of research establishments spread all over the globe (Berman and Hey, 2006). One can imagine the variety distribution and the volume of data that will be produced by each such experiment. Other fields of research which generate extremely huge amounts of data include astronomy, biological/genetic research, medical/health monitoring, climate/geological studies, and mechanical equipment function monitoring. Study of these data can result in profound new insights about life and nature.

Mega data generating research has changed the traditional pattern of scientific communication, which is built around authors (mostly individuals and small groups) who create data; publishers of scientific journals; libraries discharging the role of curators; and scientists using the published data. The pattern of communication in the mega data world needs a new model. In the new model, "the author, publisher, and curator roles are clearly present in data-intensive science, but they are performed in different ways" (Szalay and Gray, 2004, p. 98). In the new structure, the author is identified with collaborations; the data is published through web-based archives; and during the life time of a project the curatorial responsibility lies with the projects themselves. Later on, data considered valuable are transferred to national data archives. Project data management involves custom coordination of distributed data, their consolidation, standardization of nomenclature; design of data forms and web site tuning. Raw instrument data need to be transformed into calibrated and catalogued data, and even customizing. Data-driven mega scientific research has to handle scientific data in the range of terabytes to petabytes (10^{15} bytes).

TECHNOLOGY

Technology is generally perceived as the application of science to the production of material goods and conveniences. The contradictory general notion that pure science produces discoveries and technology is working out or an application of science to make practical discoveries is a fundamental misconception (Nye, 2006). It is only at the turn of the 20th century (particularly after the 1st World War) that the term technology came to be invested with the sense in which it is used today- meaning complex systems of machines and techniques. Prior to this, technology meant things like "the mechanic arts", "useful arts", "invention" or "science". The present thinking seems to be that technologies are nondeterministic, and it is the cultural choices that shape technology (Nye, 2006).

How we define the nature of science, technology, and knowledge has ramifications for the development of technology and also society. Regarding this, there are two opposing schools of thought, namely, positivism (or objectivism or rationalism) and "social construction" (or "interpretation"). Approach of positivism derives its strength from physical sciences and scientific method implying verification- a stand strongly supported by Karl Popper. The weakness of this approach is that there are many assertions of knowledge that can not be verified applying the standards of physical sciences. To overcome this difficulty social construction theory considers knowledge, including social knowledge, as the collective product of society. What is important in social construction is not the physical reality, but how a group of people define knowledge. This is shaped by the outcome of relationships, institutions and shared belief. Science is "best understood as socially constructed rather than the result of objective scientific truths about nature"- the position taken by Thomas Kuhn in his work *The Structure of Scientific Revolutions.*

The above debate on the nature of science is also applicable to the nature of engineering and technological knowledge. Technological knowledge lies midway between scientific knowledge and social applications. Similarly much of technological knowledge is socially constructed up to a limit.

Science and Technology Relation. Arts and crafts, science (in the form of simple discoveries by observation), and technology (in its rudimentary form) served as main instruments in shaping early human history on the material side. Aristotle had recognized '*techne*' (corresponding to engineering in English) as a separate branch of knowledge.

Natural science aims at discovering the laws governing the universe through scientific method. Technology, on the other hand, puts into practice particular findings of science to produce new processes, products, equipment and machines. Based on this distinction, science is divided into pure science (or pure research) engaged in discovering the nature of the world around us and applied science (i.e., technology), referring to practical applications. Applied science is further categorized into: physical technologies (e.g., mechanical engineering); biological technologies (e.g., genetically engineered plant seeds); social technologies (e.g., operations research); and thought technologies (e. g., computer technology) (Bunge, 1974). In a very general sense, one can say that relation between natural science and technology is one of *theory and practice*. The differing aims of natural science and technology result in different methods of procedures followed by them. Science provides technological sciences specific types of scientific knowledge to solve practical problems or for putting them into practice. Technology in return feeds science with technical problems needing scientific insights and also makes instruments required for scientific research (Rapp, 1974).

Technological theories are combination of *sustentative* and *operative* theories. Substantive theories are concerned with action itself and are essentially applications, e.g., theory of flight, an application of fluid mechanics used in the manufacture of aircraft. Operative theories essentially deal with the operations of men and man-machine complexes, e.g., the theory of air flights management in an airport. Operating theories are theories of action, which follow scientific method, but are not by themselves scientific theories (Rapp, 1974). Some of the characteristic features of science and technology showing their relationship (Bunge, 1974) are:

1. A theory being true in science does not vouch for its success when applied to practice. Similarly a theory may prove productive in practice, and yet scientifically invalid. There could be several reasons for this anomaly, for example, a small component of truth in a false theory may be sufficient for the success of the false theory in practice.
2. Pure science stands on discovered laws, where as technologies work on the rules of applied sciences. While laws are descriptive representation of truth, rules are prescriptive. Rules are for compliance by the concerned human agents and machines. For the success in application (say a technology project), prescriptive rules have to include manmade standards dictated by

economic, environmental and other compulsions.

3. Science makes prediction, where as technologies make forecast. In science, the research scientist is a detached operator throughout the research. In contrast, the technologist in action is an active participant in every stage of the project, indicating an attitude different from science. Predictions and forecasts are not same. A scientific prediction, which follows from an established theory, does not vary; where as a technical forecast allows desired variations in end goals by taking influential actions. Prediction is akin to stating the trajectory of a comet, and forecast is similar to plan and forecast the orbit of an artificial satellite. In predicting, the goal post is firmly fixed, but in forecast it rests with the policy-maker. The implication is that technological forecast cannot be used for controlling things or men by changing the course of events, but the policy-makers by knowing the forecast may modify the situation by changing the non-technical parameters. Because of this, technological knowledge is subjected to varying degrees of social, economic, political, managerial and other non-technical knowledge.

Technological Knowledge. In the last fifty years the nature of production of knowledge has undergone a paradigmatic change reflecting the radical changes that have taken place in the pattern of conducting scientific research, technology–industry interplay, and in the forms of communication. The changed pattern of knowledge production is sufficiently different from the traditional form. Gibbons et al. distinguish the traditional form of knowledge production by naming it as Mode 1 production (mostly in science), and the new pattern as Mode 2. Some of the distinctive features of Mode 2 production of knowledge are: a) it is a participative venture drawing actors from different disciplines and with different back-grounds; b) it is mostly site-based, meaning fixed duration projects and programmes with no pressure to get them institutionalized; c) it is context oriented and application/use bound; d) it is characterized by a constant flow of knowledge back and forth between the fundamental and the applied, between the theoretical and the practical; e) its trans-disciplinary nature of production impacts on the social diffusion of knowledge, production of further knowledge, and communication; f) first level of communication of Mode 2 produced knowledge is interpersonal, i.e. in tacit form circulating within the organization or the academia, which energizes the environment for further production of knowledge; g) there is a quality control aspect to ensure not only excellence-a prime requirement in science, but also efficiency or usefulness of the knowledge, which is assessed in terms of the contributions of the knowledge to the overall solution of trans-disciplinary problems; h) Mode 2 knowledge is heterogeneous in nature; and i) specific ordered structure rather than search for first principles becomes the main criteria guiding innovative activities in technology. Such a structure emphasizes the role of design in formulating the research and development programmes and their execution. This calls for extensive reliance on computers, especially computational modeling as important operational tools (Gibbons et al., 1994). Decisions on technological knowledge applications are subjected to varying degrees of social, economic, political, managerial, and other non-technical influences. The other major issues in technological knowledge are: diffusion and transfer of technology; the intellectual property rights; and technology industry relations, which are covered in chapters 5, 15 and 16 respectively.

SCIENCE AND THE ARTS

If art is production of beauty or a work of highest form of creative imagination, then science at the highest abstract level is also art. To a creative scientist arriving at a supremely elegant hypothesis is an artistic creation. For instance, to Einstein the formulation of relativity theory and the visualization through the mental eye how the universe appears under the relativity theory, surely, must have brought him the supreme joy of seeing a work of art of highest beauty. At the practical level many of the phenomena in nature like a black hole, which can only be perceived through mathematical reasoning and fundamental laws of science, can be presented to the world in visual form through an artist's brush without compromising their basic scientific norms. Architectural designs and cubism in art draw inspiration from geometry. Arts and science relationship appears in two forms: a) use of scientific themes and facts as the content of a work of art; and b) use of art to present scientific truths in a visual form. One example of using scientific facts in art is DNA portraits. DNA data of individual persons are being successfully used to create DNA portraits- painted or printed on coloured canvas- that can be hung on a wall (Economic Times, 2007).

SCIENCE, DEVELOPMENT AND CIVIL SOCIETY

Science, scientific research and technology are a part of society; they are a sub-set of knowledge in society. Science is linked to technology through applications. Technology is linked to economy and environment through manufacturing processes. Economy and environment in turn link technology to society (Abdul Kalam and Pillai, 2004). Creation of science and its advancement are sustained by the material and human resources spent on them by society. Thus, there is continuous interaction between science/technology, economics, environment, and society. This interaction results mostly in positive contributions to the development of society.

Philanthropy and Science. The actual and potential capabilities of science, technology, medicine, and other branches of knowledge to reduce poverty and contribute to the wellbeing of society have motivated many benefactors, both in the east and the west, to share their wealth for promoting the cause of science and other domains like technology, education, and libraries. While two prominent programmes supporting science, technology and education are described here, the others are taken up in chapter 19.

The Fulbright Program. The Fulbright Program for International Educational Exchange of Scholars, Educators, and Graduate students is one of the most prestigious programmes initiated by the American Senator, the late J. William Fulbright in 1946. It is born out of the vision and belief that educational and cultural exchanges promote peace and understanding throughout the world. It operates in 144 countries with 51 Commissions. It also awards Fulbright Prize. The programmes are administered by the Council of International Exchange of Scholars, Washington, DC. (wikipedia Fulbright). Its work in India is coordinated by the US Educational Foundation in India, New Delhi. There are a number of Fulbright Alumni Associations.

The Tata Foundations. The foremost philanthropists of India are the illustrious Tata's family funded foundations engaged in promoting causes varying from scientific research to performing arts. The trusts include: Sir Dorabjee Tata Trust founded in 1932; Jamsetji Tata Trust; JRD Tata Trust; and the Tata Education Trust. Endowment grants from Dorabjee Trust enabled the establishment of the Tata Institute of Fundamental Research, Mumbai; the Tata Institute of Social Sciences, Mumbai; the National Centre for Performing arts, Mumbai; and the National Institute of Advanced Studies, Bangalore. (*www.dorabjitatatrust*). The Indian Institute of Science, Bangalore was founded in 1909 from the philanthropy of Jamsetji N. Tata. The following extract from his letter addressed to Swami Vivekananda mirrors his concern for the development of science in India.

> "......I recall these ideas in connection with my scheme of *Research Institute of Science for India*, of which you have doubtless heard or read. It seems to me that no better use can be made of

> the ascetic spirit than the establishment of monasteries or residential halls for men dominated by this spirit, where they should live with ordinary decency, and devote their lives to the cultivation of sciences- natural and humanistic....." (Tata, 1898).

Brand Value of Science. Since the mid-nineteenth century, Western society bestowed science with the prestige it deserves. Prior to that elite status was reserved to priesthood, philosophy and nobility. Thinkers like Nicholas Copernicus and Galileo were forced to hide their scientific theories from becoming public, as their findings contradicted the long held notions about the god-centric order of the natural world. The general perception of science till then was that of an aloof activity of a few persons working in unpretentious laboratories. With the increasing realization of the value of the contributions of science and technology in ameliorating the sufferings of human beings through the advances made in fields of biology and medicine; increasing wealth through creation of new materials and services; and unraveling several mysteries of nature, which had remained unknowable until recently like the inside of an atom, functioning of organic cells, and blackhole phenomena, science and technology have gained recognition as powerful means of changing the world. Because of these achievements and the power it holds, science and scientific fraternity have been granted higher prestige by society. As a consequence, the craze for claiming status of science became pronounced among other disciplines and professions. Thus, sociology became social science; librarianship got rechristened as library science; and economics became a science eligible for Nobel Prize. The claim for status of science needed justification. Justification given was that any discipline is justified to the status of "science" provided it followed scientific approach in their activities, and fulfilled at least to some extent the criterion of objectivity. There are also other reasons for science to earn its exalted status; and one of them is the fear of the unknown. Since science holds power to make unknown known, and also predict many of the recurring occurrences in nature, it is looked upon with awe. Another reason is the human desire to accumulate wealth, which science and technology help to create. With the ever increasing population and decreasing natural resources man needs new or alternative resources, which only science, technology and engineering can help produce. A third factor is the role of science in fulfilling the natural human desire to avoid or reduce pain and sorrow caused by diseases, ill health, and natural calamities. Finally it is man's craving for new avenues of pleasure or comfort, which science and technology is able to fulfill abundantly. Though science has garnered sufficient power and a high brand value it still remains the hand maiden of the ruling class, irrespective of the system of governance.

Social Concern. Since the destruction of Hiroshima in Japan by the atom bomb, the Bhopal gas tragedy, and the Chernobyl reactor explosion understanding the relationship between science, technology and civil society has become a major concern to civil society. Prior to this, justification of racial and gender discrimination on the basis of selective application of genetics particularly in America and Nazi Germany had shown the glaring misuse of science. These negative aspects of science has drawn the attention of many thinkers and social activists towards the adverse impact of science and technology on the civil society. The issue of science versus civil welfare has become more complex with the impact of globalization, faster flow of knowledge and expertise cutting across spatial and temporal zones with a corresponding increase in risks and uncertainty facing all societies. This has led to many citizen's movements (affirmative action), both violent and peaceful, to express their grave concern over the adverse effects of science and technology on society and their impact on the environment. Allowing patenting of plant genetic materials sourced mainly from the developing countries by advanced countries and thereby depriving the indigenous populace of their rights and benefits; America's unhelpful attitude towards issues like reducing level of global warming; depriving rural population of their farm lands in the name of industrialization in developing countries are a few examples of adverse impact of science and technology on society. Some of these actions are carried out in the name of development, and free flow of trade under the banner of WTO, World Bank and other organizations. Development is taken to be sine qua non with technology, brushing aside all social and health concerns. Citizenship and knowledge claims have become the locus of affirmative action espoused by human rights activists, ecologists, feminists, pacifists and other critiques of science. They and the affected people are seeking what Shiv Vishwanathan terms "cognitive justice" (Vishwanathan, 2005, Leach and Scoones, 2005).

Cognitive justice seeks equal constitutional rights for systems of knowledge represented by indigenous knowledge, and practices derived from generations of living with nature to coexist with the high technological knowledge. Cognitive justice is not opposed to high technology *per se* but seeks the blending of the two for the common good. More importantly, it seeks science policy makers and economic policy strategists to give due consideration in their decision-making process to the concerns of the people likely to be affected by their decisions on the latter's livelihood and life style. In the existing system of governance there is no place for rights of alternative epistemologies and alternative sciences.

Social Responsibility of Science. Scientists engaged in critical areas of research, the findings of which may have dangerous consequences for society can not be absolved of their share of responsibility. If a scientist does not " take the concerned peers and people into confidence and tell them the circumstances under which his discovery may prove dangerous, his professional negligence is 'unreasonable' and 'culpable'. Also, the scientist is under moral obligation to share with his peers and the concerned policy-makers the necessary safety steps to be taken to prevent the anticipatory dangers (Chattopadhyaya, 2000, p. 108). The problem of social accountability of scientists is not that straight forward as it involves many basic issues, such as: the type of society—democratic, theocratic or dictatorship to which the scientist belongs; his own belief system, national pride and others. For instance in a war situation if the use of the scientist's findings is critical to the very existence of his country, what is he to do?

As against genuine concerns on the ill effects of some scientific inventions and technological creations, there are also people with attitudes founded on ignorance or prejudice or vested interests holding science and technology responsible for all the ills facing societies. Science and technology are really neutral in this respect. It is the human greed, hatred, and hunger for power acting in the form of social, political, economic and military policies framed and executed by man at the state/institutional levels, and not science that is responsible for the adverse consequences of science and technology.

CLOSURE

Science is the objective study of nature, its constituents, and the laws governing them. Development of science in the West goes back to the ancient Greek period, to the times of Socrates, Plato, Aristotle, Pythagoras and Archimedes. In India during the Vedic period and early centuries following it, science appears not to have taken roots due to Vedantic philosophy's aversion towards all worldly things. However, astronomy, logic, and medicine had flourished. The development of modern science is a late eighteenth century phenomenon initiated by the British. Scientific tradition began in the late 19th century by the pioneering achievements of Acharya Prafulla Chandra Ray, Srinivasa Ramanujan, Sir C.V. Raman, and a few others.

Early years of Independence laid a strong foundation for the development of 20th century science. Today, Indian science and technology is growing fast and has archived international recognition by exporting scientific talent.

Science displays a few basic features which are applicable to the whole of science. These include: a) the concept of unity of science, b) cumulativeness of science, c) scientific objectivity, d) use of precise terminology and distinctive form of communication, e) distinguishing basic research from applied research; and f) application of scientific method. The validity of some of these features like unity of science is not accepted by all. Professional associations play a distinctive role in the development of science. Kuhn opines that science grows via the rise and fall of many "paradigms", i.e., research consensus.

Scientific knowledge forms a major segment of universe of knowledge. It is deeply influencing other fields, such as philosophy, sociology, economics, and even arts and sports. Scientific and technical knowledge have become the prime pushers of economic development. It is influencing the pattern of thinking of even ordinary people, and their daily lives. Scientific knowledge is growing faster than in most other disciplines. It incorporates the vitality of science, its objectivity, directness and clarity. Study of the pattern of growth of scientific knowledge has interested both sociologists and information science people. Data is the building blocks from which science is constructed. Information and communication technology-based data structuring, data organization, and data transmission are reshaping big science, and is changing the mode of scientific communication.

Scientific advancement relies on theories and laws. A theory is constructed from hypotheses confirmed by experiments. Mathematics is built on axioms, i.e., self evident facts. Scientific method uses either inductive logic or deductive logic with the general consensus favoring the latter. Cognitive scientists are trying to unravel the mentality of scientists, and particularly the role of different forms of reasoning, conceptual change, and intuition.

Technology and science are intimately related. While basic research tries to unravel the mysteries of nature, technology by applying scientific findings develops socially useful new products and new uses for existing things. Technology has its own methodology. While science makes predictions based on theories, technology makes forecast. Adoption of a technology process is mostly governed by political, economic and managerial considerations. Today's scientific research and technology programmes rely on collaborative efforts.

Science is a child of society. It has acquired a brand value. Science and technology contribute to the development of society. Because of the disastrous consequences caused by applying certain findings of science and developmental technology, they have become the target of 'affirmative action' all over the world. This has raised the question of social responsibility of science. Science is neutral in this. The Science and technology will continue to grow with enormous consequences for society. It will reshape in new ways our style of living and the structure of society leading to 'knowledge society'.

REFERENCES

Abdul Kalam, A.P.J. and Pillai, A. Sivathanu. Envisioning an Empowered Nation: Technology for Transformation. New Delhi, Tata McGraw- Hill, 2004.

Barrow, John D. The World within the World. Oxford, Clarandon Press, 1988.

Berman, Fran and Hey, Tony. The Scientific Imperative. Pp. 13-24. *In* Foster, Ian and Kesselman, Carl. Eds. The Grid: Blueprint for a New Computing Infrastructure. Ed. 2. San Francisco (CA), Morgan Kaufman, 2004. (Indian reprint, Elsevier, 2006).

Bhattacharya, Manoranjan. Science and technology in post- independent India. *Science and Culture* 69 (5-6): 178-187, May-June, 2003.

Bunge, M. Technology as Applied Science, Pp. 19-39. *In* Rapp, Friedrich. Ed. Op.cit., 1974.

Chaitin, Gregory. The limits of reason. *Scientific American* 294 (3): 54-61, March 2006.

Chattopadhyaya, D.P. Science Value and Ethics. *Science and Culture* 66 (3-4) : 101-109, March-April, 2000. P.108.

Dampier, W. C. A History of Science and its Relations with Philosophy and Religion, ed. 4. New Delhi, Chand, 1982. (Indian reprint).

Dixon, Bernard. What is Science For?. London, Collins, 1973.

Dunbar, Kevin and Fugelsang, Jonathan. Scientific Thinking and Reasoning. Pp. 705-725. *In* Holyoak, Keith J. and Morrison, Robert G. Eds. The Cambridge Handbook of Thinking and Reasoning. Cambridge (NY), Cambridge University Press, 2005.

Economic Times (India), 2nd September, 2007, p. 14. Gene portrait spark new trend : DNA is now also gaining popularity as art. (Source: Reuters, New York).

Freedman, Paul. The Principles of Scientific Research. Ed. 2. Oxford, Pergamon Press, 1960.

Gibbons, Michael et al. The New Production of Knowledge: The Dynamics of Science and Research in Contemporary Societies. New Delhi, Sage Publications, 1994.

Heilprin, Laurnce B. Science and technology: From prescientific times to the present. *Journal of the American Society for Information Science* 46(8): 574-578, Sept. 1995.

Cf. Jones, A.L. Logic,Inductive and Deductive. New York, Henry Holt, 1929.

Kuhn, T. S. The Structure of Scientific Revolutions. Chicago, Chicago University Press, 1962. Ed. 2, 1970.

Ladyman, James. Understanding Philosophy of Science. London, Routledge, 2002.

Leach, Melissa and Scoones, Ian. Science and Citizenship in a Global Context. Pp. 15-38. *In* Leach, Melissa; Scoones, Ian and Wynne, Brian. Eds. Science and Citizens: Globalization and the challenge of engagement. London, Zed Books, 2005.

Mc Burney, Donald H. Research Methods. Ed.5. Wadsworth, 2001. (2002 reprint, Bangalore).

Cf. Medawar, Peter. The Art of the Soluble. Pelican, 1969.

Menon, M.G.K. Basic Research as an Integral Component of a Self-Reliant Base of Science and Technology. (Presidential address given at the

Indian Science Congress, 1982, Mysore). Pp. 1271-1303. *In* The Shaping of Indian Science. Indian Science Congress Association Presidential Addresses. Vol. III : 1982-2003. Hyderabad (AP), Universities Press, 2003..

Mukunda, N. The Meaning of Understanding Nature. Pp. 97-107. *In* Life, Mind and Consciousness. (Papers read at a seminar held at the Ramakrishna Mission Institute of Culture, Kolkata, India, on 16, 17 and 18 January 2004). Kolkata, The Ramakrishna Mission Institute of Culture, 2004.

Nye, David E. Technology Matters: Questions to Live With. Cambridge (Mass.), MIT Press, 2006.

Popper, K. R. Conjectures and Refutations: The Growth of Scientific Knowledge, Ed. 2. New York, Harper and Row. 1973.

Popper, K.R. The Logic of Scientific Discovery. London, Hutchinson, 1972.

Cf. Popper, K.R. Realism and the Aim of Science. London, Hutchinson, 1983.

Purver, Margery. The Royal Society: Concept and Creation. With an Introduction by H. R. Trevor-Roper. London, Routledge and Kegan Paul, 1967.

Rama Rao, P. Science and Technology in Independent India: Retrospect and Prospect. (Presidential address delivered at the Indian Science Congress, 1998, Hyderabad). Pp. 1901-1926. *In* The Shaping of Indian Science. Indian Science Congress Association Presidential Addresses. Vol. III: 1982-2003. Hyderabad (AP), Universities Press, 2003.

Rapp, F. Ed. Technology and Natural Science- A Methodological Investigation. Pp. 93-114. *In* Rapp, Friedrich. Ed. Contributions to a Philosophy of Technology. Dordrecht (Holland), D. Reidel, 1974.

Ray, Prafulla Chandra. Dawn of Science in Modern India. (Presidential address given at the Indian Science Congress, 1920, Nagpur). Pp. 82-95. *In* The Shaping of Indian Science. Indian Science Congress Association. Presidential Addresses. Vol. I: 1914-1947. Hyderabad (AP), Universities Press, 2003.

Schlick, Moritz. General Theory of Knowledge. Tr. Albert E. Blumberg. Ed. 2 (German). New York, Springer Verlag, 1974.

Sengupta, Pradip Kumar. Growth of knowledge, man and transcendence. *Science and Culture* 66 (3-4): 139-146, March-April, 2000.

Spangenburg, Ray and Moser, Diane Kit. The Birth of Science. Vol.1: Ancient Times to 1699; The Age of Synthesis. Vol.3: 1800-1895. New Delhi, Viva Books, 2006. (Indian edition).

Szalay, Alexander S. and Gray, Jim. Scientific Data Federation: The World-Wide Telescope. Pp. 95-108. *In* Foster, Ian and Kesselman, Carl. Eds.

The Grid: Blueprint for a New Computing Infrastructure. Ed. 2. San Francisco (CA), Morgan Kaufman, 2004. (Indian reprint, Elsevier, 2006).

Tata, Jamsetji N. Letter written by Jamsetji N. Tata to Swami Vivekananda on 23rd November, 1898. Source: The Indian Institute of Science, Bangalore 2009: The Centenary Calendar.

Thacker, M.S. Grammar of Scientific Development. (Presidential address delivered at the Indian Science Congress, 1958, Madras). Pp. 782-791. *In* The Shaping of Indian Science. Indian Science Congress Association Presidential Addresses. Vol. II: 1948-1981. Hyderabad, Universities Press, 2003.

Vishwanathan, Shiv. Knowledge, Justice and Democracy. 2005. Pp. 83-94. *In* Leach, Melissa et al. Loc. Cit.

www. Dorabjitrust. *http://www.dorabjitatatrust.org/*

Wikipedia. Fulbright. (http:// en.wikipedia.org/wki/Fulbright#History

World of Learning (Europa), 2005. London, Europa Publications, 2007.

14
Knowledge Resource and Power

Many of the facets and characteristics of knowledge considered so far invariably touch upon some aspect of application of knowledge to the well-being of man and progress of society. This chapter studies the resource function of knowledge, and how knowledge and its strategic employment leads to accumulation of power.

KNOWLEDGE RESOURCE

The term "resource" is increasingly finding a place in the vocabulary of decision-makers on knowledge and information related activities, and in fields as varied as education, economics and development. Hence there is a need for examining the resource function of knowledge. The dictionary meaning of "resource" is "a new or a reserve source of supply or support", and "resources" are "available means as of a country or business" (Webster's, 1981). Knowledge is a resource as it is a reserve source of supply available to mankind for their subsistence and development, and also is an available means of a society. Resource aspect of knowledge has received special attention by economists because of its being considered as an intangible asset of an economic enterprise. Boulding affirms that economic development is essentially a learning process, and that the nature and allocation of the intellectual resource is the key to it (Boulding, 1970). Implicit in this explanation is the condition that a resource must have some economic utility.

Analogy to Natural Resource. In examining knowledge as a resource, it may be helpful to draw the analogy of natural resource. While natural resources are the gifts of nature knowledge is a creation of the human mind, and a product of society. Natural resources are governed by laws of nature and man-made laws, whereas knowledge to a large extent is governed by the neural phenomena, the mental makeup of an individual, and his environment. Every human-being is endowed with certain amount of knowledge, which he employs in everyday life to support his actions. Thus, knowledge is a component of human resource. Further, it is an intellectual resource. Natural resources comprise of renewable and non-renewable resources. Knowledge is inexhaustible as any given knowledge item can be used any number of times, and it never gets exhausted. The same knowledge item can be regenerated by recording and reproducing. However, knowledge exhibits the characteristic of non-renewability, if it is not communicated or recorded. Just as natural resources need conservation, knowledge too needs to be conserved. The purpose of conservation is to ensure rational utilization of the natural environment for sustaining the highest quality of living for mankind. Measures of conservation of resources include preservation and protection, rational use, and pollution control. Knowledge is preserved through the process of communication, learning and experiencing. Museums, archives, libraries, academic and professional bodies, publishers, and performers of art serve as the agents of preservation through diffusion and dissemination of knowledge in the organized sector. Knowledge is preserved in the form of records, artefacts, pictures, paintings, archaeological finds, recorded narrations, and performances. The following measures contribute either directly or indirectly towards the rational use of knowledge:

1. Planned production, transmission and utilization of knowledge resources.
2. Controlled allocation of financial and other resources towards knowledge activities.
3. Grant of subsidies and tax concessions to knowledge producers and distributors.
4. Establishment of recording and information distribution agencies as in metrology, oceanography, census, industrial data and scientific data, to mention a few.
5. Imposition of censorship, where necessary.
6. Exercise of authority on the release, distribution and use of knowledge resources by governments, knowledge holders, and other authority wielders like parents, schools, and religious leaders.
7. Bestowing property rights, such as copyright, lending rights, trademark, and patent rights.
8. Regulating the use of insider information as in share market.
9. Enactment of laws on the public right to knowledge, and on safeguarding a citizen's right to privacy.
10. Pricing mechanism.
11. Ensuring security of data, information and knowledge transmitted in electronic form and accessed via internet, telephones, and other means.
12. Avoiding duplication of research and other knowledge creation activities, so that there is no wastage of time and efforts.

In addition to the methods mentioned above, social organization and taxonomy of knowledge, professional bodies, and knowledge distribution systems both in private and public sectors also play a part in the proper utilization of knowledge.

One of the characteristics of knowledge that distinguishes it from natural resources is, unlike natural resources, knowledge does not obey the economics law of "diminishing returns", meaning its distribution results in the growth of it (Boulding, 1970).

Knowledge is a resource, which enables economising and effective use of labour, capital and material. In other words, it conserves other resources (Cronin, 1985). Like natural resources, knowledge too has different utility values. Knowledge applied to produce goods and service, to increase productivity, to enhance an individual's earning capacity reflects economic value of knowledge; literature and art forms represent aesthetic value; drama, music, quiz and comics indicate recreational value; knowledge conveyed through prayers, discourses, sermons and codes of conduct are of spiritual and ethical value; and inventions and research as steps to further research represent scientific value (Machlup, 1980).

Knowledge Pollution. Creation of certain types of knowledge and their application can lead to activities that are considered prejudicial to the proper functioning of society. Dissemination of knowledge considered obscene, subversive, pornographic and inflammatory; promotion of unwholesome knowledge through advertising; and eulogizing knowledge about superstitious acts and barbaric customs are examples of one form of knowledge pollution. Controlling this form of pollution is beset with difficulties arising out of differing value systems held by social groups and individuals; vested interests; and arbitrary control over the flow of knowledge by authorities in power. Knowledge explosion and its consequences contribute to knowledge pollution in no small measure. In a situation of tremendous growth in knowledge output, the creation of some unverified and doubtful knowledge, choking the channels of communication, straining the tolerance capacity of the human brain to knowledge intake, and wastage of knowledge resources are inherent. Abuse of Internet, e-mail, and new forms of electronic information has become a major cause of knowledge pollution (see chapter 19). The problem with the new forms of information exposure is that it is difficult to detect the culprit sources like hackers and take remedial action because of Internet's global operation without any central control.

Nature of Knowledge Resource. The knowledge resource is of three types: a) knowledge in the minds of people (tacit knowledge), b) knowledge outside the mind existing as information and information records (explicit knowledge); and c) data. All the three forms of knowledge resources are used as input in manufacturing, trade, industry, agriculture, research and development, politics and other sectors to produce wealth as output. This input to output transformation process creates new knowledge, new technologies, and new insights, in addition to tangible wealth. The process is continuous, but the input knowledge and the output knowledge keep alternating in each cycle. Accrued wealth and knowledge, when applied generates further wealth, newer technological knowledge, and strategic knowledge which in turn result in further accrual of economic, industrial, technological, and political power to a state. Politics and international diplomacy are two areas where knowledge is applied directly to achieve power. In other cases application of knowledge resource does not result in power directly, it acts as an agent or as a factor of production.

As a resource, knowledge has an international dimension. Knowledge has no national boundaries. Knowledge produced in one country is available elsewhere. Yet, there are many impediments to the flow of knowledge, i.e., transfer of resource across national and transnational borders. McGuire points out "nations are beginning to perceive information as a natural resource and the regulation of transborder data flow as a means of protecting it" (McGuire, 1979). Groshan indicates that the technology of transborder data flow (TDF) "frees data physically from the national constraints of the regulatory arms of individual governments. Data can reside in many places at once, be moved rapidly from nation to nation, or be isolated to a single national jurisdiction almost at the will of those operating the data system. Therefore, serious problems of extraterritoriality arise in national efforts to regulate uses and applications of data within a nation's boundaries." (Groshan, 1981).

Issues involved in the transfer of this resource are complex. They impinge on economic, political, social, cultural, computer and communication policies of different nations. International cooperation plays a vital role in the conservation and rational utilization of knowledge. Providing free and universal access to knowledge is a cherished goal of enlightened international community. Often, the self-interests of sovereign states, professional groups, and multinational corporations are ranged against this universal goal. International conventions, bilateral agreements, and creation of greater understanding among the concerned parties are a few means tried to overcome or minimize these conflicts and pave the way for orderly, legal, and practical solutions to the problems of transfer of knowledge throughout the world. Exhaustive analysis of the issues involved, a thorough understanding of the implications of communication and computer technologies on flow of knowledge, appraisal of the interests and fears of different nations, and comprehensive studies on knowledge and its characteristics help in formulating polices on the distribution and utilization of this resource.

Knowledge Resource in Wealth Generation. As a resource, knowledge and information is employed to generate wealth in the form of goods and services, either directly or indirectly. Wealth generation function of knowledge is fulfilled in five ways, namely: a) sale of knowledge and information as a commodity, i.e., a directly saleable good or service (e.g., intellectual property, books, software systems); b) knowledge serving as a factor of production to enhance the production power of the other factors of production; c) developing professional services derived from knowledge (e.g., legal service, medical practice); d) by means of third party processing and transmitting information; and e) export of embedded knowledge in the form of manpower. The first three items are dealt in detail in chapters 15 and 16 respectively. A knowledge-based model for the wealth-generation system, and the last two items will be discussed now.

Knowledge-based Wealth Generation Model. Though knowledge is an intangible resource, by working on the tangible items like capital, land, and labour it converts them into wealth, the basis of all economic development. The main features of the conversion process is shown in Fig. 1.

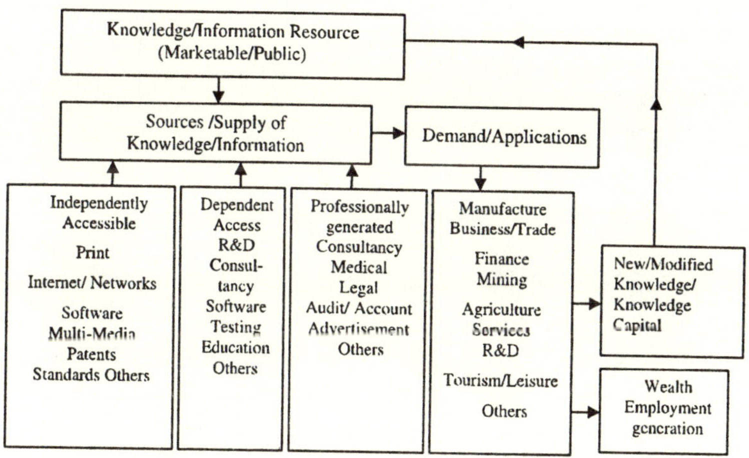

Fig. 1. Knowledge resource and wealth generation system

In Fig. 1 above, source and supply side shows the different sources of embodied and implicit knowledge, and their mode of access. It is made up of independently accessible items like print media, Internet and web sites; institution/agency dependent creators and suppliers of knowledge as in education, scientific research and technology development; and the various professional services like legal and advertising. Knowledge thus generated is utilized by the demand units for the manufacturing of goods and providing services, which accounts for the demand side of the system. Certain types of units, like software testing, and education in the source side also generate wealth directly as they have markets. However, it is the demand side constituents like industry, business, transport and communications, utilities and consumer services create wealth by efficient application of knowledge resource. The system to sustain and grow must create surplus so that the surplus is reinvested for the continuous growth of source and supply sectors of knowledge. Creation of surplus is possible only when each constituent part of the system is able to successfully compete with competitors- local, regional and global. The present day global economy has thrown open the entire world market for business and has provided unprecedented opportunities. At the same time, it has also created the forces of fierce global competition. By harnessing knowledge resource, particularly technology type, a country could come up a winner.

Third Party Processing of Information. Wide disparity in cost of processing information, availability of relevant knowledge and skill power outside an enterprise, different time zones, and affordable instant communication systems have provided business and industry the economic choice of outsourcing many of their functions, such as enquiry/call centre services, certain administrative and ancillary functions, and design to third parties, i.e., outside agencies, both offshore and onshore. This ensures outsourcing organizations the advantage of cost cutting and releasing the time of executives to concentrate on more productive functions. Business Process Outsourcing (BPO) and Knowledge Process Outsourcing (KPO) are the two widespread services employed by organizations. BPO and KPO are today estimated to be a multibillion dollar industry and generate nearly half a million job opportunities. India, with its English-speaking, intellectually trained young work-force is well placed to garner a significant portion of international outsourcing market.

Outsourcing functions may be conveniently classified under the kind of industry they serve, such as: financial services including equity, insurance research and banking; marketing research and competitive intelligence, general business research; data analytics, integration and management; research and information services in HR; intellectual property, paralegal content and services; animation and simulation services and medical content and services. The main difference between KPO and BPO are:

1. KPO emphasizes 'intellectual arbitrage', where as BPO (and also IT outsourcing) emphasize cost arbitrage.
2. KPO cuts into the traditional "core competencies" of many organizations and is non-rule based. BPO is rule-based and continuous.
3. Communication with client is more in KPO as compared to BPO wherein the back-end operations do not involve client interaction.
4. In KPO there is a clear demarcation in process complexity, the amount of intellectual intervention in the process, the skills required and the ability to scale. It also involves judgment. Business processes are essentially process-driven and rule-based (Business Line, 2008).

Human Resource Development. Human resource corresponds to labour, one of the factors of production. It is human resource, i.e., labour that uses other factors of production, like capital, land and organization to convert them into wealth. Labour has two components: physical labour and intellectual labour. In the new economic scenario, intellectual labour, i.e., the use of intellectual resource has reduced the role of physical labour resource. Defining human resource development (HRD) is slippery. A cousin of HRD is human resource management (HRM), which runs parallel to HRD in certain aspects. A major component of both HRD and HRM is knowledge resource (KR), which is also called intellectual resource (IR). 'Strategic HRD', learning organization and Knowledge Management (KM) are considered distinct parts of HRD (McGoldrick et al., 2002).

Development of KR. The role of KR in the emerging knowledge society is so critical and specialized that persons engaged in knowledge dominated activities are called "knowledge workers", the term coined by Peter Drucker. Knowledge workers are professionals with expertise in interpreting and translating ideas and technologies into realities and in problem solving. Also coming under this category are technicians, laboratory analysts, paralegals, whose works are based on theoretical knowledge acquired through formal education, not apprenticeship. Development of knowledge workers, who are practical and result oriented, calls for development of human resource programmes built on a flexible education system. Such a system incorporates basic education providing elementary education, followed by secondary and tertiary education capable of not only imparting technical knowledge, but also arousing creative and critical thinking, the two most important elements in problem solving and innovation. (Edersheim, 2007).

An intrinsic feature of KR is that it is not created instantly. It requires acquisition of knowledge, training, and task familiarization in specific work areas. It is a continuous process. KR needs to be nurtured. Knowledge manpower development takes years of nurturing through setting up of institutions and programmes to impart the requisite knowledge and skill in each area of requirement. It is a dynamic process as the goals keep on changing to suit changing environment and requirements. It needs careful planning. The prime means of developing KR are education and training. The other components of KR development are knowledge component of science and technology development, transfer of technology, information collection and dissemination (libraries, data banks, Internet and networks etc.), knowledge exchange forums, communication infrastructure, industrial needs, intellectual property rights, and the like.

Two important issues in KR development, particularly in the context of education, are public good aspect and the role of private enterprise. Prescribing the role for private sector depends on many factors, such as the resource position of the state and the priority given to IRD, political clout of the private sector, mechanisms to establish and enforce minimum educational standards, flight of intellectual capital and knowledge personnel, strategic issues such as security, and more importantly the larger national policy goals, and now global factors like WTO commitments and the World Bank dictates. Because of our overwhelming concern with economic development and equating it with human development the importance of IR in promoting social, cultural and ethical values which are so important to any progressive and peaceful society, it seems, is not well appreciated.

Indian Scenario. In India we have a good foundation of educational infrastructure and a few institutions of learning of world class. This is totally inadequate, if we are to compete in the world with some of our neighbours like South Korea and China, and make our mark in comity of nations. This calls for:

1. Large-scale expansion of educational facilities beginning from literacy level right up to lifelong education.
2. Upgradation of quality of teaching and assessment, including transparency to world standard.
3. Specific attention to be given to science and technology education;
4. Initiation of new courses, recasting existing courses to match the needs of the new economy.
5. Introduction of new modes of education like distance education, informal literacy programmes.
6. Substantial increase in funding.

7. Increasing avenues for private sector participation in the development of the sector.
8. Encourage community participation and foreign involvement in educational programmes subject to essential safeguards in place where necessary;
9. Involve Indian diaspora abroad to derive maximum benefit from their contributions (Dahlman and Utz, 2005); and
10. Reduce regional disparities.

Restructuring and expansion of higher education and engineering/ technology education is one of the primary tasks before the country. Several initiatives have been suggested or taken up in this regard by the Planning Commission (India. Planning Commission,2002) and the central government. The most recent initiative in this regard is the constitution of the National Knowledge Commission, which has submitted its recommendations (India. National Knowledge Commission, 2007). Based on the Knowledge Commission's recommendations, the central government has recently established four new Indian Institute of Technology and 8 new centrally sponsored universities. (See also chapter 21).

Development of KR in Industry. Development of KR in industrial sector follows a different framework. There is no denying the fact that business and industry in a capitalistic society are solely governed by profit motive. Hence all KR issues are evaluated and finalized by applying the standard of what contribution a particular IR initiative makes to the profit profile of the organization, its survival and growth. Since meeting competition, both global and local, is the biggest challenge facing modern liberalized and globalized economy, industry and business have realised that appropriate selection and use of IR makes the difference between a performing and a nonperforming enterprise. The first mantra to make the organization a performing one is to invest in people to raise the standard of competency in individuals to keep the organization perform optimally. This calls for development of suitable organizational structure, strategy, and management standards. The second mantra is installing *lifelong learning* programmes. Lifelong learning programmes are expected to increase the knowledge potential of employees, and add to the intellectual capital of the organization (McGoldrick et al., 2002). However, it is another matter that IR alone cannot save a company or an economy from going burst as shown by the current US financial crisis (September, 2008), and its worldwide repercussions. Economists now consider human resource, i.e., intellectual resource plus knowledge resource as an important component of an organization's asset. By assigning money value to them, they are treated as 'human capital', 'intellectual capital' and 'knowledge capital' and are included in the balance sheet of companies. Knowledge Management is dealt with in more detail in chapter 20.

KNOWLEDGE POWER

Francis Bacon's statement "knowledge is power" implies an important strategic dimension of knowledge. Knowledge by itself is not power; its strategic deployment can bestow power on its employer. According to Oxford English Dictionary the word "power" means " possession of control authority over others", "strength", "might", "dominance", " personal, social or political influence" (Oxford English Dictionary, 1993). The concept " knowledge is power" is used in the sense that use of knowledge enables one to gain control authority over others, or influence the action of others, or to become powerful. Exercise of power takes different forms such as political power, economic power, military power and spiritual power. Whichever be the form, the main sources of power are knowledge, wealth, and physical strength. Knowledge power is easily recognised in military domain. War strategies and tactics are nothing but collection and evaluation of knowledge power of the adversary, and matching them through superior action. Ability to grasp appropriate knowledge and use it effectively is a characteristic of able leadership. Whatever be the system of society - democracy, monarchy or any other form, power exists and acts in all of them.

Empowering Individuals. Power seen in a social context is of two types: power in the hands of an individual, and 'structural power'. An individual member of society, by virtue of being a member or agent enmeshed with various social relationships with other agents, enjoys every day, everywhere, certain degree of power. Besides this socially granted power, individuals can and do garner additional power through their own individual efforts. Knowledge is one of the means individuals employ to gain power. Knowledge empowers individuals by increasing their abilities to use other levers of power such as organizing ability, material wealth, communication skills, intellectual supremacy, and social status. There are various ways of acquiring knowledge. Education and training is one of the most important and commonly available means of acquiring knowledge; the other methods include self-study, experiencing, and research.

Present-day knowledge and power equation is vastly different from the past. As explained by Peter Drucker, "for decades, information was power. But to-day, with the unprecedented availability of instant information to any one with a laptop, true power comes from screening, interpreting, and translating vast quantities of information into action" (Edersheim, 2007, p. 20). The spread of information technology, globalization of economy, and changing culture are redefining the role of knowledge and information in bringing changes in society, particularly in empowering individuals. Naisbitt underscores this point when he says "information is, indeed, power, and as more and more information becomes available to individuals through telecommunications systems, individuals will be empowered as never before."(Naisbitt, 1994, p.17). This empowerment has tremendous impact on enhancing the political awareness of individuals and on the functioning of democracies. To quote Naisbitt, again, "... Because we are in a position to know all we have to know as soon as everyone else knows it— including those who represent us— we do not have to have that kind of *representativeness* any-more. We don't have to have people on the scene who have the knowledge and information to make judgements for us. We have the same information and knowledge and we are also on the scene. The only thing the representative on the scene has that the citizen at home doesn't have is knowledge of the culture of the institutions of government — and most of that culture is antidemocratic and maladaptive" (Naisbitt,1994, p. 43).

One way of depriving individuals, organizations, and nations from becoming powerful is by controlling or complete blocking of the flow of knowledge to them. By blocking the flow of technological knowledge, advanced counties of the West retain their supremacy over the developing countries.

Structural Power. Over and above the power of the individual is, what sociologists call, the 'structural power' — the power that controls and sustains society. Structural power is an organizational power. Sociology recognises two types of structural power: a) power of *the state,* and b) the power arising from the social positions of different groups in society. The power of the state is pervasive and extends over its population, and the structural units of the society. Extending its influence or power over other countries is one of the hidden policies of every state.

It is interesting to observe how structural groups of society utilise their specialized knowledge in the field to gain power. In all such cases the objective seems to be to gain exclusive power by the group to shape and control policies that govern the given area of activity as a whole, to the exclusion of others and to promote the self interest of the group. Some of the fields that have attained or capable of attaining power by virtue of their specialized knowledge are medicine, media, accountancy, certain technologies, and now education. 'Medicalization' is a typical example that shows how knowledge is employed by medical profession to garner power over the entire medical sector in modern society.

'Medicalization' of society refers to the process of extending the sphere of medical authority over many non-medical aspects of life, so as to bring them under the category requiring medical treatment, as if they are medical problems (Illich, 1975). Medicalization of women's body by the International Federation of Gynaecology and Obstetrics is a recent example. The Federation, in its 1991 Congress recommended the routine use of hormone replacement treatment (HRT) for menopausal and post-menopausal women, which raises what is purely a part of natural process of ageing to the level of a disease requiring medical treatment, as if all women suffer from the ill-effects of a lowering estrogens levels. Sometimes, the process of medicalization gets support from non-medical agencies, such as uninformed media, from ideological beliefs like ageing affects feminine beauty, and hence it is to be prevented by any means, thus making it a gender issue; and not to speak of the support from pharmaceutical industry (McLennan et al., 2000). Another example is that of childbirth which was formerly considered a natural process of life, and attended by midwives and mothers are now brought under the control of doctors.

The enlargement of the power-base of medical profession by virtue of professional knowledge is continuing through the adoption what Foucault terms 'medical gaze'. This gaze is not the one used to regulate the behaviour of individuals. Foucault argues that power and knowledge are so deeply interconnected that "there is no power relation without the correlative constitution of a field of knowledge, nor any knowledge that does not presuppose and constitute at the same time power relations (Foucault, 1977). The professional medical knowledge is imposed on population in such a way that it takes on a self-regulatory form on the part of individuals; thereby the decision of the medical profession on how individuals should behave medically becomes a sort of scientific truth and assumes the form of disciplinary power. That is how women have been self-influenced to accept HRT as an infallible truth.

The interpretation of Illach, Foucault, and a few others on the empowerment of medical profession through knowledge stated above reflects one of the negative aspects of the utilization of medical knowledge to attain power. But, a more important aspect of knowledge is that the enormous benefit the medical knowledge and the profession brings to society also results in power that is being used for the extension and up gradation of health care to society.

Conversion of Knowledge Resource into Power. The destiny of a nation is controlled by the power it wields. Power exists in four forms: political power, military power, economic power, and moral power. In the modern day context, economic power rules over the other three. If a nation or a state is economically powerful then the other forms of power follow it. How knowledge resource is used to generate wealth has been explained earlier (Fig. 1). There is a strong relationship between the development of a country and its resources- particularly knowledge resources. Abdul Kalam, former president of India, while bringing out the relationship between knowledge resource and power emphasises that a developed India has to be powered by economic development, which in turn is powered by competitiveness. The competitiveness is powered by knowledge power. The knowledge power is powered by innovation. Innovation is powered by science and technology, and technology is powered by resource investment (Abdul Kalam, http 2005). Thus, knowledge resources effectively directed lead to accumulation of power.

CLOSURE

Knowledge is a resource as it is a reserve source of supply available to mankind for their subsistence and development, and an available means of a society. Though knowledge is an intangible resource by working on the tangible items like capital, land, and labour, it enhances their production potential. Knowledge resource is inexhaustible as any given knowledge item can be put to repeat use, and it never gets exhausted, and can be regenerated by recording and reproducing. Knowledge resource needs to be conserved. Measures of conservation include preservation, rational use and controlling information pollution. Knowledge does not obey the law of "diminishing returns", meaning its distribution results in the growth of it.

Knowledge is preserved mainly through the process of communication, diffusion and dissemination. Museums, archives, libraries, educational system, professional bodies, publishers, performers of art, and now Internet serve as the main agents of preserving knowledge resource in the form of records, artifacts, pictures, paintings, archaeological finds, and performances.

Development of "knowledge resource planning" is one means of securing rational use of knowledge resource. The plan covers all aspects of knowledge— its creation, transmission, dissemination and utilization. Elements of the plan consists of setting priority knowledge sectors, budgetary provision, intellectual property rights, transfer of technology, security of data, safeguarding public right to information, security of national sensitive knowledge, infrastructure development, manpower needs, information industry and trade, international dimension, role of private sector and professional associations, and controlling knowledge pollution.

Knowledge resource (KR) is an intellectual resource (IR). IR is a major component of human resource development (HRD), and human resource management (HRM). IR is treated as an organization's intangible asset, and is reflected in the account books. An intrinsic feature of KR is that it is not created instantly. It requires acquisition of knowledge, education and training, and task familiarization in specific work areas, and is a continuous process.

The concept " knowledge is power" is used in the sense that use of knowledge enables one to gain control authority over others, or influences the action of others, or helps one to become powerful. Exercise of power takes different forms, such as political power, economic power, military power, and spiritual power. Whichever be the form, the main sources of power are knowledge, wealth, and physical strength.

Power seen in a social context is of two types: power in the hands of an individual, and 'structural power'. An individual inherits power by virtue of being a member or agent enmeshed with various social relationships with other agents. In addition, individuals can and do garner additional power through acquiring knowledge. Knowledge empowers individuals by increasing their abilities to use other levers of power such as organizing ability, material wealth, communication skills, intellectual supremacy and social status. Education and training are the most important and commonly available means of acquiring knowledge; the other methods include self- study, experiencing and research.

Structural power is an organizational power that controls and sustains society. Sociology recognizes two types of structural power: a) power of *the state*, and b) the power arising from the social positions of different groups in society. The power of the state is pervasive and extends over its population and the structural units of the society. Structural groups of society like medical fraternity, higher education, media, and others utilize their specialized knowledge in the field to gain power. The objective is to gain exclusive power by the group to shape and control policies that govern their area of activity as a whole, to the exclusion of others and to promote the self interest of the group. 'Medicalization' is an example that shows how the profession employs its medical knowledge monopoly to garner power over the entire medical sector in modern society. This can be seen from the International Federation of Gynaecology and Obstetrics 1991 Congress resolution recommending the routine use of hormone replacement treatment (HRT) for menopausal and post-menopausal women, which makes what is purely a part of natural process of ageing to the level of a disease.

Knowledge is a resource and is also a source of power. Power has no meaning unless we know how to use it. It can be used for the good of people or for exploitation and destruction. The option lies not with knowledge and wisdom, but with the human "I".

REFERENCES

Abdul Kalam, P. J. *http://www.hindu.com/2005/12/09/stories/2005120904 841000htm*

Boulding, K. E. The misallocation of intellectual resources. *Proceeding of the American Philosophical Society* 107: 117-120, 1963. (Reprinted in Boulding, K. E., 1970. Op. cit., P.151-56).

Boulding, K.E. Knowledge as a Commodity. *In* Beyond Economics. Essays on Society, Religion and Ethics. Ann Arbor, University of Michigan, 1970. (Reprint).

Business Line. KPO is about 'intellectual arbitrage'. *Business Line* Friday, 15 Feb. 2008. Zarrella, Egidio (Edge) A.B. in an e-mail interaction with *Business Line www.businessline.in/webextras* Murali D.

Cronin, B. Towards information based economics. *Journal of Information Science* 12: 129-137, 1985.

Dahlman, Carl and Utz, Anuja. India and the Knowledge Economy. Leveraging Strengths and Opportunities. Washington(D.C), The World Bank, 2005.

Edersheim, Elizabeth Has. The Definitive Drucker. New Delhi, Tata McGraw-Hill, 2007.

Foucault, M. Discipline and Punish. London, Allen Lane, 1977.

Groshan, Robert M. Transnational data flows: Is the idea of an international regime relevant in establishing multilateral controls and legal norms? Part I. Law Tech. 14: 7. 1981. (Cited by Miller, A. P. Teleinformatics...

Columbia Journal of Law and Social Problems 20: 89-140, 1986.

Illich, Ivan. Limits to Medicine. London, Calder and Boyars, 1975.

India. National Knowledge Commission. Compilation of Recommendations on Education. Chairman: Sam Pitroda. New Delhi, 2007. (Recommendations made up to Nov. 2007). www.knowledgecommission.gov.in

India. Planning Commission. Tenth Five-Year Plan 2002-2007. New Delhi, The Planning Commission, 2002. (http://planningcommission.nic.in/plans/planrel/fiveyr/welcome.html)

McGoldrick, Jim; Martin, Graeme; and Pate, Judy. Problems of Method in HRD Research: Company- based Lifelong Learning and 'longitudinality' Pp.41-64. *In* McGoldrick, Jim; Stuart, Jim; and Watson, Sandra. Eds. Understanding Human Resource Development. A Search-based Approach. London, Routledge, 2002.

McGuire, Richard. The information age: An introduction to transborder data flow. *Jurimetrics Journal* 20: 1-2, 1979. (Cited by Miller, A. P. Teleinformatics... Columbia Journal of Law and Social Problems 20: 89-140, 1986.

McLennan, Gregor, Ryan, Allanah and Spoonley, Paul. Exploring society: Sociology for New Zealand Students. Auckland, Pearson Education New Zealand, 2000.

Machlup, Fritz. Knowledge: Its Creation, Distribution, and Economic Significance. Vol. 1: Knowledge and Knowledge Production. Princeton, Princeton University Press, 1980.

Naisbitt, John. Global paradox. The Bigger the World Economy, the More is Powerful its Smallest Players. Maryborough, Victoria, Allen & Unwin, 1994

Oxford English dictionary, The New Shorter. Lesley Brown. Ed. Vol.2, 1993.

Webster's Third New International Dictionary. (Unabridged). Springfield (Mass.), Marriam-Webster, 1981.

15

Knowledge and Information as Goods

Seen from an economic perspective, knowledge and information has two facets: a) information as an economic entity, and b) the role of information in economic activities. In this context, we find in usage three terms "information economy", "economics of information", and "information economics", which need clarification. Information economy relates to the macro level (e.g., agrarian economy, industrial economy) in relation to a country or a region as a whole. Economics of information is "... more applicable to the micro level, dealing with, for example, the efficiency or input/out put ratio of a specific information service, such as, selective dissemination of information, online access, etc." (Neelameghan, 1999, p.111); it is a sub-discipline within economics. The nature of 'economics of information' may be further amplified. In economics of information, information is studied as an economic good. It deals with all economic aspects, such as production, distribution, marketing and utilization of information as an economic good. In other words, information is seen as an industry. Information economics, on the other hand, refers to the pervasive role of information in shaping all economic functions and activities. It tells us how economics is approached today, how it has provided explanations to phenomena that were previously unexplained, how it has altered our views about how the economy functions, and, perhaps most importantly, how it has led to a rethinking for the appropriate role for government in our market economy (Stiglitz, 2003). Economics of information is the theme of this chapter. When knowledge and information are produced items, they become economic goods coming under the purview of the laws of economics.

Economics, according to Adam Smith, is the study of the enrichment of revenue, i.e., how wealth is produced (Smith, 1898). This definition is too materialistic and it ignores values attendant on human actions. Hence Alfred Marshall defined economics as the study of wealth and more importantly, a part of the study of man (Marshall, 1947). A more concise definition by Lionel Robbins states that "economics is the science which studies human behaviour as a relationship between ends and scarce means which have alternative uses." (Robbins, 1935, p.16). Whether it is economics or information it cannot be studied in isolation of man's social, political, cultural and religious environment. Information, with some exceptions like highly abstract information whose practical implications are unknown and information of transitory nature, has alternative uses. It is also an instrument of production. However, information differs significantly from other types of economic goods from production to consumption.

Knowledge and information are acquired/produced by means of:

1. Direct exposure of the human mind to natural and human environment.
2. Through communication with others, and education.
3. Exposure to records.
4. Thinking process.

One may acquire knowledge incidentally, without

applying efforts or incurring cost. It is only the knowledge and information produced or acquired by spending efforts and employing resources comes under the purview of economics.

INFORMATION AS WEALTH

Both knowledge and information constitute wealth as they fulfill the criteria of wealth (as in material goods), namely, they have utility; they are relatively scarce; they are transferable, and are external (knowledge in the form of information) as shown in Table-1.

Table 1. Criteria of wealth applied to knowledge/information

Criterion	*Material good*	*Knowledge*	*Information*
Utility	Yes	Yes	Yes
Scarcity	Yes	-	Yes
Transferability	Yes	Yes	Yes
Externality	Yes	-	Yes

Knowledge behaves peculiarly in relation to the criteria of scarcity and transferability. Knowledge is scarce in the sense that it is not freely available like air, but at the same time it is not so scarce as it is widespread in human society, and in each individual. Similarly, unlike material goods, knowledge cannot be physically transferred directly from one person to another person. But, at the same time, knowledge is transferable from one mind to another through time and space via information. Knowledge being a phenomenon taking place within the brain it is internal to man (implicit knowledge), whereas information is external (explicit knowledge).

One of the basic characteristics of wealth is its utility. Utility is defined as the power to satisfy human want or desire. Information fulfils this criterion. Utility of information rests on the contents of the message or mental text conveyed by it. A musician's musical talent is not considered wealth, though it enables the musician to earn his or her livelihood. On the other hand, the results of his music ability when sold in the form of an album or charged for his concert becomes a good and is thus considered wealth. Though uncommunicated knowledge (held in the mind) does not constitute wealth, the holders of such knowledge constitute intellectual asset — a form of wealth in the modern managerial perception. Economists treat this as *human capital*. An example is the brain drain from underdeveloped countries to developed countries. Strictly speaking, it is a case of transfer of the means of producing wealth, i.e., human capital rather than the transfer of wealth itself.

Types of Information Wealth. Since information constitutes wealth, the question that follows is what type of wealth is information. Applying the classification of wealth, information is both a good and a service. Goods are anything that have utility. Information is a good because it has utility; it is a service whent it is processed and served for the benefit of others. Libraries providing information, lawyers interpreting law in a court of law on behalf of a client, the consultancy work by a psychoanalyst — all constitute service. In most of the advanced economies services sector has overtaken the goods sector. Backed by the advanced information and communication technologies, the service sector is seeing unprecedented growth. A clear distinction needs to be made between the act of service and the goods acted upon. Information is, good and making information available to others by an agency or employing it for others is a service. The implication of this distinction is that when the information service does not have a monopoly over the information served it is the value of its service, not the value of the information, that determines the economic viability of that service (Sassone, 1981). This is because the information good served is common in all competing services.

Information as a Good. Information fits into the scheme of classification of goods and may be further categorized as follows:

1. As a *free good.* Information is obtainable without payment, like air, as quite a lot of information floats free in the society.
2. As *economic good.* Information is also produced, distributed and marketed. As economic good information forms a large segment of the national economies of developed countries like the U.S.A. and Japan, and developing countries like India and China. As an economic good, information has become exchangeable.
3. As a *consumption good (primary goods)* and also as a production *good (manufactured goods)*. Information that appeals to our senses may be considered to be consumption good, e.g., a novel, music record. And information used to produce further products through research, development, and production- a production good. It would be more appropriate to treat knowledge in its original appearance, e.g., music, artistic artifacts, and education as consumption good and value added information as production good.
4. As a *single use good.* An item of information forms a single use good, if the item loses its validity or utility after a single use, e.g., insider information in stocks and shares, weather broadcast on storms and cyclones, and outdated information.
5. As a *durable good.* As most information items are not exhausted by a single use and are available for repeated use information is also a durable good.

Analogous to classification of wealth, *information* falls into the categories of *public good* and *private good,* and *information* service into *public service* and *private service.*

Information as a Public Good. Public good categorization is based on the acceptance of certain social and political value judgements. The production and distribution of public goods (also known as social goods) and services generally come under government ownership and public institutions. Machlup defines a public good as "those that can be enjoyed by more than one person at zero marginal cost" (Machlup, 1984, p.146). Information constitutes a public good and also a private good depending on ownership. Information is public good when it fulfills the following characteristics of a public good:

1. Non-rivalry in consumption. The same unit of a public good can be consumed by many individuals. Its availability to one does not diminish its availability to others, e.g., national defense. Knowledge and information can be utilized by many persons at the same time. An online information service can be simultaneously used by many.
2. Non-excludability. Once a good is provided to some individuals, it is impossible or at least very costly to exclude others from benefiting from it, examples being national defense, a public park. Exclusion can be tried through licensing, imposition of rules and regulations, membership, and other methods. When information supported by a public fund is made available to some, others cannot be excluded from having access to it. Similarly, the public library service or information generated by government research (unless secret) is available to all those who can use it, without exclusion.
3. Non-rejectability. Just as a public good exhibits non-excludability, one cannot reject a public good even if one does not want it. Information provided as a public good cannot be rejected even if some do not want it. One may not use a public library service, and yet he or she pays for it in the form of taxes to the local government authority. Information is also a good that can be enjoyed by more than one person at zero marginal cost. When the same information is also held or produced under

exclusive private ownership, the information then looses its pure public good character. Thus, information displays the characteristics of both a public good and a private good. A record, on the other hand, exhibits non-rivalry as far as its information content is concerned, but not non-excludability, as the same record is not available to others at the same time. Thus, it shows private good characteristic. Yew-Kwang Ng cites the example of books in a library, wherein it forms a pure public good item and as a good with external effects, i.e., common consumption externality, if the same books owned by an individual, but borrowed by his colleagues(Yew-Kwang Ng, 1979).

A public good can also yield a private good and vice versa. Web site information service provided by government is a public good, and so is the information on patents. The same becomes a private good when a private body uses it for private distribution. Goods and services coming under public good could also be left to private enterprise, depending on the policy of the state. Commercial databases and networks co-exist with databases and networks falling under public domain. Such a policy introduces some competition.

Just as some goods and services are considered public goods, there are goods considered public bad. Distribution of spurious information causing injury to the community is a case of public bad. So is the display of obscene posters in public places.

The public good concept of information does impact on the production, distribution and utilization of information and records. A large segment of information activities come directly under the government sector or are supported by it. How much valuable is information to the society, how much resources should be allocated to the information sector, what trade-offs are available, what can be left to the private sector, what is the loss to society in not providing a particular information good/

service are some of the important decision areas in managing information as a public good. An area of private knowledge activities in which public good concept is effectively used to some degree is Intellectual Property Rights, which is covered in later sections.

The concept of public good is related to a wider branch of economics, namely *welfare economics*. Welfare economics is defined by Mishan as "…. that branch of study which endeavors to formulate propositions by which we may rank, on the scale of better or worse, alternative economic situations open to society" (Mishan, 1969, p.13). Acceptance of the philosophy of welfare economics provides choices in the selection and formulation of national policies on information. Such policies will have to be based on information plus and information minus alternatives open to the society. These options provide information policy makers convenient evaluation criteria based on social benefit and social cost to the society. It also serves as a basis for allocation of resources to the information sector.

Grant System of Financing. The major impact of treating information as a public good will be on the allocation of resources to the information sector from public finance. Most of the money spent on research forms a part of public expenditure. These activities are either subsidized or fully met from government funds. Public expenditure on information is justified, by Boulding, for the reason that "the gains to society which come from the pursuit and transmission of knowledge are apt to be diffuse. They are not easily appropriable, and it is hard to tell who gains and who does not…. or how much each person gains. The pursuit and transmission of knowledge, therefore, has almost always been regarded as a peculiarly fit subject for the activity of government or some other agency representing society as a whole… such as an established church" (Boulding, 1970, p.147).

Allocation of funds for research, education, and

information falling under public good come under what is called "grant system" operated by governments or by endowed institutions, and not under capital or investment. In India, the grant system is operated through autonomous bodies registered as societies like the Council of Scientific and Industrial Research; grant commissions, such as the University Grants Commission; boards, such as the Central Social Welfare Board; and various academies like the Sahitya Academy. States too have similar grant bodies. The grant system has the following advantages:

1. Relative freedom of action in formulating and pursuing projects sought under the grant.
2. Dynamic leadership can succeed in projecting innovative programmes and also manage to get the necessary grants.
3. Enables drawing talent from different sources.

Some of the disadvantages of the grant system are:

1. There is no public check on the grantee's performance.
2. Strong tendency on the part of grantees to excuse themselves and each other for the possible lapses in the completion of work.
3. Lack of pure competition.
4. Unwillingness to take up imaginative and dynamic programmes, involving risks, and the tendency to opt for soft plans.
5. Tendency to select programmes that will be popular with the grantor or look glamorous irrespective of their contributions in the form of social good.
6. Political considerations influencing the selection of programmes and allocation of grants.

Peter Drucker concludes that the grant system of funding research makes scientists publication cantered by publishing in peer-reviewed journals. This inhibits sharing of information before it is published. This acts as a barrier for the type of collaborative knowledge-sharing needed for scientific breakthroughs. The scene is no different in private sector research though for different reasons, namely the need for keeping down cost and the fear of lawsuits. Thus, there is a cultural gap between scientists working in academic and research institutions in the public sector and those in the commercial sector. As a result, the scientists in the public sector look down upon the latter as lacking intellectual integrity, and the latter frown upon the former as those living in ivory towers. (Edersheim, 2007). Fierce competition does enter the grant market when there are a large number of grantees and less number of grantors with limited funds.

Return on Investment under Public Good. Benefit to the society accruing from goods such as information, education, and research is intangible. It is not easy to evaluate the utility and worth of such programmes to the society, and calculate the returns on the resources expended on them. Evaluation, in the absence of better techniques, relies on assessment of benefit accruing to the society relative to other activities. Benefit-cost analysis forms the most used evaluation technique. Consensus and expert opinions replace scientific and rational decision-making.

INFORMATION AS A COMMODITY

With the concept "value for money" gaining supremacy and the use of price as the yardstick of measurement, information too is coming under commodity scanner. To understand how this change is affecting information arena needs study. Any consumable good is considered a commodity. This definition does not suggest how to distinguish one commodity from another. For a good to be called a commodity, it must be homogeneous within itself (Robinson, 1954). A good becomes a specific commodity when it is not easily substitutable by another good and is restricted to a particular quality or grade (Mitra, 1982). Because of its homogeneous character, information in its formalized form becomes a commodity; its heterogeneous and intangible traits make it an unusual commodity; and in its non-formalized form a non-commodity. This becomes clear by considering a bibliography as an example. A bibliography consists of entries of books, articles, proceedings of conference papers etc. on the subject covered by the bibliography. Each item in the bibliography is unique and is not substitutable by another item, and thereby fulfils one of the characteristics of a commodity. Multiple copies of the same item, such as a book constitute a homogeneous good. If we consider all the items in the bibliography with other items of knowledge in the world then the collection is heterogeneous. The bibliography as a whole is homogeneous because of its subject affiliation. If the unifying feature of subject affiliation is withdrawn it becomes heterogeneous. Thus, information displays both homogeneous and heterogeneous character.

Two critical characteristics of a commodity are: a) its exchangeability, and therefore its ability to command a price; and b) it can be produced and consumed, i.e., it can be created and destroyed. Information fulfills both these criteria and hence becomes a commodity (Boulding, 1970). The price aspect of information is comparatively more complex. Not all information that is produced has a price. Though information is not exchanged for another information item or a good it is exchangeable for money. Taking public library service as an example, it is seen that the service is funded publicly and is served free, and as such it does not become a commodity. But the increasing costs of providing the service makes charging for library use imperative. Once the service is charged one is justified to consider it as a service commodity. Investing intellectual property rights to certain types of information, such as industrial inventions (patents), computer software programs, and literary and artistic works (copyright) give information a definite commodity character.

The commodity aspect of information may be considered

from another angle, namely how information is produced for the market. Consider the following information products: databases, publications, educational products, consultancy services, news services, software products, and entertainment products. All these items need to be manufactured or produced. For this capital is to be invested, raw materials are to be acquired and processed, and finally the products are to be packaged and distributed— the features that are common to any manufacturing industry. The raw material for information products may consist of: new knowledge created by research; information originating as a by-product of manufacturing, governing, and trade; and already existing information texts, such as published articles and books used in the creation of a database. Since production of information involves all the processes that go with producing and selling a commodity, information becomes a manufactured item and so constitutes a commodity.

The term commodity is applied to information very loosely. Not all information can be considered to satisfy the conditions of a commodity. John Martyn maintains that it is more accurate to apply the term commodity only to products and services of information that are manufactured and delivered at a price (Martyn, 1984). In the above sense, information becomes a commodity, i.e., an article of trade and commerce. However, the interpretation by Martyn that information service provided by information people, brokers and intermediaries such as librarians, whose main activity consists of customizing and repackaging items of information selected from a large mass of available information is analogous to service industry needs qualifying in part. A library service can be considered a service commodity only when it is priced.

Impact of Commoditization. Commodity status affects information in the following manner (Narayana, 1991):

1. Information becomes a well recognized industrial sector.

2. Profit becomes the prime motive.
3. Private sector will play a greater role in the production and distribution of information.
4. Information may increasingly come under monopoly.
5. Production, distribution and marketing aspects of information get well organized.
6. Information sector will come under some statutory regulations.
7. Information sector will become eligible for subsidies and incentives.
8. Public good aspect of information may suffer.
9. The gulf between the information-rich and the information-poor may widen.
10. Information in high and assured areas of profit will receive better research, development and marketing efforts.
11. Use of information produced both in the public and the private sector is likely to increase as a result of private enterprise. One example for this is information brokers drawing information from public sector and selling it to private parties. Information needs not satisfied by public sector services will be served by private industry for a fee (Clayton and Nissenoff, 1977).
12. May give rise to competition or cooperation between the public and the private sectors.
13. Results in greater options to an user in terms of medium, format, and packaging of information.
14. Information sector will become an important part of economy.
15. May increase demand for intermediary services and products in the information chain.
16. Information flow will come under the orbit of World Trade Organization (WTO) regime.

17. Computer and communication technology developments will have greater say and impact on almost all aspects of information production and use.
18. On the whole, the information sector will see enormous growth.

Implications for Libraries and Education. Recognition of information as a commodity will have far-reaching consequences for two major knowledge sectors, namely, libraries and education.

Libraries. Libraries, other than small private commercial services, buy information as a commodity and render, not sell them as service. When the price of the commodity rises it becomes difficult to pass on the increased cost to the customers. Libraries cannot hope to charge for their services not even on a 'no profit no loss' basis as library service is considered a public good, and they have been provided free all these years. Other professional services like medicine and law do not face this dilemma as they acquire skill and information and sell service. Their investment on information and skill is a one time investment, and updating of their professional knowledge does not call for heavy investment. Moreover, the additional cost will always be passed on to the client. Information as a commodity supplied online or by networks will affect the budget of libraries. Unlike print media products most commercial data bases and network information (excluding Internet) are supplied only on rental basis or per unit use. Rentals for some of these products will become very costly, and libraries with low budgets cannot afford them. The adverse impact will be felt more severely by developing and under developed countries. The adverse effects of monopoly may prove serious. Another area likely to be affected will be limiting the growth of libraries and library services. This will lead to a greater disparity between the information-rich and the information-poor. To combat these adverse effects of information becoming a commodity, possible solutions lie in greater cooperation and resource sharing among libraries, charging for their services, regulatory action by the government, and higher allocations from public fund. Information falling fully under commodity market is likely to bring a major change in the basic philosophy of librarianship, and in the approach to the management of libraries in the new era of Internet and globalization. Education is another area, where commoditization of information will have major consequences.

Education. Education market which treats knowledge as goods, forms a significant portion of global education sector. As a service good education is covered under the General Agreement on Trade in Services (GATS) following the pattern of the General Agreement on Trade and Tariff (GATT). The purpose of GATS is to accomplish progressive liberalization of trade in services by providing secure and more open market. Under GATS, export of education is to be negotiated between exporting and importing countries. Education is split into five categories for the purpose of negotiations: a) higher education, b) secondary education, c) primary education, d) adult education, and c) others. Trade in services is classified into: a) cross-border supply of a service, which includes courses provided through distance education or the Internet, all types of testing services, and educational materials, b) consumption abroad (students going abroad), c) commercial presence, i.e., presence of foreign investors in host countries, which relates to setting up of educational institutions and services, and d) presence of natural persons, meaning free movement of teachers who render educational services (India, 2008).

Presently, the private enterprise in education is flourishing by catering to the richer segment of Indian society. This has relieved to some extent the economic strain on the finances of the states by meeting the needs of the affordable class. The governments do exercise some control (via bargaining with private college managements) over the intake of students and fee structure. But it has neither a say in the management of colleges nor on the maintenance of academic standards. Educational regulatory bodies seem to be finding it difficult to cope up with the complex situation. Further, the mixed educational economic system seems to widen the educational gap between the rich and the poor in society. The National Knowledge Commission has addressed these issues, and has given a detailed policy framework in its recommendations. A direct effect of treating knowledge as a commodity is bestowing ownership rights in the form of Intellectual Property Rights to the creators of knowledge.

INTELLECTUAL PROPERTY RIGHTS

Intellectual property rights (IPR) are legally instituted mechanism for according exclusive ownership rights for a fixed period to the creators of knowledge over the knowledge produced by them. IPRs have a history of over 500 years and are linked with politics, economics, and geography. Historically, the institutional recognition of these rights within an international framework came into existence with the Paris Convention on Patents in the year 1883, and the Berne Convention on Copyright in 1886. Thenceforth the items coming under IPRs have grown in diversity, and now include literary creations, artistic works, photos, paintings, still pictures, emblems, models, sculpture, diagrams, maps, engineering drawings, software programmes, Internet derived products, multimedia creations, microfiche, CD-ROMs, music records, and the list is growing. Rapid changes in the pattern of production of knowledge caused by technology and the economic interests of nations have made IPR management more complex.

Economic Rationale behind IPR. In general, ideas, knowledge, and information are non-rivalries as they can be used by two or more persons simultaneously without competing. As a non-rival good information finds it difficult to extract a price in the market. In order to enable the owner to extract a price legally for his intellectual good, a scarcity factor is introduced in the shape of intellectual property right. Once IPR is granted market forces come into act on it, and with it information asymmetry. Since it is felt that society has a claim over knowledge because of social benefits accruing from the use of knowledge, there is an obligation to safeguard the public interest of free use of owned knowledge. This raised a conflict of interest. The conflict was resolved by striking a balance between the interests of the private owner of knowledge and the public interest by imposing certain restrictions on private ownership rights (May and Sell, 2006). The important restrictions are: a) allowing fair use (free of charge) by public in the case of copyrighted material, and b) limiting the period of ownership. How the restrictions operate can be seen from the following: a) an idea to become eligible for patent right, it must be new, non-obvious, and useful or applicable in industry; b) limiting copyright for the lifetime of the author plus 50 years, and a patent right for only 20 years; and c) copyright is given effect from the moment it is created, where as in a patent it is from the date of granting the patent.

The categories of items presently covered by IPRs include patents, literary and artistic creations, trademarks, geographical indicators, industrial designs, layout designs of integrated circuits, maps, trade secrets, photographs, audio-visual texts and recordings, music albums, computer software, Internet contents, databases, genetic alterations, and a few others. Separate IPR conventions/ agreements govern each category of intellectual property. These conventions frame in detail the eligibility criteria for granting IPR, duration of the right, institutional and other mechanisms for granting such rights, machinery and methods for resolving infringement of IPR s, and the obligations of each signatory country. IPR is getting complicated with the entry of computer software which combines the features of both literature and industrial products. This challenges the traditional line of demarcation within IPR. Further, the networks may demand more limited protection (Besen, 2002).

The effectiveness of patents in safeguarding the competitive advantages of new processes and innovative products to an organization is being questioned. Answer to this question will have a bearing on the organization in formulating its patent policy. The studies by Levin et al. have shown that lead-time, learning curves, scale and service efforts lead over patents in protecting the advantages (Levin et al., 1987 cited by Besen, 2002). Further, it is reported that the rate of diffusion of an innovation is related to the innovator's personality and the perceived attributes of the innovation. In a global scenario, innovativeness will be affected by the decision-makers tolerance of uncertainty, while technological innovations would be conditioned by media exposure and other communication behaviour (Vishwanath, 2005).

IPRs in India. It seems that the concept of ownership rights over knowledge, and the contingent rights to rewards were repugnant to the ancient Indian mind. But, the holders of knowledge gained indirectly by the recognition and authority it brought, and also by using their exclusive knowledge as a means of livelihood. It seems that entitlement to exclusive authorship was recognized as could be inferred from association of author's names with their works such as Manu in *Manusmruti* and Katyayana in *Sarvanukramanika* (Max Muller, 1900). Further, the cast system imposed a sort of collective rights by prescribing specific vocations to specified varnas and casts.

Coming to modern India, the patents act was first passed by the British in the year 1858. It did not have any impact on the indigenous industry due to many historical and social reasons. The act primarily served to safeguard the rights of British industry. For the British, India was a prime market for their manufactured products and a supplier of raw-materials. The Indian industry was then limited to craft production. Later, a few family run enterprises like the Tatas and the Birlas took up manufacturing, which needed limited technological backup.

However, the visionaries like Jamshedji Tata, J.R.D. Tata and Sir M. Viheveswaraiah who recognized the importance of industry and higher education were rare exceptions. Second World War brought the industrial breeze to India. After independence, successive governments and the industry recognized the economic potential of industrial research, but the implementation was too slow. Until two decades ago, whatever technology needed came via foreign technical collaborations and manufacturing under license. The situation has changed substantially in recent years, particularly after the opening of the economy and liberalization of economic policies. Still for a country of India's size and population the number of patents taken is too meagre. For the year February 2007 to February 2008, 35,067 patent applications were filed and 15, 262 patents were granted. Out of this manufacturing sector accounted for about 700 patents. Of the top 1000 technological firms 89 had not filed a single application (Economic Times, 2008). It reflects how far behind we are in promoting technological innovation and industrial research for promoting economic development. In contrast, advanced countries of the West were active in patenting Indian native knowledge and genetic materials. A comprehensive patent law was framed in 1991 (Keayla, 2005).

IPR Conventions. Important IPR conventions and agreements that are in existence are as follows:

Copyright. Berne Convention of 1886. There have been later revisions, the last one in 1975. It is now administered by the World Intellectual Property Organization. The Universal Copyright Convention under the aegis of UNESCO which came into existence in 1952 introduced the symbol © for universal copyright. India is a signatory to this convention.

Patents. Paris convention of 1883 with subsequent revisions. It was last revised in 1975.

Trademarks. Madrid agreement of 1891.

Trade Secrets. These refer to undisclosed information generally associated with industry and firms. Firms try to safeguard their trade secrets being disclosed by their employees by including a clause in the employment norms governing such disclosures (May and Sell, 2006).

The most recent and powerful agreement, in terms of impact, amongst all the IPR regimes is the Trade Related Property Rights (TRIPS) worked out under the World Trade Organization Treaty that came into effect in 1995. India is a signatory to TRIPS. TRIPS is powerful because it directly affects many aspects of national concerns, such as growth of technology; free flow of scientific information and thereby affecting growth of science; lending and copying records in different forms; providing access to Internet and databases by libraries; interests of trade, industry and development in the signatory countries (Prasad, 1998). Inclusion of items like micro organisms and genetic modifications under patentable category has opened up a new area of conflict between developed and developing countries.

Of particular concern to libraries, their users, and publishers is the issues relating to libraries digitizing their collections to virtualized form, and the use of electronic document delivery service which conflict with the interest of publishers. If these and other technical issues like electro-copying are not resolved, there is the possibility of libraries circumventing the law and information users accessing texts directly from authors through bulletin boards. This will have serious implications for bibliographic control, quality of research, and production of vetted publications (Prasad, 1998).

The Internet seems to be the soft underbelly of IPR because it exists in cyberspace; involves many countries; encompasses copyright, trademark, patents, and multimedia products. Combination of Internet and communication technologies enabling movement of information in different forms at incredible speed has made locating infringers, and taking action against them a very difficult task.

On the whole, the IPR scene of today seems to resemble a vast jungle with only a few people having a complete grasp of the intricacies of the field. With strong interest groups in the advanced countries of the West trying to safeguard and enhance their rights, and the developing countries trying for the best bargain they can get to advance their economies through transfer of technology, the IPR has moved into the arena of intense international diplomacy. In this process, you gain some and lose some depending upon how strong you are, and how best a country can articulate its position in the relevant international forums, make others recognize and accept your interests.

Once information is treated as a good, as wealth, its study involves the study of the various economic processes governing the creation of wealth. As a commodity, it was seen earlier, information takes on the features of a manufacturing industry, such as production, distribution, and consumption, which will be considered now.

PRODUCERS OF INFORMATION

Major producers of information are:

1. Information industry. This is mostly under private enterprise and is governed by the economics of the firm. The sector includes- book and journal publishing, databases and networks, radio and TV production, audio and video records, newspapers and magazines, motion picture, computer software, and other electronic media products.

2. Commerce, trade, and industry. All business and industrial concerns generate considerable data\information relating to raw-materials, production, sales, cost and others during the course of their functioning. Primarily, the information generated relates to in-house activities. Information gets incorporated in company manuals, internal memoranda, reports, correspondence with other agencies, organizational

charts and statement of objectives, customer oriented publications and others. Some of this information is required to be filed or published under statutory obligations and takes the form of company annual reports, public notice, and so on. Trade associations also generate information of interest to the group and the general public. The information thus generated could also be useful to others.

3. Private industrial research. Many private firms invest on research and development. As a result considerable amount of technical information is produced by private industry. In return they gain patent rights. The economics of research is highly complicated due to factors, such as uncertainty of the utility of the invention, waiting period, risk, and market reaction. Sometimes the government subsidizes such private efforts, e.g., by granting tax concession. Generally, the cost of research gets added to the overall cost of production (even if the research is not a success). Apart from industrial research, a number of private organizations, such as research, higher education, and academic institutions produce significant body of knowledge over a wide range of interests like education, public health, environment, economics, politics, under-developed countries, and so on.

4. Public funded research. Areas supported by such funds include scientific research, academic research, education and culture. These activities are fully or partly supported by governments. They result in the creation of public knowledge. Return on investment so made is a matter of faith. The knowledge thus created is believed to contribute to public good. The controlling authorities may put restrictions on its free flow under some circumstances.

5. Promotion of social welfare. Both governments and voluntary organizations generate information during the course of conducting social welfare activities. Issuing of publications on the rights of citizens to exercise their franchise during election

time is an example. This type of information is mostly disseminative rather than original. The intention is to create greater awareness among general public, and mould public opinion for or against a given agenda.

6. Government departments. The three branches of governance- legislative, executive and judiciary in the course of their functioning collect and also generate vast and a variety of data and information, e.g., census data, industrial licenses issued, parliamentary discussions, and judicial decisions. Government departments and their records are a rich source of information. They include personal data of citizens, e.g., income tax returns, and records of patients in government hospitals. Access to and the use of such information involve the issue of the public's right to information and a citizen's right to privacy.

7. Professional and other voluntary bodies. Considerable amount of information is generated by such organizations, e.g. annual reports and special publications of scientific societies. This information, though public, is generally meant for the members or is issued in the interest of the profession.

8. Networks generated information. To capture information from Internet, the information needs to be first created and then suitably shaped and organized before being adapted to the Internet. This is the task of content providers and portal creators, the first stages in the Internet/online value chain (Ricart-Costa et al., 2004). Contents can be divided into five broad categories: learning, business, entertainment, transactions and personal communication. As the main concern of this book is knowledge and information only learning aspect of processing is considered. It is the authors, writers, research workers and academicians, singers (called collectively "talent" in the industry) who create the content and it is the packagers, like publishers, movie producers who package the contents into books, journals, newspapers, music and photo albums etc. into finished products in the digital language. Different from creators

and packagers are portals which buy contents from creators and packagers on copyright basis for stipulated periods, aggregate them into categories through value adding processes to facilitate browsing on the Internet or other networks. Search engines such as Google, and American Online are portals in this limited sense. Institutional websites making available their library or data collections would have any way already organized their collections for online access. Commercial databases provide discipline oriented information online mostly on subscription basis with 'conditions apply'. These databases mostly contain abstract of papers and may also include full articles with facilities to supply originals, both current and archival under stipulated terms.

9. Individuals. Apart from organized sources, many individuals also create knowledge and make it available to others. The Internet has created vast opportunities for individuals to become authors and producers of knowledge. Vikipdia and numerous web sites, and blogs have become producers of knowledge.

Unique Features of Knowledge Production. Production of knowledge differs from that of other goods. Knowledge is a unique product. In the production of normal goods, the economic availability of resources and not the labour is the limiting factor. Theoretically, an automobile firm can produce cars in any numbers by increasing the factors of production, and so also a publisher any number of copies of a book. The same is not true in the case of knowledge. Increasing the factors of production does not necessarily result in increased production of new knowledge. Knowledge is a product of brain and mind. The capacity of the brain to create knowledge is controlled by unique cognitive characteristics and abilities of an individual, and the individual's environment which act as limitations. A fundamental feature of knowledge production is that the raw-material used for the production of knowledge begins with or makes use of already existing knowledge and entities in which information is embodied. Further, one may not be sure in advance whether the new knowledge created is exactly what is intended or expected; the result may turn out to be as expected or entirely unexpected, and it may or may not be useful.

A feature seen increasingly in the field of creation and application of knowledge, particularly in science and technology, is team approach. Scientific research to a large measure has ceased to be a single man's endeavor. Often, it is multi-disciplinary involving a wide range of specializations needing coordination with a number of agencies, and interpreting vast amount of data. This calls for group effort. Team approach is also finding extension in professions, such as law and medicine. In essence it is pooling of knowledge in an effort to increase efficiency and complementing research efforts. The nearest analogy to this in industry is the consortium approach and outsourcing of functions.

A characteristic of knowledge production is that knowledge once created, its production can be repeated any number of times without incurring major capital cost. This is possible due to the surrogate property of knowledge. Additional cost needed is only to cover the cost of reproduction or re-relaying. For example, the composed matter of a manuscript can be preserved in the digital form, and reprints can be taken as and when required. In contrast are the material goods whose repeat production needs the use of additional raw-material, for example in milk production, the milk cannot be stored to produce additional quantity of milk later on.

CONSUMPTION

Consumption is utilization of goods and services for satisfying human wants. Consumption involves destruction of utility or use up of a service, and not destruction of matter. As a consumable, knowledge may be consumed as a necessity, as a comfort, and as a luxury. Some knowledge belongs to the category of sustenance of life; others used to increase efficiency; and some others for their exhibitive or ego satisfaction value. As a society becomes more complex the needs and desires of its members increase, new and varied goods and services are introduced, and the mode and tempo of life changes. Consequently, some knowledge tends to become, increasingly, a necessity of life. A unique feature of knowledge consumption is that the creator of knowledge (different from producer) is also a consumer of knowledge. A major problem before a consumer of implicit knowledge is assessing the value of such knowledge beforehand.

Assessing Implicit Knowledge. It is not easy to assess the real value of implicit/tacit knowledge before consumption. For example, in seeking the advice of an expert one is influenced more by factors relating to the expert than by the exact assessment of his expertise, i.e., the validity or contents of the knowledge product. Knowledge producer factor is accounted by: a) credibility of the producer of knowledge as perceived by the consumer, and b) perceived proximity of the consumer to the producer of knowledge product. "Trustworthiness" and reputation of the producer act as de facto guidelines in arriving at consumption decision. Proximity is explained by the general human tendency to seek information from the nearest source, say talking to a colleague, than a distant or more tedious source as in consulting a database. Sometimes, experienced implicit knowledge may be evaluated by consuming the knowledge product or by sampling. Risk associated with knowledge product lies in integrating new knowledge products, processes, and practices. Some of the factors that influence implicit knowledge use are: perceived complexity, perceived relative advantage, and perceived risk associated with the knowledge product and the producer (Desouza et al., 2006).

Joint Consumption and Cost Savings. Information can be consumed jointly. Such sharing of information by groups results in net savings in the cost of acquiring information and in accrual of additional benefits due to the effects of specialization. For example, a given piece of information costs the same to acquire whether the decision to be based on it is large or small. Thus, the formula for a steel alloy has a given cost though it may be used to make one ton or a hundred thousand tons. Therefore if by joining in an organization a number of individuals can acquire separate signals which can then be used by all of them, net benefits (benefits less costs of information) increase more than proportionately to the size of the organization. Further, the cost of information is independent of the scale on which it is used (Arrow, 1979). This characteristic has a very significant effect both on the producer and the consumer of information. For the producer, it will help in assessing the demand and supply for a product, in product planning, pricing, and turnover; and for the consumer, it means lower cost and increased benefit.

Marginal Utility. The laws of economics try to explain the phenomena of creation of wealth and other related activities in society. These laws are not exact as they are based on human behaviour, and as such are probabilistic and inductive in nature. The concept of marginal utility and the law governing it are of great significance in economics, and it finds frequent application.

Law of Marginal (or Diminishing) Utility is defined by Marshall as "the additional benefit which a person derives from a given increase of his stock of a thing, diminishes with every increase in the stock that he already has" (Marshall, 1947, p. 1). Encyclopaedia Britannica defines marginal utility as the value to the consumer of an additional unit of some commodity (Encyclopaedia Britannica, 2007. Vol. 17). If we take consumption of tea by a person as an example, the total utility derived by the person increases from the first cup to every additional cup of tea consumed. But the total utility derived by the 2nd, 3rd, 4th and subsequent cups of tea will not be the same as that of the corresponding 1st, 2nd, 3rd and the following cups. The utility goes on gradually decreasing with each cup consumed. The total utility derived by the person goes on increasing up to the point of satiety that is when marginal utility becomes zero. The concept of marginal utility helps in studying the functional relations between marginal utility and supply.

In applying this law to knowledge, one encounters the difficulty of nomenclature, i.e., precise naming of the specific item of knowledge consumed. Even if one is able to overcome the constraint of nomenclature, one is faced with measuring problems. Further, there is the problem of distinguishing one unit or item of knowledge from another. Although commodities containing information may be divided into units (books are an example) information itself is difficult to divide. Ideas and information are often interrelated in complex poorly defined units (Braunstein, 1981). As these problems are irresolvable the law of marginal utility cannot be applied to knowledge.

Information (and records) also shares some of the features of knowledge. But the commodity characteristics of information should make it possible to study the behaviour of information under the law of marginal utility. Taking information as an identifiable individual item, the total utility derived by consuming one unit or several units remains the same. The utility of the information that "water boils at 100°C." remains the same irrespective of the number of times it is used. Hence the marginal utility concept becomes redundant in the case of information taken as a specific individual item. However, sensual information which appeals to our senses seems to be an exception. The total utility in the form of satisfaction derived from hearing Thygaraja's *Pancharatna* kritis or Beethoven's *symphonies* twice is more than the utility derived from hearing once. Similar is the case with fine arts and literary works. Further, it is difficult to put a satiating limit as the point of satisfaction varies with each person.

In contrast to sensual knowledge, a collection of information or records seems to behave differently. In a collection, the independent state of information gets submerged in groups and the element of choice gets introduced. The utility of the collection as a whole increases with the addition of new items to the collection. The increase in utility depends on the quantity, quality, and variety of the items added. In this case, the marginal utility concept applies to the collection as a whole or an identifiable portion of it and not to an individual item of information. The utility of a book say on 'tissue culture' to a reader remains same whether the book is read and understood once or ten times. On the other hand, the utility of the collection increases by the addition of further books to the collection on the subject. The additional books display marginal utility.

In the above example, increase in the total utility of the collection and the benefit of marginal utility from additional items contradicts the fact that using the same information (say a book) for the second and subsequent times does not add to the total utility of the information to the user. However, one could argue that reading the same book second and third time may contribute to deeper insights; but it is thinking and not the second time reading that adds to the insight. Evidently, the utility increases because of the variety, richness and availability of books added to the collection. It is difficult to say whether a satiation point is ever reached. Marginal utility concept applied to information as a collection helps in understanding the demand side of information and information products.

Marginal utility of information becomes clearer if the situation is analyzed in terms of *indifference curve analysis*. In assessing the demand for two commodities *a* and *b*, instead of finding the utility of the two items, one can find out a consumer's relative preferences for *a* and *b* or their combinations. It is assumed that greater the utility, higher is the preference. When the consumer finds that his preference for the two commodities are equal, then he is indifferent as between them. Following this approach, it is possible to establish the comparative preferences of a consumer for information and other commodities. Thus, the demand for information vis-a-vis other items like food, clothing, recreation, health-care, etc. can be established. Within the broad class of information, relative preferences for each segment, such as books, computers, television, newspapers, can be established. However, it needs to be noted that in assessing the preferences, information is to be taken in its collective form (not a specific book, but books as a class). Following this approach, it can be ascertained how much resources an organization allocates on research, information, manufacturing, advertisement etc. It can be assumed that the allocation reflects the relative utility or preference of each item to the organization. The same holds good even in the case of individuals.

DEMAND AND SUPPLY

Demand. It is the desire for a good backed by adequate purchasing power. It signifies how much of a commodity is purchased at a given price at a per unit of time. The demand for a commodity depends on many factors, such as price of the commodity, income of the consumer, price of substitutes and complements, preferences of the consumer, habit and imitation. Subject to a few exceptions, demand is governed by the Law of Demand which states that the demand for a product varies inversely with its own prices. The Law of Marginal Utility also applies to demand. The *elasticity of demand* or *price elasticity* represents the rate at which demand changes in response to changes in price (Mitra,1982). The phrase 'demand for information' represents too broad a coverage. Other than in a general sense or in the context of macroeconomics, such a broad view will not be of much help in studying demand. The demand is always for a specific categorized item of information by a given segment of users. This point is often missed in considering demand function of economics of information.

Elasticity of Demand. The law of demand does not operate uniformly in the case of all types and categories of information goods. It varies. The characteristic of information being a durable good affects demand. In the case of print media the utility lasts as long as the record lasts. Hence, the demand for print media text is of one time for that particular consumer. This limitation on demand is counter balanced by the effects of the characteristic of growth in knowledge which creates fresh demand (see Chapter 5).

The demand for information is influenced by the category of consumer and the source of financing the consumption. The demand for information falls into two distinct categories- a) individuals as buyers, and b) organizational buyers. The organizational sector consists of public sector, public good sector, and private sector. In buying a commodity an individual buyer makes a personal sacrifice, where as in the case of an organizational consumer it is the organization that makes the sacrifice. Decision to buy depends on the stake of the individual in the organization. Since this stake is largely linked to the profit in the corporate sector, the decision to buy information is subjected to rigorous scrutiny which may not be so in the case of government and the public good sector. Where information is essential for survival as in high technology industry and in certain areas of defense research demand is inelastic. In the case of technical information in print media, demand is generally inelastic or less elastic. Demand for general reading materials, e.g. novels, popular magazines bought by individuals, is relatively elastic.

Effect of Substitutes. Because of its heterogeneous character, information does not have substitutes, e.g. an article by X on the role of glutaric acid receptor genes on the memory function of brain cannot be a substitute for another article on the same subject. But elasticity of demand for information could be affected by the substitution effects of one medium for another medium of record- *container effect*, e.g., microfiche for paper, audio visual for print, and electronic media for print. Similarly, one information service could substitute another, e.g., one database for another in the same subject field.

Supply. It is the quantity of goods offered for sale at a particular price during a period of time. Thus, both demand and supply are related to price. Supply of a commodity is always at a price and per unit of time. The Law of Supply states that other things remaining constant; the supply of a product varies directly with its own price (Mitra, 1982). Apart from price, some of the other factors that determine supply are cost of production, technology employed, environment, and the philosophy of the firm producing the item.

CLASSIFICATION OF INFORMATION GOODS

Organized collection of data on industry and trade is a key input in understanding and managing an economy. A mass of dispersed data is of no use unless it is structured and ordered. Classification brings order to any collection of dispersed data. Industrial classification is a system of classification designed and applied to order industrial data. With information industry accounting for a significant portion of national economies it has its place in the general industrial classification. Information enters industrial classification only when it becomes a good or a commodity. Information poses several problems to classification because of its unusual characteristics. A study of the North American Industrial Classification (NAIC adopted by the US, Canada, and Mexico in 1997), and its predecessor the Standard Industrial Classification (SIS) gives an insight of the issues involved, and how they are addressed. Malone and Elichirigoity examine NAIC and the SIS. Selected salient features of their study are presented below:

1. In economic census, information as a thing in its ordered structure can serve as a representation of the actual and the relative importance of various aspects of the economy.

2. Information poses unusual problems because of its multiple dimensions, such as: as a process, as a good-private and public, as a service, as an activity, and as a multimedia product.
3. What imparts information the status of a commodity is the applicability of intellectual property rights.
4. The information sector has to cover information in all its forms, which must include both manufactured products (e.g., newspapers), and services (e.g., news syndicate). Inclusion of information "in all its forms" is ensured by defining the criterion of inclusion as "industries engaged in 'the transformation of information into a commodity that is produced, manipulated and distributed," (Malone and Elichirigoity, 2003, p.517). Thus, it brings into its fold printed products, software publishing, wireless communication, online news services, the Internet, and libraries.
5. One of the basic issues in the classification is whether to use more than one criterion chosen by NIC, which has lead to inconsistencies, or a single criterion as chosen by NAIC. It is another matter that NAIC flouted this principle in the 2002 revision by the insertion of "(except Internet)".
6. The two principal characteristics applied for grouping items (classes) are: a) production or supply aspect used as the criterion, and b) commodity or demand aspect served by the entities as the basis.
7. The production or supply criterion adopted by NAIC relies on inputs like labour, intellectual property right, technology and materials, and is oriented towards measuring economic productivity. The commodity oriented grouping chosen by SIS applies the criterion of similarity of use found between items, and it serves market observation better.

Information has emerged as both a measurable commodity and as a key factor of a new transnational system for classifying industrial data. This itself is a new feature of the "information economy" (Malone and Elichirigoity, 2003). NAIC is designed to meet the requirements of an advanced information economy, as such it will not be fully suitable to meet the needs of economics of information of developing economies. This calls for designing taxonomies to suit the requirements of individual countries, keeping in mind the need to be in consonance with international practices. The outlines of a model for designing such taxonomies described by Neelamehan are presented here.

A Taxonomy of Information Industry. Once information is recognized as a commodity, information sector becomes a subsector of industry. After knowing the nature of information industry and its components, relating information sector to the larger economy may be done by drawing the structure of information sector. We can arrive at the structure by constructing taxonomy of information processes on the lines of commodity segment of economy. The structure of commodity segment is developed by using product flow models, input-output tables, Leontiff coefficients, and other indicators. In constructing a taxonomy of information industry, one is confronted with a few information specific properties like: non-appropriability of information cost, increasing return feature of use of information, and indivisibility of information. These characteristics pose problems in applying the theories of resource allocation, and demand and supply based models of commodity structure to that of information. This limitation can be overcome by following an institutional perspective of information adopted by Newman (Newman, 1976 cited by Neelameghan, Oct. 1999). By applying one of Newman's propositions, information sector may be divided into: a) market supplied information meaning open market information products and services like books, newspapers, library service and online information; b) institutional information, i.e., information created by and used within an organization. By collecting and analyzing these two types of information, we can arrive at the elements constituting the sector, and their respective share. By using these data we can build the taxonomy of information processes (Neelameghan, 6 ct. 1999). By extending the collection of information production data pertaining to each type to cover a whole country, and by adding them, we arrive at the total production of information by type. Based on this data taxonomy of information goods can be generated.

CLOSURE

Information and, to a large extent, knowledge are now considered as wealth as they fulfil the criteria of wealth, namely utility, scarcity, transferability and externality. However, they differ from material wealth. Information as a good and as a service satisfies the economic criteria of both. "Public" and "private" distinction made in economics is also applied to knowledge and information. As a public good information sector benefits from public funding. The allocation is mostly in the form of "grant system of financing" prevailing in science. Return on investment under public good is not easy to assess since information, education and research are intangible goods.

Information is exchangeable, commands a price; and it can be produced and consumed, and thereby fulfils the critical characteristics of a commodity. Commodity status affects information and information services in a number of ways, and among them are: a) information comes under industrial sector; b) profit motive predominates; c) private interests will dominate information sector, and may also come under monopoly; d) will be subjected to statutory regulations; e) becomes eligible for subsidies and incentives in some cases; f) public good aspect of information may suffer; g) the gulf between the information-rich and information-poor may widen; h) high margin and assured profit segments of information will attract private investment; i) market for information products will expand and information sector will see enormous growth; j) consumer will have greater information options in terms of medium, format, and packaging; k) demand for intermediary services and products may increase; l) globalization and World Trade Organization regime will severely impact on information flow; m) computer and communication technology developments will become the determining factor in the production, distribution and use of information. Libraries and education sectors will be affected most by commoditization of information.

The commoditization entitles creators of knowledge to ownership rights, i.e., intellectual property rights (IPR) over the knowledge produced by them. IPR includes patent rights, copyright, trademarks right, geographical indicators, and rights covering artistic creations, music compositions, industrial designs, trade secrets, and a few others. IPR involves a compromise between safeguarding the public interest of free use and rewarding the creator for his efforts through grant of ownership. Compared to industrially advanced countries production of IPR items like patents, and copyrights in India is meagre. Internet seems to be the soft underbelly of IPR because it exists in cyberspace, involves many countries, and encompasses all forms of IPR.

Three fundamental economic concepts– production, consumption, demand and supply become applicable to information as a commodity, as an industry.

Major producers of information are: information industry comprising of print media, multimedia and network generated information; industry and commerce which produce information relating to their in-house activities or to fulfil statutory obligations; private and public funded research; social and political organizations/activities; legislative, executive and judicial bodies; professional associations, and individuals.

Production of knowledge differs in several ways from that of other goods. Some of differences are a) increasing the factors of production does not necessarily result in increased production of new knowledge; b) production of knowledge makes use of existing knowledge, and existing entities in which information is embedded; c) in research there is no guarantee that the output knowledge will be the same as the one planned at the beginning; d) scientific and technological knowledge production is increasingly becoming collaborative programmes; and e) intangible characteristic of knowledge enables reproduction and repeat use of the same knowledge without incurring additional cost.

There is no destruction in the consumption of knowledge. The creator of knowledge (different from producer) is also a consumer of knowledge. For a consumer of implicit knowledge, assessing its value before hand is one of probability. In the selection of a knowledge source the consumer is influenced by a number of factors, such as reliability of the knowledge holder, nearness of the source, and perceived risk. Information can be consumed jointly (i.e., sharing) and thereby by saves cost. While the law of marginal utility cannot be applied to knowledge, it is possible to study the behaviour of information and records under this law due to their commodity characteristics. Marginal utility of information becomes clearer, if the situation is analyzed by applying *indifference curve analysis* from which we can establish the preferences of a consumer for information relative to other items.

The law of demand does not operate uniformly in the case of all types and categories of information goods; it varies. Further, the demand for information is influenced by the category of consumer and the source of financing the consumption. Where information becomes an essential item demand is inelastic. Because of its heterogeneous character, information does not have substitutes. However, effects of substituting information in one medium for another can affect elasticity of demand for information.

Digitalization of information, and the new forms of communication employed to deliver information have added a new dimension to the study of knowledge and information as goods. With its single-minded pursuit of commoditization of knowledge and information capitalism is powering the creation of a seemingly new dehumanized digital society.

REFERENCES

Arrow, K.J. The Economics of Information. *In* Dertouzos, M. L. and Moses, Joel. Ed. The Computer Age: A Twenty-year View. Cambridge (Mass.), MIT Press, 1979. P.310.

Besen, Stanley M. Intellectual Property. Pp.348-51. *In* The New Palgrave Dictionary of Economics and the Law. Ed. Peter Newman. Vol. 2. London, Palgrave Macmillan, 2002.

Boulding, K.E. Knowledge as a Commodity. *In* Beyond Economics. Essays on Society, Religion and Ethics. Ann Arbor, University of Michigan, 1970. (Reprint).

Braunstein, Yale. Information as a Commodity: Public Policy Issues and Research. Pp. 9-21. *In* Mason, R. M. and Creps, J.E. Jr. Information Services: Economics, Management, and Technology. Boulder (Colo.), Westview Press, 1981.

Clayton, Audrey and Nisenoff, Norman. Potential Impacts of Automation and User Fees upon Technical Libraries. Arlington(Va.), Forecasting International Ltd.,1977. (NTIS PB 271-418).

Desouza,Kelvin C., Awazu, Yukika and Yun Wan. Factors governing the consumption of explicit knowledge. *Journal of the American Society for Information Science and Technology* 57(1):36-42, Jan.1,2006.

Economic Times (Bangalore). Sunday, June 8, 2008, p.1. Mfg. cos. lead in filing patents. *Shantanu.sharma@timesgroup.com*

Edersheim, Elizabeth Haas. The Definitive Drucker. New Delhi, Tata-McGraw-Hill Publishing, 2007.

Encyclopaedia Britannica, The New. Ed.15. Chicago, Encyclopaedia Britinica, 2007. Vol. 17. Pp. 916-952: Economic Theory.

India, 2008: A Reference Annual. New Delhi, Government Publications Division, Ministry of Information and Broadcasting, 2008.

Keayla, B. K. Amended patents act: A critique. *Combat Law* 4(2). June-July, 2005.

Cf. Levin, R.C. et al. Appropriating the returns from industrial research and development. Brookings Papers on Economic Activity 3: 783-820, 1987. (Cited by Besen, Stanley M. Op. cit.).

Machlup, Fritz. Knowledge: Its Creation, Distribution and Economic Significance, vol.3: The Economics of Information Human Capital. Princeton, Princeton University Press, 1984.

Malone, Cheryl, Knott and Elichirigoity, Fernando. Information as commodity and economic sector: Its emergence in the discourse of industrial classification. *Journal of the American Society for Information Science and Technolgy 54 (6): 512-520, 2003.*

Marshall, Alfred. Principles of Economics: An Introductory Volume, ed.8. London, Macmillan, 1947.

Martyn, John. Information as a commodity. *Assistant Librarian* 77: 76-79, 1984.

Max Muller, Ed. and Tr. The Upanishads: Part I. London, Oxford University Press, 1900. (Reprint: Delhi, Motilal Banarasidass, 2000.). P. lxvi. (The Sacred Books of the East Series. Vol. 1).

May, Christopher and Sell, Susan K. Intellectual Property Rights: A Critical History. Boulder (Colorado), Lynne Riener, 2006.

Mishan, E.J. Welfare Economics: Ten Introductory Essays. New York, Random House, 1969.

Mitra, J. K. Economics (Including Economic Planning). Micro and Macro. Ed.2. Calcutta, World Press, 1982.

Narayana, G.J. Information as a Commodity: An Inquiry into the Characteristics of Knowledge. Ph.D. Thesis. University of Poona, Pune, 1991.

Neelameghan, A. Information economy and knowledge society: An introduction. Part 1: Definitions and indicators. *Information Studies* 5 (2): 107-124, April 1999.

Neelameghan, A, Information economy and knowledge society: An introduction. Part 3: Economics and policy aspects. *Information* Studies 5(4):249-260, Oct. 1999.

Cf. Newman, G. An institutional perspective of information. *International Social Science Journal 28:*466-92, 1967.

Prasad, K.N. Intellectual property rights. *Information Studies* 4 (2): 67-104, April, 1998.

Ricart-Costa, Joan E.; Subirana, Brian; and Valor-Sabatier, Josep. Sources of Information Value: Strategic Framing and Transformation of the Information Industries. London, Palgrave, 2004.

Robbins, Lionel. An Essay on the Nature & Significance of Economic Science. Ed.2. London, Macmillan, 1935.

Robinson, Joan. The Economics of Imperfect Competition. London, Macmillan, 1954.

Sassone, P.G. A Theory of the Market Demand for Information Analysis Center Services. Pp. 23-38. *In* Mason, R.M. and Creps, J.E. Jr. Information Services: Economics, Management, and Technology. Boulder (Colo.), Westview Press, 1981.

Smith, Adam. An Inquiry into the Nature and Causes of the Wealth of Nations. London, George Routledge, 1898.

Stiglitz, Joseph E. Information and the change in the paradigm in economics, Part I and II. *American Economist* 47 (2): Fall 2003 (6p).

Vishwanath, Arun. Impact of personality on technology adoption. *Journal of the American Society for Information Science and Technology* 56 (8): 803-811, 2005.

Yew-Kwang Ng. Welfare Economics- Introduction and Development of Basic Concepts. London, Macmillan, 1979.

16

Information as a Factor of Production

The previous chapter dealt with knowledge and information as an economic good and its implications. Production and consumption aspects of information as a commodity were also considered. This chapter will examine information as a factor of production, and how it will affect the other factors of production. In other words, here we deal with information economics, that is, the study of the impact of information on the working of an economy and the economic processes. How knowledge and information are guiding the course of development of economics is the content of this chapter. Economic theories are generally considered to fall into classical and neo-classical versions. The foundation of classical theories was laid by Adam Smith. The neo-classical theories are a product of the last forty years. Lord Keynes is the most prominent contributor to the neo-classical theories. The first part of the chapter treats information in the light of classical theories of economics, which will be followed by the information view of economic activities in the post-Keynesian era.

Knowledge interests an economist in two ways: knowledge as an input to production, and the production of knowledge. The accumulation of knowledge, the accumulation of capital, and the effort to economize are the three proximate causes of economic growth. They are equally important and mutually interdependent. Knowledge as a factor in economic growth contributes in the form of : a) technological knowledge about things and living creatures and as social knowledge about man and his relationship with his fellowmen. While the former contributes to production, the latter teaches how to manage large scale organizations or creating institutions which favour economizing effort (Lewis, 1955). Knowledge is now considered a social resource- a resource derived not directly from nature but from human invention and social organization (Chiaraviglio and Gehl, 1974). Presently, economics is engulfed by knowledge and information revolution, a revolution on a global scale continually supported by computer and communication technologies. In the expanding knowledge networks on which economic growth rests, information is the neuron and communication the nervous system.

In economics land, labour, capital and organization are identified as the four factors of production. This schema does not recognize information and knowledge factors explicitly although the role of knowledge is implicit in organization. Land being geographic space, its role in production vis-à-vis information needs no explanation. Information in relation to the other three factors needs examination.

INFORMATION AS CAPITAL

Capital is a resource used in the production of goods produced by human labour, which can be used for further production. It consists of assets which earn money or provide utility. Some of the important characteristics of capital are:

1. Capital is productive. Capital increases the productivity of labour, and can produce new goods.
2. Capital is prospective. Capital accumulated is expected to result in income or utility.
3. Capital is the result of labour.

4. The main source of accumulating capital is savings, i.e., excess income retained after meeting consumption.

Applying the characteristics of capital, it is seen that knowledge is also capital, but of a different type. The concept of knowledge as capital is also interpreted slightly differently, when it is said that: a) economic development is essentially a learning process (Boulding, 1970); b) organization, information channels, and "capability" have the characteristics of capital in the economic sense (Lamberton, 1984); and c) technological knowledge has far greater influence over production compared to that of other traditional factors of creating wealth.

Unlike traditional pattern of production modern economies need to invest heavily on knowledge, besides money capital, to produce goods and services, and to gain competitive edge. Knowledge is the product of human labour, and its application results in the production of repetitive goods or new goods. Thus, knowledge shares with capital its goods obtaining property. Scientific and technical information, in particular, has enormous capability to produce a variety of goods and services, and to increase the productivity of labour. Further, application of accumulated knowledge results in the creation of new knowledge, which acts as an investment and results in income or utility. Creation of knowledge is the result of human labour as is the case with capital in creating wealth. Applying the criterion of savings, it is seen that information does not depend on savings for the reason that knowledge remains available for use even after consumption, i.e., knowledge remains an inexhaustible saving.

Information as capital differs from money capital in one vital sense, namely, that capital buys the three other factors of production- land, labour and organization, where as information do not buy them directly. In recent years, knowledge and information is considered as a human resource or human capital. Other things keeping constant, the competitive advantage and entrepreneurial performance of a firm or an enterprise depend on human capital. This is more so in the global level competition. Knowledge functions both as a means of enhancing production and as an end good. Information can be "regarded as an investment in the individual who is transformed by relevant information into a more effective factor of production. Information may, therefore, be acquired and stored as an investment rather than consumed as a product,..."(Prodrick, 1980, p.91). This interpretation ignores goods producing property of information, corresponding to goods obtaining characteristic of money capital. On the contrary, money capital is analogous in many respects to information capital. The money capital is "built upon knowledge— the knowledge that one can obtain goods and services without the need to exchange something with intrinsic value" (Feinman, 1981, p.54).

Intellectual Capital. Late twentieth century (post-Keynesian era) saw the beginnings of post-industrial society in the West. It also saw the domination of knowledge and information use in the economic development of nations. This was primarily due to: a) technology becoming the underpinning force in the production of goods and services, and in managing organizations; and b) the overriding impact of newer forms of information transmission facilities like the Internet and other ICT enabled services in conducting transactions. With this, the traditional concept of production which gave priority to capital and labour was over shadowed by the importance of acquiring knowledge through learning, training and education; and applying the acquired knowledge in all economic activities, more so in fields driven by technology. Since it is the human mind that acquires, stores, and applies knowledge, the holders of such knowledge in the organization constitute the human resource of that organization. This resource needs developing, maintaining, sharpening and applying, which is the essence of human resource development activities. As the worth of an enterprise is assessed in terms of its assets, human resource too is treated as an asset. Hence the value of 'human capital' and 'intellectual capital' is increasingly appreciated and valued by industry, economics, and governments. However, there is also some hype and exaggeration added in describing the importance of these two assets.

Intellectual Capital (IC) is defined as the total knowledge combining implicit knowledge embedded in an organization and its people, and the knowledge artifacts held by the organization. In the past, many experts equated IC with Knowledge Capital, Knowledge Management, and Organizational Learning. Human capital is invariably considered an important segment of IC. A more comprehensive view of IC includes Customer Capital, Social Capital and Structural Capital (Khan, 2008). Customer capital is the goodwill of customers towards a particular good or service, their producers and suppliers as well as customer loyalty to a given product or service. Social Capital is the value derived from social exchanges between employees, between the organization and its customers, and between the enterprise and its other stakeholders (Leena and Van Buren, 1999). Structural Capital refers to mechanisms and structures enabling the organization's employees to optimize their intellectual performance. Structural Capital items include information constructs like databases, organization charts, processes, manuals, strategies and other components whose value is higher than material value (Ross and Edvinson, 1997). In the modern day accounting practice, IC gets included in the balance sheet, i.e., the financial statement reflecting the assets of an organization. Without the inclusion of IC, the balance sheet will not depict the total assets and their value (Edvinson and Malone, 1997). IC is used as an important tool by firms to evaluate the worth of their enterprise. Particularly in the case of knowledge based industries like software, and in art productions the value of IC asset is seen more important than other forms of assets.

Human capital is defined as "the knowledge, skills,

competencies and attributes embodied in individuals that facilitate the creation of personal, social and economic well-being" (Centre...., 2001, p.18). Besides acquired knowledge and skills, innate mental capacities, certain traits of motivation and behaviour, and characteristics such as physical, emotional and mental health of individuals are also taken to be a part of human capital. Development of human capital takes an inclusive approach by including preschool learning, formal education and training, work place training including specially designed informal learning programmes at work or participation in various professional networks, and informal "on-the-job" learning. It also emphasises the importance of lifelong learning.

Human capital in industrial and economic enterprises acquires an organizational characteristic. Knowledge management, manpower management, research, development and innovation, technology induction are linked with human capital. Stocks of human capital in healthy enterprises always remain dynamic due to constant changes associated with enterprise growth. These changes are caused by introduction of new technologies, changing industrial environment, policy changes within the enterprise, employee turnover due to retirement, voluntary exit, hiring and firing, enterprise's policy on cooperation and competition, and mergers and acquisitions. However, "....the highly specific, culturally bound, non-communicative, tacit and heterogeneous dimensions of human capital are not easy to encapsulate in such aggregate measures of human capital" (Centre....., 2001, p.20).

Stock and Flow of Information. Economists are interested in studying the stock and flow of capital and of goods. Knowledge and information too can be considered in terms of stock and flow. Stock refers to the sum total of knowledge held by an individual, a given community or organization or the society at large, at any given period of time. Stock of knowledge is built as a consequence of the cognitive phenomena of the human brain and is accounted by the growth of knowledge. The flow of knowledge refers to the transfer of knowledge in the form of information and is related to the spread or diffusion of knowledge. Knowledge held by individuals in their minds and information contained in the records of archives, in all the books held in libraries, in the Internet and web sites, and other knowledge artifacts represent the stock of knowledge. On the other hand, the process of communicating, transferring and disseminating information from the creators of information to users employing various means and forms represent the flow of knowledge/information (Machlup, 1984). Manipulative characteristics of information affect the flow of information. The depletion of knowledge is mostly caused by death and human incapacitation.

Computing the stock of knowledge and determining the rate of its flow is beset with many difficulties. While knowledge in the mind, i.e., tacit knowledge, cannot be computed in physical terms, the stock and flow of information (with some exceptions) can be measured quantitatively, e.g., in terms of number of books, number of journal articles published in a year, the number of hours spent on Internet or k-bytes of data stored in computer memory. Both stock and flow can be assigned money value which then forms a measure. The concept of stock of knowledge and flow of information becomes useful in planning and controlling knowledge as a resource, in the allocation of funds to various sectors of societal activities, in determining the effects of flow of knowledge, and in computing the information component of Gross National Product. Often, planning a new information facility begins with deciding the initial stock of information records to be collected and the quantum of flow, i.e., circulation of records. In assessing the economic worth of a business concern its stock and flow of knowledge, nowadays, are included under assets, particularly in knowledge based industries.

INFORMATION AND LABOUR

Information accounts for the intellectual part of labour, the other parts being manual, skilled and managerial. Labour is measured in man-hours or output, whereas information in terms of its economizing power which is quantifiable or significance which is not quantitatively measurable and yet easily perceived. The cost of labour may be viewed from two angles, namely, that of employees and employers. In the former, cost refers to the cost incurred in acquiring the qualifications, skill and experience. Whereas in the case of employers, it refers to the compensation paid. But in both the cases, we cannot afford to ignore the value generated. Knowledge impacts on labour and labour market in the following manners :

Occupational Mobility. Knowledge and skill brings mobility to the labour market. Acquiring new or additional knowledge, skill and experience enables people to move from one field of employment to another or from a lower position to a higher position. The mobility range is not limited to one specific geographic location, but encompasses a wide area from villages and towns, to states and continents.

Division of Labour. Specialization of knowledge and its practice give rise to division of labour. Distribution of existing knowledge in society and the growth of new knowledge influence the labour market. Application of new technological knowledge is the single most agent that leads to specialization of labour. Industries and services based on out-dated technology will not be able to withstand competition, which results in their extinction or in wasteful employment of labour. Specialization increases employment potential. To give an example, in most advanced economies and in developing economies like India service sector has overtaken manufacturing and agricultural sectors put together. Service sector accounts for a larger share of total employment, but at the cost of physical labour. Technology centered service sectors making use of advanced information, computer and communication systems have replaced the blue-collar labour employed earlier. To give another example, the use of ready-mix concrete and construction machinery has made large-scale employment of labourers redundant in Indian building industry. Impact of specialization on labour are felt in areas ranging from the need for rehabilitation of labour to that of wider issues of welfare economics.

Decreasing Role of Physical Labour. Enhanced application of technical knowledge decreases the role of physical labour in society, and thus affects the labour market. For example, the use of Internet and e-mail has reduced to the minimum the employment of mail operators. In technologically advanced countries like Japan, robotics is gradually replacing human labour. Market for personnel with specialized knowledge is increasing whereas the demand for unskilled labour is decreasing. This is bound to create more labour conflicts and greater social unrest in countries like India, unless immediate steps are taken to address these issues. For advanced economies, outsourcing of skilled jobs to developing countries has already become a major political issue.

Knowledge Component of Labour Cost. The cost of labour includes the cost of acquiring knowledge and skill. Acquiring specialist knowledge is becoming costly. One important reason for a specialist's services to cost more is that the specialist is required to invest heavily in terms of time and money to acquire specialist knowledge, experience and skill. Another reason is the relative scarcity of a specialist's knowledge and skill. Some of the other features of knowledge and labour relationships are:

1. While labour cannot be transferred to another labourer (can be to a machine), information can be transferred.
2. Increase in population results in increase in the total stock of knowledge and information in society. The growth in population does not lead to scarcity of information, but may cause distribution problems.

3. Death results in the loss of labour hours, but not in the loss of knowledge as the latter can be stored and retrieved in the form of information and records.
4. Universal equality of knowledge is not possible, but providing equal opportunities to acquire knowledge is achievable. It is possible to achieve economic socialism, but not knowledge socialism. Providing better facilities and increased allocation of resources towards dispersal of information create more opportunities for acquiring knowledge, but actual acquisition depends on the mental quality and capacity of the individual.
5. The factors that are conducive to efficiency, i.e., the productive capacity of labour, are also the factors that are conducive to the acquisition and application of knowledge. Some of the conducive factors that contribute to efficiency of labour are: appropriate social and political environment, climate, health, food and hygiene, education, income and standard of living. But this is not always true in the case of knowledge.

Making choice is a crucial element in economics, both theoretical and applied. Informed choice underlies economic decision-making and intelligent human action, however imperfect the decision-maker's accumulated knowledge may be. Thus, stocks of knowledge and flows of information guide the choice and decisions that result in economic action (Machlup, 1984). An offshoot of this requirement is the greater emphasis laid on management information systems in business and industry, think-tanks, and advisory functions in governments

INFORMATION AND ORGANIZATION

The function of organization is the co-ordination of the factors of production in working units. Broadly, it represents management. Organizing is the effective use of information in meeting organizational changes and exercising organizational options through decision-making. These take place in an environment of uncertainty. Communication is central to organization. Thus, information occupies a central position in organization.

In all organizational setups information is distributed in its functionaries at different levels. Controlling the organization is controlling the flow of information in the organization. Managerial function is that of integrating the information held at different levels in the organization and in the external environment into a cohesive force, and making it an instrument of effective actions to achieve objectives.

SCIENCE, TECHNOLOGY AND INDUSTRY

Scientific knowledge and technological information are crucial to industrial development, economic growth and social wellbeing. In today's world technological knowledge has become the most powerful economic force pushing into background the other factors of production in creating wealth. Economies survive if they are able to withstand competition, and this ability depends on how we exploit science, technology and the knowledge generated by them. To appreciate this fact, it is necessary to understand how scientific and technical knowledge is exploited to serve as the most important factor of production. Further, as never before, science is linked to technology; technology is linked to economy and environment through the manufacturing processes; and economy and environment link technology to the society (Abdul Kalam and Pillai. 2004).

Science and Industry. Scientific research leads to generation of new ideas, which on application leads to technical knowledge. By applying technical knowledge industry produces new goods or services. The translation of an idea into a product goes through three phases- a) selection of relevant scientific findings and theories derived from basic research, b) technical research, i.e., applying scientific findings and principles to solve specific technical problems or to produce new things; and c) development work that converts technical research into products or solutions to problems. In the development phase, and to a lesser extent in technical research phase, commercial decisions become decisive. Industry on its part provides the challenge to research, invests funds and converts the results of research into economic goods or services.

Allocation of Resources. Industry looks for direct profit. As the basic research does not directly lead to profit, the industry will not invest on it. Thus, research becomes a charge on the public fund, and the returns a public good. Basic research is entrusted to universities and institutions created for such research, fully or partly supported by government. The output of technical research is a commodity with potential profit built into it. The industry would invest only in such ventures which result in a patentable commodity. The patent system conveys monopolies not only upon the inventor, but also upon the developer, and later upon the commercial producer. Investment on development research involves risk.

Technical Manpower Development. Technology-based development calls for the creation of manpower at various levels and disciplines- from skilled labour to competent managers. To supply the needed personnel establishment of vocational training centers, technical schools and colleges, costing and management training establishments, and institutions of higher learning becomes necessary.

Pro-technology Environment. Technology quickly takes firm roots in societies which are pragmatic and conscious of the value of efficiency. Economic backwardness of the underdeveloped countries can be traced to over population, limited natural resources, mass illiteracy, unproductive deployment of capital, and over-demand for jobs in government bureaucracy than in industry. Capital investment in local trade and money-lending takes higher priority than that of investment in industry. High technology and laissez-faire work culture do not go together. It requires a major attitudinal change on the part of employees and authorities in responding. For example, if an e-mail query addressed to a company remains unattended for long or transferring the query from one agent to another endlessly, the very purpose of installing the system has no meaning. In the political system though based on universal franchise until recently 'ma-bap' culture was evident in the employer-employee relationship, which was not conducive for technology growth. In taking advantage of technology for industrial growth, many developing countries also face the problems of overcoming the consequences of social prejudices, cultural inhibitions, and religious taboos. All these factors give strength to the argument that capital will be less productive in the less developed countries because fruitful use of capital depends on ever improving technology, and the growth of knowledge is slower in the less developed countries (Lewis, 1955).

Supporting scientific research based on sound economic and social criteria is crucial to a country's progress. Investing on research by developing countries having meager resources seems a luxury. However, if they do not invest in research they will remain perpetually backward. Hence a sound investment policy is needed.

Innovation and Incentives. Scientific and technical research is only a part of innovation. Innovation is as much a part of organization as information is. It is the organization and people in it who convert the results of research into wealth. By itself, neither a science and technology plan nor a heavy investment will result in industrial and economic growth. Creation of a progressive and pro-entrepreneurial environment is vitally important. This calls for the development of innovative spirit in economic, political and social spheres. Creation of new and effective instruments, organizational structures and social institutions to cope with the changing complexities of enterprises and altering environment are as much a part of innovation as inventions are. Development of innovative organizations, innovative attitude, and innovative strategies is a part of the management of innovation. Innovative ability can be furthered by providing suitable incentives. Apart from material incentives, individuals are influenced by higher motivational factors like the urge to succeed, desire for achievement and prestige. Organizational culture, including relative freedom to work, plays an important part in promoting innovative spirit. Environment of monopoly or competition affects the growth of innovation. Opinion is divided on the exact role of each environment. One view is that incentive to innovate is greater under competition than under monopoly (Arrow, 1962), and the opposite view is that innovative spirit flourishes better under monopoly (Demseetz, 1969). However, the element of challenge which is more in competition appears to provide a better incentive to innovate.

Technology and Information. Industrial growth in modern economies depends upon technology, the application of which results in new products and gives a competitive edge to an industry. Social knowledge results in the creation of efficient organizations and promotion of social welfare. Technical information is an input in technology application. The major issues in the utilization of technology are:

1. Understanding the relationship between science and industry.
2. Allocation of resources.
3. Creation of a pro-technology environment.
4. Training of personnel.

Modern day technologies are complex. They involve cooperation between scientists; between basic research laboratories; technical cooperation agreements between firms; technology transfer within multinational companies; development of international networks involving enterprises, government establishments and university laboratories within the programmes totally or partially funded by state; transaction on intellectual property rights; trade in high technology products; and foreign direct investments. These new features of science and technology have given rise to what is called 'technoglobalism'. "Big science" is a good example of technoglobalism. Some of the features of high technology projects are : huge investment, expensive equipment and facilities, cost-sharing, and access to scientific knowledge across a wide spectrum of disciplines. They generate vast amount of information, which need to be processed, stored, disseminated, interpreted and utilized. These factors are of vital importance in formulating national technology and industrial policies. They have also to consider how each one of these factors affect traditional trade, competition and investment policies. At the local level each industrial enterprise has to devise its own strategy dictated by the vision of the firm, available resources, and the environment weighed in the background of information (Drilhon, 1992).

Further, the national technology policy have to have sub-sector policies on related issues, such as human resource development, higher education, research training, international mobility of students and young scientists. A component of this technology scenario is 'research networks', both national and international. The main features of such networks are their emphasis on the coordination and collaboration between groups in existing institutions with a view to ensure more effective and flexible functioning of research system. Research networks are often designed to reach a critical mass of human, equipment, and financial resources in some areas to bring together complementary skills and abilities (especially in multi-disciplinary research) and to facilitate the circulation and diffusion of scientific information and data to potential users (Drilhon, 1992).

MULTI-ROLE OF INFORMATION

The study of the various economic characteristics of information discussed above shows that information displays the dual roles of a free good and an economic good; a good and a service; a public good and a private good; a commodity and a non-commodity; an agent of production and a product by itself; and a production good and a consumption good. Thus, information assumes dual and even multi-roles depending on the context. This makes the study of information complex and at the same time interesting.

CORPORATE INFORMATION

Economic organizations, including firms, during the course of their working not only collect information from various external sources, but most importantly generate plenty of information within. The value and utility of corporate information to the society at large is an important issue. The corporate information is made up of information which is purely of interest to the particular corporate body holding that information, and information of significance to sociologists, government policymakers, economic research workers management study, research institutions, historians and others. This raises a number of fundamental questions, such as: a) Is such information only of archival value or does it have other applications? b) Whether such information be made available to public or not? c) What information to be made available and how much of it? d) What should be the organizational setup to collect, maintain and provide access? e) Should access be free or at a charge? f) Should firms deposing their information be compensated? g) Is there a role for the government? h) Should corporate information become a part of the national network? i) What protection measures are needed to ensure that information is not exploited by individuals, firms and foreign agencies in manners inimical to national interest? These issues are not resolvable to the satisfaction of all because of :

a) the nature and requirements of the global economy, b) the power of information and communication technology to provide instant universal access to information and the involvement of issues relating to destruction of information integrity, illegal exploitation of information, and cyber crimes.

FROM KNOWLEDGE ECONOMY TO KNOWLEDGE SOCIETY

Knowledge and information are playing key roles in shaping the economics of the twenty-first century. The role is determined by a complex system of flow of information across the globe transmitted through computer terminals and communication facilities at incredible speed. Knowledge as the new factor of economics is redefining the status of other factors of production- capital, land and labour. In today's global economy information acts as a surrogate for material goods in most of the national and international trade transactions. Many national economies are integrated with international economy, and any change in either of the two finds immediate impact on the other because of instant transfer of information. Information transfer decides efficiency and competitiveness of industrial and business enterprises with serious consequences for national economies as a whole and on labour, employment and standard of living in particular. Information as a factor of production has overtaken the importance of all other factors of production, namely capital, land, labour and organization. It has become a powerful and pervasive instrument of creating wealth in new ways. Knowledge and information have become the prime agents of changing twentieth century industrial society into knowledge society of the twenty-first century.

Knowledge economy is defined as "an economy that creates, disseminates, and uses knowledge to enhance its growth and development" (Dahlman and Utz, 2005, p. xvi). The objective of knowledge economy is to harness and use new and existing knowledge to improve the industrial productivity in all sectors of the economy. The ultimate goal of knowledge economy is to increase overall welfare and not just high-technology industries (Dahlman and Utz, 2005). For the attainment of knowledge economy education and human resource play pivotal roles. Knowledge economy requires a different type of people than the traditional work force. It is driven by "knowledge workers", a term coined by Peter Drucker. A knowledge worker is one who is professionally qualified whose forte is interpretation of knowledge, its translation, and problem solving. In addition, knowledge economy needs supply of a large number of knowledge technicians in fields such as computer and communication technologies, laboratory analysis, paralegal assistants and the like (Edersheim, 2007). Development of technology plays an equally important role in moving towards knowledge economy.

It is apt to present here the pristine analysis of a nation's progress made by Dr. A.P.J. Abdul Kalam, the former president of India at the inaugural session of the World Knowledge Platform recently. He observes that a nation's economic development is powered by competitiveness; the competitiveness is powered by knowledge power; the knowledge power is powered by technology and innovation; the technology and innovation is powered by resource investment; the resource investment is powered by revenue and return on investment; the revenue is powered by volume and repeat sales through customer loyalty; the customer loyalty is powered by quality and value of products; quality and value of products is powered by employee productivity and innovation; the employee productivity is powered by employee loyalty, employee satisfaction and working environment; the working environment is powered by management stewardship; and management stewardship is powered by creative leadership. The Economic prosperity, security and peace of a nation in turn is bound by a system of ethics and values beginning with the parents and subsequently committing the two to family, society and nation. Parental ethics and values come from value based education and creation of clean environment that leads to righteousness in heart (Abdul Kalam, 2008).

As observed by Abdul Kalam, a knowledge economy is only a means to an end. The end goal is to usher in a knowledge society- a society that is enlightened, healthy and well-off, just and equitable. A knowledge society is much more than a knowledge economy, whose main objective is to create wealth through the application of knowledge acting on resources employing efficient and effective organizational skills. The knowledge society stands for a way of life and values founded on knowledge economy and guided by spiritual, ethical, social, intellectual and philosophical knowledge (Dahlman and Utz, 2005). It is to be brought about by : a) social transformation for a just and equitable society; b) wealth generation; and c) protection of knowledge, not only generated in research laboratory but by communities as traditional knowledge. This is to be achieved through education with the support of information technology, connectivity and appropriate positive governance (India, Planning Commission, 2002). (See also chapters 14 and 21).

CLOSURE

The study of information as a factor of production occupies a central place in information economics. Information functions as a means to increase efficiency, enhance production, and produce new goods and services, and as an end in itself- the end being a good. Information, as a factor of production works on the traditional factors of production-capital, land, labour, and organization- to maximize their impact on production, distribution, marketing and other economic functions.

In a technology driven economy, knowledge and information is taken as a part of human capital, and knowledge an asset. Other things keeping constant, the competitive advantage and entrepreneurial performance of a firm depend on human capital. Included in human capital is intellectual capital, which is the sum of implicit knowledge embedded in an organization and its people, and the knowledge artifacts held by the organization. The concept of stock and flow of capital is also applicable to information. Stock refers to the intellectual capital, and flow refers to transmission and diffusion of knowledge. Stocks of knowledge and flows of information guide the choices and decisions that result in economic action.

Information accounts for the intellectual part of labour, the other part being physical. Labour is measured in man-hours or output whereas information in terms of its economizing power. Knowledge affects labour market through creation of higher occupational mobility; increasing division of labour by specialization; and decreasing the role of physical labour in work. Universal attainment of equality of knowledge is not possible, but providing equal opportunities to acquire knowledge are achievable. The cost of labour includes the cost of acquiring knowledge and skill.

The function of organization is to co-ordinate the factors of production in working units. Broadly, it represents management. Managerial function is that of integrating the information held at different levels in the organization and in the external environment into a cohesive force, and making it an instrument of effective actions to achieve set objectives. These take place often in an environment of uncertainty. Information helps in reducing uncertainty. Information and communication are central to organization. Managing an organization is becoming managing the flow of information, and exercising knowledge options in the organization.

Scientific knowledge and technological information are crucial to industrial development, economic growth, and social wellbeing. Firms cannot survive unless they are innovative. Development and application of technology involve several issues, important among them are: science and industry relationship, investment on research, technical manpower development, creation of a pro-technology environment, and managing information. Technology, economic development, education and manpower development, and social wellbeing are interlinked.

Knowledge and information are the main forces that are driving modern economies, which are called information economies or knowledge economies. What characterizes knowledge economies is not just the use of information for producing new goods and services, but also the use of information as a factor of production to enhance the most efficient use of other factors of production- capital, land, labour and organization.

REFERENCES

Abdul Kalam, P. J. " Dr. Kalam stressed the need to evolve CSR ethics". *Economic Times*, 31st Jan. 2008, (From Dr. Kalam's address to the First International Summit jointly organized by the Corporate Affairs Ministry and the ASSOCHAM).

Abdul Kalam, A.P.J. and Pillai, A Sivathanu. Envisioning and Empowered Nation: Technology for Transformation. New Delhi, Tata-McGraw-Hill Publishing, 2004.

Arrow, K.J. Economic Welfare and the Allocation of Resources for Invention. Pp.609-625. *In* National Bureau of Economic Research. The Rate and Direction of Inventive Activity. Princeton (NJ), Princeton University Press, 1962.

Boulding, K. E. The Misallocation of Intellectual Resources. Pp. 151-57. *In* Boulding, K.E. Ed. Beyond Economics: Essays on Society, Religion and Ethics. Ann Arbor, University of Michigan, 1970. (Reprint).

Centre for Educational Research and Innovation. Organisation for Economic Co-operation and Development, Paris. The Well-being of Nations. The Role of Human and Social Capital. Paris, OECD, 2001.

Chaiaraviglio, Lucio and Gehl, John. Some notes on the planning of research in the information discipline. Pp. 202-07. *In* Zunde, Pranas. Ed. Information utilities: Proceedings of the 37th ASIS Annual Conference. Washington (DC), American Society for Information Science, 1974.

Dahlman, Carl and Utz, Anuja. India and the Knowledge Economy: Leveraging Strengths and Opportunities. Washington (D.C.), The World Bank, 2005.

Drilhon, Gabriel. Science & Technology Sans Frontiers? Organization for Economic Cooperation and Development. Paris, The OECD Observer. Issue No.175, April/May 1992.

Demseetz, Harold. Information and efficiency: Another viewpoint. *Journal of Law & Economics* 12: 1-22, 1969.

Edersheim, Elizabeth Has. The Definitive Drucker. New Delhi, Tata McGraw-Hill, 2007.

Edvinson, L. and Malone, M. Intellectual Capital: Realizing Your Company's True Value by Finding its Hidden Brain Power. New York, Harper Collins, 1997.

Feinman, Stephen. Regulation of the STI Industry: A Historical Basis and Some Possibilities. *In* Mason, R.M. and Creps, J.E. Jr. Information Services: Economics, Management, and Technology. Boulder (Colo.), Westview Press, 1981.

India. Planning Commission. Tenth Five-Year Plan 2002-2007. New Delhi, The Planning Commission, 2002. (http://planningcommission.nic.in/plans/planrel/fiveyr/welcome.html)

Khan, Shaniz. Intellectual capital and the perceived relevance of the balance sheet as a value measure for corporations. *Journal of the American Academy of* Business12 (2): 83-91, March, 2008.

Lamberton, D.M. The economics of information and organization. *Annual Review of Information Science and Technology* 19: 3-30, 1984.

Leena, C.R. and Van Buren, H. Organizational social capital and employment practices. *Academy of Management Review* 24 (2): 538- 555, 1999.

Lewis, W.A. The Theory of Economic Growth. London, Allen & Unwin, 1955.

Machlup, Fritz. Knowledge: Its Creation, Distribution, and Economic Significance. Vol. 3. The Economics of Information and Human Capital. Princeton, Princeton University Press , 1984

Prodrick, Gerald. The peculiar and complex economic properties of information. *Canadian Journal of Information Science* 5: 89-92, 1980.

Ross, G. and Edvinson, L. Intellectual Capital Navigating in the New Business Landscape. New York, New York University Press, 1997.

17
Information as Economic Signals

Over the last forty years, information-centric study of economics called "information economics" has emerged as a new subdiscipline of economics. Information economics has enabled us to explain some of the economic phenomena, which the traditional economic theories could not explain satisfactorily. The most striking impact of the information approach has been in examining the appropriate role for government in economies and larger society. The fundamental belief underpinning the modern capitalistic economics from the days of Adam Smith is that free market leads to efficient outcomes, and it works best when there is no government intervention or least intervention. This stand is being questioned now. Information economics calls for a better understanding of issues like national level economic polices and initiatives, bankruptcy, corporate governance and the role of government action on decision-making (Stiglitz, 2003). Information is embedded in economic activities, and it also serves as an economic signal. Information signals serve four main purposes: a) as an input for planning, b) help in conducting the economic activity; c) serve as a diagnostic tool, and d) help in devising remedial measures in case of disruptions in implementation.

By studying the nature, strength and effects of the information signals embedded in an economic activity we get the insight of its functioning. The signals also forewarn of any fault-lines developing in the activity. As most of the economic activities are of a continuous nature, the information gets generated continuously. Hence the information signals are to be monitored continuously throughout the life cycle of the activities. Information signals fall into two broad categories, namely, macroeconomic signals dealing with national and global economies; and microeconomics concerned with markets, market-makers, households, and the like.

MACROECONOMIC SIGNALS

Planning and managing national economies are dependent on the use of macroeconomic information signals generated by various sectors of an economy. These signals are of numerous types representing the different segments and features of the economy. The signals are mostly in the form of statistical data, indices, and ratios. Some of the signals are: gross domestic product (GDP), per capita income, industrial production data, lending rates and spread, cash-reserve ratio in banking and financial institutions, market capitalization and stock indices in share market, unemployment and labour figures, tax collection and revenue growth picture, internal and external tariff and trade data, educational statistics, and many others. The budget is the foremost instrument that signals time-bound targets to be achieved in each area of the economy, and the means of attaining them. Other sources of signals are vision statements, plan documents, evaluation reports, and the like. Drawing inferences in time from the signals, and acting thereupon as necessary is the key to macroeconomic management.

The consequences of failure to act on the basis of signals either by dogma or due to ignorance is illustrated by the current U. S. subprime crisis (September 2008), and its conductive effects on the global financial system. This crisis has highlighted again the role of governments in the management of economies. A basic tenet of the classical economic theories and the inbuilt "self regulating" mechanism in a free enterprise economic system, advocated by the Austrian neoliberal economist Fredrich Hayek in his work *The Road to Serfdom,* emphasize that economic development will be faster, if it is left to free market play without any role or least role for the government. The free market model followed by the U. S. and many other countries ignores one of the fundamental duties of a government to regulate economy in order to safeguard the interest of the taxpayers and vast majority of its citizens, when the free market acts irresponsibly guided by sheer greed or folly or both. Analyzing the current crisis, Percy Mistry attributes market and regulatory failure as one of the causes (Mistry, 2008). Market failure occurs due to lack of appropriate regulatory mechanism in place, or not reading the macroeconomic information signals properly, and failure to take immediate corrective actions. Information signals indicate the state of health of an economy at any given point of time. The signals also form the input for arriving at decisions at the macro-level.

INFORMATION AND MARKETS

In studying markets and firms, the policy emphasis has now shifted from competitive equilibrium paradigm to that of information paradigm. The standard models relied only on scarcity side of information problem, ignoring other aspects like information problems faced every day by consumers and firms in areas such as price and quality of products on sale, quality and efforts of labour hired, and the returns of investment projects. Information is involved in all markets, commodities, insurance, securities, banking, stocks and shares, public good, intellectual capital, and many others. Decision-making is pervasive not only in firms and households, but also in political processes. Information is a crucial input that affects decision-making. This has led to a reassessment of the impact of information imperfection or asymmetry of information in an economy and in society (Stiglitz, 2003).

Information Asymmetry. Information asymmetry exists in all segments of societal activities involving participation between citizens and their governments, between professionals and their clients, sellers and buyers, in the tax systems, in the labour market, in banking, in insurance, in political processes, and others. Existence of information asymmetry in markets is only a special case of information disparity in society. For example, in the matrimonial field often the contracting parties do not have all the information about the other party before solemnization of the marriage. In essence, information asymmetry refers to a situation where one person has more information than the other relating to a given situation. Information asymmetry could be the result of either disparity of information between the contracting parties created by unequal access to information or due to concealing a part of the information or both. Often, this gives scope for exploitation of the informationally less privileged by the more privileged either by design or ignorance, or by chance. Two cases of information asymmetry are cited below as examples:

1. An insurance company issuing a health policy at a premium meant for a person of normal health without knowing that the policy holder is suffering from a congenital disease puts the insurance company into loss or in litigation in case of a claim.
2. The paracetamol-based pain-killer tablets are sold in the market under different names and brands with varying concentrations of paracetamol. By not disclosing the contents and the concentration of the main ingredient by the manufacturer, the consumer is not certain whether he is paying the right price.

In economics, information asymmetry is defined as the gap that occurs when buyers and sellers are not equally well informed (Spence, 1974). The reasons for the existence of imperfect information could be many. The information gap may be large in some markets or may be less in some others, but it exists. Information imperfection and the public good aspect of management are two main causes of corporate problems. Informational asymmetries cause problems because it limits the range of contracts that can be drawn up. Contracts must be based on information that both parties can be presumed to have at some relevant point of time. Informational gaps resulting from asymmetrically located information can lead to inefficient market performance and in some instances to the collapse or nonexistence of a market (Spence, 1974). Information asymmetry in developing countries leads to less efficient allocation of resources, which affects adversely flow of information, than in advanced economies. Weak information flow results in poor institutional arrangements (Lakshmanasamy, 2003). Public good aspect puts restrictions on management. Classical economic theories could not account satisfactorily the effects of asymmetry in an increasingly technology-based economy.

The major flaw in formal economic modeling has been the assumption that information was perfect, although it was known to be not so, but ignored as of no consequence. Stiglitz and others showed that even a small amount of imperfection could profoundly affect the nature of equilibrium. What distinguishes markets with imperfect information from that of perfect information is that actions (including choices) convey information, market participants know this, and this affects their behavior (Stiglitz, 2003). Under imperfect information paradigm, markets are nearly never Parato efficient. Imperfect models are difficult to construct as imperfect information appears in infinite ways. This further complicated the modeling equilibriums- between lender and borrower, employers and employees, and so on. Hence all earlier models were based on perfect information resulting in lack of credibility.

It is difficult to establish perfect information equilibrium between the seller and the buyer. Information asymmetry can be created by market to exploit market power. On the part of the manufacturers and traders taking the following measures reduces the information gap between the seller and the buyer, and limit the adverse effects of information asymmetry: a) educating the consumer of his rights and instituting protection measures; b) instituting agencies and mechanisms by governments and voluntary organizations to look after the interest of consumers; c) dissemination of consumer information through advertisement, publicity, brand name, price, word of mouth, and other means, d) issuing guarantees by firms for their products and services about the quality, and against product failures; e) conveying authenticity and identification of products to a consumer by using trademarks and brand names by the manufacturer; f) firms providing expert advice on the technology used in the product, spare parts and their supply, and about the needed infrastructure, all of which can help the consumer to compare and contrast different competing products and services and make his choice. For firms, the cost of information search acts as one of the decisive criteria in opting for the dissemination approach. Disclosing facts accurately and providing incentives to tell the truth by companies about their products and services eliminate or reduce information imperfections, and positively counter any adverse propaganda by competitors. In the Internet commerce, the emergence of a new type of intermediaries called "infomediaries" who by studying and matching unbiased the needs of individual customers and the market provide inputs to the buyer to make judicious choice.

Transparency helps create a level-playing field and thereby denies selective disclosure of sensitive information for a consideration. But transparency is disliked by certain sections of bureaucracy and politicians as it reduces their power for showing favoritism and receipt of reciprocal illegal favours. The best method of preventing transparency is by imposing secrecy under specious arguments. Secrecy is an artificially created scarcity; it gives rise to rents. Selling information for a consideration becomes an ingenious art. Economics of information and social reality tell us that problems arising out of unscrupulous means like secrecy cannot be fully eliminated, but the situation can be improved by instituting suitable laws and institutions to enforce information access.

Regulatory measures help bridge information gap in consumer world. General sources of consumer centered information are : direct observation of the product; information in the form of labels, product literature and media announcements; direct experience gained by use; and information gained through third parties (e.g., consumer reports). Indirect sources include information provided by trade associations and consumer forums. Information signals are also derived from prices, warrantees and service guarantees provided by manufacturers and dealers, seller's reputation, and advertisement about products. When these information sources do not fully meet the information requirements about markets, government may enter to overcome market failures through regulatory measures (Magat, 2002). Some of the examples for information regulation are: making it compulsory for manufactures to bring to the notice of consumers about the health hazards of smoking; legally binding manufactures to compulsorily display manufacturing date and expiry date, price data, risks if any on medicine bottles and packages. The most important measure has been the passing of consumer safety acts by governments. It is not that information regulation will fully prevent market failures, for government may not find it always easy to acquire and communicate the relevant information, and the cost of collection may also act as a deterrent for government action.

Providing consumer information has its complexities. The main problems center round: a) too much information or too scanty information hinders consumers to arrive at rational decision; b) cost and time factors involved in collecting and communicating information may inhibit providing information in time; c) highly technical nature of available information may make processing of information difficult for general consumers. This emphasizes the need for presenting information in understandable form. In the absence of full and correct information, consumers tend to make their decisions solely based on one or two characteristics (Magat, 2002). The impact assement of various consumer information provisions like use of symbols, product labels, consumer response to advertisement have been the subject of a number of consumer information theories.

In India, transaction costs are so high that creating a level playing ground for all for acquiring market information on equal footing by creating transparent and open information system is not a workable proposition. The workable solution lies in creating ethical and moral consciousness, patriotism and national character. Deprivation of information and education to certain sections of society due to historical reasons, like caste system, as it happened in India is a major cause of information asymmetry. This is gradually rectified by introducing reservation in employment and education fields. Reservation implies discriminatory privileges and hence may be condemned on efficiency grounds. But this is a narrow interpretation of the concept of the pecuniary efficiency of a system. Reservations not only rectify a historical injustice, but is in the interest of building continuing social harmony, which is so essential for economic development (Brahmananda, 2001). Imperfections in information may be reduced greatly by introducing stringent segmentary and discriminatory devices. Since enforcing such measures contain the risk of large-scale interference with freedom that we may accept inefficiency than forego freedom.

INFORMATION AND FIRMS

The conventional theories of economics are based on flow of material. In recent years, there is a growing trend to study economy as a system of structured information flow. Economic institutions are perceived to-day as instruments for allocating decision-making responsibilities and structuring information flow. Structure of institutions at a given time represents the social response to economize on information costs. As communication costs decrease due to technological progress institutions expand their geographical reach, thus leading to further economic development. Firms constitute a major segment of any economy. The structuring is effected by firms, which specialize in processing information needed to proper allocation of resources.

In a general sense, firms may be considered as specialized intermediators mediating between factory owners and householders as consumers. Though the textbook view of intermediation is production, when analyzed from the standpoint of information-based view of economy, it turns out to be organization of trade. The key constituent in the organization of trade is market-making firms. Market-makers coordinate the decisions made by households and producers of goods and services. Coordination itself is an information function with two-way flow of information, where as flow of material is unidirectional.

Intermediation. In retailing, intermediation involves both material and information flow, where as pure market-makers deal only with information flow. In a mixed economy (as in India) market-making is undertaken by the private firms and also by state enterprises. Information in market-making is related to several other features, such as ownership, labour, information costs, and organization of market-making.

Decision-making power is generally confirmed by ownership, and so ownership becomes the instrument for exploiting information in one's possession. The market-maker extracts rents, i.e., returns, from this information by buying and then reselling the product. In this way, he covers his costs of collecting information out of the profits on sales. The retailers acquire ownership from the market-maker, and adds his own local knowledge of the market. On the other hand, the producer exploits information by buying labour from his workers and converts it into products that he owns. An important implication of ownership is that the possessor of information tries to guarantee the buyer through the medium of information about the quality and other characteristics of the product, a point well made out by Stiglitz (Stiglitz, 2003). However, in practice the owner's right over the resources gets established by the way the property rights are defined and how well the effects of externality are covered.

Investment in research. Research is one of the most important determinants of accelerating the tempo of economic growth. If the problem for developed countries is one of investing in research, for the developing countries it is catching up with the more advanced countries. Many of the issues that are central to economics of information are also relevant to understanding research and development, such as the problems of appropriation, the fixed cost portion of investment in research which give rise to imperfections, and the public good nature of information. The important role of research and innovation in market economics is yet to be fully researched. It is observed, that in general, government intervention makes market equilibrium efficient (Stiglitz, 2004).

DIMINISHING RETURNS OR INCREASING RETURNS

Diminishing returns, i.e., negative feedback begets corrections that lead to predictable equilibrium- that is what classical economic theories say. These theories failed to explain satisfactorily the effects of technology adoption on the principles of economics. The main reasons were: a) classical theorist's preoccupation with market equilibrium in terms of supply versus demand, cost versus benefit, and so on; and b) the complexities involved in collecting, analyzing and interpreting information pertaining to technology and economics interface (Pool, 1997). For understanding modern high-technology economics it is increasing returns economics, i.e., positive feedbacks is the best method.

In many parts of the economy, stabilizing forces generated by diminishing returns do not seem to operate. Instead, positive feedback magnifies the effects of small economic shifts. Diminishing returns imply a single equilibrium point for the economy, but positive feedback (increasing returns) makes for many possible equilibrium points. Decreasing returns applied to resource-based economy (e.g., agriculture and mining) worked well because cost of production, by and large, remains unaffected by organization and economy of scale. Knowledge based segment of an economy is largely subject to increasing returns. Technology-based industries need large initial investments on research and development, and tooling, but the cost decreases due to incremental production. With increased scale of production unit cost slides down and increases profit. There are additional benefits which include: a) scope for further cost reduction due to gaining of manufacturing experience which leads to improvement in production processes; b) the experience gained in manufacturing one product may be utilized to make new products based on the same or similar technology; c) information exchange pertaining to a product that gets well established influences other consumers, thereby increase sale and profit.

Economic activities that hinge on increasing returns should be modeled not as static, deterministic problems, but as dynamic processes based on random events unrelated to the technology used and natural positive feedbacks, or nonlinearities. This is because even small random events further influenced by positive feedback over a period of time often determine the eventual outcome. Once random economic events select a particular path, the choice may become locked-in regardless of the advantages of the alternatives. This can be partly explained by the principle of least effort, and psychological aversion to change, besides the power of increasing returns. Once a person is satisfied with a particular product or service, he or she will be reluctant to change over to another one even if the latter product is technologically superior. This lock-in effect is a factor to be considered where there is a choice of competing technologies. Once a high technology product gets established in a competitive market "success breeds success" phenomenon implied in Zipf's law begins to operate (see chapter 4).

Positive and negative feedback concepts have grave implications for the formulation of policies in areas ranging from product and process development, research and development (R&D) policies, pooling of resources in joint ventures, marketing networks, technical knowledge and standards. Increasing returns theory influences tactical decision-making in the selection of technology, R&D initiative, and timing. Government economic policy-making need to be guided by the composition of economy. Modern economies are generally made up of a high technology industrial sector and the traditional natural resource dependent segment. Policy for the technological sector is guided by increasing return mechanism and is proactive, where as in traditional sectors the policy approach is dictated by decreasing returns and is reactive. Negative feedback economy relies on open market mechanism, anti-monopoly and no-subsidy measures leaving R & D decisions to individual companies. Policy for high technology sector necessitates promotion of technological R & D at the national level, encouraging joint ventures, creation of marketing networks and strategic alliances (including world-wide). These will help establish industry/product standards, and in exploitation of information and technology to gain competitive edge internationally. In this scenario, protectionism leads to a no-win situation to all the participants.

A technology that improves more rapidly and more people adopt it stands a better chance of survival due to a "selectional advantage". But, any random incident, even if it is trivial, can nullify the advantage. The positive feedback theories are beginning to portray that the economy is a process-dependent, organic and continuously evolving phenomena; and not a simple, deterministic and predictable mechanism as depicted by traditional economics (Arthur, 1990).

INFORMATION COST. ORGANIZATION STRUCTURE

Decision-making power, and the direction and pattern of flow of information decide the type and the organizational structure of each unit. Impact of information costs is reflected in the origin of government bureaucracy, shaping of factory system, development of global market, structuring and restructuring of trade (Casson, 1997).

The elements of cost of information get included in labour contracts. However, it is not easy to calculate the cost of information involved in the various subunits of a task. Even if it is possible to fix the information cost for each subunit, the cost of arriving at it will be extremely high. The influence of information costs on the specificity of contracts also applies to market transactions. Market-makers try to reduce the information cost in trading. One method of doing it is to substitute versatile goods for specific goods. If the cost of collecting information is high, then there is a trade-off between the cost of collection and the quality of decision-making. There is also the problem of deciding how much information to be collected. Inadequate information leads to lop-sided decisions, and too much information collection is wasting managerial resources. There is an organizational problem of division of labour in collecting and organizing information. Division of labour into more number of task groups leads to more specialization, which in turn imparts greater dynamism by way of increasing relevancy of information collected and its effective use. However, any specialization and increase in the number of people collecting information increase the communication cost to be invested in integrating information. These impact on the organization structure of both overall economy and individual firms. Communication costs can be lowered by standardization of procedures.

It is advantageous to the firm if the synthesizer of information is also the decision-maker. Then it is easier for him to encode his synthesis in the form of a decision than to simply share his synthesized knowledge with functional specialists. Synthesis of knowledge involves both tacit information of unique and unfamiliar nature gathered mostly from external sources and explicit information obtained from specialist functionaries/divisions of the firm.

In economizing information costs to the firm, an important consideration is to decide when and at what stage collection of information pertaining to a situation must be terminated. Sequential collection of information and the stage of synthesis enable the synthesizer to decide whether he has in his stock adequate information needed for making decision on the given situation/problem. Adding of additional information results in diminishing marginal returns. The cost of information and investment are interrelated. Cheaper information cost encourages investment.

Information cost and Transaction Cost. It is generally assumed that information cost is covered in transaction cost. Information cost and transaction cost are independent of each other, but closely connected (Casson, 1997). Transaction cost is cost incurred for establishing the transaction, and cost incurred to ensure that the contract is fulfilled, i.e., information content of the transaction is fully implemented to the letter and the spirit. In a property transaction, the title deed transferring the ownership rights and information collected about the property form the information cost, and the brokerage paid to the intermediary, legal fees incurred in drafting the deed, and the registration charge constitute transaction cost.

A major portion of information cost goes towards establishing ownership of property and safeguarding property rights (Casson, 1997). Information about property rights is the vehicle through which banking system, insurance business, and corporate units by virtue of shareholding in the company establish ownership. Coordination of information in these sectors has also to deal with trusteeship characteristics of resources entrusted to them.

All transactions are preceded by interactions between individuals and/or organizations engaged in search, coordination, and supervision of numerous information involving activities in the transaction or exchange, such as price, terms of contract, customization, warehousing, tax implications, and so on. The feedback from the interactions helps identify transaction costs. Transaction costs serve as important criteria in decision-making in areas such as outsourcing of activities, design of optimal organization structures, and cost of information gathering in the market. Use of Internet and associated facilities bring down information access cost tremendously (Ricart-Costa et al., 2004). At the same time, it also involves risks associated with Internet crimes and security of data.

Most of the transactions we enter into in daily life, in organizations, and in trade are contractual. In addition to contractual transactions, we are also bound by many conventions established by society. For example, a red signal at a traffic junction signifies a 'stop'. Conventions are coming together of people to set up common understanding to regulate their transactions; it is a sort of tacit agreement by which all the participants are bound to abide, (Sugden, 2002). Conventions reduce uncertainty in transactions. A lower degree of uncertainty in turn reduces information asymmetry leading to savings in transaction cost. Thus, the notion of convention is closely related to that of transaction cost (Warneryd, 2002).

Imitation. The term 'imitation' is interpreted in different ways: as a human instinct, as a learning method, an optimal response to a particular type of uncertainty, and as a fundamental social process. Imitation is an act of copying with or without the consent of the innovator. Imitation is one of the avenues of obtaining information belonging to others without taking the trouble of himself discovering information. It is a means of economizing information cost. The originator may employ several strategies based on his own behaviour and anticipated responses of imitators to his strategies, as well as calculated secrecy or disclosure through anonymity of his behaviour. He can still make a profit by outsmarting the imitators. Imitation raises many other issues of entrepreneurship that are yet to be understood. While imitator saves the cost of discovering information, the discoverer is cheated from full enjoyment of his rights. The latter aspect may discourage organizations from investing on the production of innovative knowledge. When the original owner refuses to part with the information, for some reason, imitation is an easy alternative. Imitation is a cheaper alternative to acquire innovative information rather than re-creating it. Imitation carries risk as there may be difference between imitation and the original (Casson, 1997).

Rational imitations may lead to the formation of conventions. When one chooses to imitate the choices of others against his own perception formed by limited information, it gives rise to what is called 'informational cascade'. Such a cascade is based on weak information and its behavioural impact may last for a long time. At the same time, even a small change or information exposure can alter the consumer behaviour (Hirshleifer, 2002). Successful entrepreneurship depends on one's own knowledge of markets, knowledge of technology, knowledge of people, and knowledge of the firm.

COORDINATION

Coordination is the process of achieving harmonious integration of the activities of different individuals in an organization or a group. Coordination is essential to the effective functioning of any organization. Without proper coordination no institution, mission or economy can properly function. Coordination requires information transmission and motivation. Organizations cannot function unless each individual in the organization receives information informing his role, and in turn the relevant information from the individual is coordinated and used effectively. Transmission of information goes hand in hand with incentives. In economics, quite often prices symbolize the mode of transmitting information, e.g., wages in the case of workers, price in the case of sale transactions. Coordination of information arises in every economic activity including decision-making, planning, flow of organizational authority, mergers and de-mergers of firms, and statutory reporting to authorities (Campbell, 1995).

A broader view of economy shows that a network reflects the flow of information that is used to coordinate the flow of material goods and services. Seen from the angle of markets and firms, a network may be seen as a distinctive high-trust method of coordination and from the viewpoint of coordination, network is essentially an institutional alternative to the market and the firm (Casson, 1997).

It is reasonable to think that wider dispersion of information will improve coordination, and improved coordination leads to higher stability of the market. Yet, some of the most information rich economies are most susceptible to instability. Innovative information also needs collection and organization. From the world of knowledge, the knowledge items appropriate to the field of activity of a firm need to be demarcated. Such information is often subject to political jurisdiction covered by intellectual property rights and embargos. Prospecting for information of innovative potential is one of probability. If there is competition among discoverers of new knowledge, the cost of acquiring them comes down. The principle of diminishing returns applies to innovative information. Coordinating investment in innovative information calls for a different strategy than in information used in general working. Maintaining secrecy of information or sharing it is one of the decisive choice factors in planning of coordination. Trust among the involved parties is a basic factor that influences sharing of information.

From the perspective of neoclassical economics, information may be divided into factual information and conceptual information. Factual information is the most common type of information that surrounds economic transactions, market makers and firms, including retailers. Factual information may be further divided into persistent information and transitory type of information. This classification has important implications in understanding the different roles information play in establishing the significance of each type of information in the work of coordination, methods of storage, and use of information.

COMPLEXITY, VOLATILITY AND UNCERTAINTY

What distinguishes modern economy from the earlier economy is the sheer complexity. Complexity is caused by the large-scale application of technology, the driving force that is shaping the economy. A modern technology project needs support from a multitude of other technologies, integration of thousands of parts, employment of large manpower with different skills, huge investment, outsourcing of items and services, large-scale coordination, intricate organizational structure and managerial expertise. Outcome of complex systems are not completely predictable, and hence involves decisions on how much uncertainty is acceptable. On the technological side, the problem is about understanding of scientific and engineering principles and designs, which calls for expert advice, a function of information. Because of availability of different technological and design parameters choices are to be made between competing technologies, and between available means to adopt it. Thus, the study of complexity enters information economics. Any modern technology is the product of a complex interplay between its designers and the larger society in which it develops. Non-technical issues exert influence on the development of simplest technologies, and more so in sophisticated branches like computers, and genetic engineering. Complexity is a new feature of today's technology applications causing uncertainty about the consequences of the technology on society (Pool, 1997). In economic transactions information complexities vary with the type of transaction, and hence, the transaction cost too varies. For example, information complexity in the merger of two companies is not the same as in booking a hotel room on Internet.

A salient feature of modern economic activity is volatility in the functioning of the economy, especially in the market-oriented activities. Volatility may be traced to several causes, the prime cause being the impact of technological advances and the communication revolution. Volatility introduces uncertainty into information, which impacts on the cost of obtaining information. To cope with information uncertainty demands a different mental framework, particularly at the level of policy making and in interpreting information signals. Knowledge workers have to reorient their horizon to adjust to the frequent economic shocks injected by the economy.

Information and Uncertainty. Knowledge is incomplete, fragmentary and provisional in character (see chapter 3). Uncertainty results from this characteristic of knowledge. The impact of this characteristic is apparent in the field of economics. Uncertainty is a feature of many markets and information helps in reducing it. To give an example consider the case of Mr. B buying 50000 equity shares of TELCO at Rs. 2000/- per share influenced by a news channel report that the company has secured a huge export order at a favorable price. The next day, the share price crashes due to the decision of the government to raise the prices of diesel oil and petrol. This illustrates a simple effect of uncertainty. All decision makers whether they are individuals or corporate managers or administrators have to deal with uncertainty. Misinformation and lack of information may lead to uncertainty, whereas information reduces it. When there is uncertainty, there is usually the possibility of reducing it by the acquisition of information. There is a distinction between *economic variables* like price, i.e., those variables of interest to an economic agent and *signals*, i.e., other variables. A variable represents values of changing or uncertain factors (Arrow, 1973).

Uncertainty affects the present and the future outcomes, but the past often provides a clue to the future behavior under normal conditions. The seriousness of the consequences of uncertainty depends on the nature of the uncertainty factor, the degree of uncertainty, and the field of activity. The nature of uncertainty in science is different from that of uncertainty in commerce, which is different from that of uncertainty in individuals. Uncertainty may relate to the behaviour of known factors or to that of totally unknown factors. Uncertainty are of various types of which two important types are: a) market uncertainty, and b) technological or event uncertainty (Hirshleifer and Riley,1979). The effects of uncertainty could be adverse, beneficial or of no consequence. Dealing with uncertainty involves:

1. Recognition of uncertain factors (problem variables).
2. Ascertaining the probable effects of uncertainty (value).
3. Reducing uncertainty (solution).
4. Preparing to meet the effects of uncertainty due to known factors (contingency plans).

5. Coping with the consequences of uncertainty due to totally unknown factors (no solution in advance).

Decision-making under uncertainty assumes vital importance in economics and in management. Heuristics, theory of probability, other statistical methods, and hunch are some of the means employed in managing uncertainty. A key input in all these methods is information

SUBSTITUTION OF INFORMATION FOR GOODS

Using information as an intermediate substitute for goods is a common feature in many market transactions. Just as money has purchasing power over goods, information has delivering power over goods in intermediate transactions as could be seen in the following example. A firm A in Singapore contracts to buy 60,000 tons of tea from Tata Tea Ltd, Mumbai (India), and the buyer then sells the commodity to another firm B in London, which in turn sells it to a company C in Warsaw (Poland). The commodity is directly dispatched from Mumbai to Warsaw bypassing Singapore and London. In this case, information acts as a substitute for tea in the physical transfer of the commodity except in the last transaction. Intermediate ownership transfer is effected by transfer of information signals. Information substitution for goods derives its unique advantage by bridging time and space, and replacing material. It is likely that information substitution will replace most of traditional methods of transfer by means of instantaneous storage and transmission of large amounts of data and information cheaply over large distances through electronic mode. Already, in a large number of national and international trade and banking transactions information is substituting commodities and funds by involving only information exchange.

Procedural Conformity. Economic information to be accepted as valid must follow prescribed procedures. On the contrary, validity of scientific information depends on repeatability of experimental results and supply of mathematical or empirical proofs, and not on authentication. The truth of the information that Halley's Comet was visible to the naked eye on the earth in 1980 does not depend on the recorder, the date of recording, and any witness to the record. It can be established by calculating the orbital period of the comet. The truth of an economic event that took place some time in the past cannot be established by mathematical proof or experiment. Economic, social and political information to be accepted need formal authentication by social instruments created for such purposes. This is because economic, social and political events are not experimentally repeatable as it is impossible to create the exact environment under which the event took place. Even if repeated, it is unlikely to give the same results equivalent to the original results in all respects. Reliability of many of the economic contracts depends on mutual trust among the contracting parties or on formal recording. To ensure truth of the events and reliability of such information, social instruments like norms of procedure, rules, regulations, and forms of recording have been devised. The following examples illustrate the point:

1. Imprinting © or 'Copyright' on the work establishes an author's intellectual property rights.
2. A sale deed is not legally valid unless the execution of the deed fully complies with all the set procedures.
3. In a court of law, oral evidence is not accepted unless it is made under oath.

The instrument of procedural conformity tries to:

1. Provide sufficient safeguards to the enforcement of transactional obligations.
2. Lay down uniformly applicable standard procedures for effecting deals and in enforcing compliance with the terms of the deal.
3. Help in verifying facts and in establishing truth.

Procedural conformity norms invest information signals

with the requisite sanctity and authority. Sanctity comes from social customs, religious and moral conventions. Authority is transferred by executive and judicial processes. Some of the adverse effects of the instruments of procedural conformity are:

1. Prescribing a plethora of procedures, rules and forms breeds inefficiency and corruption.
2. It gives rise to delay and infructuous expenditure.
3. Control passes on to bureaucracy and into legal domain.

A system that works more on mutual trust than on bureaucratic norms and form filling appears to provide reasonable freedom for action and also sufficient safeguards. Benefit-cost analysis forms the most important decision criterion in dealing with situations of breech of contract. Any decision as to the course of action to be followed will rest on the trade-off between various options.

CLOSURE

Information performs signalling function in economics. Information is embedded in all economic activities, and any change in the activity is reflected by a change in their information state. Information signals are mostly in the form of statistical data, indices, and ratios, as well as in the form of measures such as price, unit cost, and so on. Information signals serve four main purposes: a) as an input for planning; b) help in conducting the activity; c) serve as a diagnostic tool; and d) help in devising remedial measures in case of disruptions in implementation. By studying the nature, strength and effects of the information signals embedded in an economic activity we get the insight of their functioning. As most of the economic activities are of a continuous nature, information gets generated continuously. Hence, it is essential to setup mechanisms to monitor information signals on a continuous basis.

The major flaw in formal economic modelling has been the assumption that information is perfect, although it was known to be not so, but ignored as of no consequence. It has been shown by Stiglitz and others that even a small amount of imperfection could profoundly affect the nature of equilibrium.

Macroeconomic planning and implementation relies on economic signals like: GDP, production statistics, employment data, growth projections, export-import figures, and a number of other signals. Budget is one of the foremost originators of economic signals.

In microeconomics, information signals show the state of health of markets and firms. Information signals play an important role in many economic activities and features like: information asymmetry, technology application, market volatility and uncertainty. Asymmetry of information is a common feature of all market functioning. Reducing asymmetry is a significant issue facing markets, customers, and regulators.

If diminishing returns (negative feedback) ruled resource-based economy, it is increasing returns (positive feedback) that rules knowledge-based sectors of economy. Information cost is a significant factor in economics and market functioning. Information cost and transaction cost are independent of each other, but are closely related. Imitation is a means of economizing information cost.

Decision-making power, the direction, quantum and pattern of flow of information in an organization represent its type and structure. Without proper coordination of information no institution, mission, or economy can properly function. It is involved in all economic functions like decision-making, planning, flow of organizational authority, mergers and demerges, and statutory reporting to authorities. Coordination is also communicating and motivating. Quite often prices symbolize the mode of transmitting information. Complexity, volatility and uncertainty are three salient features of modern economic functioning. In all the three features information acts as a causer and as an effectible. Information and information signals often substitute goods in numerous economic transactions like transfer of money, sale and delivery of goods. Economic information in transactions, and in reporting to become valid must conform to prescribed procedures. The grave consequences of failure to monitor information signals, and act upon them in time are illustrated by the U. S. subprime crisis (September 2008), and its conductive effects on the global financial system. Economic signals thus, serve as a new mode of analyzing economic functions and conducting economic activities. In other words, economic signals provide a new approach to the study of economics.

REFERENCES

Arrow, K.J. Information and Economic Behavior. Stockholm, Federation of Swedish Industries, 1973.

Arthur, W. Brian. Positive feedbacks in the economy. *Scientific American 262(2): 80-85, Feb.* 1990.

Brahmananda, P.R. India: Asymmetry in committee's information. *Business line* (Cheinnai). October 13, 2001.

Campbell, Donald E. Incentives, Motivation and the Economics of Information. New York, Cambridge University Press, 1995.

Casson, Mark. Information and Organization: A New Perspective on the Theory of Firm. Oxford (U.K.), Oxford University Press, 1997 (Paperback, 2001).

Hirshleifer, David. Informational Cascades and Social Conventions. Pp.300-307. *In* Palgrave Dictionary of Economics and the Law. Newman, Peter. Ed. Vol. 2. New York, Macmillan, 2002.

Hirshleifer, J. and Riley, J.G. The analysis of uncertainty and information. An expository survey. *Journal of Economic Literature* 17:1375-1421, 1979.

Lakshmanasamy, T. New information, new institutions and economic development. *The Asian Economic Review* 45 (3): 425-439, Dec. 2003.

Magat, Wesley A. Information Regulation. Pp. 307-311. *In* Palgrave Dictionary of Economics and the Law. Newman, Peter. Ed. Vol. 1. New York, Macmillan, 2002.

Mistry, Percy S. What bailout? The treasury will earn profit. (The Global Financial Crisis. Part III). *Business Standard,* Tuesday 7, Oct. 2008.

Pool, Robert. Beyond Engineering. How Society Shares Technology. New York, Oxford University Press, 1997.

Ricart-Costa, Joan E.; Subirana, Brian; and Valor-Sabatier, Josep. Sources of Information Value: Strategic Framing and Transformation of the Information Industries. London, Palgrave, 2004.

Spence, A,M. An economist's view of information. *Annual Review of Information Science and Technology* 9: 57-78, 1974.

Stiglitz, Joseph E. Information and the change in the paradigm in economics, Part I and II. *American Economist* 47 (2): Fall 2003 (6pp.); 48(1): Spring 2004 (17pp.).

Sugden, Robert. Conventions. Pp. 453-460. *In* Palgrave Dictionary of Economics and the Law. Newman, Peter. Ed. Vol.1. New York, Macmillan, 2002.

Warneryd, Karl. Conventions and Transaction Costs. Pp. 460-465. *In* Palgrave Dictionary of Economics and the Law. Newman, Peter. Ed. Vol.1. New York, Macmillan, 2002.

Access and Servicing

18

Users and Information Processes

Information in its record form, such as books, journal articles, newspapers, computer records, albums, recorded CDs, and the like need processing and managing to facilitate users of the texts in exploring information for their purposes. Processing of information texts differs from, but is related to some of the cognitive and intellectual processes described in chapter 4. Cognitive processes are directly involved in the creation of knowledge or in changing an existing knowledge structure, whereas information processing acts upon information already created. Processing of information and the working of human memory follows distinctive patterns. Most of the intellectual processes described below are designed to simplify things for the brain and to increase its operational efficiency. Thus, there is a psychological explanation behind these processes. In abstraction, the explanation is that human mind remembers only the gist of the matter or experience rather than the particulars of what one experiences. The hypothesis behind interpretation is that people interpret information by making inferences, and then remember the inferences as part of original interpretation. The cognitive basis of integration of information is that we abstract meaning of an event/text, and that meaning is put together with the rest of our knowledge to form a coherent whole (Benjafield, 1996). The economic principle behind different intellectual processes is to increase efficiency and reduce cost in acquiring and utilizing information. Information processing may be done by mediatory agencies like libraries, search engines, newspapers or by end users of information, such as reporters, consultants, lawyers, advisors, research workers, imparters of education, managers, administrators, and individuals in their daily encounters. Functions of libraries, lawyers and consultants are explained further to show how different process act.

A library collects information records in different media, such as books and journals and makes them available to users. In order to do this, it must collect the documents, analyze their subject contents, find the terms to surrogate the document, describe them, store them, and provide retrieval devices. The database compiler analyses the documents, evaluates the contents for their significance, abstracts/extracts the information contained in them, may store the original documents and even reproduces the abstracts and the originals for clients. A lawyer correlates the aspects of the case to the relevant laws, interprets the issues in the case in terms of applicable laws, cites the previous interpretations and judgments, and summarizes the case. A management consultant analyses the problem entrusted to him, collects all the relevant outside and in-house information that has a bearing on the problem, evaluates, interprets and correlates the various factors represented by the information, arrives at the possible solutions, summarizes his findings and may submit the findings in the form of a report. The investment advisor collects, analyses and stores investment information, evaluates them, compares them with alternative investment avenues and advises his clients. The analysis of work in the above cases shows that processing of information consists of methods or processes of searching, collecting, analyzing, and organizing information and information texts. This is also true of information processing by individuals and governments. Amenability of information and its texts to cognitive, linguistic and physical processing is a characteristic of information. Processing of information must be geared to the relevant information facets of the end users of information and their information needs.

USE AND USERS OF INFORMATION

Several important aspects of knowledge, its characteristics and use have been discussed in earlier chapters. Use of information by individuals and organizations are considered here.

Utilization of Information. Broadly stating, information is used to promote material well-being, social well-being, and spiritual well-being, which may be further detailed into: a) information for advancing frontiers of knowledge; b) creation of wealth; c) decision-making and management; d) social and personal development; e) recreation and entertainment; and f) spiritual attainment and development of values.

Use of information takes place either in a personal context or in an organizational and larger societal context or in their combination. Ultimately, the use of information takes place at the level of the individual.

Information is used by individuals in a personal context for: a) personal satisfaction, b) earning a livelihood, c) self-development, d) entertainment, and e) exercising one's citizen related rights and discharge of obligations (i.e., "citizen information"), and others. As an example, citizen information is further analyzed to show the complexities of servicing information. Citizen information includes information on hospitals, nursing homes and health hazards; environmental pollution; consumer protection against misleading or false advertisement; risks and hazards of shopping; social concerns covering alcoholism, drug abuse, birth control, special services for youth, handicapped and minorities; educational facilities; political decisions on political issues including the attitudes of candidates for public offices towards public issues (Jones, 1985). Access to this type of information is mostly through the enquiry desks or "help lines" at the concerned agencies; and nowadays through outsourced call service centers. Non-availability of, and inefficient access to this type of information generally lead to exploitation of ordinary citizens, and corruption in public services and utilities. This leads to lack of accountability by service providers and inefficiency. Whether "we are citizens or slaves to ignorance may depend upon our ability to obtain and use the available information."(Wessel, 1975, p. 4.). Availability and use of citizen information has not received much attention in India. The problems of access to citizen information is far more serious in India than in the developed countries. Processing of information to meet citizen information generally centers round query type answers regarding factual information, and supply of texts relating to rules, laws and practices.

In the societal and organizational context, information uses fall broadly into the categories of: a) education, research and development, b) arts and crafts, c) creation of wealth and increasing productivity, d) political, social and moral development, e) management and control, and f) entertainment and leisure. In the context of information in management, the most basic function of information is to control action in an organized system and thereby operate the organization (Scarrott, 1989).

Analyzing information into its basic use components indicates the following compulsions behind using information:

to know	to create	to confirm	to satisfy self
to explain	to destroy	to support	to satisfy others
to decide	to refute	to confuse	to manage
to improve	to control	to mislead	to blackmail

to influence to empower to change to predict

Psychology of Users. Utilizing information is affected by many factors including: a) previous experience, b) time factor, c) perception, d) false perception, e) differences in logical thought, f) social factors, and f) language (Kemp, 1976). To the above must be added another important factor, namely, motivation. The psychology and purpose of use influence the method of processing and supplying of information. The methods vary from the rigorous approach employed by disciplines such as science to that of less rigorous, factual and instantaneous approach as in meeting the information needs of routine life. Handling of information (knowledge) may be categorized into: proto-scientific, everyday casual, expert way and the "political" way (van Lohuizen, 1986). A new revolutionary development affecting psychology of use is the ccoming into age of electronic communication of information, particularly the use of Internet as a mass media. This has created a number of new social, economic, and psychological basics affecting users of information and psychology of use.

Producers of electronic form of communicating texts are constantly introducing new features into the communication format. It is becoming more informal, more abbreviated, and matter of fact. For example, in e-mail communication of pragmatic information non-linguistic cues like aural and visual compositions and gestures— a psycholinguistic advantage in interpreting a message which is part of the face-to-face communication— cannot be transmitted. This disadvantage is tried to be overcome to some extent by using semiotic techniques like use of keywords or phrases. This drawback can be further reduced by continued and frequent interaction which facilitates enhanced awareness of their communication partners (Menchik and Tian, 2008). It is not beyond our imagination to expect that advances in technology may soon find a method of transmitting aura, as visual element has already become a part of teleconferencing.

User Studies. In business and industry marketing is a vital function, since what is produced needs to be sold. Selling needs knowing the psychology of the customer, their needs and preferences in relation to the commodity or service produced—an activity covered by market research and analysis. What is true of business is also true of information, but with a major difference. Although information in its record form is a physical entity, its value and use lies in its knowledge content, which is intangible. Yet the results of analysis and research on the use and users of information can be employed to maximize the use of information- an area of study, named "use" studies (Kunz et al., 1977), and "information needs and uses" (Dervin and Nilan, 1986). Insights gained through user studies serve as invaluable guidelines or feedback to process and package information records, to communicate and disseminate their contents. However, these studies deal mostly with the use of information by individuals in an organizational context using information systems. Utilization of information by users is the final objective of all information activities. The processing of information and the exploitation of the manipulative characteristics of information are to serve the purpose of maximizing the use of information. Information processes are to ensure that the information supplied is relevant and is of value to the user.

POST-PROCESSING OF INFORMATION

Work analysis of handling of information by different categories of persons and professions shows the use of following important processes and techniques listed in Table 1.

Many of the processes and techniques listed in Table-1 like analysis, correlation, and interpretation are used by all persons, and they form an integral part of general thinking process. Some of the techniques and processes like indexing, surrogating, and translating have become specialized and professionalized. And a few others processes like coding and programming fall under machine systems. These processes and techniques are further explained in brief.

Table 1. Some of the important processes and techniques used in processing information

Type	*Process/technique*
1. a) Intellectual processes (general)	Description, abstraction, extraction, summarization, paraphrasing, reviewing, explanation, analysis, synthesis, interpretation, interrelation, correlation, interpolation, comparison, illustration, valuation, evaluation, structuring, editing.
b) Intellectual processes (retrieval)	Coding, indexing, classification, structuring, surrogating, arrangement, alphabetization.
2. Language related	Translation, transliteration, communication, alphabetization.
3. Physical processes	Storage, transference, reproduction, formatting, citation, arrangement, suppression, destruction, dissemination.
4. Machine processes	Programming, Information Architecture, Knowledge representation.
5. Others	

Description. It is giving an account in words of a given concept, thing, work, event or situation. Description enables one to get a picture of a given item. Description could take different forms like narrative— short as well as exhaustive; follow different approaches, such as chronological, and thematic; and could be made more effective by use of audio, visual, and other means, such as pictures, slides etc. Certain words have the power to represent or describe more comprehensively the contents of a given text better than others (Wren and Martin, 2003). In information science such words are known as "descriptors" or "keywords" and they serve as principal information access and information retrieval tools. In journalism, describing an event, situation or account of a transaction to another agent or authority is reporting.

Abstraction, Extraction. Summarization. These are primarily concerned with volume-wise reduction of a given information text without modifying the basic thought contents. It is a selection process. They are intended to reduce noise, avoid repetition, and bring greater clarity. They are time and labour saving processes which enable faster transmission of information, and increase the user's power of grasping and also save his time.

Abstraction. It is the art of making a brief summary of the essential content of a record, such as an article, book, speech, report or other works by presenting the main points as in the original, but having no independent literary value. An abstract can be indicative, informative, critical, or written from a particular point of view (Reitz, 2004). An abstract usually appears at the beginning of a technical paper, thesis or conference proceedings. It is a concise description of the problem addressed, the methodology followed in resolving the problem, the findings and conclusions. It is a distillate that reflects the entire work, highlighting the critical issues raised in the text (Warrier, 2008). Abstracting could take different forms depending upon the objective of making the abstract.

Extraction. It is to take out a portion from an information text based on some criteria or to fulfil a specific purpose. In the information context, extraction refers to one or more lengthy quotations from a book or other work set within the main text of another work. In a more general sense, any piece taken from one work and used in another, sometimes to represent the whole (Reitz, 2004). An *excerpt* is an extract, generally longer than a quotation.

Summarization. A summary is a shortened version of a text, discarding explanations, examples and elaborate technical details. It is usually given at the end of the text. In summarizing, we keep in view the persons to whom it is made and it is to serve their purpose. A summary follows a persuasive style to help the user of the summary by highlighting important points in the text. Summaries take different forms such as: executive summary to help the decision-maker; general summary to provide the reader an overall picture of the text without highlighting or ignoring any particular aspect; and legal summary to help judges to evaluate a case. The summary maker may disagree with some of the views in the original text, but he is not allowed to distort the original views. Nowadays, computer programmes providing instant summaries to a given length of text are available (e.g., MSWord: Tools-Autosummarize). However, these 'autosummaries' miss the value of human judgment, which employs cognitive and linguistic skills to assess the critical points needed for decision-making (Warrier, 2008).

Review. A review in the context of academic, research or literary publication is an evaluative account of the literary or research work. Such reviews are undertaken before the publication. Sometimes an author may submit his work to his peers to examine the worth of an academic or research work to find its suitability for publication. The reviewer assesses the work in terms methodology applied, the experimental details given, if any, validity of the conclusions drawn, and the completeness of the text in terms of references etc. The reviewer, always a knowledgeable person in the field, may suggest to the author to modify the text, if necessary. A post-publication review is done to bring to the notice of intended audience through newspapers, magazines and journals or electronic media about a newly published book, artistic performance or exhibit. A review can be critical, descriptive, reportorial or comparative. Reviews could be of different genre like book reviews, annual reviews, quarterly reviews, and *literature review.*

A literature review is done as a part of a research programme resulting in an academic thesis. The reviewing involves selecting available documents, published and unpublished (pertaining to the research/academic topic), containing information, ideas, data and evidence written from a particular standpoint to fulfill certain objectives or explain certain views on the nature of the topic and how it is to be investigated, including effective evaluation of these documents, in relation to the research being proposed. Before initiating work on the project one needs to know what knowledge/ information already exists on the subject, and thereby equips himself with the required information background (Hart, 1998). Literature review is also known as literature survey.

Analysis. It is a basic step in all information processing work. It is an intellectual activity on which many other functions of information depend. It is through analysis that one can know the contents or subject matter covered by a given information text, ascertain the context, relevance, currency, reliability and utility of information contained in the text. It is possible to correlate the different aspects and ascertain the significance of different items of information contained in a text only after analysis. Analysis is the first step in classification, evaluation, and decision-making.

Correlation. It is to establish the relationship between concepts, and between ideas contained in a given text or with an outside text. In correlating, one has options in the selection of criteria of relationship, such as cause and effect, similarity.

Interpolation. It is to alter a given text by inserting new or additional matter. It is intended to supply a missing item in a text to make it complete.

Interpretation. Used in a general sense, interpretation refers to explaining the contents of a text in a simple manner. In the cognitive sense, interpretation is a particular way of thinking. Where a text contains a concept which is amenable to different explanations, to interpret is to bring out those explanations to give a better or a new insight of the text.

Comparison and Contrast. To compare is to examine the character or qualities of two or more persons, things or text items especially for the purpose of showing or discovering similarities or differences. Contrasting is to compare two like objects by means of which dissimilar qualities are made prominent. To alter or corrupt (a text) by inserting new or foreign matter (Webster's, 1993).

Structuring. To give form to a text or thought contents so that it becomes organized into a pattern is the purpose of structuring. Different parts of a system are organically integrated to make it a meaningful whole. By indicating the components and the relationship between them, the structure enables us to study the properties of the system. Organization of knowledge relays on structuring.

Editing. Editing is the intellectual process of ensuring that any written text (even a letter or a note) at the time of its final presentation is in a readable form and format, conveying the contents of the text in an orderly way, following the rules of grammar. It is the process of converting a draft into a final text. In publishing industry, editing is a specialized function entrusted with the task of preparing the manuscript or transcript submitted for publication by an author or reporters for final publication following set editorial standards and guidelines. Editing for movies, music records, electronic network, newspapers, and others have developed on specialized lines keeping with their distinctive features.

Valuation. Information has value; it can be valued and evaluated. The nature of value depends on the user of information and the purpose for which it is sought. Thus, information could have esteem value, apparent value, use value, aesthetic value, positive value, negative value, and other values. The process of valuation makes use of certain economic concepts, which are discussed in a later chapter. In most cases, information gets its value only when someone uses it. Hence, use value is a better method of establishing value of information. Value of information to individuals in their social context, other than in social behaviour, has not received much attention although it is of great importance. Value of information is also dependent on the information environment. Every time information is acted upon there will be an alteration in the value of the outcome information. Manipulative processes alter the value of the input information. The value adding processes do not change the intrinsic worth of a given chunk of information. This process can only facilitate access and filter information to suit specific requirements.

Evaluation of Information. It is the process of assessing the value or suitability of information in relation to the requirements of a specific task or programme or user. Value of information cannot be considered in isolation of the user of that information, the ultimate evaluator. Information gets evaluated at different stages- by the creator, the producer, server, and the user of information. Without evaluation, providing access to useful and relevant information is almost impossible. Fruitful evaluation employs either exchange value or use value of information. Both these values are related to benefits- pecuniary and non-pecuniary, resulting from the use of information. Evaluation of information helps in avoidance of wasteful expenditure of time, efforts and money involved in going through a mass of unevaluated information, unevaluated in relation to the specific requirement of the user. Since making precise evaluation of given information is often difficult, the evaluator keeps the probability of use in mind.

Coding. Coding is a system of symbols designed primarily to restrict comprehension (as of a message) to particular individuals. It is a system in which arbitrary meanings are assigned to letters, numbers, words or other symbols and often used to procure brevity as well as secrecy. Coding in computer technology (and software systems) refers to a specialized system of symbols developed for introducing information and instructions to a computer (Webster's, 1993). A class number (in library) is a code designed to indicate the subject of a book.

Indexing. It is the process of alphabetically arranging lists of headings consisting of the names of persons, places, and subjects treated in a written work or other forms of records with page numbers to guide the reader to the place in the text where information pertaining to the heading is found (Cleveland and Cleveland, 2001). Indexing is not limited to records. An index may be provided to locate information about any item in an organized collection such as a museum of art, museum of toys. Sometimes an index can also serve the purpose of a detailed contents list, if the items in the text are covered comprehensively by the index. Indexes are of different types, such as: name index, subject index, book index, periodicals index, permuted title index, string index (e.g., keyword in context), citation index, classified index, coordinate index, cumulative index, newspaper index, multi-media index, faceted index, first-line index, and others. A concordance is also an index to the words occurring in a complete text.

Indexing helps in locating a particular item of information in a text or a required document in a collection. It is alphabetical in arrangement and is based on natural language terms. However, in an automated system indexing need not follow alphabetical arrangement. Access to information through subject is the most sought approach (the other being author) in information access systems, which is fulfilled by indexing by subject. Indexing language, i.e., the access or search terms with their in-built semantic and syntactic features may be of either natural language or controlled language. A natural language indexing is one, wherein the index terms are taken from the text or title or abstract of the text. A controlled or artificial language is one wherein the designer of the indexing system or the indexer provides formalized and organized concepts in the form of words or codes (Aitchison, 1982). Lists of subject headings, thesauri, authority lists of keywords are examples of controlled language indexing terms.

A controlled language indexing, not excluding

classification, has to take care of two types of relationships — between words, and between subjects (semantic and syntactic features). Foskett sees three types of semantic relations: equivalence, hierarchical, and affinitive/associative with further categorization as given below (Foskett, 1977):

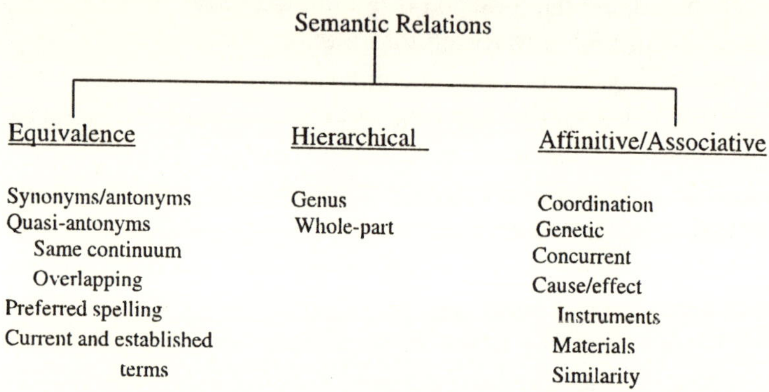

Fig. 1. Semantic relations in controlled language indexing

Use of 'See', 'See also', 'Broad term', 'Narrow term', 'Related term', 'Used for' are some of the indexing devices employed to take care of some semantic relations.

Syntactic relations establish the role of terms in coordinating different concepts and in properly expressing a concept or subject so that indexing improves the relevance of retrieved items. Pre-coordinate indexing methods like rotation of keywords, cross referencing, permutation and shunting of words, and Preserved Context Indexing System rely on syntactic relations. Indexers and designers of indexing systems can benefit greatly from linguistic research for example, the concept of "epistemes" or "constructional meanings" make "the meaning of a systematic constructive work more than the sum of the meanings of its constituent alone" (Bloch, 1953). Indexing is one of the methods employed in IR. A closely allied technique to indexing is classification. Indexing by natural language terms and by classification schemes with artificial notation are similar in structure, controls and uses. Hence, both of them can be regarded as parts of the generic category of indexing systems (Buckland, 1983).

Indexing system followed by web sites, and other electronic media collections is called "hypermedia indexing". A hypermedia index is in electronic form that allows users to search nonlinearly by associations. An user identifies an item through nodes and links between the nodes established electronically. The indexing aspects are transparent to the user. It is the human skill that analyses the given text and makes indexing decisions in establishing the nodes and connections. Internet indexes are indefinable. They are rarely called *indexes*, although they are indexes. These exist in traditional forms, in hypermedia forms, in automatic forms, and in implicit forms (Cleveland and Cleveland, 2001).

Classification. Classification is a process of sorting of objects based on some criteria selected among the properties of the classified objects. Selection criteria and the basis of selection largely determine the quality of classification. How we conceptualize and classify objects is influenced by our socio-cultural background, domain specific knowledge, and our theoretical inclinations- the study of which falls under psychology and social anthropology. Classification for library and information purposes is concerned with a normative theory of classification that indicates criteria for ordering documents that optimize retrieval (Hjorland and Pederson, 2005). Classification of knowledge also finds use in the arrangement of topics in general encyclopaedias. Ecyclopaedias, which arrange items in an alphabetical order, have employed classification independently to facilitate systematic survey of all branches of knowledge and to help those interested in the complete study of a topic. An example of this is the 15th edition of the New Encyclopaedia Britannica. It provides a classification approach to knowledge through Propaedia or outline of knowledge. This detailed classified table of contents is in 10 parts. The 10th part covers the branches of knowledge or the 'circle of learning' subdivided into 5 main divisions- logic, mathematics, science, history and the humanities, and philosophy.

Library/Bibliographic Classification. Features of the world of books are hardly compatible with the philosophical classification of knowledge. Hence any classification to serve library purposes has as for its primary objective the practical task of systematic arrangement of books on the shelves so that access to them becomes easy. Further, a library classification must enable access through subject. Schemes of library classification in common use are the Dewey Decimal classification, the Universal Decimal classification (UDC), the Library of Congress Scheme of classification, and the Colon classification. Library classification schemes of theoretical interest are Brown's Subject classification, Bliss's Bibliographic classification, and that of Cutter's Expansive classification.

Library classification schemes are found to be enumerative or synthetic or a combination of both. An enumerative scheme assumes a universe of knowledge and divides it successively into narrower concepts. In a synthetic scheme classes are derived by combining terms representing concepts drawn from different schedules. Use of different schemes of classification in practice has hampered universal bibliographic control of information. 'The Broad System of Ordering' classification tries to overcome the problems arising out of the incompatibility of the different schemes by providing switching facilities. Library classification schemes need to have notation to show the sequence of classes in the scheme. The notation must have a self-evident sequence. A good notation must fulfill several criteria, such as user friendliness, mnemonics, hospitality, expressiveness, and flexibility. A poor or complex notation can mar a good classification as is the case with the Colon scheme.

Classification for Bibliographic Control. Abstracting, indexing, and bibliographic services play a very important role in providing access to current and cumulative information, particularly in research, law, business, finance and education. Degree of utility of such services is affected by the structure, organization, and display of items and entries followed by the service. Classification determines the structure and organization. Classification for bibliographic purposes has to consider the level of specificity to which classes should be divided, and the needs of retrieval and browsing.

Classification in Search Engines. Access to, and retrieval of information in electronic media texts and web engines employ word-based natural language information processing methods (NLIP). Words used in large texts reflect different and changing paradigms or cultural worlds, which accord well with the general psychology of users of information. One of the most important IR research technique is *relevance feedback*, which exploits term distribution information along with relevance judgment on viewed documents to modify queries. It relies on the selection of properties of basic data features, such as simple terms and the values they can take through weighting. Relevance feedback has raised a fundamental question, that is whether classification in the conventional, explicit sense, is really needed for retrieval in many, or most, cases, or whether classification in general (i.e. default) retrieval context has a quite other interpretation. The retrieval advantage of the technique is due to the weighting, which has been absorbed by search engines and not the classification (Jones, 2005).

Retrieval. Use of stored information from large collections becomes impractical unless means are devised to locate, i.e., identify, select and retrieve the stored item when required. When the volume of stored information is not large or when the information is homogenous as in a book, information can be retrieved through simple devices like contents list or index. When the collection is large, varied, used by many persons and over a period of time, developing retrieval devices becomes complex. Information retrieval occupies a core position in information handling activities as in libraries, databases and large abstracting services. Garvin estimates that when there is a problem, 90 percent of the work is in finding the source and 10 percent of the work is in using the source material to get the answer (Garvin, 1980). Information retrieval (IR) forms a major branch of study in information science.

Although the beginning of the development of IR techniques is traced to retrieval of documents from a collection in a library, the modern subject of IR is characterized by the emphasis on retrieval of information relevant to a request, rather than direct specification of a document (Heaps, 1978).

IR techniques employ the surrogate property of information in which terms are used to represent subject content of a text. IR mechanism in document retrieval takes the form of pre-coordinate or post-coordinate indexing. Retrieval of documents could be by author, title, subject and other data elements or what is now called as "metadata". In the retrieval of information from texts, the most commonly sought approach is by subject. Fig. 2 shows the basic mechanism of IR. Retrieval could be by manual methods or automated, i.e., through computer.

Automated retrieval works on the principle of symbol manipulation through programmed instructions to compare, recognize, and identify words in the text. Retrieval is achieved by scanning for words through character matching, and linking words that have broader or narrower relationship, and words that have special meanings when used in association with other words. It is based on identification of textual words rather than on an understanding of them. Advances in parallel programming have made it possible to incorporate, in a limited way, the human functions of judgment and experience into a purely automated system. Expert systems are already in use in some automated IR systems. Such systems have the advantage of examining language for structured qualities not easily deduced by intuitive means. Further progress in this direction can be expected to follow from developments in the field of artificial intelligence.

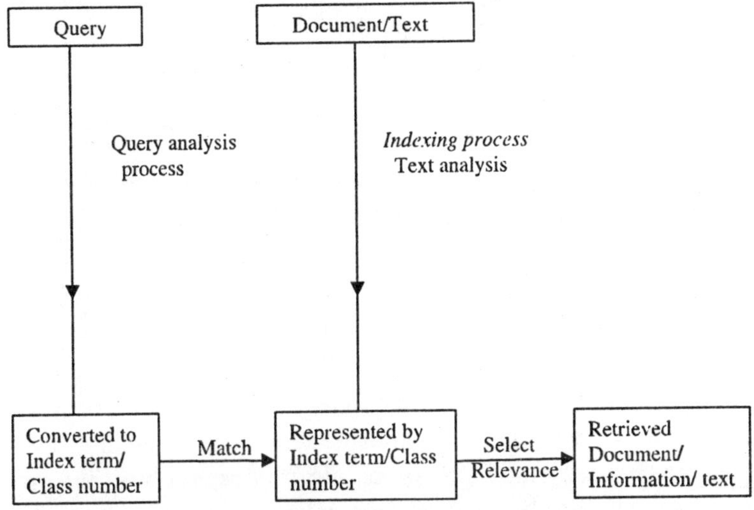

Fig. 2. Basic mechanism of IR

Alphabetization. It is arranging items or entries in the conventional order of the letters of a language. Alphabetization can be letter-by-letter, ignoring punctuation and divisions between words, or word-by-word. In arranging large texts, as in dictionaries and indexes, it is essential to explain at the beginning the rules and the pattern followed in alphabetizing so as to guide the user in locating the item without creating ambiguity.

Translation. It is to convert a text in one language or form of representation into another language or system of representation. Translation is an important means of increasing the use of information. Without translation access to knowledge presented in different languages is impossible. Efforts to develop machine translation have seen considerable success, but a total solution to the translation problem is still far away.

Transliteration. It is to represent a text in one language

script to the script of another language. The change is with respect to the letters and characters (script) of language and not the language (and the phonetic part), e.g., a Sanskrit text written in English script. Transliteration saves one from learning the script of another language, though not the language itself. Employing transliteration a person whose language script is not developed for the computer is able to send an e-mail by using the Roman or other language scripts of the computer keyboard.

Storage. Information can be stored externally. Knowledge is stored in the human mind. Unless recorded, knowledge communicated in the form of information is transitory. Only when information is stored it will be available for use at a later date. In the earlier days there existed the tradition of oral communication, and storage was through memorizing. Symbolic representation of information through writing, i.e., graphic records, made storage of information in physical form possible. Storage has two aspects: physical aspect relating to storage surface/form like paper, and mental factor corresponding to medium of expression like language. To store information in physical form various options are available, ranging from common print on paper to digital storage in the computer memory, in CDs and DVDs. Convertibility from one physical medium to another has become common and has added to our convenience and ease. Storage serves two main purposes, namely, archival and current use. Before storage, records need to be collected. This is the first function of libraries, archives, museums, and now networks. Storability is related to many other characteristics of information records. Records will be examined in further detail in the next chapter because of their importance in the utilization of information.

Formatting. The term 'format' generally refers to the physical features of records and recording. But, format has also a communication dimension. The purpose of formatting is to make records aesthetically appealing, easy to use, highlight portions of the content that are significant, which need proper designing and editing. The communication domain of formatting is concerned with the use of appropriate form of presentation- pictorial, narrative, poetic, dialogue; and design of conceptual framework of presentation, and its translation into physical presentation. Use of alliteration and meter in poetry, inclusion of charts and figures in texts are examples for communication elements in formatting. Search engine developers and web site designers are also engaged in improving the format of texts to ensure efficient access and smooth display of contents for easy reading.

Suppression. Destruction. Censorship. These processes deprive access to information. While relegation and discarding are voluntary actions, suppression is dictated by an external agency such as the State. Destruction and relegation of information is dictated by the operation of the law of diminishing return and the limitations imposed by space and time considerations. Suppression of information from public may be necessitated by the security requirement of the state arising out of political, moral and cultural expediencies of the ruling class or the community; and sometimes due to the need to prevent harm being done to the interest of the originator of the information. Suppression raises important moral and legal issues, free access to such as information vs. cont rolled access, determination of what is harmful information, the rights of citizens to information and the right to safeguard individual's privacy. While unnecessary restrictions inhibit the free flow of information, and thereby its utilization; free access to sensitive or harmful information may endanger the security of the state, adversely affect the moral and cultural values of the community, and affect profit and ownership rights in the case of commercial enterprises.

Dissemination. It is a process aimed at creating greater information awareness in society by providing enhanced access to information, i.e., spreading knowledge. Major dissemination agencies are libraries, archives, museums, print and electronic media, Internet and web sites, citizen information units, and extension services. Industry has to disseminate information about their products and services to attract clientele. These agencies have developed distinctive methods and techniques of dissemination of information making use of some of the information processes described in this chapter and outside it. Advertizing is one of the most important methods of dissemination. A dissemination service may be individual oriented or group oriented. The methods of dissemination used range from display of book jackets by libraries and bookshops to sophisticated advertisement programmes designed by marketing people. Audience preferences and user psychology are major factors to be considered in designing a dissemination programme.

Reproduction. Information texts can be reproduced by using manual, mechanical and electronic methods. Reproduction could be in formats, sizes and colours different from that of the original. This property of information has a tremendous impact on the storage, transferability, cost, dissemination, and use of information. The technology has reached a stage where reproduction in a few seconds of a text generated in space or at a continental distance away from the recipient has become common. An economic issue related to reproducing items/texts is intellectual property rights like copyright.

Arrangement. To arrange is to put in a convenient or desired order of all the elements, themes, and other contents that go to form a text. Arrangement is to serve the intended purpose.

Programming (Computer). A computer is an information processing machine. The machine needs to be provided with detailed instructions on how it is to carry out the processing of information. The set of instructions written for the computer to follow is called a "programme". The process of writing the programme is called "programming". The programmes constitute the software. Computers work on the principle of representing and manipulating symbols (characters). In digital computers the symbol is represented by binary digits 0 and 1 corresponding to one of two states- on or off of an electronic circuit, which the machine senses. A software is usually written in a special language which the computer can understand and translate into binary language. Software languages are of two types : a) machine-like languages called "assembly" or "low-level" language which is more compatible with the way a computer operates, and b) high-level languages which are patterned on natural language like English usage. Weather it is low-level language or high-level language, the computer requires a special programme called either a compiler or an interpreter. The special programme enables the computer to convert user code into binary code, and high-level language into binary code. Most computers are provided with a standard packaged operating system written in assembly language or high-level language thereby freeing the user from file management, programme location and other chores (Thomas, 1987). The most common high-level languages in use are C++ and JAVA. Pragramming is a continuously developing area.

Information Architecture. Information created by the originators need to be adapted/ organized for the network. This process is called *information architecture* (I A). IA is the process of designing, implementing and evaluating information spaces that are humanly and socially acceptable to their stakeholders (Dillon, 2002). Earlier, IA meant designing of web sites, but now finds wider applications and includes navigation and labelling. Its coverage is not limited to linear information texts, but includes multimedia, animation, and other forms of information. It is a multidisciplinary process needing knowledge of computer science, information systems, information organization, user and usability studies, and skills ranging form graphic design to communication and writing (Latham, 2002).

Citation. In literary sense, citation refers to any written or spoken reference to an authority or precedent or to the verbatim words of another speaker or writer. In library usage, citation means a written reference to a specific work or a portion of a work (book, article, dissertation, report, musical composition etc.) by a particular author, editor, composer, etc. that clearly identifies the document in which the work is to be found (Reitz, 2004).

Citation and referencing are two distinctive features of information texts. They are not restricted only to recorded information. Citation or source authority is also an integral part of hearsay information. Referencing differs from citation in that it may include items not cited in the text, e.g., list of names of publications given under "further reading" in textbooks. Citation links information with authority, precedent, author, subject, time, stage of development, index and bibliography, prestige or value. All these types of relationships have practical utility. Religious and moral actions make use of authority by quoting texts. For example, the Vedas, the Upanishads and the Smruthis constitute the source of authority in Hinduism. Legal and government actions often depend on precedents. Citation establishes the relationship between information texts produced by different persons (except in self-citations), having different, same or similar subjects and produced generally at different periods of time. Research proceeds from the stage of development of previous work. Citing reputed sources enhances the prestige of a work or shows its importance and reliability. Citation study is an important branch of bibliometrics and scientiometrics. Citation property of information is used in collection development and in IR in libraries, in sociometric study of information, and in mapping of knowledge. Published citation indexes are valuable research tools.

CLOSURE

Most information activities flow from the processing

characteristics of information. Processing is in the context of use and user of information. Use of information takes place either in the personal context, or in the organizational context, or in the larger social context, or in their combination. Ultimately, the use of information takes place at the level of the individual. Ensuring reliability, currency, relevancy, and comfort ability in use of information and information records are essential elements in processing information. Processing facilitates recording of information, its communication, dissemination and use. Every user of information is also a processor of information, but his processing is limited to his information situation. Being aware of psychology of use of information, and information needs of users serve as invaluable guidelines to process and package information records, to communicate and disseminate their contents.

Processing of information has become a specialized function, and has been the focus of exhaustive studies. Processing of information for professions, industry, trade, governance, and other focused groups has given rise to a number of professions and trades such as librarianship, information science, knowledge management, script writing, translating, programming, information architecturing, publishing, content providing for media and search engines, and many others.

Some of the information processes are intellectual in nature requiring good grounding in information science techniques, communication skills, good writing, besides a fair knowledge of the discipline. Information and communication technology application has revolutionized the field of information processing. Information processing is both an art and a science depending on the process.

REFERENCES

Aitchison, J. Indexing language. Classification Schemes and Thesauri.Pp. 207-26. *In* Anthony, N.J. Ed. Handbook of Special Librarianship and Information Work, ed.5. London, Aslib, 1982.

Benjafield, John, G. Cognition. Ed.2. Upper Saddle River (N.J.).Prentice-Hall, 1996.

Bloch, Bernard. Linguistic Structure and Linguistic Analysis. Pp. 40-44. *In* Hill, A.A. Ed. Report on the Fourth Annual Round Table Meeting on Linguistics and Language Teaching. Washington (DC), Georgetown University, 1953.

Buckland, M.K. Library Services in Theory and Context. New York, Pergamon Press, 1983.

Cleveland, Donald B. and Cleveland, Ana D. Introduction to Indexing and Abstracting. Ed. 3. Greenwood Village (Colorado), Libraries Unlimited, 2001.

Dervin, Brenda and Nilan, Michael. Information needs and uses. *Annual Review of Information Science and Technology.* 21: 3-33, 1986.

Dillon, Andrew. Information architecture in JAIST: Just where did we come from? *Journal of the American Society for Information Science* 53(10): 821-823, 2002.

Foskett, A.C. The Subject Approach to Information, Ed.3. London, Clive Bingley, 1977.

Garvin, A.P. How to Win with Information or Lose Without It. Washington (DC), Bermont Books, 1980.

Hart, Chris. Doing Literature Review: Relating the Social Science Research Imagination. London, Sage Publications, 1998.

Heaps, H.S. Information Retrieval: Computational and Theoretical Aspects. New York, Academic Press, 1978.

Hjorland, Birger and Pederson, Karsten Nissen. A substantial theory of classification for information retrieval. *Journal of Documentation* 61(5): 582-597, 2005. (60 years of the best information research).

Jones, Karen Spark. Revising classification for retrieval. *Journal of Documentation* 61 (5): 598-601, 2005. (60 years of the best in information research).

Jones, M. G. Citizen's rights to information: The role of the government. *Information Services & Use* 5:37-47, 1985.

Kemp, D.A. The Nature of Knowledge: An Introduction for Librarians. London, Clive Bingley, 1976.

Kunz, Warner, et al. Methods of Evaluation of Information Needs: A Critical Review. Munchen, Verlag Dokumentation, 1977.

Latham, Don. Information architecture: Notes toward a new curriculum. *Journal of the American Association for Information Science 53(10): 824-830, 2002.*

Menchik, Daniel A. and Tian, Xiaoli. Putting social context into text: The semiotics of E-mail interaction. *American Journal of Sociology* 114(2): 332-370, Sep. 2008.

Reitz, Joan M. Dictionary for Library and Information Science. Westport (CT), Libraries Unlimited, 2004.

Scarrott, G.G. The nature of information. *Computer Journal* 32: 262-266, 1989.

Thomas, Theodore K. Comp. ASM Computer Source Book: A Colletion of Outstanding Articles from Technical Literature. Metals Park (OH), American Society for Metals, 1987.

van Lohuizen, C.W.W. Knowledge management and policy making. *Knowledge: Creation, Diffusion, Utilization* 8: 12-38, 1986.

Warrier, B.S. Learn the art of summarizing. *Hindu, (The) May 25, 2008.* Education supplement, p.2.

Webster's Third New International Dictionary of English Language. Cologne, Merriam-Webster, 1993.

Wessel, A.E. Computer-Aided Information Retrieval CAIR). Los Angeles Melville Publishing Co., 1975.

Wren, P.C. and Martin, H. High School English Grammar and Composition. New Edn. Revised by N.D.V. Prasad Rao. New Delhi, S.C. Chand & Co, 2003. (Original Copyright 1936).

19

Libraries, Internet and Web Sites

Preservation and transmission of knowledge continuously from one generation to successive generations shape the history of civilization. Libraries, archives, and museums are institutions that mirror the cultural heritage of man. Without knowledge, and information- the surrogate of knowledge, it is almost impossible to survive and progress. This is because human beings are "active, information...seeking and information... using organisms, not as prior views held, passive receivers of stimulation" (Reynolds and Flagg, 1977, p.15). Individuals and societies are increasingly becoming totally dependent on external sources for vital information (Artandi, 1979). Society created libraries and similar institutions to fulfil the knowledge/ information needs of individuals and society. Information needs of military, scientific research and industry during and after the Second World War necessitated refinement of library and information service segments giving birth to information science, and later on to Knowledge Management.

LIBRARIES

Libraries are one of the oldest social institutions created by society to collect, store and service human created records in all forms for the wellbeing of society. Apart from libraries, there are other types of modern institutions, such as archives, museums, planetariums, arboretums, botanical gardens, and aquariums that are also engaged in collecting special types of records, human artefacts, and other types of nature's creations. Institutions like museums and botanical gardens provide opportunities basically to experience the collection besides disseminating information about their collections. They are all parts of the cultural, knowledge, and educational heritage of mankimd. The coverage here is limited to the domain of libraries and information only.

HISTORICAL PERSPECTIVE

The term "library" is derived from the Latin word "liber" for book. In Greek it is "bibliotheca", and in Sanskrit " Granthalaya". The precise origin of libraries is not known. The study of library history and allied disciplines shows that the "instinct to preserve, the passion to collect and the desire to control have been dominant influences in the genesis and growth of the library idea in the history of civilization" (McGarry et al., 2003, p. 371).

The concept of library took concrete form when man started creating records of his thoughts and deeds, and the number of such records grew, thereby necessitating the need for taking care of them. In course of time, the custodian function with added responsibilities got institutionalized and became library practice. The custody of knowledge, both in its oral and written forms was vested with prestige; and the task became an honoured assignment. Development of libraries is directly linked with the development of recording.

Recording is thought to have begun in the historic age. And so must have been the beginning of libraries in its rudimentary form with archival function as the main aim. The evolution of libraries from the ancient times up to the invention of printing is linked with the search for suitable writing surface and recording tools. Around fourth millennium BC Sumerians of Mesopotamia (present day Syria, Iraq and Turkey) invented writing on clay tablets using stylus for recording. Libraries flourished in cities like Nineveh. In about 3000 BC Egyptians of Nile Valley began using papyrus scrolls made from reeds for writing, which later spread to Babylonia, Greece and Rome, and the practice continued up to 300 AD. The library at Alexandria (about 297BC) contained thousands of papyrus scrolls. Parchment or vellum sheets made from hide of sheep appeared around second century BC and filled the libraries of Greek and Roman empires. Black ink was prepared by mixing lamp black with water and glue, and red ink was made-up of red ochre (iron oxide) mixed with water and glue. The concept of book as we know now is traced to *codex* formed by hinging together two or more wax covered wooden or ivory leaves in the fourth century AD in Europe. The writing tools of the ancient world consisted of feather and quills, wooden and metal stylus (Johnson, 1970).

The libraries of ancient civilizations were created mainly to meet the needs of religion and theology, but later on became the repositories of state records relating to wars and treaties between kingdoms, ownership of land, taxation, state laws and the like. Later on libraries also became depositories of records of genealogy, family histories, and other civil events. Libraries were mostly parts of monasteries and the state, and aristocracy had their own collections (Johnson, 1970). Though paper was in use in China at the beginning of 1st century AD, it reached Europe only in 1100 AD. This gave enormous fillip to writing and also to copying on paper of earlier manuscripts written on other types of materials. European libraries during middle ages (476 AD to 1400 AD) saw a general decline, although Christian monasteries continued to copy and collect religious texts found in various locations.

The invention of printing by Johannes Gutenberg of Germany in mid-fourteenth century laid the foundation for large scale production of books in various disciplines. This necessitated establishing numerous libraries. The real impetus to the growth and development of libraries came from the European Renaissance (1400 AD-1700 AD) and the Industrial Revolution that followed (1760 AD-1830 AD). Renaissance released intellectual forces that provided the creative and adventurous environment needed for flowering of arts, literature, science, philosophy, education, political awareness, commerce, and exploration of the New World. The Industrial Revolution was fuelled by scientific advances and technical innovations, which transformed Europe from an agrarian society to that of an industrial society. This large-scale change in many fronts necessitated creation of and dissemination of knowledge on a wide scale to meet the demands of all-round development. The required scientific and technical manpower, and skilled workers could only be met by remoulding and enlarging the then existing system of education. Book was one of the key instruments in this transformation. Libraries became leading agencies for disseminating knowledge and information. This is the beginning of the modern day library development in Europe. Later, this trend spread to other continents and European colonies.

India. In ancient and medieval India literacy through books was the privilege of Brahmins and Kshatrias (warrior class) within the confines of the monastic organizations and privileged chambers. Later, the entry was open to upper strata of officials of the court and scholarly individuals. Collection of manuscripts and their preservation became a part of teaching institutions like "patashalas" (schools) and higher centers of learning situated in centres like Nalanda and Taxila (Vikramasila), and monasteries and royal courts. Fa-Hsien, the Chinese traveler who was in India from 399 AD to 414 AD has recorded in his dairy that important *Mahayana* monasteries maintained libraries of Buddhist texts. Libraries or manuscript collections have existed much before 400 BC as Panini the author of Sanskrit grammar mentions 'granthas' by different authors. During the Muslim rule libraries continued to be built and maintained by the Sultans, kings and emperors. Babur, Humayun and Akbar were great lovers of books and had maintained imperial libraries. All manuscripts were in Persian language (the court language) written on paper. The writing covered various topics, such as affairs of state, law, art, literature and crafts. Libraries remained the luxury of the royals and nobles, with the exception of madrasas (religious schools) which maintained religious texts (Datta, 1970).

Modern library story in India began in early nineteenth century when with the active support of Europeans, public libraries were established in Calcutta (1836), Madras (Chennai) and Bombay (Mumbai). This was followed by the establishment of the Imperial Library in Calcutta under the Imperial Library Act 1902. Later on public libraries were established in other major cities like Bangalore, Hyderabad, Lucknow and Patna. The first public library system, in its modern form, was established in India in the then princely state of Baroda around 1910. Maharaja Sayajirao Gaikwad III, the then ruler of Baroda invited W. A. Borden, the Librarian of the Young Men's Institute, New Haven, Connecticut of America to start a public library network for the entire state. Borden before returning to America in May 1913 had established the central library and a system of libraries covering cities, districts and villages of the state. He also initiated a staff training programme for libraries by conducting classes (Krishan Kumar and Patel, 2001). Later on the idea of creating public library systems through legislative act spread to other states with S.R. Ranganathan playing an important role in selling the idea to state level leaders. By the year 2001, ten states- Tamil Nadu (Madras), Andhra Pradesh, Karnataka (Mysore), Maharashtra, Manipur, Kerala, Haryana, Mizoram and Goa had public libraries act in place. However, the public libraries in all the states are in bad shape, and they need to be rehabilitated in terms of collection, library technology application, and services rendered.

The development of special libraries, and to some extent academic libraries, has progressed comparatively well due to government initiative, better funding, proper guidance and necessity. The establishment by the then British government organizations like the Survey of India (1767), India Meteorological Department (1875), Archaeological Survey of India (1861), Botanical Survey of India (1890), and others not only collected large amounts of data and information, produced specialized literature in their respective domains, but also set up libraries or nucleus of them to support their activities. After independence in 1947 by adopting the twin policy of planned economy and rapid industrialization by Jawaharlal Nehru, the first prime minister, the development of science, industrial research, and education got tremendous support. As a result top ranking institutions like the Department of Atomic Energy (1954), the Department of Space, the Defence Research and Development Organization, the reorganized and enlarged Council of Scientific and Industrial Research with a chain of laboratories, and agricultural and medical research institutions came into existence (India, 2008). Growth of libraries in these fields kept pace with the library standards of the West. Similar development took place in the field of education with the establishment of numerous universities, institutions of technology and higher learning, and the University Grants Commission (1956). Universities also took care of library education by opening library schools/ Departments of Library Science. The establishment of the Indian National Scientific Documentation Centre (INSDOC) renamed as the National Institute of Science Communication and Information (NISCAIR) at Delhi in 1952 as a subunit, and later upgraded to a full unit of the Council of Scientific and Industrial Research, New Delhi, and the creation of the Documentation Research and Training Centre (DRTC) at Bangalore in 1962 by the Indian Statistical Institute, Calcutta have contributed significantly to the training and research in information science/ documentation, and to the development of international contacts in the field. Regarding professional guidance and leadership, the Indian library world had the services of a pioneer and a great visionary in S.R. Ranganathan, and in B.S. Kesavan, a dynamic personality.

RECORDS

It was stated earlier that the development of libraries are directly linked with that of records. The raison'detre of libraries is the records and the need to manage them. Therefore, there is a need to know more about records, their characteristics and role, at least briefly. Records can be copied, reproduced and accessed by several persons at the same time. Thus, records facilitate distribution of information besides enabling private knowledge to become public knowledge. These characteristics pertain to the response-potential of information stated by Shera earlier. Records constitute an important means of carrying public knowledge. Popper's linking records with objective knowledge has been mentioned in chapter 1. Information, unless recorded, has extremely short existence. Records stay as long as they can be physically preserved, and knowledge so long as human memory can retain it either individually or collectively. Shera emphasizes, in the context of librarianship, that information is to be understood as "any graphic manifestation of intellectual activity; ..." (Shera, 1972, p.208).

The technology of printing/recording has advanced from ink and acoustic waves to laser printing. Recording/transferring information through electrical charge has given rise to the electronic media wherein information expressed in natural language form is first transformed into the binary code language, and then transmitted through electrical charges at the receiver's end. At the receiver's end the message gets decoded into the original natural language text- all done electronically. However, its effects, both physical and psychological, on the user of electronic media records cannot be ignored.

Characteristics of Written Records. A record to

serve its purpose must fulfil several requirements depending on the use envisaged. Some of the important requirements currently demanded from records are that they must satisfy the criteria of: a) storability, b) durability, c) compactness, d) identifiability, e) accessibility, f) transportability, g) reproducibility h) convertibility, i) affordability (cost-wise), and j) user friendliness.

Electronic media records impose additional demands, such as: a) high density storage capacity; b) high-speed processing capacity; c) system compatibility; d) reliability of infra-structure facilities and hardware; and d) security of data. In addition, electronic media record demands from the user some amount of system operation skill, and some psychological adjustment towards computer usage. This is not a major issue with the younger generation as they are initiated to computer literacy programmes at the level of elementary education in many countries. It is unlikely that non-print media records, including electronic, will provide the same ease of use as that of the print on paper medium at least in the near future. The electronic media in spite of its tremendous advantages, such as: high capacity storage of information in an incredibly small volume, enormous manipulative ability, and instant access to information anytime and anywhere, is unlikely to totally replace the print medium for the following reasons:

1. The human nature tends to follow the principle of least effort. There is no substitute to a book or paper as far as ease of handling is concerned. Because of its stand-by itself character, the use of a print medium text does not require any equipment or power supply, or any other help.

2. Human beings' inherent liking for freedom of movement/action. Print media provides that freedom; it does not tie down a reader to a particular place, time or environment. Further, a print record can be easily disposed off after one's use is over.

3. People like variety. Print provides a variety of colour, form and size. One would not like to restrict oneself to a single medium whether it is electronic or print.
4. Existence of different segments of users. Because of the wide disparity in literacy, economic standing of individuals, absence of infrastructure needed to support network access, there will always be a significant proportion of the world's population which will depend on the print media.

However, where there is a need for real time manipulation of texts, and the need for saving storage space as in large and complex organizations electronic media is cutting into print media. This is because of what Kibirige calls the artefact condition of information in a print media as against the "live" state of information in an electronic media. For, "live information may be modified as it is being transmitted, whereas artefacts are in a static state" (Kibirige, 1983, p.5). The only way of overcoming this limitation in graphic media is by bringing out new publications.

THE CORE OF LIBRARIANSHIP

A close scrutiny of the development of libraries from ancient times to the present day shows certain core themes or values common to all libraries. These features represent: philosophical, physical/technological, cultural and social, intellectual, managerial, and international aspects of libraries.

Philosophical and Theoretical Aspects. The purpose or philosophy of libraries is to bring about "...interfacing between records of knowledge, and the actual as well as potential users by a mediator, in an organizational set-up employing some document description and retrieval techniques" (Narayana, 1991, p.87). The mediatory role of libraries with the possible exception of public libraries is losing ground because of the direct access facilities provided by the Internet and other online services. There is division of labour in the organization of information services. Besides libraries, there other agencies involved either directly or indirectly in information collection and servicing activities, and they are: a) data centres, b) information centres, c) knowledge management units, d) producers of secondary information sources (i.e., abstracting and reviewing), e) tertiary sources of information, i.e., indexing agencies, f) information consultants and information brokers, g) educationists to some extent, and f) extension services. The division of labour based on the category of user segments constituting society that are being served prompts the type of information material to be collected and served by the library to meet the requirements of particular segments of users. Thus, we have public or community libraries; school, college and university libraries; special libraries; parliament libraries; government libraries; industrial libraries; libraries for the blind, different types of media libraries, church and temple libraries, map libraries, and the like. The type of library also determines the level of processing of information records, the variety and the depth of services to be provided. Apart from the development of overall philosophy of libraries and other knowledge processing professions, theories have been evolved on the various aspects of information/ knowledge processing, application and use, such as classification, indexing, and impact of information.

Physical and Technological Aspects. The physical aspects are related to location and housing of libraries, functional space allocation, design of furniture, and equipment. Library architecture demands special type of designing library buildings. The uniqueness of the physical format of books necessitated designing of special type of storage. It is only after trial and experience gained over a period of time the modern practice of using racks with shelves arranged in rows, separated by aisle space became standardized. The now out of use unit card of 3" X 5" and the catalogue cabinets to hold them have their own stories to tell. The other functions of physical nature include acquisition, and the physical organization of the collection with sub-functions of location, shelf order and maintenance.

The first technological development in the history of libraries is the use of clay tablets, the writing surface invented by Sumerians in the 4th millennium. The 2nd and the 3rd revolutions appeared in the shape of the introduction of paper into Europe in the 11th century AD, and the invention of printing press by Gutenberg in about 1450 respectively. We are now in the fourth revolution caused by computer and communication technologies, and (particularly) the Internet. The technological side of libraries are undergoing a tectonic change with the digital word overtaking the world of print, and information becoming as mobile and widespread as the mobile phone.

Application of computing technology in libraries began in 1970s initially to mechanise/automate circulation function, later extended to cover other functions like acquisition and cataloguing. This area of activity came to be referred as *library automation*. Libraries have advanced from the automation of internal functions to an integrated approach encompassing online catalogues, web sites, networks, e Books and e Journals under what is called *library information system* (LIS). The aim is to provide a "one-stop" desktop access point for materials held both locally and internationally. The LIS includes the integrated library marketplace and the online database industry. The LIS, as of now, includes: Integrated library systems; Online databases; Web-based resources; Digital library collections; ebooks and e journals (Kochtanek and Matthews, 2004).

Intellectual Theme. The main thread here is the intellectual organization of the collection, i.e., designing mechanisms to access documents, to retrieve information, and also to provide information in the desired forms. From the beginning, librarians had to handle three basic intellectual processes in managing a collection- describing the records held or added; and arranging them for storage, peruse and recall; and providing information— the functions of cataloguing, classification, and reference service respectively. The Sumerian libraries that consisted of cuneiform scripted clay tablets (3600 BC), Assyrian libraries (3000 BC), and the Alexandrian Library (332 BC) had all applied these basic processes (Harris, 1995). Beginning of mid-nineteenth century saw extraordinary increase in the growth of books, journals and newspapers. However, it was in the late twentieth century that the growth became stupendous. It is during this time that new forms of records, what is now called multi-media products, began to appear. Further, the scientific world needed access to information, at the article level, contained in thousands of journals appearing in different languages. The publications grew in volume and variety, and the task of organizing and providing comprehensive access to them became complex. The solution to the problem, put in library parlance, thus became one of "bibliographic control". Primarily, bibliographic control deals with cataloguing, classification, and bibliographies- the intellectual core of librarianship.

The last fifty years has seen a number of initiatives- some successful and some failures- to standardize, make seamless and streamline the intellectual part of librarianship. One of the Ideas was to avoid every library repeating from start the intellectual work of classification and cataloguing a document it acquires, if the data or entries are made available by a an apex body or other agencies. One example is the printing of the US Library of Congress (LC) catalogue entry on the back of the title page of a book. Even, if the purchasing library is not following LC practice or Decimal classification, the entry provides all the data elements, subject of the document, and the author's name in a standard form, which can be made use readily by the cataloguer/ classifier. This aspect is further covered under cooperation, and international librarianship.

Cataloguing. A catalogue is an organized set of

bibliographic records that represent the holdings of a particular collection (Taylor, 2000). Cataloguing is the process of generating the catalogue. When the processing is done electronically, the catalogue is called a "database", and the processing "encoding". Cataloguing codes are framed to avoid inconstancies in representing bibliographic elements, and hiding of items from the user of the catalogue. The well-known cataloguing rules include the Library of Congress's *Rules for Descriptive Cataloging in the Library of Congress (1949)*, and the earlier *Rules on Printed Cards* (1899 through the 1930s), the *Anglo-American Cataloguing Rules* (AACR, AACR2, AACR2R, and AACR2R98), American Library Association (ALA) *Catalog Rules (1908)*, ALA *Cataloging Rules* (1941), ALA *Cataloging Rules for Author and Title Entries* (1949), and the *Classified Cataloguing Code* (CCC) by S.R. Ranganathan (1938). The most scientifically developed rules are Charles A. Cutter's *Rules for a Dictionary Catalog* (1904), and the CCC with its nine cannons or principles.

Catalogues generally are of two types: classified or alphabetical depending upon the form of arrangement of entries in the catalogue. In a classified catalogue entries for an item are found under the notation representing the class under which it is classified. Intellectual part of cataloguing consists of a descriptive phase and a subject allocation phase. Descriptive portion takes care of identifying and describing a document through the selection of bibliographic elements like names of authors, editors and translators, full title, imprint details, and physical features of the document, if needed. The subject part of cataloguing consists of finding the subject content of the item and specifying the subject by means of a classification number or subject headings or keywords. Though the cataloguing process looks simple, it is not so because of the complexities found in the world of records. Cataloguers maintain "authority lists" to help them maintain consistency and reliability.

Records in digital form need a different technique for

encoding information and it should be in a machine readable form. The encoding system so designed is Machine-Readable Cataloging (MARC). MARC 21 is the latest version issued in 1999. The Standard Generalized Mark-up Language (SGML) is an international standard frame of rules used for designing mark-up languages that describe the structure of a document. Mark-up languages developed by using SGML are called Document Type Definitions (DTDs). Text Encoding Initiative (TEI), Hyper Text Markup Language (HTML), and Encoded Archival Description (EAD) are often used DTDs for bibliographic work. SGML has issued Extensible Markup (XML), a subset of additional rules that solve the problems found in using SGML and HTML (Taylor, 2000).

Classification. It is known that the Assyrian libraries in the 7th and 8th centuries BC had their collections catalogued and arranged by subject (Harris, 1995). As early as late 17th century, the German philosopher mathematician Leibniz had thought of a classification scheme for bringing out a biannual bibliography of books *Nucleus librarium*. His views on cataloguing and indexing were widely adopted by contemporary librarians (Glynn, 2004).

Coming to recent period, Melvil Dewey's invention of Decimal Classification (DC) for arrangement of books in libraries, and its wide use in many countries is considered a significant development in library classification. The Universal Decimal Classification (UDC), based on DC and developed by the International Federation for Information and Documentation (FID) served special libraries well. The Colon Classification (CC) invented by S.R.Ranganathan brought new insight to classification. The intellectual contributions to the theory of classification made by the Documentation Research and Training Centre, Bangalore (DRTC), and the Classification Research Group, London have left deep impact on the theory of classification.

What is pertinent here is classifying, i.e., processing the

records, such as books and other information materials acquired by a library by applying the chosen scheme of classification and not classification scheme or its theories. Classifying is a continuing intellectual activity in all libraries where the classifier is required to use his knowledge of the classification scheme, analyze the contents of the document to be classified for its subject, and arrive at the exact subject/ subjects covered by the document in order to assign the appropriate class number or subject heading (keyword in free-text processing) selected from the scheme.

Reference Service. The reference service function of a library combines an information function and a service function. Information function consists of finding and making available the requisite information to the reader, who seeks it, or direct the user to the source of availability; and a service function consisting of a communication act, and the act of information delivery. A reference service includes "answering substantive questions, instructing users in the selection and use of appropriate tools and techniques for finding information, conducting searches on behalf of the patron, directing users to the location of library resources, assisting in the evaluation of information, referring patrons to resources outside the library when appropriate, keeping reference statistics, and participating in the development of the reference collection" (Reitz, 2004, p.602). The standard of the reference service is an important indicator of the value of a library to its stakeholders, and its standing in the community of users. Providing an efficient, effective, and sustainable reference service is intellectually very demanding.

The role of reference librarians is undergoing change, particularly in the educational libraries. The provision of Internet and web service access has become a part of library service. The user population is increasingly accessing Internet and web sites, and ready information reference sources like Wikipedia as the first access point. How will the reference librarian effectively participate in these online societies? In the new era of Internet and mobile phone, a good deal of information transactions between the reader and the reference librarian are likely to be through e-mail, SMS, voice-mail and other computer/ telecommunication modes. The Internet and the newly emerging technologies place the user at the centre of his or her information universe, exercising significant control over what information enters that universe and how it is used. The reference librarians will adapt to the new technologies and the changing behaviours and expectations of users. They will continue to play a significant role by adding value to information seekers' experience by helping them find what they need and can use in the complex larger shared information universe (Rettig, 2006).

Bibliographic Service. Primarily it consists of reformatting and repackaging of information, and dissemination of information. The bibliographic service of a library may cover a wide range of instruments such as "Alerting Services" also known as "Selective Dissemination of Information", compilation of bibliographies on select topics on a continuous basis or on topics requested by patrons as one time compilation; bring out regularly, in print and online, lists of publications added to the library. The entries in a bibliography may be limited to an index entry or may also include abstracts. Bibliographic service being a costly service, and with the availability of access to various online services and web sites, libraries now generally limit the bibliographic service to issuing of list of additions made to the library.

Managerial Functions. To fulfil their functions all organizations need to be managed, and libraries are no exception to this. Enlightened management of organizations begins with the statement of mission of the organization from which the objectives are detailed. Managing then consists of marshalling the required resources and applying them to realise the objectives as per the set framework. This is generally accomplished through the processes of planning, organizing, staffing, leading and controlling. There are four features that are distinctive to the management of libraries and information, and they are: a) intangible nature of knowledge and information, b) libraries are service organizations; c) generally libraries are found to be parts of a larger organization with the library head vested with limited internal autonomy. Hence, the head of library is bound by the philosophy, culture, structure, rules and policies of the parent organization; d) libraries form one of the important links in the larger chain of information-knowledge system. In assessing the impact of libraries on society one must not "over emphasize the role of libraries and information services in the totality of information transfer, of which probably 80% takes place outside of any formal mechanism" (Cleverdon, 1980, p. 124).

Cultural and Social Dimension. Libraries, archives and museums have long been considered to be a part of the cultural heritage of a society. Their contents mirror the cultural history of the group. In addition, libraries have a symbolic value— symbol of scholarship, culture, and to some extent prosperity. Having a separate study room (library) in the house adds both utilitarian and prestige value to the house. Cultural symbol of libraries seems to be one of the reasons why libraries are destroyed or established, when one culture tries to dominate or influence another culture.

Social facet of libraries is mainly represented by the changing role of libraries, and in the extension of library access. Access to libraries, once the preserve of kings and highly placed functionaries of the court, as was the case in the early phases of library development, was later enlarged to include higher echelons of society. The changeover from the limited access to the wider public access to libraries occurred with the acceptance of the concept of libraries as social institutions providing free access to the entire society. Thus, came into being public library systems supported by taxation to fund them. By mid-nineteenth century, contributions of libraries to the social and economic development of a country were realized by the North American and many European countries whether they were democratic, socialistic or dictatorial by constitution. The public library's social responsibility got redefined when it extended its role to supplement the efforts of individuals and those of developmental programmes set by the state. The second change was the recognition that libraries have the social obligation of catering to the needs of special groups, such as minorities, and physically challenged (e.g. Braille for the blind). Thirdly, cooperation between libraries became an acknowledged activity of a library. The two critical turning points in the history of public library movement were the transition of libraries from their limited service concept to that of a truly public service, and the change over from closed access to open access system.

LIBRARY COOPERATION

Cooperation is a characteristic of social organizations. Cooperation between libraries is not a new phenomenon. As early as 10th century AD, Liu Xin had compiled *The Seven Epitomes*, a union catalogue of the imperial libraries of China (Yitai and Gorman, 2000). What have changed are the forms of cooperation. It has taken new forms ranging from the traditional interlibrary lending of publications to that of cooperative acquisition of library materials, central storage of less used materials, formulation of World Science Information System (UNICIST) concept, development of International Standard Book Number (ISBN), and International Serials Data System (ISDS). To facilitate interlibrary borrowing compilation of union catalogues of library holdings, especially of periodicals and special materials, became necessary to help identy and locate an item in the collections of participating libraries. A fine example is the Ohio College Library Center (OCLC), Ohio (USA) established in 1967, which has set new standards on library cooperation and bibliographic research. The practice of bringing out bulky volumes of union catalogues is now extinct, and the earlier card catalogues have been replaced by Online Public Access Catalogues (OPACs) providing access to a library's collection (database), and other information like loan and reservation status via a terminal. The Computer and communication technology revolution enabled interlinking of databases of different libraries into networks.

Library Networks. Many definitions of a network are available in library literature. The National Commission on Libraries and Information Science (NCLIS), USA defines a network as coming together of "two or more libraries and/or other organizations engaged in a common pattern of information exchange, through communications, for some functional purpose" (NCLIS, 1975, p.82-83). A true network employs computer and communication means, and the information exchange may include sharing of resources, services and information. The wide use of computers by libraries since 1970s resulted in their collections being stored in a machine readable form (digital form), i.e., database replacing the physical catalogue. Such a database may be of composite nature covering different forms of records— books, journal articles, theses, reports, CD ROMs, photos, audio-video records, e-books, e-journals and so on, or may be restricted to a particular type of record, say e-books. Interconnecting computers and computer systems located at different places by telecommunication services has enabled linking of individual databases to form networks accessible by users of all libraries in the network. Initially such library networks provided only bibliographic data including location information, thus serving mainly the union catalogue function. In the same period, major international abstracting and indexing services such as Chemical Abstracts also appeared as online databases. Later, many networks expanded their functions by including collective (or consortia) acquisition of resources on behalf of the participating libraries, undertaking centralized processing, providing document delivery services, and information alert services besides serving the basic bibliographic function. A network could interact with the users via e-mail, chat, SMS and video conferencing. Networks are categorized in to : a) Local Area Network (LAN) which is limited to a small geographic area like a campus or a single building, Wide Area Network (WAN) in which the libraries are geographically dispersed across a country or continents, and c) Metropolitan Area Network (MAN) whose area of operation is limited to a city. Presently, a large number of international networks are in operation. An example for a comprehensive network having international scope is OCLC, which is described below:

OCLC's WorldCat and FirstSearch. WorldCat is an online union catalogue of records ranging from the ancient clay tablets to e-books and web sites, representing hundreds of languages with 9000 national and international institutional members accounting for over 57 million records. FirstSearch is an online service providing access to research databases consisting primarily of journals. Both are international in scope and widely referred. OCLC has contributed substantially to research on bibliographic topics, metadata, and the future of MARC format (Wedgeworth, 2004).

India. Development of library networks was initiated in the early 1980s by the National Information System for Science and Technology (NISSAT). Since then, a number of library networks have been established covering different disciplines, regions and cities (IGNOU, 2005; Jebaraj and Devadoss, 2004). The latest network to be established is the National Knowledge Network (NKN) based on the recommendation made by the Knowledge Commission. The first phase of the network was inaugurated in April 2009 (India. National Knowledge Commission, 2007; Hindu, April 10, 2009).

Standards. Effective functioning of a network needs common agreement between participating libraries, adoption of a standard format by all libraries in the network, and the requisite infrastructure in place. The first Machine Readable Cataloging format (MARC) was created by the Library of Congress, Washington, D.C. in 1965, and since then several versions of MARC have appeared. MARC is a cataloguing format designed for computer processing of library records. To make MARC universally applicable and compatible with other systems, it was necessary to standardize bibliographic details. International Standard Bibliographic Description (ISBD) was developed to ensure standardization in presenting bibliographic data. MARC21 is the most used format. The contributions of international organizations like IFLA and UNESCO in promoting library cooperation and network formations in general, and in developing countries are detailed under international librarianship.

INTERNATIONAL LIBRARIANSHIP

From historic times libraries have fulfilled an international function. The Museum collection of the great Alexandrian Library (297 BC) had attracted scholars from Egypt, Greece and Israel who were also employed to copy and translate manuscripts (Harris, 1995). With the rise of Roman power collection building continued. With the decline of Roman Empire (476 AD) the church took over the custodianship of Christian scholarship. Christian monasteries built up large ecclesiastical libraries to serve their religious purpose. This led to build-up of large collections of manuscripts by copying and exchange of duplicates (Harris, 1995). With the spread of Christianity to countries in Latin America, Africa and Asia monasteries came to be established in those countries, and with them libraries. However, it is the Islamic Middle East under the rule of Khalifs of Baghdad (8th and 9th centuries) became the centre from where ideas and knowledge from the East flowed into Europe. Library collections in Bagdad (762 to mid-thirteenth century), particularly the one attached to the Bayt al-Hikma (the House of Wisdom), had built-up massive collections of manuscripts covering a wide range of subjects, in a dozen foreign languages, and attracted scholars from Asia, Africa and Europe (Lerner, 1999). From these collections Hellenic scholarship was rediscovered, texts were translated by European scholars and transmitted them back home. It is this knowledge that sustained Renaissance movement (Harris, 1995). Nearer Home, libraries of the universities of Nalanda and Takshashila attracted scholars from abroad, a fact documented by Fa-Hsien (399-414 AD), the Chinese scholar who had visited India. Kashi (Varanasi) was another centre of Vedic scholarship that attracted scholars from far and near.

In the nineteenth century, the international dimension of libraries attained explicit recognition. Many national library associations, such as the American Library Association (ALA) founded in 1876 included international relations in its purview. Given the unity of scholarship, national libraries being lead libraries found it necessary to develop or participate in international library movement. Libraries came to be recognized by political powers as suitable agencies for extending academic, social and cultural influence over others. The establishment of British Council Libraries, and library and information centres by the U.S. in India are examples for this. To address the problems of libraries specific to a region, a number of regional library associations have come up. These include the European Bureau of Library, Information and Documentation Associations (EBILD) covering countries of the European Union; the Commonwealth Library Association (COMILA) representing British Commonwealth countries; and the Congress of South Asian Librarians (CONSAL). However, the international dimension of libraries found forceful expression with the coming into existence of three ventures: the International Federation of Documentation (FID), the International Federation of Library Associations (IFLA), and the United Nations Educational, Scientific and Cultural Organization (UNESCO).

FID. Two Belgian lawyers, Henri Lafontaine and Paul Odet founded the International Institute of Bibliography (IIB) in 1895 with the objective of promoting the development of universal bibliographic control, and setting bibliographical standards. In 1924, IIB was reorganized as a federation of national centres for bibliography, and in 1937 it was renamed as the International Federation of Documentation (FID). The FID worked in three main areas: development of bibliographic standards; compilation of an international bibliography; and general bibliographic research. A major success of FID was the development of Universal Decimal Classification (UDC), a scheme based on Melvil Dewey's Decimal Classification adapted to suit classifying scientific literature. In the area of international bibliography, it started the *Universal Bibliographic Repertory (1895)*— a universal catalog of books, and the *Reportire Encyclopedique de Dossiers* (1907)— an index of pamphlets, newspapers, and journal articles. Its journal the *Review of Documentation* was devoted to the dissemination of research in the area of documentation and related fields. FID ceased to exist in 1992. However, the maintenance of the UDC continues, which was taken over by UDC Consortium in 1992 (Glynn, 2004). FID during its life time served as a beacon to scholars, librarians, and institutions interested in organizing and controlling scientific literature throughout the world.

IFLA. The International Federation of Library Associations and Institutions with its Secretariat in The Hague, Netherlands was founded in 1927 in Edinburgh. IFLA was completely dominated by European and North American interests until 1976. It is now a broad based international organization with representations from over 140 countries. Programmes of IFLA are organized under eight major divisions representing different types of libraries and activities, and "Round Tables" representing specialized interests. The International Association of Metropolitan Libraries (INTAMEL) is one of the Round Tables. Presently IFLA has two core programmes: a) Preservation and Conservation (PAC) which takes up research on preservation of library and archival materials, and disseminates information on the "best practices"; and b) Advancement of Librarianship (ALP) which sponsors seminars and training programmes in developing countries aimed at advancing the profession in those countries.

Earlier, IFLA had three other programmes: a) Universal Bibliographic Control and International MARC (UBCIM) which was taken over by the National Library of Portugal in 2003. Under this programme IFLA published a series of manuals for International Bibliographic Descriptions (ISBDs) in the 1970s; b) the Universal Availability of Publications (UAP). The UAP established at the British Museum with the objective of making available access to all types of materials and bibliographic data on the widest scale was closed in 2003; and c) the Universal Dataflow and Telecommunications (UDT) project sponsored by the National Library of Canada (NLC), under which IFLA became a global library network connected via IFLANET. The NLC intimated the termination of sponsorship of this project in 2003. A number of associations representing special groups like the International Association of Music Libraries (IAML), and the International Association of School Libraries (IASL) are members of IFLA. IFLA is supported by UNESCO in carrying out some of the latter's library programmes (Wedgeworth, 2004). IFLA continues to be a leader in library matters at the international level.

UNO and UNESCO. The United Nations Organization (UNO) and its specialized agencies like the Food and Agricultural Organization (FAO), the World Health Organization (WHO), and the International Labour Office (ILO) have included in their objectives setting up of institutions and mechanisms to facilitate the flow of scientific, technical and managerial information and know-how among member countries. Programmes and projects under this include the development of international and national information systems and services (e.g., AGRIS) and technical assistance missions to developing countries to establish or support information facilities in their respective fields (Neelameghan, 1999).

UNESCO. Assisting member countries in the development of libraries is one of the objectives of the United Nations Educational, Cultural, and Scientific Organization (UNESCO), which was established at Paris in 1946. This function is looked after by its Division of Libraries, Documentation and Archives. The library programme flowed from the General Information Programme (PGI) established by the UNESCO General Council in 1971. The PGI had chalked out four areas of interest for action: national information policy; standards and norms; national library infrastructure; and training and education. Around 1990, the PGI became a part of the Information Society Division of the Communications and Information Sector. With a shift in focus, the PGI became Information for All (IFAP), which is aimed at harnessing the power of information and communication technologies (ICT) to advance libraries within a communications network. Due to shortage of funds, its library programmes are now limited mainly to supporting policy documents for public and school libraries (Wedgeworth, 2004). It recently launched the UNESCO Network of Associated Libraries (UNAL) aimed at safeguarding the recorded memory of humanity with a number of pilot projects in member countries. In 1997, it convened "The International Congress on Ethical, Legal and Social Aspects of Digital Information (INFOETHICS). UNESCO supports the development of computer networking and the training of informatics specialists through its Intergovernmental Programme (IIP) (World of Learning 2006). The UNESCO has recognized IFLA as its main contact point with professional library associations and makes annual grant to it (Glynn, 2004). The Division has sponsored regional informatics networks in Africa (RINAF), Arab States (RINAS), Asia-Pacific (RINSEP), and Eastern Europe (RINEE) besides holding international conferences and training programmes for librarians through bodies like IFLA.

PHILANTHROPY

Benefactors have played an important role in the development of libraries, particularly since the beginning of the twentieth century, when expansion of library service was the need of the time in North America and Europe. Rapid reconstruction of national economies after the First World War, and the need to raise political and social awareness among the people called for development of libraries on a large scale. This cause was supported by funding the establishment of libraries through private philanthropic foundations and endowments. In India, some of the princely states like Mysore encouraged philanthropists to advance the cause of education and health care. Two great educational institutions of India- the Indian Institute of Science, Bangalore (1909), and the Benaras Hindu University at Varanasi (1916) founded by Jamsestji N. Tata and Pandit Madan Mohan Malaviya respectively are the results of benefaction.

The Carnegie Foundation. The most significant philanthropic contribution to the cause of libraries was made by Andrew Carnegie of Carnegie Steel Company, USA with the founding of the Carnegie Corporation of New York in 1911. It funded the establishment of hundreds of public libraries in the US and other English speaking countries. It also worked actively in improving the standard of library education in America. It is from the Carnegie Grant, the first graduate library school was started at the University of Chicago. The Corporation has continued to support new and novel initiatives in the field of public libraries, sociological research, and university libraries. Since 1998, the Corporation is supporting a number of programmes aimed at extending public library service, university libraries, and higher education for Women in Africa under its international development program (Wedgeworth, 2004). The other prominent philanthropic efforts whose programmes include advancement of libraries are:

The Rockefeller Foundation, New York. It was established in 1913 by John D. Rockefeller, his son, and F.T. Gates with the objective of identifying the underlying causes of human suffering at their source and finding remedies. The present emphasis is on harnessing the creative forces of globalization for the wellbeing of humanity. It also awards fellowships and scholarships (*www.rockfound*; Wikipedia. Rockfellor).

The Ford Foundation of America. It was established by Edsel Ford and Henry Ford in 1936. One of its programmes is to advance human achievement through knowledge, creativity and freedom. An initial grant from the Ford Foundation enabled the establishment of the Council on Library Resources (CLR) in 1956, later renamed as the Council on Library and Information Resources (CLIR). The Council funded a number of innovative studies and projects which generated new thinking on the development of libraries. The creation of the *Index Medicus* by the National Library of Medicine, the forerunner of latter-day international medical databases, owes to the studies initiated by the Council. It also supported research on the preservation of paper. It continues to initiate and support research that can have creative impact on the development of libraries. It administers the annual Bill and Melinda Gates Foundation Access to Learning Award (Wedgeworth, 2004; http://fordfound.org/about/guidance.cfm).

The Fulbright Program. It is covered in chapter *13. A* number of librarians from India have benefitted from the Fulbright Programs.

The George Soros Foundation. George Soros established the Open Society Institute (OSI) in 1993 with the aim of supporting and creating open societies through the establishment of democratic institutions. The OSI office in New York develops programmes that are implemented by local Soros Foundations located in over 50 countries. The foundation's thrust towards libraries consists of promoting study tours to American and Western European libraries, and exchange programmes for librarians working in Eastern Europe, Russia, the Baltic countries, and African countries to give them a first-hand knowledge about the role of libraries in democratic societies. It has an ambitious agenda for libraries, publishing, and strengthening of universities.

The Gates Learning Foundation. It was established by Bill and Melinda Gates in 1997 to help bridge the digital divide. The Gates Learning Foundation with which the Bill and Melinda Gates Foundation was merged in 2000 works towards improving health, education and libraries worldwide. Its programme to connect every public library in the US with computers was completed in 2003. It also offers scholarships (www.gates).

In India, the premier philanthropic support to the cause of education, healthcare, arts, science and social sciences has come from The Tata Foundations described in chapter 13.

Sarada Ranganathan Endowment for Library Science (SRELS). It was established by S.R.Ranganathan at Bangalore in 1963. It is the first philanthropic endowment set up in India by a librarian for promoting the cause of libraries. The main objectives of the trust are to keep the Colon Classification updated, and to revise S.R. Ranganathan's works as and when warranted. The trust arranges annual lectures by eminent scholars on library science and related topics. It also brings out publications on library and information related topics of current interest.

THE FUTURE OF LIBRARIES

The greatest challenge facing libraries is how they will adapt to survive in a world dominated by the Internet. Until recently, libraries were largely concerned with print media and its related forms like traditional audiovisual texts and microforms. Luddites had predicted the death of print media with the arrival of the Internet and networks, but they have been proved wrong. In fact, Marshall McLuhan in 1960 had predicted that "The book is dead" (Shuman, 2001). But the print media and the book publishing industry is flourishing along with the electronic media. However, the libraries have not become redundant yet, but sure to become so unless they modify their missions and redefine their roles. In this scenario, the first to suffer has been the special libraries and academic libraries. The mediatory function of bringing together the researcher and the book is becoming superfluous to a large extent due to the direct access to records provided by the Internet. This trend seems irreversible. It is no more necessary for research workers and academic users of institutional libraries to visit their libraries housed in large buildings with rows and rows of stacks to borrow publications or consult in situ. Their information requirements are met online at their desks, and the Internet does connect them to information sources available anywhere in the world, provided the institutions can pay for the service. The only functions left with special libraries seem to be that of record keeping and archival tasks with some technical processing. Knowledge "gate keeper" function is still open, more so given the volume of information accessible through the net, the manner of their structuring data, and lack of quality control over Internet served information. A major problem with the Internet is that a simple query on the net may result in thousands of hits, from which how one is to select items that are pertinent, authentic, and useful (Shuman, 2001). The situation is different in the case of public libraries.

Public Libraries. It seems that the scope and opportunities for providing public library service have increased even in the era of cyberspace. The scope has widened primarily because of economic and intellectual inequality in society, which has created the information-rich and the information-poor divide. At the same time the world of information is getting more complex with the Internet accessed information accounting for an overwhelming share of the total information stock. Libraries do have a major role in reducing this gap.

Public libraries have adapted to the new situation by provisioning Internet access to their clients, thereby meeting the information needs of informationally neglected segments of society. The real challenge and opportunity to public libraries lie in discharging their a) educational function, and b) supporting rural and marginal community development function, which are stupendous tasks.

Educational Function. Public libraries and school libraries have an important educational function to fulfil, namely, to promote "information literacy". The need has arisen because of complexities of digital information world, information overload, and providing equal opportunities to all in gaining knowledge. Information literacy cause is reinforced by the ".... needs of the information society for competent information consumers, and to meet the requirements of the knowledge economy for a responsive and informed workforce" (Andretta, 2005, p.5). Carrying out this task primarily falls on libraries, educational institutions and other primary developmental agencies working at the grass root level of society. The young generation is to be taught not only in accessing digital information, but also in developing analytical and evaluation skills to ascertain suitability of information in terms of reliability, purposefulness and effectiveness. This initiative aimed at inculcating lifelong learning trait is termed "information literacy". Information literacy and "computer literacy" are sometimes used synonymously, but the former is more comprehensive in scope and includes the latter. Information literacy is an enlargement of earlier concept of library/ bibliographic literacy.

Service to Rural and Marginal Communities. Although, discharging the community development function of libraries is limited to a small percentage of the population in the developed countries, it forms a major work field in developing and underdeveloped countries. Planning library service to rural segment differs from that of urban sector, in that it is more demanding and requiring a different strategy. The framing of such a strategy has to take into consideration the social structure, cultural factors, economic realities, and possibly the need for unorthodox solutions. For achieving effective results rural libraries and their extensions services have to coordinate their work with that of other agencies- both governmental and voluntary organizations involved in rural development. The main challenge is that of establishing appropriate proactive relationship with the masses. This requires a good understanding of the rural realities, rural psychology, and tapping indigenous community knowledge. Based on that understanding libraries have to reorient their methods of disseminating information by adopting information technology instruments like Internet, broadband wireless technologies, such as WiMAX communication, and other multimedia devices coupled with the local communication forms to suit the audience/readers. There is a need to take into consideration in planning the critical role of woman (Neelameghan and Chester, 2007). From libraries, we move on to the world of Internet and web sites which are changing the entire pattern of our thinking and living.

INTERNET AND WEB SITES

The idea of making available all information available in the world in a single compendium was behind the creation of encyclopaedias. Even encyclopaedias and library collections with their catalogues put together do not make up a single source of all information in the world, and accessible to all. Only hope was the creation of a mechanical devise that could accomplish this purpose. In the mid-fifties of last century, Dr. Vannevar Bush conceived of such an instrument, and called it "Memex". Bush's imagination has become a reality in the shape of Internet (Shuman, 2001). How this has come about is the story of the Internet. It is the invention of computer and the advances in communication technology that revolutionized the entire field of information generation, processing, transmission and access. Today, it is the Internet, the World Wide Web and the mobile phone that control the movement of information throughout the world. Alluding to Internet, Shuman observes that "only a few truly revolutionary events can be said to have completely and irreversibly transformed the growth of recorded knowledge in the Western world" (Shuman, 2001, p. 11). The Internet and the agencies involved in providing internet access are described briefly.

Internet, World Wide Web (WWB) and other networks take us to the world of information and similar categories of items like e-books, and digital video texts either by a click of the mouse on a computer or by a few touches on the mobile telephone. There is no human intermediary to encroach on our operational environment; and the exposure to information is direct and non-intermediary. In contrast, in a library or information centre there is the human intermediary to guide us to reach our information item. One may not use or need the direct assistance of library staff, yet the library plays a mediatory role by intellectual processing of information texts by collecting, ordering, and servicing them in a human environment. The mediatory role gets limited once the collection is accessible online. In the non-mediatory exploration of the information world, to tap information items one is tied to the screen. The joy of enjoying serendipity effect is reduced, and the charm of intent walks between the rows of shelves. In the cyberspace one is assured of exclusive environment, unlimited freedom to play on the screen, speed of access and reach. All this we owe to one main invention, the invention of computer.

Computer Revolution. The first general purpose computer ENAIC (Electronic Numerical Integrator and Calculator) was built by Mauchly and Eckert in 1946 at the University of Pennsylvania under the sponsorship of U S Army. Compared to the present-day computers ENIAC looks like belonging to the dinosaur's era. UNIVAC-1 was introduced to the market in 1951 and proved successful. This was followed by 701 machine built by IBM. IBM introduced 360/370 mainframe computer in 1953, which overshadowed other machines in the market manufactured by companies like Digital, Sperry, Honeywell and Burrows. The real revolution started around 1982 with the introduction of microprocessor based Apple I, and later Apple II microcomputers. In 1981, IBM introduced the microcomputer with the name Personal Computer (PC), which at once became very popular. Taking advantage of a legal lacuna other countries, particularly some Asian countries, started large-scale copying of IBM PC and marketed them at affordable prices. With the introduction of laptop machines use of computers has become a universal phenomena (Castells, 2000). All the time, software development kept phase with the hardware development. The first generation programming languages like COBOL, FORTRAN, and BASIC, were replaced by more sophisticated and user friendly languages like JAVA and C+ +. Internet revolution became possible because of the rapid devolvement of computer and communication technologies.

THE INTERNET

The Internet is an enormous network of networks of globally linked computers that enable users to search for and retrieve information from all over the world. Its history goes back to the Sputnik era. It came as a US response to the launching of Sputnik satellite by the Soviet Union. The US Defence Department's Advanced Research Projects Agency (DARPA) gave concrete shape to the idea of designing a communication system that can withstand a nuclear attack. As a result ARPANET, the first computer network combining packet-switching communication technology and digital technology became operational on September1, 1969. This online network initially had four universities as its nodes. Later, it was made accessible to scientists of other research centres cooperating with the US Department of Defence. In course of time, the ARPANET became the communication channel for military and scientific work besides being used by scientists for their personnel communication. It was followed by a number of technological and administrative developments, such as separation of MILNET used for military applications from ARPANET dedicated for scientific use, founding of a scientific network CSNET by the National Science Foundation (NSF) of America and BISNET in collaboration with IBM for the use of scholars in non-scientific disciplines—all these nets working on the backbone of ARPANET. This network of networks was called ARPA INTERNET and later INTERNET. In 1990, following the closure of ARPANET, the NSFNET of NSF took over as the backbone of INTERNET. There is confusion over the institutional authority coordinating the activities of the Internet. In spite of the establishment in 1998 of a new American-based regulatory body named the Internet Corporation for Assigned Names and Numbers (ICANN) to coordinate Internet activities there is no clarity on the authority. Now it has reached the UN's World Summit on Information Society seeking an international arrangement (Castells, 2000; www.theinternet).

The creation of hypertext mark-up language (HTML) which provides flexibility to accommodate different computer languages on the Internet; development of hypertext transfer protocol (HTTP) to establish smooth communication links between the web browser and the web server; and the finding of uniform resource locator (URL)- a standard address format are the enabling features of Internet functioning. In 1992, Netscape Corporation of USA developed Netscape Navigator, the first reliable Internet browser, replacing Mosaic. Mosaic was developed by Marc Anderson and Eric Bina who distributed it free. New developments in telecommunication and computer technologies have blurred the distinctions between decentralized stand alone microcomputers and mainframes. Database server and application servers made it possible to access the Internet from any location using portable devices. Access through PC, mobile phone, satellite-connected personal digital assistants (PDAs) Internet access, voice transmission, video conferencing, and other types of communication have become common utilities. It is expected that the combination of bio-molecular and chemical nanotechnology will revolutionize chip making to enhance the versatility of computing to an unimaginable degree. To capture information from Internet the information needs to be first created by someone, and then suitably shaped and organized, which is done by Content Providers and Portals before it becomes available on the Internet (Ricart-Costa et al., 2004). This aspect has been dealt with earlier in chapter 15.

The World Wide Web. It is a part of the Internet with its own independent identity. The Web was developed by the European Laboratory for Particle Physics in the early 1990s and is credited to Tim Barnes-Lee. It is a special software system run on the Internet linking millions of web sites/homepages spread across the world, and its use is still growing. The web sites account for more than three fourths of Internet traffic. It is a hypertext system in HTML format with links from one document to any other document stored in any PC anywhere in the world, and works on HTTP protocol. A web page may have not only text passages, but also other features like, audio visual texts, pictures, software, which can be downloaded. Linking of one document with another document does not infringe upon copyright of the owner of the document. No one has complete control over the links (Kent, 1996). Capacity of the web is limitless. The network of documents in the web are so vast, the route taken to establish a link is difficult to predict. In a sense web is limitless publishing activity spread across the globe enabling any individual or a group to become an author or content producer. There are millions of web sites, which putout information- scholarly, serious, ephemeral, genuine, doubtful and fraudulent. They are installed by information companies, government departments, individuals, all types of institutions and organizations, political groups, activists, social movements, criminals, terrorist outfits, and many others all of which are available to anyone who has access to an Internet connection. Any transaction on web has to complete two special programmes- one by web server running on the host computer, and the other by the browser, a programme attached to the access or PC. The server manages a web site hosting documents on the WWW. The browser seeks the document from the server and displays it on the screen. Out of the nearly 80-90 browsers available in the market, the most popular browser is the Internet Explorer from Microsoft (Castells, 2000).

Online Services. The Internet and online services are similar in some ways, but not same. Online services are large networks belonging to private initiatives, which are accessible only through membership and serve as a gateway to Internet. In contrast, Internet is a communication system that is linked to millions of computers owned by tens of thousands of companies, schools, government departments, and individuals. From an online service one can freely access Internet (Kent,1996).

Internet 2. A second version of Internet is under development. Named Internet 2, it is a high-performance network to serve the needs of education, research, and the next generation public Internet. It is developed by a non-profit consortium supported by IBM, Qwest, Cisco, and 3Com with active participation of 200 universities, 70 corporations, and 45 non-profit bodies, and US Government departments. The original Internet 2 project was founded informally in 1996 as the University Corporation for Advanced Internet Development (USAID). Later the name was changed to Internet 2. An important objective of Internet 2 is to monitor, filter, and limit all traffic on the network. Subsequently, *Abilene Network*- a high-speed Internet Protocol (IP) research and education network was established through collaboration among Qwest,

Cisco, Nortel Networks, Indiana University, and Internet 2. Internet 2 is not intended to replace the Internet, but to serve as a specialist Internet designed to meet the needs of scholars, scientists and educationists (Wikipedia; and www.com.qwest). The idea is to create a decongested Internet by eliminating the high volume popular functions like e-mail, chat and commercial websites which are currently cluttering the Internet (wikipedia.internet2; www.quest/internet2).

The Internet is such a versatile medium that one can use it not only for accessing information on any topic under the sun, but also to send and receive e-mail, chat over the Net, read newspapers online, conduct sales, make home purchase, book airline tickets and hotel reservations, watch favourite sports event, hear music, select a spouse, hunt for employment opportunities, learn online, telecommute, outsource services, conduct live conferences on the screen, interview candidates for selection, become an author and publisher, identify locations through city maps via global positioning system (GPS), get prayers offered to a deity, match horoscopes, diagnose diseases and prescribe medicine, operate personal finances, transmit money, indulge in stock market, advertise your views and wares, hatch a terrorist attack, spread rumours, gamble online, propagate pornography, commoditize sex, lay traps to cheat gullible, steal personal identity and use them for illegal gains, plagiarize texts, hack others' sites, spread virus, and many more activities. However, it is important to note that the Internet and the web as distributed networks with no central point or authority to control, are "vast, unedited, uncensored compendia of 'information', not all of which is knowledge, some of which might not be deemed acceptable for all people to view or access, and certainly, not all of which is true or verifiable" (Shuman, 2001, p.14). The Internet is put to a remarkable array of uses and misuses.

Web 3.0. Currently developments are on to create the third generation Web 3.0, which is also called Semantic Web.

It is to supersede the presently popular Web 2.0, which is mostly designed to facilitate web-based services like social-networking, video-sharing, wikis, and blogs. The prime feature of Web 3-0 is to bring in 3D experience. Its application will be more towards focused groups with enormous scope for commercial exploitation. It is expected to be of virtual reality location where consumers will have free-play. The Semantic Web depends on the use of a declarative ontological language like OWL to produce domain specific ontology, which machines can use to reason about information and make new conclusions, not simply match keywords (Fawzi,2006. http://). Although, Web 3.0 is still in a developmental stage there are conjectures made about creating Web 4.0.

Drawbacks. The following are some of the negative aspects of Internet and Internet accessed information highlighted by Shuman in his book *Issues for Libraries and Information Science in the Internet Age.*

1. The enormous quantity of information flowing in the Net makes focussed search difficult. Being drowned in a mass of information- relevant and irrelevant, useful and not so useful- to keep one's intellectual balance of mind is a real challenge. It is easy to loose one's way in the labyrinth of information, get frustrated, and feel unsatisfied when searching for a specific item of information.
2. There is no guarantee about the reliability of the information posted on the web. A lot of it may turn out to be malicious, misinforming or even totally false. "Feeding frenzy" conditions in the information arena caused by the right of access to full information by one and all does not allow applying "need to know" and other quality standards.
3. Selfishness of individuals inhibits sharing of information. The aspect of distribution of information for public good is totally ignored by people who receive or produce information. Information capable of fetching high

monetary returns may not enter Internet and thus not accessible.

4. Information posted may be skewed or even hopelessly inaccurate. There is the danger of crediting accuracy, fairness and truth to information just because it has appeared in the Net. This is particularly so with young people who are yet to learn the need for critical evaluation of the information they are exposed to.

5. Information appearing in the Net may be biased or suppressed due to the operation of monopoly effects caused by mergers, acquisitions, hostile takeovers and insolvencies occurring in the information industry. Further, it leads to less competition of new sources and a general homogeneity of those sources' view point. But, this is a common feature of industries as a whole.

6. Any information appearing in the Net it is unless downloaded and preserved may be lost forever. On the Net the longevity of information is short, may be six months.

7. Web may be used by individuals as an excuse to avoid person to person contact. Government departments, institutions and firms by directing enquirers to their web sites eliminate person to person contact. The web sites giving pre-recorded answers to 'frequently asked questions' may not have satisfactory answers to the query. The human voice comfort is sacrificed for the sake of efficiency and economy.

8. The principle of least effort may dissuade searchers of information on the Net to pursue with their search or tap other sources, if response is too slow or due to interruptions.

9. E-mail recipients are often subjected to "flaming", the sending of messages of anger, scorn, threat, and reproof causing irritation, disgust and anger. Such messages may

also be spread to other sites- acts which are against the spirit of Internet ethics.

10. Acts of dishonesty. Examples are cheating, plagiarism, spreading of false alarms- say a bomb is planted in a particular public place.
11. Reduces one's critical faculties in evaluating the net served information. This is not entirely the fault of Internet. The problem can be attributed to information explosion, and one's intellectual capacity to analyse and absorb information.
12. Naiveté, gullibility, or both.
13. Constant use of Internet, even a few hours a week, can affect on the psychological wellbeing of the user causing, in psychologist's terminology, "information fatigue syndrome". The adverse effects may show up in the form of headache, feeling of loneliness, insomnia, social withdrawal, and even depression. The cause may be attributed to the difference between the living in a natural environment and the virtual world of the Net.

It is difficult to identify and control abuses, as Internet is controlled by none and has no office or any director/manager who could be approached for remedies. No foolproof remedies are available to netizens in spite of the development and availability of many antivirus, data security solutions, and access barring filters. Common law remedies are available, but enactment of specific laws against cyberspace crimes are always lagging behind. The critical issue raised by the Internet revolution is ".... Will the Net enhance individual autonomy or infringe upon privacy? Will it increase people's economic independence- or expand corporate power?" (Samuelson, 2000, p. 45).

CLOSURE

History of libraries goes back to fourth millennium BC,

when Sumerian libraries maintained records on clay tablets. It was the Renaissance followed by the Industrial revolution that provided the real impetus to the growth and development modern libraries in the West. The modern library story in India began in early nineteenth century, when public libraries were established in Calcutta (1836), Madras (Chennai) (1840), and Bombay (1857) (Mumbai). This was followed by the establishment of the Imperial Library in Calcutta under the Imperial Library Act 1902. The first genuine public library system in India came to be established in the princely state of Baroda around 1910. The development of special libraries, and to some extent academic libraries, has progressed comparatively better due to government's role, proper guidance and necessity.

Segmentation of user populations according to their types of needs led to the creation of different types of libraries. The electronic media coupled with the communication technology advances radically changed the information world, and with it the orientation of libraries.

All libraries have in common certain core features or values, which have evolved over time. These features represent physical/technological, cultural and social, intellectual, managerial, and international functions of libraries.

The physical aspects are related to location and housing, functional space allocation, furniture and equipment, and the physical organization of the collection. The major technological developments that changed the course of library development were: the invention of clay tablets as the writing surface, the introduction of paper, the invention of printing, and now the computer and communication technology revolution, which has given the Internet. *Library automation* led to computerisation of specific library functions. Presently libraries are in the *library information system* phase, which covers the entire range of information resources, materials, and services.

The intellectual part in the functioning of libraries is mainly accounted by intellectual organization of the collection for providing users with access to the collection, and bibliographic control. From the beginning, librarians had to handle three basic intellectual processes in managing a collection- describing the records held and added; ordering them for access and recall; and reference— the functions of cataloguing, classification/retrieval, and reference service respectively. Libraries in the last fifty years have seen a number of initiatives to standardize, make seamless and streamline the intellectual processes in libraries. Library cooperation has taken a number of modes including centralized acquisition and processing, and creation of library networks.

The distinctive features of library and information management are: a) libraries are to cope up with the intangible nature of knowledge and information, b) libraries are service organizations; c) generally they are parts of a larger organization, and hence they are bound by the philosophy, culture, structure, rules and policies of the parent organization; and d) they form an important link in the larger chain of information-knowledge system.

Libraries, archives and museums have long been considered to be a part of the cultural heritage of a society. Their contents mirror the cultural history of the group. Social facet of libraries is mainly represented by : a) the libraries' role in increasing awareness in society; b) recognition of their social obligation of catering to the needs of special groups, such as minorities and physically challenged; and c) acceptance of cooperation between libraries as necessary to serve readers better. The two critical turning points in the history of public library movement were the transition of libraries from the limited view of service to that of a real public service, and from closed access to open access system.

From historic times libraries have fulfilled an international function. IFLA and UNESCO are two major international organizations which work for the development of libraries, bibliographic control, and library education and research. Philanthropy has contributed significantly in furthering the cause of libraries.

In the technology driven new information order with its Internet, web sites, e-publications and multimedia dominating the information world a frequently raised question is about the future of libraries. It appears that while the importance of special libraries in their present form will decrease, the scope for public library service will enlarge. This is because meeting the information needs of information have-nots, the rural community, and the indigenous people, which have been neglected so far, calls for immediate attention.

From the first computer ENAIC installed in 1946 to the Internet 2 is an extraordinary technological progress that has transformed the world of information. While Internet, over a short period of about 25 years, has become the central nerve controlling information flow in many societies, the World Wide Web has become the memory bank of those societies. The rosy world of Internet and networks is also the home for cyber crimes, computer virus, hash, and sometimes unreliable information.

Knowledge and information are now considered as the most valued resource. If information explosion mirrors the activities of an expanding human universe, then a globalized world reflects a shrinking universe filled with intangible knowledge and tangible information. From clay tablet to printed book, and from printed book to electronic bit is a long fascinating voyage; and so is the journey from library to data processing, and from data processing to cyber space and back.

REFERENCES

Andretta, Susie. Information Literacy: A Practioner's Guide. Oxford (U.K.), Chandos Publishing, 2005.

Artandi, Susan. Man, information and society: New patterns of interaction.

Journal of the American Society for Information Science 30: 16-17, 1979.

Castells, Manuel. The Rise of the Network Society. Ed.2. Oxford (UK), Blackwell Publishers, 2000. (The Information Age: Economy, Society and Culture- Vol.1.).

Cleverdon, C.W. Communication networks, their impact and effect on the nature of the profession. *In* Taylor, P.J. Ed. New trends in documentation and information. (Proceedings of the 39th FID. Congress, Edinburgh, 1978). London, Aslib, 1980.

Datta, Bimal Kumar. Libraries and Librarianship of Ancient, and Medieval India. Delhi, Atma Ram, 1970.

Fawzi, Marc. Evolving Trends. http://evolving trends.wordpress.com/2006/06/ wikipedia-30- theend of google/

Mc Garry, Kevin, Feather, John and Sturges, Paul. Eds. International Encyclpaedia of Information and Library Science. Ed.2. Libraries. Pp. 371-374. London. Routledge, 2003.

Glynn, Tom. Historical Perspectives on Global Librarianship. Pp.1-17. *In* Kesselman, Martin Alan and Weintraub, Irwin. Ed. Global Librarianship. New York, Marcel Dekker, 2004.

Cf. Harris, M.H. History of Libraries in the WesternWorld. Ed. 4. Metuchen (NJ), Metuchen, 1995.

Hindu, The, April 10, 2009. "Step towards knowledge society sans boundaries". Reporter: Priscilla Jebaraj.

IGNOU. Indira Gandhi National Open University. School of Social Sconces. Master's Degree in Library and Information Science. ML11- 103: Fundamentals of Information Communication Technologies. 2005.

India 2008: A Reference Annual. New Delhi, Publications Division, Government of India, 2007.

India. National Knowledge Commission. Compilation of Recommendations on Education. Chairman: Sam Pitroda. New Delhi, 2007. (Recommendations made up to Nov. 2007). Also at www.knowledgecommission.gov.in

Jebaraj, Franklin David and Devadoss, Frederick Robin. Library and information networks in India. *Library Philosophy and Practice* 6 (2): 1-8, 2004.

Johnson, Elmer D. History of Libraries in the Western World. Ed. 2. Metuchen (N.J.), 1970.

Kent, Peter. The Complete Idiot's Guide to the Internet. Ed.3. New Delhi, Prentice-Hall of India, 1996. (Indian reprint. Original publisher Que Corporation).

Kibirige, H.M. The Information Dilemma: A Critical Analysis of Information Pricing and the Fees Controversy. Westport (CT), Greenwood Press, 1983.

Kochtanek, Thomas R. and Matthews, Joseph R. Library and Information Systems. From Library Automation to Distributed Information Access Solution. Westport (CT), Libraries Unlimited, 2004.

Krishan Kumar and Patel, Jashu. Libraries and Librarianship in India. Westport (Ct.), Greenwood Publishing, 2001.

Cf. Lerner, F. Libraries Through the Ages. New York, Continuum Publishing, 1999.

Narayana, G.J. Library and Information Management. New Delhi, Prentice-Hall of India, 1991.

NCLIS. National Commission on Libraries and Information Science (NCLIS). Towards a National Program for Library and Information Services: Goals for Action. Washington (DC), US Superintendent of Documents, 1975.

Neelameghan, A. Information economy and knowledge society : An introduction. Part 2: Information access: International and national aspects. *Information Studies* 5(3): 169- 196, July 1999.

Neelameghan, A and Chester, Greg. Knowledge Management in Relation to Indigenous and Marginalized Communities in the Digital Era: National Conference on Library and Information Studies (NACLIN 2007). Colombo, Sri Lanka, 8-9 March 2007.[on CD]. Proceedings. html

Reitz, Joan M. Dictionary for Library and Information Science. Westport (CT), Libraries Unlimited, 2004.

Rettig, James. Reference Service: From Certainty to Uncertainty. Pp.105-143. *In* Nitecki, Danuta A. and Abels, Eileen G. Ed. Advances in Librarianship. Vol.30, 2006. Oxford (UK), Academic Press/ Elsevier, 2006.

Reynolds, A.G. and Flagg, P.W. Cognitive Psychology. Cambridge (Mass.), Winthrop Publishers, 1977.

Ricart-Costa, Joan E.; Subirana, Brian, and Valor-Sabatier, Joseph. Sources of Information Value: Strategic Framing and the Transformation of the Information Industries. London, Palgrave, 2004.

Cf. Samuelson, Robert J. "Judgment Calls: The Internet and Gutenberg," *Newsweek*, 24 Jan. 2000.

Shera, J.H. The Foundations of Education for Librarianship. New York, Wiley-Becker and Hayes, 1972.

Shuman, Bruce A. Issues for Libraries and Information Science in the Internet Age. Englewood (Colo.). Libraries Unlimited, 2001. (Indian edition, 2005).

Taylor, Arlene G. Wynar's Introduction to Cataloging and Classification. Ed. Westport (CT), Libraries Unlimited, 2000, Indian ed. 2005.

Wedgeworth, Robert. International Library Organizations, Pp.19-31. *In* Kesselman, Martin Alan and Weintraub, Irwin. Ed. Global Librarianship. New York, Marcel Dekker, 2004.

www.gates.http://www.gatesfoundation.org./about/Pages/foundation-timeline.aspx27th March, 2009).

www.Quest/internet 2. http://www.qwest.com/about/qwest/internet2/faqs.html

www.rockfound. http://www.rockfound.org/aboutus.shtml

www.the internet. http://www.foreignaffairs.com/articles/61192/kenneth-neil-cukier/who- will-control-theinternet 26Mar.2009

Wikipedia.Internet2.http://en.wikipedia.org/wiki/Internet2.html

Wikipedia. Rockfeller. http://en.wikipedia.org/wki/RockfellerFoundation

World of Learning (Europa) 2006. Ed. 56. Vol. 1. London, Routledge, 2005.

Cf.Yitai, G. and Gorman, G.E. Libraries and Information Services in China.

Lanham (MD), Scarecrow Press, 2003. P. 3-4.

20

KNOWLEDGE MANAGEMENT

The emerging knowledge-based society of the 21st century is initiated and sustained by knowledge and information acting as the dominant force of production. Information as a commodity has brought about a conceptual change in managing industrial organizations. The creation, transmission, dissemination and utilization of knowledge is no more an adjunct function in managing industries and business. The world of knowledge and information is growing in complexity and are in a state of flux. To bring order, ensure efficient and purposeful utilization of knowledge, to harness knowledge for increasing organizational efficiency, and thereby adapt to the new competitive global economy new approaches are evolving. One such approach is Knowledge Management (KM).

Advent of Knowledge Management. The Industrial and Business (I&B) environment have tremendously changed and continue to change fast since late 20th century. The major forces acting in the new environment are:

1. Multiple impacts of science and technology on the lives of people, working of professionals, functioning of governments, conducting business, and industrial growth.
2. Continuous changes caused by increasing new developments in information, computer and

communication technologies (in particular the Internet, networks, and cell phones), and their effects on all human endeavors, and more so on all economic activities. This has introduced enormous speed, mobility, and choice in functioning of organizations. Consequently, change itself has become the only constant.

3. Globalization of trade and commerce in the new World Trade Organization (W.T.O.) treaty era.
4. Changing nature of competition.
5. Volatile pattern of customer behaviour and increasing stress laid on customer satisfaction.
6. Recognition of intellectual capital of an I&B enterprise as an asset, whose accumulation adds to the worth of an enterprise.
7. Society and also I&B increasingly becoming knowledge based.
8. Opportunities laid open with the creation of new products, new services, new fashions, fads and tastes.

It is this challenging situation that provided the right moment for the advent of KM and the hope that KM will offer solutions for many of the problems.

WHAT IS KNOWLEDGE MANAGEMENT?

Knowledge Management is an interdisciplinary domain. It takes its place along with other I&B practices like Total Quality Management (TQM), Business Process Re-engineering BPR), and Learning organization. Abell and Oxbrow define Knowledge Management as the 'creation and subsequent management of an environment which encourages knowledge to be created, shared, learnt, enhanced, and organized for the benefit of the organization and its customers" (Abell and Oxbrow, 2001, in the glossary). However, in the perception of corporate world, according to the results of a survey of 1000 top German and 200 top European companies, 55.5% of the participants discerned Knowledge Management as a part of corporate culture, which supports the active exchange of information, knowledge, and experiences between employees and departments; and 47.3% of the participants considered it as a company oriented method, in which the sum of procedures that determine the generation, distribution and application of knowledge to achieve organizational goals (Mertins et al., 2003).

KM is distinct from Information Management (IM). While IM deals mostly with explicit knowledge, KM is more concerned with tacit knowledge, its strategic and tactical applications to the entire organization. KM takes an integrated approach to the use of the intellectual capital of an enterprise. The main objective of KM is to make the enterprise a knowledge based organization that values creativity and innovation, allows people to learn from failure, and makes people in the enterprise realize the interdependence of work, people, and knowledge (Abell and Oxbrow, 2001).

Knowledge Management, like any other applied discipline, has its philosophy and theories that provide the intellectual base, and an application part devoted to techniques and processes, their development, and practice. An inclusive view of KM developed by David G. Schwartz is presented in Fig. 1.

In this layered view of KM, the core (first ring) is made up of key philosophers, philologists, economists, and philosophers of science, their theories and their exploration of knowledge. It is from these fundamentals, KM processes like knowledge creation, integration, maintenance, sharing, dissemination, and functions of knowledge acquisition, organization and distribution (second ring) draw their theoretical strength and integrity. The third ring represents the context and environment— organizational, social, and managerial with which the processes have to contend with to deliver the desired theory driven KM results. The environment is made up of

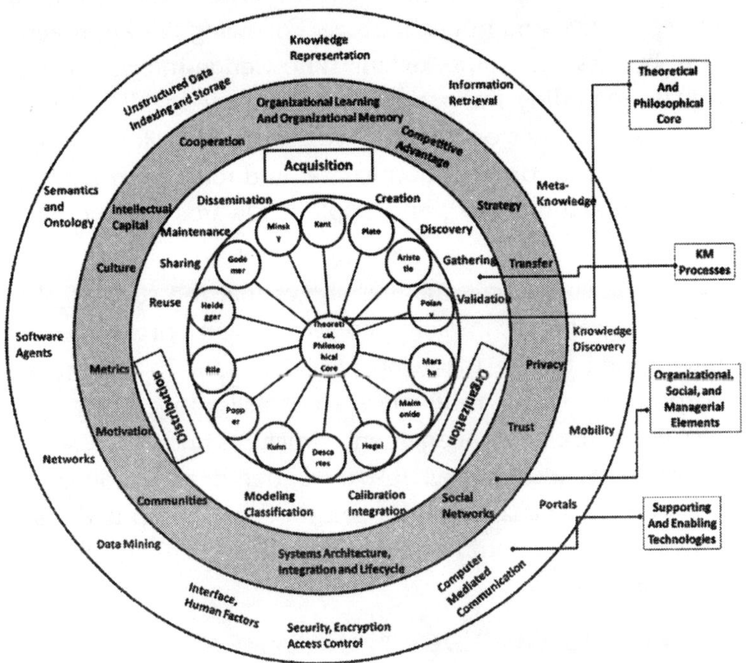

Fig. 1. Layer upon layer of Knowledge Management

(Adopted from David G. Schwartz. Aristotelian View of Knowledge Management. In Encyclopedia of Knowledge Management, London, Idea Group Inc., p.10. Copyright © 2006. Reprinted by permission of the publisher).

elements like trust, motivation, culture, intellectual capital, organizational learning, social networks, systems architecture, competitive advantage, and the like. Final ring shows the enabling technologies, like knowledge representation, knowledge discovery, networks, portals, software, computer-mediated communication, information retrieval, meta knowledge, data mining, and many others needed to support and implement the processes. The KM schema presented in Fig. 1 is dynamic as the layers keep on enlarging in keeping with technological advances, and emergence of new social concepts.

The elements and features shown in the figure are only representative and not exhaustive. Following this approach we can bypass, to some extent, knowledge-information-data debate regarding the granularity of knowledge. The focus of KM thus becomes one of how we process knowledge to make it viable for an organization to use, and reuse, and manage it as a tangible resource, and apply it towards specific actions (Schwartz, 2006).

The survey cited earlier shows that the success of any KM programme implementation in an organization is determined by the following critical factors, in the order of: corporate culture, motivation and skills, involvement and attitude of the top management, structures and processes, and information technology. KM is rendered as a consultancy service. In organizations KM setup generally forms a distinct unit or group within the Human Resource Development Division.

APPLIED KNOWLEDGE MANAGEMENT

Schwartz's vision of KM in Fig.1 represents the framework of KM, and the philosophical and theoretical foundation on which it stands. What is of interest to industry is the working part of it, i.e., applied KM. Applied KM is focused on the creation of new knowledge, and channelizing the flow of knowledge in the organization. In other words, how knowledge is made to circulate in the organization, and what that circulation means to the organization, which are shown in Fig. 2.

Knowledge acts through the people and personnel in the organization. It is the people who carry the tacit knowledge and apply it in their assigned functions and tasks, such as manufacturing or producing, marketing and servicing, management of finance and accounts, and others. The tacit knowledge so applied is to positively advance the functioning of an organization and its activities in the core areas of productivity (P), benchmark (B), decision-making (D), innovation (I), problem solving (P), and satisfaction or harmony (S), i.e., PBDIPS. As a result of the input knowledge acting on the organizations' functions and activities, the existing stock of tacit knowledge changes due to additions and deletions of knowledge items in the mind or gaining of new insights.

One of the most significant parts of in situ application of tacit knowledge is the new experience that may be gained, and the picking up of new learning that may be involved in the process. Thus, the modified tacit knowledge with the addition of explicit knowledge becomes the new input through the process of sharing and learning. Further, the modified tacit knowledge may be turned into explicit knowledge. The new knowledge consisting of both tacit and explicit versions will add to the organization's stock of assets in the form of intellectual capital, structural capital, and social capital. The entire process is facilitated by the use of computer and information technology

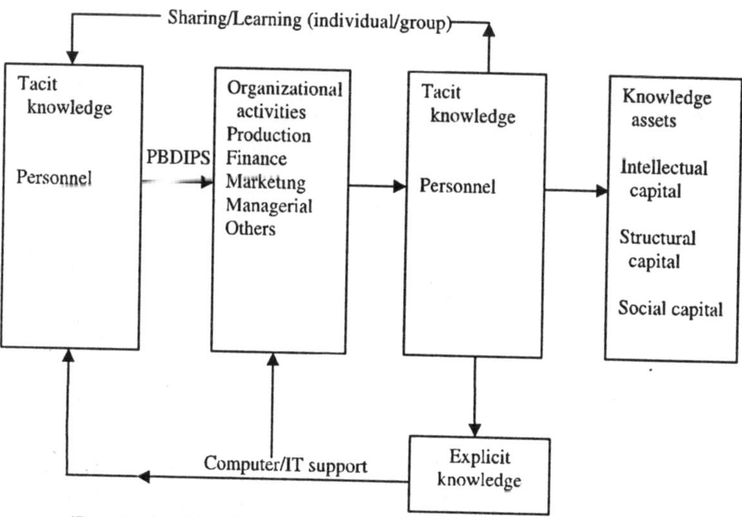

(P= Productivity, B= Benchmark, D= Decision making, I=Innovation, P=Problem solving, S= Satisfaction).

Fig. 2. Application side of KM: Flow and effects of knowledge.

as the supporting system. Internally generated explicit knowledge supplemented by explicit knowledge received through external sources will become a part of the tacit knowledge, which serves as the new input. It becomes an ongoing continuous process.

It is seen from the above figure that the principal objectives of KM are to help in: increasing productivity, decision-making, problem solving, generating creative ideas, to strive for benchmark, and enhance the level of satisfaction in the organization. In other words, the objective is to make the organization knowledge-based. These objectives are achieved through KM functions of sourcing of knowledge (S), sharing/learning of knowledge (S), applying knowledge (A), asset (knowledge) formation (A) and, computer/IT support building (C) or SSAACs for creating a knowledge-based organization as shown in Fig. 2). Each of these functions is further explained.

KNOWLEDGE IN KM: SOURCING

In contrast to the traditional epistemological view of knowledge as individually centered neural phenomena, KM considers knowledge as "a practical tool for framing experiences, sharing insights, and assisting with practical tasks" (Aarons, 2006, p. 167). Further, the effects of knowledge are judged by their impact as an organizational resource, which includes the *factual* knowledge of the individuals within the organization as well as their *practical* knowledge, *tacit* knowledge, and *technological* knowledge. Knowledge within a collaborative environment and its distributed features are of particular importance to KM. It takes an inclusive view of knowledge by drawing from the works of philosophy of science and social epistemology relating to methodology used in the creation of scientific knowledge, collaborative research, analysis of complex systems, shared features of knowledge, as well as the situatedness of the knower and other findings applicable to organizational environment. Thus, KM is structured on the foundations of individual knowledge, social knowledge, shared knowledge, collaborative knowledge and distributed knowledge (Aarons, 2006). KM sees knowledge as dynamic force acting not only through individuals, but also through organizational knowledge where there must be movement for knowledge to be transferred or shared. Further, the special features of KM processes, namely, the creation of knowledge, the intentional elicitation of knowledge, and the ability to share knowledge artifacts make KM distinct from the classical view of the organization of knowledge, and the history of information management (Mclnerney, 2002). .

Knowledge management also treats knowledge as a resource, which an enterprise acquires, creates, and uses. The resource view of knowledge is seen in three perspectives: a) knowledge as an object or product which needs to be identified, collected, and organized as codified knowledge for use in the organization. Such a collection may take the form of databases and uses Information technology for processing, sharing and disseminating information— the traditional perspective; b) knowledge as a dynamic process— a continuous process of creating, adopting, learning, applying and sharing/ communicating knowledge, and is sensitive to the demands of time; and c) knowledge as a complex self-organizing system. Here, knowledge evolves as a response to the changes in the organization as well as changes in the external economic, social, political, and ecological environment surrounding the organization. The system perspective insists on deliberate actions on the part of the organization to influence and shape the environment (Haravu, 2002). The choice of perspective made singly or in combination by an organization depends on several factors including the perception of the top management.

In KM programmes, comments Mclnerney, it is "the knowledge artifact, or the thing, that is managed, not knowledge itself, and the knowledge representation must reflect the action of knowledge acquisition" (Mclnerney, 2002, p.1011). Knowledge goes beyond mind activity; it is based on sensory experience and physical activity as well as mindful cognition (McInerney, 2002). It is essential to distinguish between tacit knowledge and explicit knowledge. The former is subconscious, personal with insights, judgments and assumptions being a part of it where as explicit knowledge is formally articulated through words, gestures and symbols. KM places high importance on harnessing tacit knowledge for organizational benefit. Tacit knowledge is of two types: a) knowledge in mind which can be laid down as rules and practices, and b) knowledge which is only felt and can be expressed only by demonstration. Most expertise is made up of tacit knowledge of non-expressible nature that can be made known only through actual implementation guided by heuristics, i.e., rules of thumb. It is the descriptions of the successfully solved "actual" cases by experts applying their expertise that can serve as the foundation for the establishment of "best practices" (Blair, 2002). Insights, past experiences and others' expertise, which are to be extracted out of peoples' mind, when applied to relevant information results in knowledge most valuable to an organization (Krishna Kumar, 2000 a). Experts are generally reluctant to part with their expertise unless there is sufficient motivation. One form of motivation is recognition. Organizations may motivate experts by giving ownership and credit to the contributions made by them. Experts seem to value peer acclaim more than monetary incentives (Krishna Kumar, 2000 b).

The constant transformation of tacit knowledge into explicit knowledge and explicit knowledge into tacit knowledge occurring in an organization, and how to capture them, convert them into useful applications, and ultimately turn them into the organization's asset are major tasks in KM. This takes us to the study of the new ways of creating knowledge in organizations. Earlier, knowledge creation was an exclusively human preserve. But now knowledge, subject to limitations, can also be created by means of applying artificial intelligence, and information technology techniques. Two such techniques used by KM are knowledge discovery in databases (KDD) and data mining. KDD is used on data sets for creating new knowledge through model building, or by finding patterns and relationships in existing data and manipulating them. KM makes use of both KDD and data mining. Data mining is mostly used for carrying out descriptive and predicting applications, and makes use of machine leaning, artificial intelligence and statistical algorithms (Wickramasinghe, 2006).

Organizations internally generate large amounts of data and collect information from external sources. Data in its descriptive form is called *metadata*. Collecting, storing, analyzing and disseminating this data is one of the important functions of KM. The accumulated data is a part of the knowledge resource of the organization and is included in its assets as intellectual capital (Gillman, 2006). Disseminating and sharing of this resource is efficiently achieved by creating web sites and portals through which the organizational personnel, clients, customers and public can easily access what the organization wants to inform and share. Portals by virtue of content organization, structuring of information and tagging make access and sharing of information easy and user friendly (Woods et al, 2006).

Locating expertise is one of the common problems encountered in life. It is equally true of organizations and firms. Whenever a problem needing the application of a particular skill or knowledge arises one thinks of seeking assistance from the experts in the field. If the problem is critical, it needs to be attended immediately; there is no waiting period. Searching the source of expertise and skill becomes complex in large organizations, particularly when the help is needed at once. Last minute search situation can be avoided by maintaining a "knowledge inventory" or "knowledge map" similar to a ready reckoner. Such an inventory provides an explicit tabulation of the organization's knowledge assets with the listing of individuals and their expertise included. Development of resourceful "knowledge workers" with specialized skills and analytical mind to assess quality, reliability and relevancy of each source of knowledge beneficial to the organization becomes an important task. Possessing knowledge workers who can create value through effective decision-making in the most complex of environments featuring change, uncertainty and differing organizational cultures is crucial to KM (Blair, 2002). Knowledge maps can also be used to develop necessary strategies and techniques to manage knowledge, and in tactical decision-making.

Expressed in terms of knowledge, the core activities in KM, according to the survey cited earlier, were: a) identification of relevant knowledge, b) setting knowledge goals, c) generation of new knowledge, d) storage of knowledge, e) distribution of knowledge, and f) applications.

KNOWLEDGE TRANSFER AND SHARING

It was stated earlier that learning and sharing of knowledge is a key function of KM. Learning and sharing of knowledge takes place through transfer of knowledge. There are different interpretations in concluding when knowledge transfer is complete between the transferor and the transferee. According to some, knowledge must both be communicated and applied before it has been transferred; to a few others, transfer has occurred if the recipient of knowledge has the capacity to apply it; and to many others, transfer is complete, if it has been cognitively transferred, meaning that the recipient has understood or made meaning out of it. All these interpretations are useful depending on context (King, 2006). The process of transferring knowledge is generally called communication.

Communication. Human communication is complete when knowledge, skill or insight is transferred from one person to another, and the receiver is able to successfully reconstruct the knowledge thus transferred to him. Communication is of two types: face-to-face or real-time interactions, and delayed, usually media-based (virtual) interactions. Knowledge transfer is more than communicating information (facts, situations, developments) or emotions (e.g., fear commitment). Communication to become effective needs appropriate environment, which includes the elements of trust, body language, time-factor, and many others. Without supply of context information does not become knowledge. Communication of knowledge between experts and decision-makers could be affected by a number of factors. These factors may be categorized under: a) expert related problems, mainly caused by knowledge asymmetry, use of specialist jargons, and ego problems; b) manager related problems due to the manager's inability to frame clearly the problem and to state what the manager expects from the expert; c) differential behaviour and attitude factors like mutual feedback; d) problems relating to interaction situations; and e) constraints imposed by differing organizational specific factors like vesting of authority, tasks and priorities of the manager and the expert (Eppler, 2006). In an organizational context, interdepartmental communication can make all the difference between well coördinated, harmonious working of departments aimed at achieving goals, and departments working tangentially resulting in a dysfunctional organization. Ineffective organizational structure, personal rivalry, lack of trust among functionaries, and keeping objectives vague are some of the factors that adversely affect smooth and purposeful flow of communication in an organization.

Learning. Learning at work is an important element in KM. Such learning, apart from traditional initiatives, ranges from learning through team programmes to organization-wide efforts aimed at making learning organizations. Need for relearning is not an uncommon feature especially in established units. When there is large-scale change caused by : introduction of new techniques, such as Total Quality Management (TQM), and Business Process Recycling (BPR); introduction of new equipment and machinery; major organizational restructuring due to mergers and de-mergers; and significant cultural changes relearning becomes compulsory (Gold et al., 2002). The other forms of learning include training programmes, seminars, e-learning, and face-to-face learning. As important as learning is de-learning. In the dynamic world of business and industry things keep changing. Hence, continuing the old processes, practices and methods in the changed environment affects the organizational viability in a competitive world. Hence unlearning should be a part of the organization's knowledge strategy, and KM is to help identify areas needing unlearning (Haravu, 2002). De-learning is not easy to implement because of factors, such as : a) the general tendency of opposition to change, and b) continuous practice over a period of time has the tendency to become a habit, which is difficult to overcome.

Learning Environment. Knowledge flourishes in a free environment, and more so in a human environment. The question is how free and congenial is the organization's environment for free flow of knowledge and information. It is an irony that on the one hand, we are dehumanizing the learning environment by making it impersonal, machine dictated and byte centered; and on the other hand, a lot of resources and time are invested to re-humanize the same environment to make it more condusive for live interpersonal and group knowledge encounters and associations. Unless these obstacles are overcome, attaining the goal of creating a knowledge based enterprise will remain only a vision.

KM nurtures knowledge growth process by increased exposure of people to various learning options at different levels. KM employs both online learning and conventional methods; builds user friendly communication channels for the smooth flow of knowledge. Having acquired knowledge, its application in decision-making, development, and building relations across the enterprise is expected to energize the organization. Successful implementation of learning programmes leads to a positive change in the mindset of people in the organization, and increase their commitment to function better by applying the knowledge newly learnt. If the process of learning, creation of knowledge, its use and reuse becomes an organization-wide phenomena, it will make the enterprise a truly knowledge-based organization.

Sharing of Knowledge. Sharing of knowledge is a key component in KM. The objective is noble, but institutionalizing it is a challenge in an organizational setup. There are several impediments in the way. Among the obstacles are: a) those related to knowledge sharing process, and b) those related to the creation of a learning environment.

Knowledge Sharing Process. Trust among people in an organization is a prerequisite for sharing knowledge and experience. It is on trust that knowledge culture is built in an organization; and creating trust is one of the most difficult parts of KM (Mclnerney, 2002). Ultimately, sharing of knowledge is between two or more minds, and involves a good deal of understanding, shared values, and common interest between the participants. However, this sharing process differs to some extent when applied to a group. Decision to share or not to share depends to a large extent on the individual's mental make-up, his value system, organization culture, and other social, cultural, and psychological factors. A few questions associated with sharing of knowledge are: a) Why one wants to share his or her personally held knowledge with others? b) What will the individual personally gain or lose in the bargain? and c) With whom the individual is required to share the knowledge, and how is the equation between the two? Answers to these questions will decide the choice. Knowledge sharing takes two forms: sharing within the organization, and between the organization and its environment. Sharing of knowledge includes both tacit and explicit knowledge. People may use face-to-face contacts as well as telephone, Internet, and other ICT- based systems. "Communities of Practice" (CoP) is one means of sharing knowledge especially in large multinational organizations. Organizational structure also determines the strength and the channels through which knowledge exchanges take place. Motivation and material incentives are important factors that influence a person's attitude towards sharing (Reychav and Weisberg, 2006).

Communities of Practice. An important feature of KM is establishing, maintaining, and facilitating communication between experts and novices in the organization. One of the means designed to achieve this is through promoting Communities of Practice (CoP). For Communities of Practice to succeed there must be willingness on the part of the experts and the novices to share information with each other (Blair, 2002). Communities of Practice in an organizational context, is a means of promoting learning and building competence. Social and professional bonds tie members together. An organization can exploit these bonds for enriching the internal work culture by promoting the concept of CoP. This is not easy as participation in CoP is voluntary. Many CoPs disappear after sometime or become a part of the formal organizational structure, and in the latter case they lose their original goal of knowledge sharing informally. They tend to become project teams. While a project team is bound to a particular project, CoPs are bound by socio-technical ideals of inclusivity with fluid boundaries. It is the wide-ranging domain interests, different experiences, and work cultures of participants that encourage mutual exchange of ideas, creative thinking, and development of problem solving skills (Coakes and Clarke, 2006). Several aspects of CoP, such as evaluating the contribution of CoP to an organization, psychology of participants, organizational response to CoP are not easy to assess. Seen pragmatically there could also be some doubt as to whether we are exaggerating CoP contributions to an organization, and its sustainability across the entire range of industries (Coakes and Clarke, 2006). What is now called by the grand name of CoP has been practiced by scientific community since long, and it has contributed to progress of science in no small measure. It is successful in science because there is a fraternal relationship among scientists, strong domain identity, and clear norms of scientific research.

Organizations create, collect and make use of all types of information records- data, text, images, schematics, video, audio, web pages as ancillary sources of explicit knowledge. For facilitating sharing of this explicit knowledge organizations need to install database management systems. With these one can access a wide variety of places and sources through interconnected networks, storage systems, user platforms, and interfaces linked through an efficient and cost-effective communication system involving high bandwidth communication channels, a common multimedia communication protocol, and other enabling technologies (Blair, 2002).

APPLYING KNOWLEDGE

KM achieves its objectives by applying KM processes and techniques through raising the level of knowledge (relevant to the task) of people engaged in carrying out the organization's functions and activities. These functions include production and manufacturing, finance, marketing, managerial and others as shown in. Fig. 2. KM process is relevant to every function or activity of the organization as the scope for increasing efficiency will always be there; there is always a better way of functioning; and there is no limit to innovation. A key function in any organization, factory or firm is production or manufacturing, and hence is the most fertile area for applying KM techniques and methods.

Production Process. The focus of KM in industrial and business enterprises is on the production processes. Production is the primary activity in such enterprises followed by marketing and others. The survival and growth of an enterprise largely depend on economizing cost of production, distribution and marketing, i.e., "Supply Chain Management" and/ or product improvisation and introduction of new products vis-à-vis market competition and customer satisfaction. Production engineering emerged in the mid-twentieth century with the objective of increasing productivity by streamlining the manufacturing processes, bringing efficiency, standardizing procedures, sustaining quality, controlling cost, installing prudent financial procedures following scientific methods. Development of new techniques and tools to plan, to measure, to move, to improve, to design and redesign, and to cut cost became a part of this approach. This was not sufficient to meet the challenges or take on the market forces of the digital era. The new requirements gave rise to the development of more advanced systems such as "Supply Chain Management", "Customer Relationship Management", "Human Resource Development", and "Think Tank". These systems constitute an exclusive approach, as they concentrate their attention mostly in their own particular areas of specialization or work.

KM processes and techniques are applied, as stated earlier, to accomplish PBDIPS, i.e., productivity increase, benchmarking, improved decision-making, innovation, problem solving and raising satisfaction level in the organization (Fig. 2). Every successful application and completion of any or all PBDIPS goals not only accomplish the desired objective, but most importantly result in the creation of new tacit knowledge and additional insights, some of which may get converted into explicit knowledge. The newly created tacit knowledge together with the accompanying explicit knowledge adds to the existing knowledge asset of the enterprise. The new knowledge becomes the new knowledge input, thus the whole process becomes cyclic. KM addresses the issues by taking a holistic view of the enterprise functioning from production process to post-marketing. More importantly, it follows an integrated approach to people and processes. KM is knowledge centered and aims to make the I&B enterprise a knowledge based organization.

Benchmark. A critical function of KM is the management of knowledge about best practices whether it is in the mind as human capital or intellectual asset/ property. Best practices are the methods followed by those enterprises and industries, which produce goods and services efficiently, economically, and bring maximum satisfaction to all stakeholders. Bench marking is the activity of perceiving, sharing, and adoption of best *practices*. KM aims at obtaining maximum value from best practices. Ideally, best practices must strive to become world class. Transferring leading practices are not easy. Using knowledge "in a structured and organized way is one of the key factors that determine corporate success. The goal is to share and apply knowledge faster and more efficiently than your competitors" (Camp, 2003).

Feel of KM at Work. After reading through the expanding body of KM literature one generally gets the feeling that they are long on information about KM, but short on giving a feel of the real-time impact of KM application, and actual picture of in situ working of KM. However, the following representative accounts give us a feeling of KM at work.

Henkel K. Ga of Germany. The KM team of the company "mines" "pieces" of knowledge from the workers, employees and experts in the company by interviews, and the wisdom portion of it is transmitted for sharing. Knowledge is extracted from each interest area, namely technology, product launches, brands, systems, suppliers, e-commerce, innovation, time to market (Haxel, 2003).

Nano Project of Tata Motors. How the KM principles and procedures actually worked in the design of Nano car is given by Mr. Wagh, the principal designer. KM application consisted of: a) constant redefining of performance specifications as the project went on; b) "leveraging" the collective knowledge as a solution; c) sharing of knowledge, which reminded one of a "melting pot of ideas", and bringing homogeneity of ideas needing the use of "concurrent engineering in real time"; d) provoking every participant to come up with smart engineering solutions, which were used as inputs. In summary, it was more important "to have people young between their ears and flexible than just young blood" (Economic Times, 2008). Though this account pertains to a project team, it brings out clearly the elements of KM in action.

Knowledge Based Organization. There is always a better method of completing a job, managing a business or running an industry. Similarly, one can always find solutions even to the most intractable of problems. The key to these "better methods" and "solutions" lies in the application of knowledge and skill. For large-scale successful application of knowledge in an enterprise the enterprise must breathe knowledge. Knowledge must become an integral part of the corporate culture, i.e., imbibed in the minds of people who form the enterprise. Ad hoc knowledge application is not the solution.

To enhance the level of appropriate knowledge in an enterprise KM has to fully tap the existing knowledge resources within the enterprise. This knowledge is in the minds of people and is not limited to any one functionary or hierarchical level. The goal is to make the tacit knowledge held by individuals widely available across the enterprise to become enterprise knowledge to be shared, enhanced and enriched. By this process a large pool of knowledge is created. This pooled knowledge, which is an intangible asset, becomes an important part of the intellectual capital of the enterprise.

A knowledge based organization is called a *learning organization* or *inquiring organization*, although the two differ in their approaches. Both believe and stride to improve an organization's competency through widespread application of all forms of knowledge. A learning organization believes in reactive approach, whereas an inquiring organization follows a proactive approach by continually inquiring into the problems and the organization's knowledge environment. The focus of an inquiring organization is learning, and the accompanying growth of organizational memory. It takes a customized approach, and uses different forms of enquiry to suit the particular nature of organizational form (Hall and Croasdell, 2006). Sustaining a learning organization demands institutionalization of knowledge seeking, sharing and applying knowledge among all people in the organization, and the continuous development of an organizational culture that values knowledge. At the same time, one has to remember that applying knowledge just for the sake of applying has its own hazards.

KNOWLEDGE ASSET CREATION

KM is concerned with different types of intellectual assets, which are intangible. The important among them are intellectual capital, structural capital, and social capital.

Intellectual Capital (IC). Both KM and intellectual capital of an organization are tied to knowledge. IC is a form of capital, where as KM is a form of labour. IC differs from conventional money capital as the rules of money capital are not always applicable to IC and vice versa. KM as a form of labour in its conventional sense cannot be managed directly as other resources are managed. Further, knowledge by itself is now recognized as a factor of production like labour. Ariely concludes that:

"Knowledge, and managing all of its elements (knowledge creation, sharing, and transfer, etc.), becomes part of the organization's intellectual capital. The intellectual capital is then transformed through its value to the organization (a matter of perception, as discussed, dependant on the eye of the beholder) into the organization's owned intellectual property so that it can be protected.

Explicitly exploring knowledge management as a mechanism that moves us toward intellectual capital and property allows the KM processes to become part of the intellectual capital itself" (Ariely, 2006, p.286).

Knowledge is inherent in people and in interactions. Treating knowledge as a part of human capital "leads to the idea that managing knowledge is part of the structural capital (although not limited to structure). So, successful KM is in itself part of the organization's intellectual capital in addition to the knowledge incorporated in it as a process and in its people. But in order to fully understand the relationship between KM and IC, which surrounds the transformation of knowledge and managing it into value; we must consider the meaning of value within the dual contexts of KM an IC." (Ariely, 2006, p. 283).

Measuring Intellectual Capital. Intellectual Capital (IC) is an intangible resource, which the companies exploit to gain competitive advantage over others and also to increase the value of their assets. Intellectual capital is knowledge based, and hence KM is concerned with its development and management. In order to manage IC, it is necessary to measure and evaluate the asset. Current methods in use to measure IC are either based on monetary terms or on a system of indicators, such as practical experience of employees, and other non-financial or qualitative quantities. Monetary and quantitative methods are based on a company's book value and its market valuations. The resultant of subtracting the book value from its market value is taken as the value of the IC. Another method is by comparing the market value of an intangible asset with the cost of its reproduction, which gives a quotient called Tobin' Q. Other type representative methods include : return on assets (ROA), calculated intangible value (CIV), and value explorer. ROA is arrived at by dividing the average pre-tax earnings of a company by the average of its tangible assets for a particular period of time, which is then compared with its industry average. Multiplying the difference by the company's average tangible assets gives the average annual earnings from the intangibles. Dividing the average earnings by the company's average cost of capital or an interest rate gives the estimated value of the intangible asset. The value explorer method relies on identifying the components of IC, and then evaluating them directly in financial terms either individually or as a whole (Schindler and Jaitner, 2003).

Non-financial methods employ indicators (which enable comparison) to show the human capital of a firm which go to create a company's intellectual assets consisting of processes, patents, trademarks etc. Other models include structural capital and customer capital besides human capital. There is no single statutorily recognized and universally applied standard of measuring IC, which could be used for accounting and reporting uniformly across industries. A way-out is to express tacit knowledge in terms of explicit knowledge comprising of quantitative data and qualitative information.

INFORMATION TECHNOLOGY SUPPORT

To accomplish its functions KM makes use of Information Technology (IT) as an enabler. IT is a prerequisite for any large scale implementation of KM. Besides IT, KM draws support from other disciplines including Artificial Intelligence, expert systems, statistics, behavioural psychology, production engineering. Information Systems (IS) and Information Management (IM) play only a secondary role in KM, although KM employs some of their basic techniques and uses IS as a support for explicit knowledge, i.e., information. KM acts more at the mental level than at the information plane (Natarajan and Shekhar, 2001).

Computers and Information Technology. Use of computers in business initially began for automating transaction processes. This was later extended to serve higher level functions of decision-support systems (DSS) and expert systems (ES). The earlier expectations that DSS and ES would improve human decision-making or replace it completely have been belied. In contrast, KM does not try to replace or supplement human decision-making by DSS or ES, but rather try to encourage and facilitate human expertise. The reason behind this realization is that ES can capture information, but not the knowledge behind it (Blair, 2002).

Albert and Hoffman have listed 25 KM tools under the heads: 1. Abatracting (machine based); 2. Agent technology consisting of software programmes based on Artificial intelligence; 3. Business intelligence tools, such as Multidimensional analysis software, and Data mining tools; 4. Case-based reasoning derived from individual cases; 5. Categorization of documents using semantic algorithms of analysis, statistical procedures, and neuronal nets; 6. Clustering for grouping data and documents; 7. Content Management Systems (CMS) for creating, editing, managing, and publishing a variety of contents; 8. Collaborative functionality for retrieving knowledge from collaboratively generated information; 9 Collaborative filters for extracting evaluated knowledge from experts, and Communities of Practice; 10. Collaborative workspace to create a common electronic area, where groups accomplish learning tasks; 11. Creativity support through Brainstorming, Mindmapping tools and other techniques to generate creative and innovative ideas; 12. Data analysis for generating new knowledge through pattern recognition, classification and forecasting; 13. Data warehousing; 14. E-learning/and "Computer Based Training" (CBT); 15. Electronic Document Management; 16. Groupware to enhance knowledge sharing and collaboration between employees through e-mail, scheduling, work flow automation and others; 17. Information retrieval tools for search and manipulating data and information; 18. Knowledge discovery from databases using techniques like data mining, Text mining and Data warehousing; 19. Knowledge maping of both tacit and explicit knowledge in the organization; 20. Knowledge portals, customized and general, for accessing various knowledge sources and distribution of knowledge throughout the organization; 21. Semantic functionality for searching relationships between different text contents and contexts through automatic categorization, semantic networks, linguistic analysis, and other methods; 22. Skill management for identifying available skills and skill-holders within and outside the organization so that they can be immediately tapped when required; 23. Text analysis; 24. Text mining; and 25. Workflow Management System for integrating KM with the business processes of a company (Alwert and Hoffmann, 2003). Software packages on the application of many of these methods and technologies are readily available in market. Customer designed packages to meet specific requirements of a given KM solution are also available.

RESERVATIONS AND CRITICISMS

Knowledge management is not free from criticism. These criticisms and reservations have generally come from information science people. The criticisms include (Streatfield and Wilson, 1999):

1. The stakes of vested interests in promoting KM. They include– a) IT concerns interested in promoting their products and solutions; b) Information professionals hoping to increase their professional status by exploiting the glamour associated with the term "knowledge" in Knowledge Management, and c) Specialist industrial and business consultants trying to expand their market span.
2. Knowledge, unlike a commodity, is not amenable to management, at least directly. We can only manage information about the tacit knowledge held by an organization's people. Such information to be managed is necessarily incomplete because the boundaries of

personal knowledge are fuzzy and continually changing as individuals get out of touch or extend their knowledge (Streatfield and Wilson, 1999). Further, as George Por observes "knowledge is not a 'thing' that can be 'managed'. It is a capacity of people and communities, continuously generated and renewed in their conversation, to meet new challenges and opportunities. People responsible for knowledge value creation can be inspired and supported, but they cannot be 'managed' as people were managed in industrial era, as mere extensions of the machinery" (Por, 1997 quoted by Streatfield and Wilson, 1999). Since knowledge is embedded in human mind, managing embedded knowledge through KM endeavors seems impalpable to skeptics and critics of KM (Mclnerney, 2002 , p. 1013).

3. IT enabled KM ignores humans in the process of knowledge creation (Malhotra, 1997).
4. The reliance of KM on an exclusive IT-based static and syntactic notion of knowledge ignores the dynamics of knowledge phenomena in organizations and people in them (Davenport and Prusak, 1997).
5. KM has certainly "been 'hyped' beyond its ability to deliver clear benefits in all applications. Some of Knowledge Management has been simply an enthusiastic renaming of existing management practices...."(Blair, 2002, p.1028). In Blair's final analysis, Knowledge Management "is not an end in itself, it is a means to a further end. For the goal of Knowledge Workers is not so much to 'manage knowledge' but to solve problems" (Blair, 2002, p1028).

Extending the Field of Application. Presently, Knowledge Management is mostly applied in industry, and to some extent in military and hospital management. There are several other areas where knowledge management may be applied to great advantage; and one such area is rural development. This may not be easy as the domain of rural development is comparatively more diffused than that of an industrial unit. Some specialists may also feel that Information Management rather than KM is more suited for rural development.

CLOSURE

Knowledge Management (KM) evolved in the latter half of the twentieth century to enable industrial and business organizations to meet the challenges of a globalized economy driven by competition. The objective of KM is the creation and subsequent management of an environment which encourages knowledge to be created, shared, learnt, enhanced, and organized for the benefit of the organization and its customers. The discipline of KM consists of a theory part that provides the intellectual base, and an application part devoted to the development of techniques, processes and their use.

The theoretical part is derived mainly from the insights of knowledge drawn from philosophy, philology, economics and sociology of knowledge. From these fundamentals KM processes like creation, integration, sharing and dissemination of knowledge, and KM functions of acquisition, organization and distribution of knowledge draw their theoretical strengths. It studies the environment— organizational, social, cultural, and managerial in which the processes are applied.

Applied KM is focused on the creation of new knowledge, and channelizing the flow of knowledge in the organization. The emphasis is on tacit knowledge. The tacit knowledge so applied is to advance the functioning of an organization and to increase efficiency in its activities, particularly in the core areas of PBDIPS— Production, Benchmark, Decision-making, Innovation, Problem solving, and Satisfaction or organizational harmony. It is a continuous process. KM objectives are achieved through the functions of SSAAC- sourcing knowledge, sharing and learning of knowledge, applying knowledge, asset formation, and computer-based support building.

KM treats knowledge as an organizational resource comprising of factual knowledge, practical knowledge, and technological knowledge held by the organization and its people in the tacit and implicit forms. There is constant transformation of tacit knowledge into explicit knowledge and vice a versa. The aim is to capture them and convert them into useful applications, as well as turn them into knowledge assets (human and intellectual capital) of the organization. To achieve this KM employs knowledge discovery in databases, data mining, computer assisted learning, artificial intelligence, algorithms, knowledge inventory, portals, and a host of other methods and tools.

One of the key elements in KM is knowledge transfer and sharing. KM employs learning in all its forms, and sharing of knowledge between personnel at all levels of the organization as the main instruments in bringing desired changes. To advance learning it employs conventional, as well as newer methods of learning, like online learning. Encouraging people in the organization to participate in Communities of Practice is one of the important means adopted to encourage sharing of knowledge. Information and Communication technology is the backbone of KM in handling knowledge and information. The ultimate objective is to make the organization knowledge-based.

In a complex competitive world no one doubts the important role of knowledge in organizational problem solving, rendering a competitive edge, and in enhancing the value of an enterprise to all its stakeholders. KM could play a decisive role in transforming an existing enterprise into a knowledge centered organization, provided its limitations are recognized, and taken into account, while implementing KM. There is some amount of hype about KM, as is the case with many of the soft sciences. At present KM application is mostly oriented towards industry and business. The principles and practices of KM are valid to all organizational activities even outside industry, and hence one can benefit from extending its use to other areas formally or informally.

REFERENCES

Aarons, Jeremy. Epistemology and Knowledge Management. Pp.166-172. *In* Schwartz, David G. Ed. Op cit.

Abell, Angela and Oxbrow, Nigel. Competing with Knowledge: The Information Professional in the Knowledge Management Age. London, Library Association Publishing, 2001.

Alwert, Kay and Hoffmann, Ingo. Knowledge Management Tools. Pp.114-150. *In* Mertins, Kai ; Heisig, Peter; and Vorbeck, Jens. Eds. Knowledge Management: Concepts and Best Practices. Edn. 2. Berlin, Springer, 2003.

Ariely, Gil. Intellectual Capital and Knowledge Management. Pp.281-286. . *In* Schwartz, David G. Ed. Op cit..

Blair, David C. Knowledge management: Hype, hope, or help? *Journal of the American Society for Information Science and Technology* 53 (12): 1019-1028, 2002.

Camp, Robert C. (In his Foreword to the First Ediion). *In* Mertins, Kai; Heisig, Peter; and Vorbeck, Jens. Eds. Knowledge Management. Concepts and Best Practices. Ed.2. Berlin, Springer, 2003.

Coakes, Elayne and Clarke, Steve. Communities of Practice. Pp.30-33. 2006. *In* Schwartz, David G. Ed. Op cit.

Davenport, T.H. and Prusak, L. Working Knowledge: How Organizations Manage What They Know. Boston (MA), Harvard Business School Press, 1997.

Economic Times. The ace designer behind Nano. Wagh belongs to a new crop of engineering whiz kids *The Economic Times* Saturday 12th January, 2008. Pp.1-2. (Reporter: Nandini SenGupta).

Eppler, Martin J. Knowledge Communication. Pp. 317-325. *In* Schwartz, David G. Ed. Op cit..

Gillman, Daniel W. Data Semantics. Pp.97-104. *In* Schwartz, David G. Ed. Op cit.

Gold, Jeff; Watson, Stuart; and Rix, Mike. Learning for Change by Telling Stories. Pp.166-181. *In* McGoldrick, Jim; Stuart, Jim; and Watson, Sandra. Eds. Understanding Human Resource Development. A Search-based Approach. London, Routledge, 2002.

Hall, Dianne and Croasdell, David. Inqiring Organizations. Pp.244-250. *In* Schwartz, David G. Ed. Op cit..

Haravu, L. J. Lectures on Knowledge Management: Paradigms, Challenges and Opportunities. Neelameghan, A. Ed. Bangalore, Sarada Ranganathan Endowment for Library Science, 2002.

Haxel, Christoff. Foreword to the First Edition. P. xvii *In* Mertins, Kai ; Heisig, Peters and Vorbeck, Jens. Eds. Knowledge Management: Concepts and Best Practices. Edn. 2. Berlin, Springer, 2003.

King, William R. Knowledge Transfer. Pp. 538-542. *In* Schwartz, David G. Ed. Op cit..

Krishna Kumar. (a) What is Knowledge? (Reporting in) *PC Quest* March 2000. Pp.48-49.

Krishna Kumar. (b) Managing knowledge. (Reporting in) *PC Quest* March 2000. Pp. 53-54.

Mclnerney, Claire. Knowledge management and the dynamic nature of knowledge. *Journal of the American Society for Information Science and Technology* 53(12): 1009-1008, 2002.

Malhotra, Y. Knowledge Management in enquiring oganisations. Pp. 293-295. In Proceedings of 3rd American Conference on Information Systems. Indianapolis (In.), 15-17 Aug. 1997.

Mertins, Kai; Heisig, Peter; and Vorbeck, Jens. Introduction. Pp. 1-14. *In* Mertins, Kai; Heisig, Peter and Vorbeck, Jens. Eds. Knowledge Management: Concepts and Best Practices. Ed. 2. Berlin, Springer, 2003.

Natarajan, Ganesh and Shekhar, Sandhya. Knowledge Management Enabling Business Growth. New Delhi, Tata McGraw-Hill, 2001.

Cf. Por, George. 'Why Knowledge Management is an Oxymoron'. Community Intelligence Labs. 1997. (Cited by Streatfield and Wilson, 1999. Loc cit.)

Reychav, Iris and Weisberg, Jacob. Human Capital in Knowedge Creation, Management and Utilization. Pp. 221-229. *In* Schwartz, David G. Ed. Op cit.

Schindler, Robert and Jaitner, Arne, Intellectual Capital: Measuring Knowledge Management. Pp.151-175. *In* Mertins, Kai; Heisig, Peter; and Vorbeck, Jens. Eds. Knowledge Management: Concepts and Best Practices. Edn. 2. Berlin, Springer, 2003

Schwartz, David G. Aristotelian View of Knowledge. Pp. 10-16. *In* Schwartz, David G. Ed. Op cit.

Schwartz, David G. Ed. Encyclopedia of Knowledge Management. Singapore, Idea Group Reference, 2006.

Streatfield, David and Wilson, Tom. Deconstructing 'Knowledge Management'. Aslib Proceedings 51(3): 67-71, 1999.

Wickramasinghe, Nilmani. Knowledge Creation. Pp. 326-335. *In* Schwartz, David G. Ed. Op cit.

Woods, Steven et al. Dissemination in Portals. Pp. 115-121. *In* Schwartz, David G. Ed. Op cit.

Fulfillment

21
Knowledge Society

Before the term "knowledge society" gained currency, the term "information society" was in popular usage. The predominant role played by information in a technology environment, supported by computer and communication technologies, in subordinating the importance of other factors of production in the economy led to the concept of information society. The advanced countries in the West, and possibly Japan included, have progressed from the stage of industrial society to that of information society in the late 20th century, and more particularly since 1990 (Hill, 2005). Another name for it is "postmodern society" or Postmodernism. By analogy, a knowledge society is one whose economy is directed by the widespread use of knowledge, and knowledge becoming the single most decisive factor in bringing change. However, the terms knowledge society and information society need further clarification. When we say "agricultural society", "egalitarian society" or "theocratic society" the message is clear, which is not so in the case of "information society" and "knowledge society" because of the noun and not adjective qualifying "society". Castells makes a clear distinction between "informational society" and "information society" in his work *The Rise of the Network Society*. He argues that information society emphasizes the role of information, i.e., communication of knowledge in society, which is there in all societies to varying degrees. In contrast, "informational" indicates "the attribute of a specific form of social organization in which information generation, processing, and transmission become the fundamental sources of productivity and power because of new technological conditions emerging in this historical period" (Castells, 2000, p. 21. Note 31). He further adds that networking logic is a key feature of informational society that explains its basic structure, which takes us to the concept of "network society". Following the analogy of "informational", knowledge society should be "knowledgeable society" which does not convey the intended meaning behind knowledge society. The correct usage should be "information-based society" (for short "information-b society"), and "knowledge-based society" (for short "knowledge-b society"). Following the popularity of the names, information society and knowledge society are retained in the text. Even though the two usages seem to be near synonyms there is difference between the two.

Distinction between Information Society and Knowledge Society. The distinction between the two is not apparent at the surface. The two concepts are closely linked to each other. Hill implies that the distinction can be gauged by the meaning and contents represented by the respective terms "information" and "knowledge" (Hill, 2005). The distinction becomes clear if we take Knowledge Management view of knowledge. In Knowledge Management, the emphasis is on tacit knowledge, i.e., knowledge embedded in the minds of people. Application of tacit knowledge in enterprises implies sharing of knowledge, collaborative thinking, and more of interpersonal and inter-organizational knowledge contacts, which should result in more effective and efficient organizations. The same holds good when tacit knowledge is applied to a larger body called society with its numerous entities. On the other hand, information society implies the emphasis on the employment of information- an external agent/devise, which does not carry the same intensity or meeting of mind effect on the outcome.

The Nature of Knowledge Base. In understanding the basics of a knowledge society, it is pertinent to dwell upon the nature of knowledge base of a knowledge society. Jacques Chevalier in the context of "Social Analysis of Systems" states that at present, the knowledge base of the knowledge society consists of knowledge resource generated, accredited or communicated predominantly in scientific, corporate and university-based settings that exclude and ignore many other segments of society. A true knowledge society has to engage all human beings without exception in the application and cogeneration of knowledge. Such a system draws on the information, imagination, skills and meaning, and reasoning of many people, seeing their different views and the methods they use as "living knowledge" that has a potential to advance the common good on universal scale. This implies keeping the object of enquiry is socially relevant and following collaborative approaches (Chevalier and Buckles, 2008). Hence, the inquiry has to cut across boundaries by fostering understanding and dialogue across institutions, classes, professions, disciplines, generations, and genders in pursuit of common ground. Such an approach reconciles tension between quantitative versus qualitative information, efficiency versus participation, accountability versus adaptability, and simple verses advanced methods. It is only then, "we can arrive at the essential points common to all genuine forms of human inquiry" (Proust, 2008, p.81).

INFORMATION SOCIETY

The picture of information society largely evolved from the brushes of Fritz Machlup's, and Marc Porat's depictions of the changing scenario of the Western economies characterized by the application of knowledge and information; Daniel Bell's painting of the *postindustrial society;* Alvin Toffler's, and John

Naisbitt's caricature of the new society evolving under the impact of information and communication technologies (Machlup, 1979, 1980-84; Porat, 1977; Bell, 1976; Toffler, 1970, 1980; and Naisbitt, 1982). However, there are differences in defining what constitutes an information society, its structure, behavior, characteristics and effects. Whether we are already in an information society or on the threshold of it remains disputed. Adding further to the confusion is the new phrase "knowledge society". The idea of information society can be perceived through different, but related perspectives: economic perspective, religious and cultural perspective, socio-technical perspective, and value perspective. Alternative to this is the theories of information society presented by Frank Webster in which he presents five perspectives— technological, occupational, spatial, cultural, and economic (Webster, 2002).

Economic Perspective. Central to this perspective is that knowledge and information are the prime factors guiding economic development and growth. Knowledge is considered an intellectual resource. Employment of computer, Internet, web-technology, and other electronic forms of communication in all economic spheres information energizes other factors of production to yield optimum results. As a consequence, service sector of an economy dominates more and more over manufacturing and other sectors of the economy. It is a changeover from industrial economy to that of a knowledge-based economy. To put it simply, it means "adopt information and knowledge or perish". In contrast to industrial society, information society means that: a) Information and information-based services form the main single source of national income; b) Information generation and supply is the main source of employment; c) Generating new information and new information services is a major occupation; d) Information is valued above tangible goods; and e) One strives to make the maximum use of information (Hill, 2005). The main problems in this scenario are: there is bound to be exaggeration in the actual economic worth added by the information sector to the overall economy; it is not easy to segregate informational and non-informational domains of economic activity; it presents a homogeneous picture of the economic contribution made by a heterogeneous set of economic activities, which gives an incorrect picture of the contributions of each sector. Putting a price tag to overcome the problem of valuation will only hide the real value dimension of information (Webster, 2002).

Religious and Cultural Perspective. Religious and cultural factors have strong impact on the formation of one's attitude towards his or her concept of society. Collectively these attitudes may develop into an ideology or dogma, which may promote or inhibit a society becoming a knowledge society. For example, it seems impossible for theocratic societies (found in many of the Middle East countries) to embrace the concept of a knowledge society as perceived by the Western or secular mind. On the other hand, is the fact that the spread of secular knowledge in a traditional society may largely modify the existing social norms and value systems, and thus create conditions that are supportive of a knowledge society.

Webster reasons out the cause for culture determined information society to the pervasive hold of media remitted information, and the impact of anywhere, anytime personal and interpersonal informational intercourses on the society. Social intercourse involves greater degree of information content than before. It is information of all types bombarded from all sides is shaping fashion, individual life styles, and the social values. Such a society is an information laden society, where information is received and exchanged instantaneously and its social and cultural adoption too is immediate. He concludes that experientially the idea of an information society is easily enough recognized, but a definition of the new society is haphazard than any of the notions stated so far.

Socio-technical Perspective. The National Working Party on Social Inclusion in the Information Society set up by the

IBM describes Information Society as, "a society characterized by a high level of information intensity in the everyday life of most citizens, in most organizations and workplaces; by the use of common or compatible technology for a wide range of personal, social, educational and business activities; and by the ability to transmit and receive digital data rapidly between places irrespective of distance" (INSINC, 1997 cited by Hill, 2005, p. 315). Webster identifies the technical perspective from the visible features of the information society created by the cable and satellite television, widespread use of computer (particularly Personal computers) and communication instruments, new office technology processing (particularly online services) and CD ROMs. The socio-technical assessment of the present knowledge society shows that, unlike its predecessors, it is to an unprecedented extent the product of its own action, which power may not be evenly distributed throughout the society. The balance between the power of nature and the power of society, i.e., the human capacity to control nature has tilted enormously toward the latter (Stehr and Meja, 2005). The objection to the technology defined information society, Webster points out, is that technology is an asocial phenomena which cannot define a social world.

Communication technologies in the knowledge society bring groups and individuals nearer, while regions, cities and villages remain isolated. In the present knowledge society the "world opens up and creeds, styles and commodities mingle, yet the walls between incompatible convictions about what is sacred do not come tumbling down" (Stehr and Meja, 2005, p. 15).

Value Perspective. In this, the criteria of identifying a society as information society is through the assessment of the impact of information and knowledge on the cultural values, faith systems, ethics and life styles of people. The emphasis is on assessing how pervasive is the change brought about by knowledge application, and its consequences for the individual and the society as a whole. Intercultural effects induced by new modes of communication systems and the capacity of globally accessible information to alter cultural and social values, and styles of people is taken as the most important criterion of identifying an information society. Value perspective includes the importance of goodness value, ethical values, democratic values, and other higher level values in shaping a society.

Occupational Persptive. The prime author of information society, one that is symbolized by knowledge workers is Daniel Bell. According to Bell, the knowledge society is manned and managed by knowledge workers. The people constituting the new work force bear the designation 'symbolic analysts', 'knowledge experts' or 'informational labour'. Their main job is to create and use knowledge/information in an endless cycle. The 'occupational perspective' is faulted on the ground that it is based on a count of raw numbers of 'information workers'.

Spatial Perspective. The fundamental feature of the information society in the spatial perspective is the overwhelming impact of information networks— a spatial or geography linked phenomena. The networks philosophy has shaken the very concept of traditional organizations rigidly bound to specific locales and time frames. In the information society homes, offices, businesses, recreational spots, and even religious and spiritual centres are all conneted to one another by information networks. Castells observes that "*our societies are increasingly structurd around a bipolar opposition between the Net and the self*" (Castells, 2000, p.3). This has profound effects on one's organization of time and space. The question raised against this perception is "Where is the logic in calling a society an information society merely because of the overwhelming presence of networks?"

Forces Behind Knowledge Society. The present concept of knowledge society is driven by: a) capitalism, b) globalization, c) liberalization of economy, d) wide spread use of information and communication phenomena, especially digital communication and networked information, e) social, cultural and religious attitude of a society, and f) stage and state of development of a society in terms of natural resources, intellectual resources, educational standing, and level of technology development. All these factors are interlinked. Capitalism aims at maximizing the creation of wealth, and is solely wedded to private enterprise. Maximizing the creation of wealth is achieved by economizing the use of input in manufacturing, creation of new products and services, and expanding into new markets; which are possible only by adoption of technology, use of new knowledge and existing information in effective ways. Globalization has integrated trade and commerce into a single world market. An inherent feature of global market mechanism is the element of competitiveness. To achieve the competitive edge industries have to invest on knowledge and technology to find the best way of economizing in possible ways, such as outsourcing of operations and products; minimizing information and communication costs; enhancing creative talent in the organizations; continuous study and evaluation of different markets, and trade policies of individual states. The success in this venture will depend on how efficiently and effectively one collects, analyzes, transmits, and employs knowledge and information. To operate successfully in the new global market instant communication and transfer of massive and varied types of information across the globe is a prerequisite, and so is the movement or exploitation of intellectual talent. To survive and progress in a globalized competitive world liberalization of economy is a must. It releases creative energies of entrepreneurs and industry to concentrate on the task of creating wealth rather than spending time and resources to overcome the state installed and other barriers that curb initiative and inhibits industrial progress. A problem with the economic version of knowledge society represented by globalized capitalism is that once an agent becomes a part of the system, the agent will be so carried away by its hypnotic power of garnering money, and more money that all other values and issues, such as the needs of the poor, environmental safety, and the common good aspects of society vanish from the view. The present global economic turmoil (September 2008) illustrates this point well.

In contrast to industrial society, a critical characteristic of a knowledge society is the pervasiveness of knowledge application implying flow of knowledge and information across inter-organizational and intra-organizational networks spread out widely across time and space. This enables organizations to pay instant attention to problems, take immediate decisions, and communicate information for immediate action. Internet, web sites and other networks constitute the central nervous system of the information society. Another feature of the information society is the convergence effect. Convergence "is the outcome of a complex interplay between such factors as advances in the information and communications technologies, the liberalization and deregulation of trades and capital markets, and the development of global competition. It has led to the blurring of boundaries both within and between industries, for example between computing and telecommunications and between computer hardware and software industries, between communications and broadcasting..." (Martin, 1995. p.136). Convergence assigns a new role to knowledge and information in the form of identifier, coordinator and troubleshooter. On the other hand, convergence of disciplines, i.e., unity of knowledge (akin to unity of science) is a reality in knowledge society. This has opened up increasing opportunities for application of the findings of one discipline in another field of knowledge, hitherto unimaginable, examples being— unisex marriage laws; feed-forward concept in economics; and DNA imprint as personal identification mark.

Stage and State of Development of a Society. A knowledge society can take off only when that society has attained a state of minimum economic development, and a takeoff-stage in terms of educational standard of the people, R&D support, political maturity and stability, innovative sprit in people, a work culture built on the principles of efficiency, effectiveness, and at least a minimum level of trust in its people and governance. A prerequisite for knowledge society is that the state of development of information, communication and technology is such that it sustains the massive movements of information created or available in society overcoming time and space separation.

FACTORS DETERMINING KNOWLEDGE SOCIETY

A knowledge society is determined by the criteria of how far knowledge has become an integral part of everyday life of citizens, and in what ways knowledge is put to use by them; and not solely by attaining the state of a knowledge-based economy or by mere wide spread use of information networks. Some of the conditions required for the creation of a knowledge-based society are:

1. A high rate of literacy (including computer literacy), if not total literacy.
2. Knowledge and information dissemination services, and extension services providing access to information either free or at affordable cost to all citizens. This calls for creating an effective public library system covering the entire population.
3. Widespread use of Knowledge Management not only in industry and business, but in all major areas of societal activities.
4. Reliable computer and communication infrastructure to support Internet and web site access, communication and control in organizations.
5. Well developed general and technical education system, and support for two-way transfer of technology.
6. Encouraging innovation and production of intellectual property.

7. Conducive environment and support for knowledge creation activities, such as scientific research, academic research, medical research, and others.
8. Using technology as the base in all wealth creating activates- industry, commerce, agriculture, etc., and to replace humans wherever desirable.
9. A responsible and pro-active democratic system of governance. A non-democratic egalitarian society can also become a knowledge society.
10. Effective e-governance.
11. An independent judiciary capable of delivering justice at affordable cost without undue delay.
12. Belief in the goodness of knowledge-based society.
13. Application of knowledge in all activities must be a conscious act and not a chance or spur of the moment act.
14. Mechanisms- regulatory, industrial, social and others to monitor the working of each sector of the knowledge society, and a machinery in place to initiate immediate appropriate measures to maintain stability in case of major disturbances.
15. Certain minimum ethical values in the whole society.
16. Support from international bodies like UNO, UNESCO, FAO, and WHO to help those societies intending to become knowledge societies.

A few of the factors that are detrimental to the growth of a knowledge society are:

1. Uncontrolled population growth.
2. Lack of proper work ethics.
3. Economic and social exploitation of masses. The problem with unbridled capitalism is greed, which can destabilize the whole society.

CONTRADICTIONS IN KNOWLEDGE SOCIETY

The current phase of knowledge society seems to have many contradictions which are stated below. A few of the contradictions arise from the characteristics of knowledge and information.

1. The knowledge society is sustained by knowledge workers and computer literacy at the base level. The same knowledge society accounts for a significant percentage of digital illiterates.
2. While there seems to be a shortage of knowledge workers in select knowledge fields in many of the knowledge societies in the West, a number of knowledge workers in the developing countries are seeking employment opportunities in the West and their own advancement. Avenues of emigration to knowledge societies are restricted by the emigration policies of the host countries, of course for valid reasons.
3. The impact of knowledge on the recipient is determined by how information is presented and the time of presentation. ICT technology has evolved a number of techniques (e.g., multimedia presentations, SMS service, and video conferencing) and yet, effective and exhaustive access to relevant information is made difficult by the flood of ephemeral, unsubstantiated information clogging information highways. This is a case of poverty of relevant information amidst plenty of Information.
4. In the present knowledge society "the world opens up and creeds, styles and commodities mingle, yet the walls between incompatible convictions about what is sacred do not come tumbling down" (Stehr and Meja, 2005, p.15). The communication technologies are bringing together people from across the world surmounting the barriers of language, religion, race and gender. On the other hand, one may not know who his or her immediate

neighbor is. Anyone can today instantly acquire the bit of information about the existence or nonexistence of water on the planet Mars, but in all probability may not know the source of water flowing in his tap and its purity. We are becoming more and more a part of the global community, and at the same time getting far removed from the local community. A large number of people are made to live lonely lives.

5. Knowledge societies have developed all the technologies, weapons systems, and strategies and tactics to wage a war or prevent an attack, and yet are unable to evolve a foolproof and workable system that can identify a terrorist and prevent his entry into its territory. Similarly, a knowledge society may have all the knowledge and the technology to cure even the most dreaded disease, but many a medical man does not want to prescribe a simple natural remedy, because it is not profitable or he has not cared to know as it does not have the glamour of a super specialty.
6. National or local culture in a knowledge society is supposed to flourish under the power of communication networks, and greater circulation of social and cultural knowledge. Yet, the social and cultural destabilization is spreading fast due to media led commercial interests. Local languages are yielding place to English language.
7. Increasingly time has begun to control life instead of man controlling time. One of the reasons behind the success of man to come to the present level of progress is his ability to control space and time by applying his inventive genius. But today in the knowledge society the pressure of keeping schedules is becoming so acute that time has begun to control him.
8. A feature of the knowledge society is the increasing scientization of all aspects of human activities and the

domineering influence of experts in the organization of societies (Stehr and Meja, 2005). As a consequence, with the clever use of the media even a trivial function or tasking may be raised to the level of an expertise.

We "are increasingly a dissatisfied society, not just because we have been urged to complain and have learnt to sue if something goes wrong" (Hill, 2005, p. 318). Why should this be so in a knowledge society when pleasures are easily accessible to all those who can afford, and many other means of satisfying mind and body in real or virtual forms are available anytime, anywhere?

Martin after studying the claims made by many that information society exists here and now, says that in the absence of credible evidence; the prevailing reality tends to indicate that "information society has remained little more than a catchphrase or a slogan, more a matter of rhetoric than of reality" (Martin, 1995, p.1). This assessment seems valid equally, if not more, when applied to knowledge society.

KNOWLEDGE SOCIETY AND INDIA

The idea of information society or knowledge society has become popular with a section of the elite in some of the developing countries like India. This popularity is based on the criteria that : a) service sector of the economy has now grown more significantly compared to manufacturing, agricultural and other sectors; b) use of Internet and telephony is catching up with the masses; and c) software sector is well established and is booming; and d) the country's stock of intellectual resource, i.e., skilled and educated manpower is rising, which are facts. But a knowledge society, in its true sense, has to fulfill not only the above stated criteria but something more. The additional criteria include:

1. One of the prerequisites of a knowledge society is an appropriate mindset of people towards responsible

behavior and a sense of responsibility. In this, leadership holds the key. A pervasive negative work culture is not the mark of a knowledge society. One example for negative work culture is seen in the lack of response from individuals and organizations to successive e-mails and telephone calls received from valid clients— not an infrequent experience in some societies, including India, hoping to become a knowledge society. A nation where one fourth or more of the population lives below poverty line cannot make up a knowledge society, unless there is positive work culture and improvement in their standard of living. In such a situation, any advancement towards attaining the goal of knowledge society is likely to end up in a society with dual cultures surviving side by side in antipathy.

2. Where feudalism in new forms (e.g., scores of cars filled with officials and hangers- on following ministers, political leaders, and glamorous celebrities in their errands and creating roadblocks) found in many developing countries like India flies against the ethos of a knowledge society.
3. A knowledge society is not sustainable, where corruption at all levels negates all other gains. No doubt that in many of the Western societies known to be knowledge societies high-stake corruption exists, but it is limited only to higher levels. By this, the common citizen's daily knowledge behavior is not directly disrupted.
4. Acquiring a cell phone or access to Internet largely for ephemeral use even by the entire population does not mean that knowledge is used as an instrument for progress contributing to the effective functioning of a knowledge society. On the contrary, it could be the symbolization of a nation of talkers and not doers, and wastage of society's time.
5. Rise in per capita income and a high GNP growth rate

is a characteristic of a knowledge-based economy, which is not an equivalent of a knowledge society.

6. Unchecked population growth without corresponding increase in resources is one of the major negative factors blocking the way to knowledge society. Any reference to population control has become a taboo in some societies including India.
7. Level of literacy and knowledge society are intimately related. A low literacy rate deprives large sections of people taking active part at the information access level in the knowledge society.

From the above stated facts it would be wrong to conclude that underdeveloped countries can never become a knowledge society. What it means is that there are impediments in the way, which can be removed. In our case, most of the essential pre-requirements of a knowledge society are already there, some in a nascent stage. What is needed now is our immediate attention and action to raise the level of homogeneity in society by addressing issues that have not received the attention to the extent called for. Four such issues are discussed here— e-governance, the problems of marginal people, emancipation of woman, and talent development for export.

E-governance. Given India's rural poverty and backwardness, to rise to the level of knowledge society, e-governance is a fundamental necessity. Because of their agricultural dependency, lack of infrastructure, needs of schooling, healthcare, and employment rural people and local bodies look for government's guidance and support. These problems can be attended satisfactorily by governments only through putting in place a properly planned and executed e-governance structure. There is also a need for change of attitude in government servants from the prevalent passive and even negative attitude to proactive attitude. Hence training programmes for government servants particularly for those placed at the government-people direct interface points assume importance. At present most state governments have setup e-governance, which are in different stages of working. Notable among them are Andhra Pradesh and Gujarat. Contact of people with the government arise predominantly in connection with land records, land tax payment receipts, birth and death certificates, cast certificates, below poverty line certificates, forming loans, subsidized food coupons (ration cards), job cards (under the National Rural Employment Guarantee Act), dwelling site allotment (under Indira Gandhi Awas Yojana), and the demand for infrastructure facilities. This provides fruitful opportunities for joint participation of IT sector and governments (Joshi, 2009). In this national endeavour, information and knowledge management people, including librarians have a stake in the successful implementation of the e-governance programmes.

Rural and Marginal Community Development. Unlike Western developed societies where the issue of marginal communities is limited to a small percentage of the population, it forms a major issue needing accelerated action in developing and underdeveloped societies. This is because in the latter two societies the majority of people live in the countryside; they are relatively poor; literacy rate is low; they are mostly engaged in traditional forms of agriculture, animal husbandry, and producing rural handicrafts; and they lack infrastructure facilities. It is also necessary to recognize the distinctive groups like indigenous or tribal people whose needs and approaches to life are distinct from that of general rural category. Action plans for rural segment differs from that of urban sector, in that it is more demanding and requiring a different strategy. The planning of such a strategy has to take into consideration the social structure, cultural factors, economic realities, and the need for unorthodox solutions. For achieving effective results, it calls for a multidimensional approach combining the traditional methods as well as information and communication technology based solutions. The objective must be to raise the level of knowledge in the rural masses to that of the desired standard of the knowledge society. The task is not merely acquiring knowledge, but to motivate them to apply the knowledge so gained for productive purposes, and to raise their standard of living. Such an action plan covers all major areas including education, healthcare, agriculture, poultry, water management, rural industries, environmental protection, transportation, social welfare, and local culture. Several schemes have been initiated by the central government, the state governments, and voluntary agencies. There is need for greater coordination between the agencies involved. The main challenge is that of establishing appropriate proactive relationship with the people. This requires a good understanding of the rural realities and rural psychology, and deep involvement. Libraries and other information dissemination agencies do have a major role to play in this. Unless we harness the power of technology, and more particularly the instruments like Internet, audio visual aids, other modern communication means, and local talent achieving the goal of reaching the rural sector will remain distant. In this task Knowledge Management does have a vital role to play (Neelameghan and Chester, 2007).

Emancipation of Women. This is a complicated issue found in many societies. No knowledge society can function successfully or can be called a knowledge society unless the women members of the society are empowered to take their rightful place in the society, and contribute to the societal wellbeing. In a country like India with its hoary past, cast system, religious and racial composition there can be no single solution to the problem. State intervention can ameliorate the status of women a good deal, but not completely unless there is a social transformation in the society. In the context of this writing, we are concerned more with the lot of women coming under the working class, and not with the educated class of women. Even a cursory observation of the lives of construction women labourers provides a vivid picture of the problem. There is discrimination in wages paid to them compared to the male workers, sometimes coupled with male harassment. A more serious problem is the seasonal nature of their work. The labourers and their families migrate from their villages to urban centres after sowing or harvesting season, stay in open spaces (the builder or the contractor does not provide a living place, although the law may say otherwise) near the construction sites, which keeps changing, and move back to their villages at the end of summer. This cycle repeats every year. After the construction work, she has to cook for the family and take care of the children. In such a situation one can imagine what care she can give to her children, look after their education and health care. The situation with the women farming labourers, comparatively is much better, but the problem remains. Providing education for their children is a primary problem, next only to earning a livelihood and healthcare. Formal methods of solving are unlikely to work, and the state has to think of imaginative, unorthodox means of solving them. Rojgar Yojana initiated by the central government is one such programme. The concept of starting village information centres under the e-governance has the potential to help bring in the necessary changes as education and information can instill self confidence, and show them the path to become economically self-supporting.

Talent Emigration. The needs of talented manpower in knowledge societies will be enormous. This manpower is made-up of people who put knowledge and machines to work to produce new products and services. At present, the demand for such manpower exceeds supply in most western knowledge societies. This is because the growth of working population in those countries is not keeping pace with the needs of replacement and development. There is high movement of intellectual labour (besides outsourcing) from countries like India, China and other developing countries to knowledge societies in the West. Because of this, it has become inevitable for many knowledge society regimes to relax their immigration policies to attract skilled and professionally talented manpower from countries outside their borders by liberalizing work permit quotas, and by attracting foreign students for higher education. After the completion of their studies many of them are allowed to stay back and work in the host country. Many among them seek long-term stay visa in the new country, and citizenships in due course of time. This transfer of manpower resource is working out generally to mutual advantage. The receiving country benefits as its immediate needs of intellectual and skilled manpower needs are met, and the host country benefits from the inflow of income, and also by the intellectual and commercial contacts developed between the two countries through immigrants. Sometimes it does create tension between the local populace and the immigrants, which is unavoidable to some extent. One of the features of a knowledge society is the enormous opportunities it holds for the movement of talent and skill globally. A characteristic of an industrial society is the substitution of a large physical labour force by a combination of machinery and a small work force of skilled labour. As knowledge societies progress there will be further replacement of human skill and natural intelligence by robots, cyborts, and artificial intelligence. This interim period should be utilized by India to build and strengthen its own knowledge society base.

India Towards Knowledge Society. The present political dispensation has set the goal of making India a knowledge society. Keeping this mission in mind, the Prime Minister Manmohan Singh constituted the National Knowledge Commission (NKC) under the Chairmanship of Sam Pitroda in June 2005. The goal before the Commission was to recommend steps needed to make India a knowledge society. This is attested by the Commission's publication titled "towards a knowledge society. Three Years of the National Knowledge Commission" (India. National Knowledge Commission, 2008). The terms of reference of the Commission were:

1. Build excellence in the educational system...and increase India's competitive advantage in the fields of knowledge.
2. Promote creation of knowledge in Science & Technology laboratories. Improve the management of institutions engaged in producing "Intellectual Property".
3. Promote knowledge applications in agriculture and Industry.
4. Promote the use of knowledge in making government an effective, transparent and accountable service provider to the citizen, and promote widespread sharing of knowledge to maximize public benefit.

The Commission organized its task under action heads that included— right to education, different aspects and branches of education, science and technology, private- public partnership in education and research, intellectual property, traditional knowledge, quality of life-tools, libraries, National Knowledge Network, and others.

Commenting on the implementation of the NKC, the "Daily News and Analysis" observes that for making India a knowledge society, it is imperative that we must:

1. Try to build quality institutions, achieve a reasonable degree of contestability in economy and in polity. An outward orientation is necessary for creating, diffusing and adapting knowledge. It is necessary to institutionalize economic and governance reforms.
2. Stress on strong education and training in science and technology, and reforming educational policies and regulations. Increase the supply of educational manpower and maintain quality. Preserve and apply traditional knowledge after subjecting it to scientific enquiry.

Without this power a knowledge society cannot exist. The consequences of knowledge economy are far-reaching. Knowledge economy affects everyday lives of people, and is visible in the changes it has brought in social, cultural, political and other spheres of life.

Information society, and for that matter knowledge society, is analyzed and defined following different reference points. These reference points are: economic, socio-technological, religious and cultural, value, occupational, and spatial perspectives. Each of these perspectives is faulted for different reasons. The present concept of knowledge society is driven by: a) capitalism, b) globalization, c) liberalization of economy, d) wide spread use of information and communication phenomena, especially digital communication and networked information, e) social, cultural and religious attitude of a society, and f) stage and state of development of a society in terms of natural resources, intellectual resources, educational standing, and level of technology development. All these factors are interlinked.

The prerequisites for a knowledge society are: a minimum level of industrial and economic development, a high level of educational (particularly technical) attainment, R&D growth, political maturity and stability, people's innovative sprit, a work culture built on the principles of efficiency, effectiveness, and at least a minimum level of trust in the people constituting the system. Equally important is the development of information, communication and technology structures that can sustain massive and multi-dimensional movement of information created or available in society. There are several contradictions in the existing knowledge society; the major one among them is the several divides in the society, such as educational, racial, and gender.

The idea of information society or knowledge society has become popular with a section of the elite in some of the developing countries, including India. If India is to march towards knowledge society it has to tackle first some of the basic issues facing the country. The issues relate to: a) change in the mindset of people towards information, its access and utilization, which are linked with literacy and education; b) development of rural India and supporting below the poverty-line families living in urban India to make them self supporting through the application of knowledge means. The central government and the state governments have to expand e-governance and village knowledge centeres with the participation of the private sector, c) change in the laissez-faire/ negative work culture presently existing in the country; d) check the mushrooming population growth, which is the root cause of many of our problems; f) reduce the rampant corruption, which is eating into the vitals of the nation; and g) emancipation of woman. In this context, the recommendations of the National Knowledge Commission are very relevant.

REFERENCES

Bell, Daniel. The Coming of Postindustrial Society: A Venture in Social Forecasting. Ed.2. New York, Basic Books, 1976.

Business Standard, March 14/15, 2009. P.III. E-INDIA! (Reporter : Priyanka Joshi).

Castells, Manuel. The Rise of the Network Society. Ed. 2. Oxford (UK), Blackwell Publishers, 2000. Vol. 1.

Chevalier, Jacques, M. and Buckles, Daniel J. SAS : A Guide to Collaborative Inquiry and Social Engagement. International Development Centre, Ottawa. New Delhi, Sage Publications, 2008.

Daily News and Analysis. Media: Movement Towards a Knowledge Society. The Need of the Hour. April 1, 2009. http://www.knowledge commission.gov.in

Hill, Michael W. The Impact of Information Society: An Examination of its Nature, Value and Usage. Ed. 2. München, K.G. Saur Verlag, 2005.

India. National Knowledge Commission. Towards a Knowledge Society. Three Years of the National Knowledge Commission. New Delhi, National Knowledge Commission, 2008. Also at www.knowledge commission.gov.in (Accessed 10th April, 2009).

Cf. INSINC Working Party. The Net Result. Social Inclusion in the Information Society. London, IBM, 1997.

Machlup, Fritz. Knowledge: Its Creation, Distribution, and Economic Significance. 3 Vols. Princeton, Princeton University Press, (1980, 1982, 1984).

Machlup, Fritz. The Production and Distribution of Knowledge in the Unites States. Ed.2. Princeton, Princeton University Press, 1979.

Martin, William J. The Global Informaion Society. London, Aslib Gower, 1995.

Naisbitt, John. Megatrends : Ten New Directions Transforming Our Lives. New York, Warner Communications, 1982.

Neelameghan, A and Chester, Greg. Knowledge Management in Relation to Indigenous and Marginalized Communities in the Digital Era: National Conference on Library and Information Studies (NACLIN 2007). Colombo, Sri Lanka, 8-9 March 2007.[on CD]. Proceedings. html

Porat, Marc. The Information Economy : Definition and Measurement. Washington (DC). US Department of Commerce, Office of Telecommunications, 1977. Publication 77-12(1).

Porat, Marc. and Proust, Marcel. Thinking Across Boundaries. Pp.81-82. *In* Chevalier, Jacques M. Loc cit.

Proust, Marcel. Thinking Across Boundaries, Pp.81-82. *In* Chevalier, Jacques M. Loc cit.

Stehr, Nico and Meja, Volker. Introduction: The Development of the Sociology of Knowledge and Science. Pp.1-27. *In* Stehr, Nico and Meja, Volker. Society & Knowledge: Contemporary Perspectives in the Sociology of Knowledge & Science. Ed.2. New Brunswick (NJ), Transaction Publications, 2005.

Toffler, Alvin. Future Shock. London, Bodley Head, 1970.

Toffler, Alvin. The Third Wave. London, Pan Books, 1980.

Webster, Frank. Theories of the Information Society. Ed. 2. New York, Routledge, 2002.

Index

C

D

E

F

G

H

T